THE CHRONOLOGY OF WORDS AND PHRASES

By the same authors

Dictionary of Idioms

Dictionary of Proverbs

Dictionary of Word Origins

THE CHRONOLOGY OF WORDS AND PHRASES

A Thousand Years in the History of English

Linda and Roger Flavell

KYLE CATHIE LIMITED

First published in Great Britain in 1999 by
Kyle Cathie Limited
122 Arlington Road
London NW1 7HP

ISBN 1 85626 249 9

A CIP catalogue record for this book is available from the British Library.

Edited by Caroline Taggart
Designed by Gavin Pretor-Pinney
Typeset by SX Composing DTP, Rayleigh, Essex
Printed and bound in Singapore by
Kyodo Printing

To John and Anna

Contents

......

INTRODUCTION

......

At the end of a book (for that is when Introductions are written), it is always a good moment to take stock. In fact, it is really at the end of a series of four dictionaries. The three previous ones, as etymological guides to idioms, proverbs and words, shared a lot in common. Entries began with a particular term in the language, and went on to trace its linguistic origins. We did what most dictionaries do: focused on the word and its linguistic origins, and we brought in some of the contemporary social, literary or political history in so far as this was necessary to explain the origin or use of the expression.

The book that you have in your hands is somewhat different. Instead of beginning with the word and perhaps going on to the historical world for clarification, the direction here is from events in the world to their impact on language. One book that does this type of thing is Hughes (for details, see the Bibliography) and another the estimable Baugh and Cable; but neither is in dictionary format. Other books, such as Grun and Gossling and the delightful Little, follow a time-line style of presentation, but do not concern themselves with the linguistic implications of historical events. What this book sets out to do is to look at historical events and investigate what the results were on the English language. This led to a very simple plan of presentation. Over ten centuries, we have chosen roughly ten dates per hundred years, and explored the linguistic ramifications of what happened as a result. So it is chronology that organises the material, and not an alphabetical list of words. Of course, for ease of reference, we have provided at the back of the book an index of main words within each entry.

Although there is this major difference between *The Chronology of Words and Phrases* and other dictionaries that we have compiled, there is much that is in common. For instance, we have tried to find interesting happenings, unusual word stories, good quotations. We have done our best to be scholarly, but have tried to avoid pedantry. We have sought to be reliable but not dull. We hope you agree!

So far, we have rather generally referred to an 'event' or 'happening' that triggered a word or expression. But what, in this context, is an 'event'?

Sometimes, it is possible to be very precise. In September 1653, a wall some half a mile long was built across Manhattan Island in New York. Its ditches and palisades were to provide protection from the native Americans, and from Oliver Cromwell's troops, who were imminently expected. Although we may not recognise it, we hear of this 'event' nearly every day in our news and financial bulletins. As you have doubtless guessed, this wall was situated on what we now call Wall Street. There are similar stories in our *Dictionary of Word Origins* – you might look at *serendipity* (which can be pinpointed to 28 January 1754) or the engaging but sadly apocryphal 24-hour origin of *quiz*. There is no need to go to other books, however. Some of the entries in this one relate to very specific events. If you browse through, you will find a number.

But an 'event' is rarely one specific incident, from which a word or expression immediately comes. Often, it derives from an evolving process. There is usually an on-going story which we try to tell, frequently unfolding over decades. For example, Niepce and Daguerre were early contributors to photography, and over the next century their successors have given us the still and moving picture industries we know today. In a way, it is a little arbitrary which of a number of key dates we actually chose. In fact, the one we chose (1827 – see page 200) is fundamental, but there were other options. For quite a different approach, we chose 1095 as the date to talk about the influence of the Crusades on English, and then returned to the theme at subsequent important moments (see **1192** and **1204**, pages 54 and 57). We followed a similar procedure with one of the most important dates in world history: 1492. As every school child knows:

In 1492,
Columbus sailed the ocean blue…

…and discovered America. We pick up the early influences of the New World directly for a second time in the entry for 1519, but very many of the subsequent entries up to the present day are indebted in one way or another to events on the American continent.

Sometimes it is an individual who makes the impact. Many literary 'greats' have marked our language. Obvious cases we have treated have been Shakespeare and Spenser – selecting the year of their death to discuss their linguistic influence. Of course, there are many others we could have chosen, but considerations of space forced some omissions. For those who are interested, our other dictionaries look at some of these.

Genius is manifest in other ways. Wycliffe provided the first full translation of the whole Bible into English, with immense implications for life and language over succeeding centuries (see **1382 & 1388**, page 92). Caxton changed the world, too – we choose the publication of the first printed book in English (1474) as the moment to celebrate. Other flashes of inspiration come from an unknown source. Around 1410, some anonymous person in Germany worked out how to do wire drawing, making possible the mass production of pins. Nobody knows precisely who invented spectacle lenses (we deal with the story under Roger Bacon in 1268, see page 68), but so important was this discovery that one authority recently rated it amongst the top ten of the millennium. It meant, for instance, that leadership could now remain with the over-40s. Failing eyesight was no longer a bar.

In some instances, it was quite impossible to be precise. We resort to 'c 1350' as a general mid-century date, to signal two changing social trends, the first concerning style of dress, the second the establishment of shops in most towns. This is a device we have used in various other places. Some 'events' simply do not lend themselves to the discreteness of a precise date.

The overall format of the book is very simple. The dates we have selected appear in chronological order, over the last millennium. The brief summaries of each historical event that head each article appear in the Contents, also in chronological order. This should make it easy for you to check whether or not we have covered a person or event that interests you. At the end of the book is an index of the key words we deal with. Mostly, these are the headwords in each entry, but we add other expressions that are dealt with in the text. There is also a Bibliography at the end of the book.

The format of each entry is the same in each case. After the date we have chosen, there is a summary phrase about the 'event'. The next section gives the historical context. It is deliberately brief – just enough to set the scene. In our anxiety not to write an extended essay (which would have been very easy, given the fascination of the topic and the wealth of sources we looked at), we do hope that we have not made too many sweeping generalisations. We have listed some of our sources in the Bibliography, so if we have whetted your appetite, you could take it further from there.

The entries go on to the expressions we deal with. 'Expression' covers phrases and sayings, as well as words. These relate to the theme of the event. They are not exhaustive entries, in that we do not claim to look at all imported Arabic words, for instance, under 1492. The expressions we choose are representative, but more importantly they are interesting. At least, we found them so, and hope that you do also. Not every word stems directly and immediately from the historical 'event'. We gave ourselves discretion to range rather more widely. Clearly, we would go backwards to look at the origins in Latin or Old English of terms that might now be being used in a new way. We also on occasion go forward, to pursue the word down the centuries, in its shifts of meaning, until we reach its contemporary senses.

As we trace the expressions down the years, we try to give a flavour of their uses by means of quotations. Again, there is no attempt to be comprehensive, by illustrating every sense or even the use in every century. Our goal has been to find a quotation that appealed to us in some way, and again we hope that you agree with us.

You will sometimes come across short 'postscripts' in the text, introduced by a bullet point (•). These are intended to take up incidental comments related to the main words, but not quite central to the theme of the entry. They act as an indication of the ever-increasing web of connections that surround any expression. Should you feel the urge, the Bibliography is a guide to help you pursue the tantalising side issues and red herrings that abound in etymology. It is not without reason that one eminent linguist described the subject as 'the Old Curiosity Shop of linguistics'.

Perhaps our favourite comment on our past books is one from the editor of an academic journal. We were nominated for an annual book prize, which we didn't win. However, he did say the dictionary was the book on the short list that most kept him from doing what he should have been doing! We also know from correspondence and from the feedback generated by previous books that very many people take delight in the stories at the back of our language. In this book we have tried to tie these much more firmly to the historical situation in which they were coined. We do feel that this must be done with care, however. We have not indulged in our own speculation, unless we say so, and we have tried to chart a safe course through the at times conflicting origins, to the best of our academic abilities. In that respect, we hope you hold a sound guide in your hands. It is not a perfect one, none the less! That is something else earlier books has reinforced (although we knew it already). Our correspondents have been generous in helping us to get something quite right, or to correct a mistake that has crept in. Once more, to these same ends we welcome your comments and even your brickbats.

We alone are responsible for the book before you. But we are indebted to so many others – our publisher, our encouraging editor, and supportive friends and family. Perhaps especially we owe a huge debt of gratitude to those who have gone before, and prepared the magnificent reference works that we could not do without. Every entry has called for extensive reading, to enable us to grasp the historical and linguistic dimensions more thoroughly. We would like to pay special tribute to these (of which a selection is in the Bibliography), and we trust we have never knowingly misused or misquoted them. We continue to marvel at the depths of scholarship and erudition in major sources, such as the *Oxford English Dictionary* and the *Encyclopedia Britannica*, and in the lesser known ones, such as Ayto and Skeat (see Bibliography).

In sum, in the words of a rather voguish modernism that holds some truth – enjoy!

LINDA AND ROGER FLAVELL
August, 1999

1066

THE NORMANS BEGIN TO ERECT CASTLES

......

The early years of Norman occupation saw a frenzy of castle building. Strategic sites in even the remotest regions of the kingdom were swiftly fortified using forced labour. Some were military camps and lookout posts, others provided security for a Norman lord and his henchmen:

> *[The Normans] filled the land full of castles. They cruelly oppressed the wretched men of the land with castle works and when the castles were made they filled them with devils and evil men . . .*
> (ANGLO-SAXON CHRONICLE, 1137)

Such fortified residences, centres of military presence and local administration, were a feature of feudalism in western Europe and particularly in northern France. The fact that the English possessed no such easily defended strongholds is a contributing factor to the success of Norman settlement. The Bayeux tapestry depicts the Normans in 1066, as they disembarked on the south coast, busily constructing the first castle at Hastings as a defence against Harold and his armies.

CASTLE

The early castles were raised in a hurry and were not permanent structures. Most of them were of the motte-and-bailey type. The 'motte' was a great mound of earth and rubble with very steep sides and a flattened top. The mound was surrounded at the bottom by a deep ditch and protected at the top by a stout palisade of earth and timber. A wooden tower was built within the palisade. Here supplies and weapons were stored and the inhabitants would crowd to defend if the castle were under attack. Adjacent to the motte was the 'bailey', a spacious enclosure which contained outbuildings, byres and stables. The bailey, too, had steep sides and was protected by a ditch and a palisade. Entry to the bailey was over a timber bridge. The motte could only be reached by a second bridge spanning the ditch between it and the bailey. Should an enemy manage to penetrate the bailey, this second bridge could be raised or destroyed, thus isolating the motte for its easier defence.

The trouble with these earlier castles was that the wooden palisades were relatively easily breached by chopping them down or by fire. Later castles used stone, which made them much more impregnable. With subsequent refinements to the art of castle building, most sieges were concluded not by direct assault but by hunger or sickness, or even by treachery.

The word *castle* reflects this notion of fortification for it goes back ultimately to Latin *castrum*, which meant 'fortified place'. A diminutive noun *castellum*, 'fortress', which was derived from this, found its way into Old Norman French as *castel*. The rapid construction of castles throughout England in the years immediately after the Conquest made such an impact on the population that within a year or two the Norman word *castel* had passed into English:

When the king was informed that the people in the north had gathered together and would oppose him if he came, he marched to Nottingham and built a castle there, and so on to York, and there built two castles, and also in Lincoln, and in many other places in that part of the country.
(ANGLO-SAXON CHRONICLE, 1068)

DUNGEON
The great White Tower at the Tower of London and the keep at Colchester are unusual for being constructed of stone during the reign of William the Conqueror. In the early twelfth century, however, when the urgency to impose Norman rule had passed, many of the wooden fortifications which were of royal, military or administrative significance were replaced by permanent structures. Local materials gave way to stone, sometimes brought in from a distance. Wealthy barons began to construct mighty square tower-keeps of dressed stone to accommodate their households. Such towers were known as *donjons*. This word goes back to Latin *dominus*, 'lord', from which the noun

dominium, meaning 'domain, possession', was derived. In Late Latin this had evolved into *dominiō* or *domniō* and denoted 'the lord's tower'. Old French borrowed the term as *donjon*, which initially signified 'the lord's keep-tower' and later also 'a dark underground prison', because not only was the tower the lord's ultimate security, but while he lived protected above, prisoners of war languished in the chambers beneath. The Old French word *donjon* together with its two meanings was borrowed into Middle English in the fourteenth century. Here the spelling *dungeon* soon began to evolve (found early in Chaucer) but is now only applied to 'an underground prison chamber'. The archaic spelling *donjon* is reserved to denote 'a castle keep'.

• The English word *keep* began to be used for 'a donjon-tower' during the sixteenth century and was possibly a direct translation of the Italian word *tenazza*.

BELFRY
Castle defences were difficult to break through, and a number of siege-engines were devised for this purpose. The 'trebuchet', which worked by means of counterweights and was designed to hurl stones, was one such. A *belfry* was a wooden siege-tower, originally a simple structure intended to shield soldiers attempting to penetrate a fortification, but later to carry an array of offensive equipment. The term *belfry* was borrowed into Middle English as *berfrey* by way of Old French *berfrei* in the thirteenth century. It soon evolved into *belfry* for phonetic reasons, and the connection of the first syllable with 'bell' led to a siege tower becoming a 'bell tower'. A similar change, in form and meaning, happened in French.

c 1070

WILLIAM THE CONQUEROR INTRODUCES THE FEUDAL SYSTEM

......

William of Normandy's conquest of England in 1066 met strong opposition, particularly in the north. When it was finally complete in 1070, William set about imposing the feudal system of his homeland upon his conquered territory.

Regarding all land as his own by divine right, he confiscated the holdings of Saxon landowners and distributed them amongst his loyal Norman barons. In return the barons swore allegiance to the king and pledged to serve him by supplying him with a number of knights according to the terms of the grant. In order to meet these obligations the barons, in turn, might divide their estates, using grants of land to secure the loyalty and service of a knight. Indeed a tract of land, thus divided and subdivided, might support several such contracts. Feudalism, then, was a pyramid system of interdependent political and military relationships, each guaranteed by oaths of loyalty and homage; William granted directly fewer than 180 land holdings, yet he had on call over 4,000 knights.

HOMAGE

A vassal was granted a fief (a grant of land) only on condition that he paid *homage* to his lord. In a formal ceremony the vassal, kneeling, declared himself the lord's 'man' by pledging fealty (loyalty) to him and undertaking to fight for him. Indeed, the word *homage* derives from Latin *homō* (stem *homin-*), 'man'. It came into English by way of Late Latin *homināticum*, 'the service of a vassal', and Old French *homage*. In modern English *homage* is used figuratively to denote 'respect or reverence publicly manifested for a person or an idea':

Call it a homage, call it parody (though heaven knows how you could tell), Fowler has written a damned fine Vonnegut novel – audacious, sparky and very funny. Nice one, Kurt.
(Review of THE ASTROLOGICAL DIARY OF GOD in THE TIMES, 10 April 1999)

BARON

In Norman England a *baron* was a man, of whatever rank, who was vassal to the king himself. He was a tenant-in-chief who ruled his estates much as the king ruled the country and whose wealth enabled him to run his household on a lavish scale. *Baron* like *homage* is derived from a term that means 'man', in this case medieval Latin *barō*. The term came into Middle English through Anglo-Norman *barun* and Old French *baron*. The particular sense of *barō* was a 'man' in relation to another person. It could, for instance, mean 'husband' as opposed to 'wife'. In a feudal context it meant 'servant' as opposed to 'king' and was a statement of feudal relationship. *Baron* did not become a title until 1387 when Richard II created John Beauchamp *Baron* of Kidderminster. Over subsequent centuries, the title lost some of its great prestige (Henry VI created large numbers, thus rather debasing the currency), but it still retains today considerable cachet. *Baroness* was the honour the former British Prime Minister Margaret Thatcher was granted in 1992.

Barons constitute the lowest order of nobility. More impressive these days are commercial *barons*. The term's modern application to a 'magnate' or 'influential businessman' arose in America in the first quarter of the nineteenth century. Its use is usually defined by a qualifying word, as in *drug baron* or, in the case of Henry Clay Frick (founder of the Frick Collection in New York), *robber baron*:

> *Henry Clay Frick was the bête noire of the*
> *robber barons, which is a bit like being Satan*
> *amongst so many devils. The Pittsburgh*
> *Gradgrind made his millions out of steel,*
> *coke and beating up the labor unions. The*
> *most famous instance is the five-day sit-in*
> *that took place at the Homestead steel mill*
> *in 1892. Frick simply sent in 300 of his*
> *thugs, provoking a bloody scrimmage in*
> *which 14 people were killed.*
> (Vanessa Letts, CADOGAN GUIDE TO
> NEW YORK, 1991)

FEE

In the eleventh century a knight was no more than a lowly military retainer in the service of a baron but, under the feudal system, the reward of a fief, or fee, from his lord raised his status to that of landowner. In Anglo-Norman and then Middle English, *fee* denoted 'a grant of land bestowed upon a vassal by a lord in return for loyalty and service'. It was the equivalent of Old French *fé, fié, fief*, which came from the medieval Latin *feodum, feudum*, 'the use of land or property of another granted as a payment for service'. The source of these words was Germanic, possibly the unattested Frankish *fehu-ōd*. This was a compound of *fehu*, 'cattle', and *ōd*, 'wealth'. Since the ownership of cattle indicated wealth, derivations from *fehu* developed the sense of 'possessions, property'.

Besides land, a man might be given the heritable right to a paid office (the

keeping of prisons, for instance) which was held *in* or *of fee* in return for feudal loyalty. The remuneration such an officer was entitled to claim for his services was also called a *fee*. Thus, from the second half of the sixteenth century, the term came to denote 'a charge made for an occasional service rendered'.

• *Feudal* came into English in the seventeenth century as a term used by commentators on the system it describes. It was derived from medieval Latin *feudālis* from *feudum*.

• *Feud* meaning 'ongoing hostility between two parties' is unrelated to *feudal*. Their spellings coincided in the seventeenth century. *Feud* comes from the unattested prehistoric Germanic *faikhithō* which meant 'in a state of enmity'. From this, Old High German derived *fēhida*, 'enmity, hatred', which was borrowed into Old French as *fede* or *feide*, and from there into northern Middle English around the turn of the fourteenth century. During the sixteenth century the term became current in English but was differently spelt, inexplicably appearing as *food* or *fewd*.

KNIGHT

Knight is Germanic in origin. In Old English the word simply meant 'a youth', but by the tenth century it had come to denote 'a male servant'. Just after the Conquest *knight* was more specifically applied to 'a military retainer' of the king or a nobleman but, as the feudal system got underway, fiefs were offered to retainers in return for specified periods of military service and the term came to denote 'one who serves as a mounted soldier in return for land'. A knight in receipt of a fee from a baron or subtenant was responsible for the purchase and maintenance of a war-horse and armour and for the expenses of his armour-bearer or squire. He devoted forty days each year to military training or, if his lord was called to war, the knight served him on the battlefield for an equivalent period at his own expense. Once the feudal system became fully established, however, *knight* took a further shift in meaning when it was applied to 'one raised to noble military rank'.

At the age of eight or nine a lad of good birth intended for a military career would be sent from home and apprenticed to a knight in another household. Here he would serve first as a page, attending to his master's personal needs and learning the genteel manners and values expected of a knight (see **courtesy**, page 41). Then in his teens he would become a squire, maintaining his lord's horse, armour and weapons and accompanying him into battle until eventually, around the age of twenty, he 'won his spurs' and was dubbed a knight (see **chivalry**, page 38). Thus military knighthood was not a hereditary rank but one achieved through merit, even by princes.

During the fifteenth century, however, warfare began to change for the mounted knight in armour. English bowmen helped ensure victory at Agincourt, cannon were being developed (see **1346**, page 80) and the feudal custom of knight service was dying out, with lords accepting payment instead and using it to hire professional men. From the sixteenth century onwards the rank of knight ceased to be a military one and instead became an honour used by the monarch to reward services to the sovereign or country. The person thus elevated was entitled to prefix his Christian name with *Sir* (a shortened form of *sire*). This is still the case. In modern Britain pop singers, sportsmen and, of course, civil servants commonly bear the illustrious title.

BACHELOR

A knight rich enough to lead a company of vassals into battle under his own banner was known as a knight banneret. The term *knight bachelor* was reserved for a young knight who was not experienced or wealthy enough to lead a fighting force and did not, therefore, merit a banner. Instead he was distinguished by a pennant whose point was ceremoniously lopped off when his fortunes changed. The comparative inferiority of the rank has led to speculation that *bachelor* was derived from *bas chevalier*, literally 'low-ranking knight'. However, all that can be stated with certainty about the origins of the word is that it was borrowed from Old French in the thirteenth century. The earliest record of Old French *bacheler* dates back to the eleventh century when it appears in LA CHANSON DE ROLAND. To account for the term, etymologists have postulated an unattested Vulgar Latin *baccalāris* which was in some way connected to Latin *baccalāria*, 'division of land', and the derived adjective *baccalarius*, used to describe 'one who worked for the farmer', but this too is speculative.

Whatever its origins, *bachelor* is alive and well in modern English. From its beginnings as a 'young knight' the word went on to denote a 'junior', as opposed to a 'master', in other fourteenth-century institutions: in the trade-guilds, for instance, and also in the universities where *bachelor* still refers to 'one who has graduated with the lowest or first degree of a university' (see **degree**, page 44). Its application to 'an unmarried man' dates from the late fourteenth century (see **spinster**, page 76). Let the old knight in Chaucer's MERCHANT'S TALE (c 1387) have the last word as he woefully laments his unmarried state:

> 'Noon oother lyf,' seyde he, 'is worth a
>   bene;
> For wedlock is so esy and so clene,
> That in this world it is a paradys . . .
> And trewely it sit wel to be so,
> That bacheleris have often peyne and
>   wo . . .'

• Feudalism was supported by the manorial (or seigneurial) system. This was an economic and social arrangement in which peasants were bound to their lord, receiving his protection and holding their land in perpetuity in exchange for labour, produce and taxes. The manor (from Old French *manoir*, 'dwelling', from Latin *manere*, 'to remain') was central to the system. Typically it comprised an estate of arable land, meadows, pasture and woodland. It had a fortified manor house (with its kitchens, bakery, brewhouse, cellars, stables and workshop) and at least one village of peasant dwellings, often with a church and a mill. Altogether this formed an economic unit that was almost completely self-sufficient.

VILLAIN

The manorial system had originated on the great estates of the late Roman Empire, where labourers were allotted their own parcels of land to work on behalf of their master. The peasants were eventually compelled by imperial decree to remain on those lands in perpetuity but in return, although they came under the control and authority of the landowner who directed many aspects of their lives, he had no power to evict them. Estates were centred around the *vīlla*, the landowner's 'country-house' or 'farm'. It is suggested that Vulgar Latin had the unattested term *vīllānus* which literally meant 'one who belongs to a villa' and hence 'one who works on an estate'.

Feudal manors operated along the same lines as the Roman villas, and the term *vīllānus* was borrowed first into Old French and then into Anglo-Norman as *vilain, vilein,* to denote 'a feudal serf'. Both forms were absorbed into Middle English in the fourteenth century and were used interchangeably. Since those who occupy the lowly ranks of society are generally despised, they soon became terms of reproach passing from 'one who has base manners and instincts' eventually to denote 'a person with criminal tendencies'. In order to discriminate between the 'serf' and the 'scoundrel', the two forms began to part company, such that *villein* was applied to the former while *villain* became the rogue.

By the mid-nineteenth century the word had gained a literary twist. The *villain* had become a character in a novel or play whose base motives were central to the plot, hence the phrase the *villain of the piece*. More recently still, since the mid-twentieth century *villain* has been something of a vogue word in the vocabulary of television policemen and detectives. After all, it carries with it a whiff of something more sinister than the humble criminal. John Mortimer is a playwright, a novelist and a former practising lawyer and QC. Rumpole is his most famous fictional character, in print and on television:

> *I have written elsewhere of the Timson family, that huge clan of South London villains whose selfless devotion to crime has kept the Rumpoles in such luxuries as Vim, Gumption, sliced bread and saucepan scourers over the years, not to mention the bare necessities of life such as gin, tonic and cooking claret from Pommeroy's Wine Bar.* (John Mortimer, 'Rumpole and the Age for Retirement', in THE TRIALS OF RUMPOLE, 1979)

BY HOOK OR BY CROOK

The forests that belonged to a manor were set apart for the lord's hunting and peasants were forbidden any activity that would disturb or reduce cover for the deer. There were, however, tracts of common woodland where villeins were permitted to gather dead wood and whatever small branches and brush they could pull down with hooked poles (hooks) and lop with their sickles (crooks), to supply their daily needs. THE BODMIN REGISTER of 1525 tells us that *Dynmure Wood was ever open and common to the inhabitants of Bodmin, to bear away on their backs the burden of lop, crop, hook, crook and bag wood.*

The feudal right to firewood is the source of the expression *by hook or by crook,* meaning 'to go to any lengths, legitimate or otherwise, to achieve something'. The earliest records of the idiom date from around 1380, when the form appears to have been *with hook or with crook*. In CONFESSIO AMANTIS (c 1390) John Gower writes:

So what with hoke and what with croke
They [false witness and perjury] make her
maister ofte winne.

The idiom may have strong implications
of procurement by fair means or foul, but
under the feudal system strict adherence
to the terms of the concession was
expected. The improper gathering of
firewood and kindling was regarded as a
criminal offence and was tried in the
manor or forest court (see **1079**, page 26).

CATTLE
The medieval Latin term *capitāle* denoted
'property, principal stock of wealth'. It
was the neuter form of the Latin adjective
capitālis (the source of English *capital*)
which meant 'chief, principal', being
derived from the noun *caput*, 'head'.
Capitāle was borrowed into Old French as
chatel and from there passed into Old
Northern French and then into Anglo-
Norman as *catel*, a term denoting 'personal
property'. Since, under the feudal system,
the only property that could properly be
termed personal consisted of movable
goods, and since domesticated animals
represented wealth, *cattle* was increasingly
understood to mean 'livestock'. A late
thirteenth-century manuscript includes
under the term horses, asses, mules, oxen
and camels. It might also apply to cows,
calves, sheep, lambs, goats and pigs. Over
several centuries even chickens and bees
were included. In PLAINE PERCEVALL

(c 1590) Richard Harvey warns *Take heed,*
thine owne Cattaile sting thee not, while as
late as the 1830s Thomas Carlyle was
writing of *bovine, swinish and feathered cattle*
(CRITICAL AND MISCELLANEOUS
ESSAYS, 1839). The term did not begin to
apply more specifically to 'domesticated
bovine animals' until about the mid-
sixteenth century:

> *A charm to find who hath bewitched your*
> *cattle. Put a pair of breeches upon the cow's*
> *head, and beat her out of the pasture with a*
> *good cudgel upon a Friday, and she will run*
> *right to the witch's door and strike thereat*
> *with her horns.*
> (Reginald Scot, THE DISCOVERY OF
> WITCHCRAFT, 1584)

Meanwhile Old French *chatel* had been
borrowed directly into Anglo-Norman as
a legal term denoting 'personal property'
and in this context soon superseded the
Norman form *catel*. By the sixteenth
century, since *cattle* was tending to denote
'livestock', *chattel* passed from legal into
everyday language to refer to 'a piece of
movable property' in general. Today
chattel is most commonly found in the
phrase *goods and chattels* which refers to
personal property of all kinds. In legal
English *chattel* still denotes 'an article of
movable property' and, in past centuries,
was used as an emotive term for 'a slave'
by those who abhorred the trade in
human beings.

1070

THE CONSTRUCTION OF CANTERBURY
CATHEDRAL IS BEGUN

•••••

There is a story that one day a monk named Gregory came across some
beautiful children for sale in a Roman slave market. He made enquiries
and found out that they were Angli, 'Angles', from England, a pagan
land (see under **angling**, page 120). 'They are not Angles,' Gregory

replied, 'but Angels.' With this incident in mind, when Gregory became Pope he dispatched a group of monks to England under the leadership of Augustine to evangelise the Angles, Saxons and Jutes.

Augustine and his companions landed in Kent in the spring of 597. King Ethelbert was already well disposed to Christianity since his Frankish wife, Bertha, was a Catholic. The king provided the monks with a missionary base in Canterbury and became one of their earliest converts. Towards the end of the year, Augustine was created Archbishop of the English Church and soon afterwards built a cathedral in the city and a Benedictine monastery just outside it.

Augustine's cathedral, Christ Church, was destroyed in 1011 by one of the periodic Danish raids, but the Middle Ages was marked by a religious fervour which found expression in the construction of glorious churches of unprecedented grandeur. After the Conquest the Normans built not only castles (see **1066**, page 17) but also cathedrals and monasteries. Their first cathedral was at Canterbury in 1070:

> *King William . . . was a man of great wisdom and power . . . Though stern beyond measure to those who opposed his will, he was kind to those good men who loved God . . . During his reign was built the great cathedral at Canterbury, and many others throughout England.*
> (ANGLO-SAXON CHRONICLE, 1086)

BISHOP

Following his appointment as Archbishop of the English Church, Augustine established two further sees in 604, those of London and Rochester. Their Bishops, Mellitus and Justus, had been sent to England from Italy by Pope Gregory to help Augustine in his missionary efforts. The word *bishop* has its origins in Greek *episkopos*, a compound noun which was derived from *epi-*, 'around', and *skopein*, 'to look', and meant 'an overseer'. *Episkopos* was used outside a Church context in this general sense, and also more specifically as a title for various civil superintendents. With the birth, growth and organisation of the Christian faith, the word was appropriated to an ecclesiastical context where it denoted 'a Church officer'. Ecclesiastical Latin had the Greek word as *episcopus* but in Vulgar Latin this was corrupted to the more manageable *biscopus*, a form which then travelled into the Germanic languages, arriving in Old English by the ninth century.

The Greek prefix *arch-*, meaning 'highest status' (ultimately from Greek *arkhos*, 'chief') was added to *bishop* to form *archbishop*. The first Norman Archbishop of Canterbury was King William's respected adviser Lanfranc. He was appointed in 1070 to replace Stigand, the incumbent at the time of the Conquest, who was removed from office. Under Lanfranc the English Church gained a measure of independence from Rome and was protected from royal interference. His programme of reform included the deposition of English prelates in favour of Normans, a measure designed to stamp out corruption and strengthen Norman control.

CATHEDRAL

Construction of a Norman cathedral at Canterbury to replace that of Augustine was undertaken by Lanfranc, the first Norman Archbishop of Canterbury.

A cathedral was originally simply a bishop's church, a place where he and his clergy could conduct the prescribed services. During the Middle Ages, however, religious zeal inspired the glorification of God through buildings of grandeur and magnificence. In an article in THE HISTORY OF CHRISTIANITY (1977), Henry Sefton explains how the essential features of the bishop's church – the high altar, bishop's throne and priests' stalls – were partitioned off and a large area (the nave), containing an altar, a font and a pulpit, was provided for the congregation. Over time side-altars were constructed on either side of the nave which were bestowed by wealthy citizens or guilds.

In the thirteenth century such a building was known as a *cathedral church*, a term which was shortened to *cathedral* in the second half of the sixteenth century. *Cathedral*, then, was originally an adjective. Its source was the Greek noun *kathedrā*, 'chair', a word composed from *kata*, 'down', and *hedra*, 'seat' (from the unattested Greek root *hed-*, 'to sit'). A *kathedrā* was a substantial chair with arms, particularly one used by a teacher or professor and, hence, by a bishop. *Kathedrā* was taken into Latin as *cathedra* from which Late Latin derived *cathedrālis*, meaning 'belonging to the (bishop's) seat'. The adjective was used to describe the building which housed the bishop's throne, hence *cathedrālis ecclēsia*, 'cathedral church'.

Sadly, Lanfranc's Norman cathedral at Canterbury did not survive. Its choir burned down in 1174, a few years after Thomas à Becket was murdered there (see **1173**, page 49) and had to be rebuilt.

• The Greek *kathedrā* was also responsible for the English word *chair*. The Latin borrowing *cathedra* was taken into Old French as *chaiere*, 'seat, throne', and then borrowed into Middle English in the thirteenth century.

MASON

Building for permanence in stone was a costly enterprise that only the wealthiest could afford. Medieval masons were thus itinerant craftsmen who moved from one great project to another. Their search for employment was not always confined to their own land, and this accounts for the spread of technological and stylistic innovations throughout Europe in the Middle Ages.

The master mason was entrusted with both the planning and construction of a building. The man appointed from among several contenders to rebuild the choir of Canterbury cathedral after the fire in 1174 was William of Sens, a Frenchman with a fine reputation. According to the contemporary account of Gervase, one of the monks at Canterbury, he was *active and ready as a craftsman most skilful in both wood and stone.*

The origin of *mason* is unclear. Middle English borrowed the word *machun* from Norman French in the early thirteenth century, the forms *masoun* and *mason* appearing in the following century, influenced by Old French *masson*. One theory maintains that the Old French term derived from an unattested Frankish *makjo*, a derivative of the unattested verb *makōn*, 'to make'. An alternative view finds its source in the unattested prehistoric Germanic stem *mattjon-*, 'a cutter', from the root *mat-*, 'to cut', which found its way into French by way of unattested Vulgar Latin *matiō*, 'mason'.

The mason's work was not without its dangers. Gervase tells us that William of Sens was on a scaffolding one day, preparing to work on the great vault of the cathedral, when suddenly *the beams broke under his feet, and he fell to the ground, stones and timbers accompanying his fall.* William miraculously survived his fall of 50 feet (18 metres) but his injuries forced him to leave the rebuilding project. It was completed by another master mason – also named William, but this time an Englishman (see **plumber**, page 63.)

QUARRY

Choice of stone fell to the master mason. It was obviously cheaper to use stone from the nearest quarry but often this consideration was put aside. According to the monk Gervase, William of Sens imported the stone for rebuilding the choir at Canterbury from Caen in Normandy, facilitating its transportation by constructing *ingenious machines for loading and unloading ships*. (There was sometimes an artistic preference to consider. The alabaster required for the reredos in St George's Chapel, Windsor, for instance, had to be brought from Nottingham.)

To obtain the stone, quarrymen would first drive iron wedges into the rock face and then lever along the fissures with crowbars. The stone was then rough dressed with an axe and finished with a mallet and chisel using wooden templates to get the shape and size specified by the customer. Each stone bore three marks:

the first showed its position in the cathedral, and the other two were the individual marks of the quarryman and the stone cutter so that they could be paid.

The word *quarry* arose from this dressing of the stone into blocks. It was a fifteenth-century borrowing of Old French *quarriere*, which rendered obsolete the noun *quarrer*, a borrowing of three centuries earlier from the same Old French source. *Quarriere* was a derivative of the unattested noun *quarre* which denoted 'a squared stone'. This, in turn, came from Latin *quadrum*, meaning 'square'. Not all stone left the quarry in square blocks, however. During the thirteenth century some quarries began to produce ready-made tracery and statues which they supplied rough-dressed for the masons on-site to mount and finish, precursors of Do It All and B & Q. (For another sense of the word, see **quarry** in **1079,** page 29.)

1079

THE NEW FOREST IS ESTABLISHED AS A ROYAL HUNTING GROUND

••••••

In 1079 William the Conqueror took possession of a vast tract of heath and woodland in present-day Hampshire to be preserved as a royal hunting ground. It was his *Nova Foresta*, his 'New Forest', set apart for his pleasure, a reward for his diligent care and protection of the realm. Only the king, or one with royal authority, was permitted to take any of the game.

The Forest Law, a Norman regulation imposed in England and much resented, was strictly imposed to ensure that forest dwellers making their own livelihood in no way interfered with game animals, their cover or their food. Penalties for transgressing the law were harsh, and those for poaching horrific in their severity. According to the medieval ANGLO-SAXON CHRONICLE King William *established a great peace for the deer, and laid down laws therefor, that whoever should slay hart or hind should be blinded.* His successor, William Rufus, was reputedly even more severe.

FOREST, DEFORESTATION

The Late Latin phrase *forestis silva* was originally applied to the great hunting grounds of Charlemagne. The expression literally meant 'outdoor wood', *forestis* being a derivative of the Latin adverb *forīs* which meant 'outside, out of doors'. The word *silva*, 'wood', was often dropped from the phrase, leaving the adjective *forestis* to stand alone as a noun. Medieval writers distinguished the *parcus*, the enclosed woodland or park (like that fenced off by the Norman baron William de Percy at Petworth, Sussex), from the *forestis*, the unfenced tract of woodland outside its walls. *Forestis* was borrowed into Old French as *forest* (modern French has *forêt*) and from there into Middle English, where its earliest reference at the end of the thirteenth century was to the New Forest itself. When the word *forest* was applied by William and his successors to the land in Hampshire it simply denoted 'a large area of land set aside as a royal hunting preserve'. Indeed, the New Forest was not densely wooded as our modern understanding of *forest* would lead us to expect. Even nine hundred years ago it was half heathland, as it is today. *Forest* in the modern sense of 'a large area mostly covered by trees and undergrowth' became current around the turn of the fourteenth century.

The wild state of royal hunting lands was preserved by the imposition of strict Forest Law upon the inhabitants. In medieval Latin the verb *afforēstāre* was coined. This meant 'to make a district into a hunting preserve (by the enforcement of Forest Law)'. The word was taken into English as *afforest* (noun *afforestation*) at the beginning of the sixteenth century. Although it is now obsolete its opposite, *deforest*, has given rise to the very topical word *deforestation*. *Deforest* originally meant 'to remove land from the control of Forest Law', hence 'to unmake a forest'. The legal position of a forest was the land's protection. Once legal restraint was lifted the forest was physically unmade, so that, during the nineteenth century, the verb *deforest* gained the sense 'to clear land of trees', something which the human race does not seem able to stop doing:

> *In China, temperate forest occupies the south-eastern part of the country. Like many other temperate forests of the world, it has been greatly changed by centuries of intensive cultivation; in northern China deforestation is more or less complete.*
> (B Booth, TEMPERATE FORESTS, 1988)

VENISON

The Forest Law greatly restricted the lives of local inhabitants; they were forbidden to clear land for crops or even trap rabbits for the pot. All dogs were 'lawed': three claws were clipped from each paw to prevent their hunting or chasing the king's venison. Forest dwellers were, however, given certain basic rights, although these were strictly controlled. They were, for instance, given grazing rights (pannage) when the deer were not fawning and they could raise cattle and pigs. They were permitted to gather waste firewood and timber, to mend fences and buildings (heybote) but not to reduce the trees or the underwood where the deer took cover (see **by hook or by crook**, page 22). They were also allowed to cut peat for fuel (turbary). In the forest human activity was tolerated only if it did not interfere with the king's chase and the supply of venison to the itinerant royal court when it was in residence nearby.

Venison originated in the Latin verb *vēnārī*, 'to hunt'. A derivative *vēnātiō* meant 'hunting' and, by extension, 'game'. Old French borrowed this word as *venison* to denote 'the flesh of an animal hunted for food' and Middle English acquired the term from Anglo-Norman towards the end of the thirteenth century. Since a variety of animals was hunted, the word *venison* might be applied to the flesh of deer, boar, rabbit or hare. Deer were the principal quarry in the royal chase, however, and medieval cooks devised a great variety of tempting recipes using every part of the carcass. The word *venison* was so often applied to deer meat that in the late sixteenth century Manwood wrote that *amongst the common sort of people, nothing is accompted Venison, but the flesh of Red and Fallow Deere* (TREATISE OF THE LAWS OF THE FOREST, 1598). Nevertheless, those who were not quite so common continued to apply *venison* to the succulent flesh of all kinds of wild game. (English settlers in the North American colonies of the seventeenth century applied the word to bear meat, and those in nineteenth-century Australia to the flesh of the kangaroo.) Even so, by the eighteenth century *venison* was more often than not understood to be the meat of a deer and present-day English now restricts the term to this sense.

STAG

The history of *stag* is unclear. The Old English term was *stagga* and probably referred to 'a male animal in its prime'. This sense in English was certainly related to the same underlying notion, denoting 'the male of a species', in various other languages and dialects. In both northern England and Scotland, for instance, *stag* appeared in a number of fourteenth- and fifteenth-century inventories and wills to denote 'a young male horse', a use which persisted, in Scotland at least, into the nineteenth century. In later centuries the term was also applied to a male wren, cock or turkey.

The earliest appearance of *stag* to denote 'the male of a deer' comes in a twelfth-century document purported to be a charter of King Canute stating that hunting rights were a prerogative of the sovereign. The medieval kings of England used the charter to defend their right to impose Forest Law on large areas of the country by claiming an English precedent that did not, in fact, exist. It was not until the turn of the fifteenth century that the term reappeared in written form to denote 'a male deer (particularly a red deer) in its prime'. Medieval hunting treatises defined the stages of the animal's development thus:

The first yere that thei be calfede, thei be ycalle a calfe the secund yere a bulloke . . . the thred yere a broket, the iiii. yere a stagard, the v. yere a stagge . . .
(MAISTRE OF GAME, c 1400, manuscript 546 in the Bodleian Library, Oxford)

Strictly then, a *stag* was a five-year-old. In the fifteenth century the creature was sometimes termed *stag of a hart*, the word *hart* denoting 'a male deer of six years and above'. (*Hart* is Germanic in origin and may ultimately derive from a root meaning 'horn', a reference to the animal's antlers.) If such a creature became the object of royal attention, and lived to run another day, it could be elevated in rank:

If the King or Queene doe hunt or chase him, and he escape away aliue, then . . . he is called a Hart Royall.
(J Manwood, TREATISE OF THE LAWS OF THE FOREST, 1598)

With all this emphasis on 'male animals in their prime', it is perhaps surprising that *stag* has never been colloquially applied to the human male in this way. But it has to the female. Yorkshire people are never afraid to take their independent path, it seems. Halliwell's DICTIONARY OF ARCHAIC WORDS of 1850 gives the obsolete northern dialect meaning as 'a romping girl'. Since the mid-nineteenth century, however, *stag* has cropped up in American English as a slang word to describe an event or activity arranged for men only – hence the twentieth-century coinage *stag night*, to describe a bridegroom's last night of revelry with his male friends before he marries.

DEER

The New Forest was preserved for all game but particularly the wild pig and three species of deer – the red, the fallow and the roe. According to the ANGLO-SAXON CHRONICLE, King William *forbade the harts and also the boars to be killed. As greatly did he love the tall deer as if he were their father*. This writer in the Chronicle was careful to describe the larger game in the Forest as *tall deer*, because in Old English the word *dēor* simply denoted 'a beast, a wild animal' of any sort. The word can be traced back to the unattested prehistoric Germanic *deuzom*, itself derived from an unattested Indo-European term *dheusom*, which meant 'breathing creature', derived from *dheus*, 'to breathe'. As hunting rights became connected to land ownership in the Middle Ages, *deer* was from the twelfth century onwards increasingly used to specify the red, fallow and roe deer that were so jealously protected and enthusiastically hunted. By the late fifteenth century, *deer* was rarely used in its general sense of 'animal' any more but, even so, as late as 1605 we find:

> . . . *mice and rats, and such small deer,*
> *Have been Tom's food for seven long year.*
> (Shakespeare, KING LEAR, 1605)

• The word *animal* has a similar underlying meaning to that of *deer*. It comes from Latin *animalis*, an adjective which meant 'having breath', being from *anima*, 'air, breath, life'.

QUARRY

After a good day's sport it was customary to reward the hounds for their effort in the chase. Certain parts of the deer – the heart, the liver and the bowels – were spread out upon the hide for the dogs to consume. The Old French word for this portion was originally *coree*, which also meant 'intestines' (from unattested Vulgar Latin *corata*, 'entrails', from Latin *cor*, 'heart'). However, since the hounds ate from the animal's hide, *coree* was gradually altered to *cuiree*, a form which was influenced by *cuir*, 'skin, hide'. This was taken into Anglo-Norman as the unattested forms *quire* or *quere* and then into Middle English in the early fourteenth century:

> *The houndes shal be rewardid with the*
> *nekke and with the bewellis . . . and thei*
> *shal be etyn under the skyn, and therfore it*
> *is clepid the quarre.*
> (Venery de Twety in RELIQUAE
> ANTIQUAE, c 1420)

Sometime during the fourteenth century *quarry* was also applied to 'a heap made of the deer killed in a hunt'. The hunting treatise MAISTRE OF THE GAME, which dates from the turn of the fifteenth century, stated that carts should go round throughout the hunt collecting the deer carcasses and adding them to the general pile or *quarry*. At the end of the hunt the master should *leede the kynge to the querre, and shewe it hym*. From the heap of carcasses the word was later applied to meat still on the hoof when, in the early seventeenth century, it was used to denote 'a hunted animal'.

(For another sense of the word, see **quarry** in **1070,** page 26.)

1086

WILLIAM I COMMISSIONS THE DOMESDAY BOOK

• • • • • •

The Domesday Book is a testimony to William the Conqueror's capabilities and competence as a ruler. The book was a great survey of all the lands of England and of their taxable resources. It listed the ownership of the estates, their size, value, populations and livestock. The monks compiling the Anglo-Saxon Chronicle were outraged by the thoroughness of the king's commissioners, possibly because Church possessions, too, came under the same close scrutiny:

> *So very narrowly did he have it investigated, that there was no single hide or yard of land, nor indeed (it is a shame to relate but it seemed no shame to him to do) one ox nor one cow nor one pig which was there left out, and not put down in his record: and all these records were brought to him afterwards.*

And an account written by Bishop Robert of Hereford in the year of the census itself also testifies to its exhaustive enquiry whose thoroughness and accuracy was subsequently carefully checked:

> *A second group of commissioners followed those first sent, and these were strangers to the neighbourhood, in order that they would find fault with their report and charge them before the king. And the land was troubled by many calamities arising from the collection of money from [sic] the king.*

DOOM

The indigenous population of England called William's great survey *Domesday*, a fact first recorded by the Exchequer in the twelfth century. *Domesday* is a Middle English spelling of *doomsday*. The unattested Germanic root *dō-*, meaning 'to place, to set', is ultimately responsible for doom. From this came Germanic *dōmoz*, meaning 'that which is set up', and hence 'statute, ordinance'. Old English took this as *dōm*, 'law, decree', and the word also carried the sense 'judgement, sentence, condemnation'. Its genitive form *dōmes* appears in the Old English coupling *dōmes dæg*, 'day of judgement', which became *domes dei* then *domesday* in Middle English. The implication of the popular title given to the census of 1086, therefore, was that of a sentence which was final and from which there was no escape. The thirteenth-century chronicler Matthew Paris said that the book was called *Domesday* because it spared no one but judged everyone indiscriminately, just as God will judge at the end of time.

In modern English *doom* usually means 'a terrible fate', in particular ruin or death:

> *Although it had been only about ten days since the two women were murdered in Shenandoah National Park, there was already a small poster appealing for information. It had colour photographs of them both. They were clearly photos taken by the women themselves along the trail, in hiking gear, looking happy and healthy, radiant even. It was hard to look at them, knowing their doom.*
> (Bill Bryson, A Walk in the Woods, 1997)

Doom's survival owes much to writers such as Shakespeare who revived words which were at the time obsolete or near-obsolete to enrich their own expression (see **1616**, page 153).

• The phrase *till doomsday*, meaning 'for ever', has been current since the turn of the thirteenth century. It refers to the end of the world and the Day of Judgement prophesied in the Bible. People have always supposed it to be a long way off, and thus the expression gained its current meaning. In the closing months of the second millennium, however, *doomsday* became an uncomfortable possibility. According to the calculations of the sixteenth-century astrologer Nostradamus, the end of the world was expected on 4 July 1999. The fact that Nostradamus

seemed to have had some success in predicting other, less cataclysmic, events correctly gave the credulous throughout the world pause for thought. In the event, *doomsday came and went…happily without the apocalyptic results predicted by Nostradamus*, the DAILY TELEGRAPH was pleased to report on 5 July.

1095

THE COUNCIL OF CLERMONT: POPE URBAN II PREACHES THE FIRST CRUSADE

••••••

In the middle of the eleventh century the formidable Seljuk Turks began to expand their empire in the eastern Mediterranean. They took Syria and Palestine, capturing Jerusalem in 1071 and closing the holy city to Christian pilgrimage. In the same year the Seljuks defeated the Byzantine emperor at Manzikert and proceeded to invade the imperial territories of Asia Minor, subjecting the Christian population to Muslim rule. On 27 November 1095, in response to an appeal for help from Emperor Alexius Comnenus, Pope Urban II convened a council at Clermont where he exhorted western princes and Church leaders to take up arms, repel the Muslim aggressors and recover Jerusalem and the Holy Land from the infidel. Christian Europe was zealous in its response and the First Crusade was launched the following year (see **1192**, page 54 and **1204**, page 57).

CRUSADE
Deus vult!, 'God wills it'. This cry from the crowd at Clermont affirmed the Pope's impassioned exhortation that Christians should *start upon the road to the Holy Sepulchre* in order to tear it from *the accursed race*. It was to become the battle-cry of the crusading armies. At Urban II's suggestion, the Crusaders were also distinguished by a cross of red worn on the front of their tunics, a Christian emblem which inspired the word *crusade*. The Latin for 'cross' is *crux*, a word which Old French had borrowed as *crois*, 'cross'.

A verb *croiser* was derived from this. It originally meant 'to cross (two objects)' and then 'to make the sign of the cross' but with the advent of the Crusades, it acquired the sense 'to take up the crusader cross'. The verb, in turn, yielded a noun *croisee*, which was formed from the feminine past participle and which meant 'crusade'. A variant, *croiserie*, was borrowed into Middle English towards the end of the thirteenth century and *croisee* itself is found about a hundred years later.

A bewildering choice of forms became available to seventeenth-century writers wishing to make historical reference to the Crusades. During the sixteenth century French had replaced *croisée* with *croisade*, the ending *-ade* being an alteration of Spanish and Provençal *-ada*, and English borrowed this new French form towards the end of the sixteenth century. Then, during the seventeenth century, English also borrowed the forms *crusada* and *crusado* from Spanish *cruzada* (a word derived from Spanish *cruz*, 'cross'). To complicate matters further, people began to blend these French and Spanish words to give *croisado* (French stem and Spanish ending). These forms all jostled for position until the appearance of *crusade* at the beginning of the eighteenth century. *Crusade* was yet another blend, this time with a Spanish stem and a French ending. With all the possibilities now exhausted, English had to make up its mind. *Crusade* swiftly won out, quenching the opposition by the end of the eighteenth century.

Meanwhile, in the second half of that century, the word was given a new lease of life when it began to be used figuratively to mean 'zealous opposition to a perceived evil':

This turgid drama is based on the true story of a Boston law firm that becomes embroiled in a costly battle against a corporation accused of polluting the water supply of a New England town. John Travolta stars as the crusading lawyer.
(Review of A CIVIL ACTION in THE TIMES, 10 April 1999)

But the word continues to be used in Christian contexts, where a *crusade* now refers to 'a zealous evangelistic outreach' against the modern enemy of blind unbelief. As for the medieval Crusades, attempts were made in 1998 to start making amends:

A group of 16 Western volunteers has arrived in Lebanon to apologise to Arabs for the atrocities committed by the Crusaders, 900 years after the Christian warriors first set foot in the Holy Land . . . Their act of repentance ends in Jerusalem on July 15 [1999], the 900th anniversary of the sacking of the city, when up to 70,000 Muslims were put to the sword.
(THE TIMES, 8 September 1998)

1105

THE COURT OF EXCHEQUER IS ESTABLISHED

......

The Treasury dates back before the invasion of England by William the Conqueror. At the beginning of the twelfth century, however, Henry I created the Exchequer, a department of state which incorporated the Treasury. The Exchequer was part of the royal household, and developed two main arms. The lower Exchequer took in and distributed money, while the upper Exchequer dealt with wider financial matters, with matters of revenue relating to the King and with some judicial affairs. Its members were of high rank. Their judicial function (originally just about pleas on revenue and financial matters, but widening in scope over the centuries) eventually gained them a place, as the Court of the Exchequer, between common law courts and the House of Lords.

The lower Exchequer is the antecedent of the contemporary Treasury, and the upper Exchequer is now a division of the High Court of Justice, after its incorporation in 1873. The head of the Treasury retains the title of Chancellor of the Exchequer.

EXCHEQUER

Twice a year, at Easter and Michaelmas, the sheriffs (*shire reeves,* 'high officials of the King in a locality') of England were expected to submit their accounts to the Exchequer. A large oblong counting table with a raised edge and a surface covered by a chequered cloth dominated the chamber in which the court sat. Here accounts were calculated by means of counters placed in particular squares on the table top. The table was known as the *Exchequer* because of the resemblance it bore to a 'chessboard', the original meaning of the word in Anglo-Norman and the earliest in Middle English. (Chess, a game of Eastern origin, had been introduced into Europe by the Moors in Spain. See **1492,** page 111.) The term originated in the Vulgar Latin word *scaccus,* which meant 'check'. From this the medieval Latin noun *scaccārium* was derived to denote 'a chessboard'. This was taken into Old French as *eschequier,* 'chessboard', arriving in Middle English by way of Anglo-Norman *escheker.* Under the Norman and Plantagenet kings the term, which was first applied to the table, eventually came to denote the department of state which contained it.

TALLY, COUNTERFOIL

When accounts were settled, the Exchequer's receipt came in the form of a *tally.* The word comes from the Latin *tālea* which meant 'rod, stick', for indeed a *tally* was just a simple, squared-off peg of hazel wood. Notches were cut into one of the tally's faces to represent the sum of money received and the stick was then split in two along most of its length. The longer piece, which included the handle, was offered as a receipt, the other, known as the *foil,* was retained by the Exchequer. The matching of the two pieces was proof of payment, hence the principal current sense of the verb *to tally,* 'to correspond, to be alike', which dates from the early eighteenth century.

The term *foil* to denote 'the portion of a tally held by the Exchequer' is first recorded in the fifteenth century. It originated in Latin *folium,* meaning 'a leaf', and came into English by way of Old French *foil.* Since a leaf is flat and thin the word was applied by analogy to other things with these properties. The term *counterfoil,* which also denoted 'the Exchequer's tally', is first found in the second half of the seventeenth century. In modern usage *counterfoil* refers more generally to 'that part of a cheque which is retained by the issuer as a record'.

Alternative terms for the two pieces of a tally, which were in use by the late sixteenth century, were *stock* for the longer part given as a receipt (see **stocking**, page 136) and *counterstock* for the portion kept by the Exchequer. Both are now obsolete.

The tally as a method of recording payment, loans and debts was finally discontinued by the Exchequer in 1782. The tallies stored by the department were later used as fuel to heat the Houses of Parliament until, on 16 October 1834, so many of them were crammed into the furnaces that they overheated, and the whole building caught alight and burned down. Subsequent parliamentarians have also found past financial records rather too hot to handle, on occasion.

• Latin *tālea* not only meant 'rod' or 'stick' but also 'cutting of a plant', a sense which yielded a number of English words such as *tailor, detail* and *entail* (see **retail**, page 87).

POUND STERLING

The sheriffs paid their accounts in silver pennies known as *sterlings* or *starlings*. A number of theories have been advanced to explain the etymology of this word. One of these attempts to connect the coin with Baltic traders, known at that time as *Easterlings*. Another states that the term was derived from Old English *stær* 'a starling', and was descriptive of coins struck in the time of Edward the Confessor which had four birds on them. A more satisfactory explanation is found in *steorling*, an unattested late Old English term which the Saxons applied to the silver penny struck by their conquerors. Some early Norman pennies had a little star stamped on one face and *steorling* means 'small star', being a combination of Old English *steorra,* 'star', and the diminutive suffix *-ling*.

When accounts were paid into the Exchequer the coins were first tested for purity and then weighed. Two hundred and forty pennies made one pound weight. The word *pound* was ultimately derived from *pondō*, a Latin measure of weight, and came into Old English by way of the unattested Germanic *pundo*. Silver had been weighed by the pound in Saxon times, so lending the term its monetary use. With the Normans and their successors came a form of reckoning such as *four thousand pound of sterlynges*. Eventually, the practice of adding the phrase *pound sterling* to a sum of money indicated that English currency was intended. The pound remained convertible into silver until the introduction of the gold standard in 1821. Two hundred and forty pence continued to make up one pound sterling until 1971, when the pound was decimalised.

1132

FOUNTAINS ABBEY IS FOUNDED

••••••

In 1098 a new monastic order was begun on bleak and inhospitable marshlands at Cîteaux, France. Its founders were a group of monks who left the Benedictine monastery of Molesme in Burgundy under the leadership of Abbot Robert. They wanted to revive strict adherence to the rule of St Benedict, which prescribed a simple life of prayer, poverty and manual labour. In 1112 the monks were joined by a zealous young nobleman, Bernard of Clairvaux, and the Cistercian Order began to expand.

In 1131 St Bernard sent a company of monks to Henry I in England. The king received them favourably and permitted them to found a house at Rievaulx in Yorkshire. The pious, hardworking little community soon attracted the attention of a group of Benedictines at St Mary's in nearby York, who began to press for the reform of their own house. By October 1132 the debate over proper adherence to St Benedict's rule had become so fierce at St Mary's that Archbishop Thurston, who had been called in to mediate, was compelled to remove the thirteen reformers and give them shelter. On

27 December the archbishop gave the group a tract of wasteland at Skeldale upon which to found a monastery. Here they endured harsh winters and extreme hardship, but survived. The abbey was admitted into the Cistercian Order in 1135 and went on to become one of the wealthiest monastic foundations in the country. Thus it was that Fountains Abbey was founded.

ABBOT, ABBEY, ABBESS

The leader of the group of dissenters at St Mary's in York was Prior Richard, and it was he who was elected abbot of the little community that gathered in the wastes of Skeldale in December 1132. He was to be their 'father', for that is what the word *abbot* means. It was ultimately derived from *abbā,* an Aramaic term which was expressive of a filial bond of intimacy and respect. In first-century Palestine *abbā* was the name children from their earliest years would use to address their fathers, and it meant 'dear father'. New Testament Christians were first encouraged by the example of Jesus to address God in this way, and in order to communicate this notion of filial intimacy, Bible translators through the centuries to the present have retained the word, giving it a place in modern English:

> For you did not receive a spirit that makes you a slave again to fear, but you received the Spirit of sonship. And by him we cry, 'Abba, Father.'
> (ROMANS 8:15, NEW INTERNATIONAL VERSION)

Jews would never have presumed to address God as *abbā* but they did honour their rabbis by extending the title to them, a use which was eventually adopted by the Christian Church. *Abbā* was taken into Late Greek as *abbás* and into Late Latin as *abbas,* 'abbot', whose accusative *abbātem* was taken into Old English as *abbod, abbud.* In the twelfth century Latin *abbātem* gave rise to a new form in Middle English, *abbat,* and this influenced Old English *abbod* to give *abbot.*

Sadly, the desolation and poverty of Skeldale and the spiritual needs of his monks were too much for Abbot Robert. It very soon became apparent that someone with more experience was needed if they were to survive, and so the community applied to Bernard of Clairvaux who, in 1133, sent one of his own monks to guide and teach them.

In order to achieve their ideal of a simple life and manual labour, the Cistercians always situated their abbeys in remote and inhospitable areas. The monks at Skeldale toiled long and hard to build their abbey, much of which was paid for by the sale of their excess produce. The word *abbey* was a thirteenth-century borrowing of Old French *abbeie.* This came from Late Latin *abbātia,* a term derived from the stem *abbāt-* of Late Latin *abbas.* (The noun *abbess* had a similar journey into English, arriving in the late thirteenth century from Late Latin *abbatissa* via Old French *abbesse.*) But although the Cistercians sought to practise austerity, the ingenuity they exercised in order to survive, together with their discipline and hard work, brought inevitable success and prosperity, and also generated the admiration of wealthy laymen who bestowed endowments upon the communities. The abbeys at Rievaulx and Skeldale grew wealthy on wool and over time brought new prosperity to deserted areas of northern England which had earlier suffered the ravages of Danish and then Norman invasions.

MONK, MONASTERY

The Cistercians wore habits of white wool, probably to spare the expense of dyeing the cloth and also to distinguish themselves from the Benedictines, who wore black. For this reason they came to be known as the 'White Monks'. The term *monk* is of Greek origin. In Late Greek *monachos* had denoted 'a religious hermit', one who lived a solitary life away from the world. The noun was the substantive use of the Greek adjective *monachos*, 'solitary', a derivative of *monos*, 'alone'. Before long, however, the noun *monachos* was also being used to denote 'a member of a religious community', a sense which eventually prevailed. The term was borrowed into Late Latin as *monachus*, 'monk', and was eventually taken into Old English as *munuc*.

Also from Greek *monos*, 'alone', came the verb *monazein*, 'to live alone'. Late Greek derived the noun *monastērion*, 'monastery', from this and Late Latin then borrowed the word as *monastērium*. Robert of Molesme named his new community at Cîteaux the *novum monastērium*, 'new monastery'. The Late Latin word has been borrowed twice into English. It first appeared in Old English as *mynster*, arriving by way of the unattested Vulgar Latin *monisterium*. *Minster* first denoted 'a monastery' and then 'a monastery church' and finally, more generally, 'a church of importance'. York, Lytchett and Wimborne are all celebrated still for their minsters. Its second appearance, as *monastery*, 'the buildings occupied by a community of monks or nuns', was a direct borrowing in the first half of the fifteenth century.

CONVENT, NUN

The Cistercian order became very successful and by the turn of the fourteenth century it had over 600 religious houses for both men and women. Modern English has the term *convent* to denote both 'a religious community of women' and 'the buildings occupied by such a community'. This particular use began to emerge towards the end of the eighteenth century. Until then *convent* could be applied to a community of either men or women. *Convent* (like English *convene, convention* and *convenience*) originates in the Latin verb *convenire*, 'to come together', whose past participle *conventus* came to be used as a noun meaning 'an assembly, a congregation'. When the word came into Middle English in the thirteenth century by way of Anglo-Norman *covent*, its principal application was to 'a religious community'. The Middle English form still exists in London's *Covent Garden*, where the monks of Westminster Abbey once grew their vegetables. The form *convent* is a latinised spelling which was introduced around the middle of the sixteenth century.

The residence for a community of nuns was known as a *nunnery*, a word which has an archaic ring in present-day English. The term first appeared in Middle English in the second half of the thirteenth century as *nonnerie* and is probably a direct borrowing of an unattested Anglo-Norman word derived from *nonne*, 'nun'. *Nun* on the other hand had come into Middle English from Old English *nunne*. It had been acquired from ecclesiastical Latin *nonna*, which was originally a courteous form of address to an elderly woman (Italian has *nonna* to denote 'grandmother') and was later respectfully applied to 'a woman devoted to religious service'. The word in its religious sense found its way into other Germanic languages and into French, hence the Anglo-Norman *nonnerie*.

CELL

All medieval monasteries, whatever the order, aimed at self-sufficiency. In his Rule, St Benedict himself wrote that a monastery should, if possible, *be built so that everything needed – water, mill, garden, bakery – is available, in order that the monks do not need to wander about outside, for this is not at all good for their souls*. The Cistercians adhered to St Benedict's ruling that no monk should travel so far from his abbey that he could not return the same day. For this reason they admitted lay brothers to the order, men from lowly walks of life who desired to share monastic life but were not constrained by the Rule. As the abbeys accumulated land given by benefactors, however, it became necessary to build *cells*, small dependent monasteries, so that monks and lay brothers could tend their more distant holdings. This use of *cell* in twelfth-century English arose from a particular and frequent application of *cella* in medieval Latin.

In Classical Latin *cella* had denoted 'small room, storeroom, temple sanctuary'. Late Latin also applied the word to 'a hermit's or monk's chamber', a use which was taken into Middle English in the early fourteenth century. Later that century *cell* began to denote 'one of several small single chambers in a monastery' and its application to 'a prison cell' evolved from this latter sense in the first half of the eighteenth century.

Classical Latin also used *cella* to denote 'a compartment' of a dovecot or a honeycomb. English applied *cell* similarly and went on to extend the word to denote other sorts of compartment. When Robert Hooke was using the newly invented microscope in 1665 to investigate organic tissue, for instance, he noticed that cork was apparently made up of many small compartments and he called these structures *cells*. In work on electricity, *cell* was first applied to one of the cavities in the trough of the voltaic battery devised by Cruikshank and subsequently to a 'vessel containing a pair of electrodes immersed in fluid' in other batteries.

• Monasteries had vast *cellars* or storehouses in which to keep their provisions. They were the province of the cellarer, the monk charged with managing the stores and catering. *Cellar* is derived from Latin *cella*. From this noun Latin derived *cellārium*, 'series of cells', a word which passed into Old French as *celier* and then into Middle English in the thirteenth century by way of Anglo-Norman *celer*. Such storerooms were not necessarily situated below ground but, since many of them were, the word *cellar* gradually came to mean 'underground room'.

1133

St Bartholomew's Fair Is Founded

······

Medieval Rome was an unhealthy spot – many people contracted malaria from the surrounding marshes. Rahere, a jester and minstrel at the court of Henry I, fell gravely ill on a pilgrimage to the city. He vowed that, if he were permitted to recover, he would reform his life and found a hospital devoted to the welfare of travellers and pilgrims and the care of the sick and needy (see **hospital**, page 52). In 1123 King Henry I granted Rahere a piece of land at Smithfield, just outside the walls of London. Here the jester built both a hospital and an Augustinian priory, of which he became the first prior. Both foundations were dedicated to St Bartholomew the Apostle, who, according to legend, was skinned alive, but who had appeared to Rahere in a dream. In 1133 the king helped Rahere still further by granting the priory a charter to hold a great fair annually at Smithfield. The tolls from the fair were to benefit the work of the priory.

MARKET

Markets have always existed for the sale and purchase of local produce. The word *market* can be traced back to the Latin word *merx* which meant 'merchandise'. A verb, *mercārī*, 'to trade', was derived from this, and its past participle gave the word *mercātus* to denote 'trade' and also 'a market'. In Vulgar Latin the noun changed to unattested *marcātus* and from there it was borrowed into Middle English as *market* around the middle of the twelfth century. Medieval markets were established by charter and carefully regulated. Tolls were demanded for permission to trade and fines imposed by the market court for any infringement of regulations. Since they were held weekly, markets could not be set up too close together for fear of damaging trade elsewhere. It was calculated that a man could expect to cover 20 miles (32 kilometres) on foot in one day before nightfall. This distance was divided by three to allow for the walk to market, buying and selling and the return journey. Thus 6⅔ miles (10½ kilometres) was established as the statutory distance between markets.

• *Market* and *merchant* are related words. Vulgar Latin derived the unattested frequentative verb *mercātāre* from Latin *mercārī*, 'to trade'. Its present participle *mercātāns* was borrowed into Old French as *marcheant*, 'trader', and then into Middle English in the late thirteenth century.

FAIR

Fairs were different from markets because they attracted merchants carrying goods from far afield, or from another country, and were held only once, occasionally twice, a year. Records of the existence of fairs before the Norman Conquest are scant but King William early encouraged their foundation. When a fair was in progress, all markets and shops in the vicinity were closed in its favour.

Fairs were strictly regulated in the same way as markets, with stallholders paying tolls to trade, and with disputes over weights, measures and quality being settled on the spot by the Pie Powder court (a corruption of the French phrase *pieds poudreux*, 'dusty feet'), an assembly of merchants which met for this purpose for the duration of the fair. Vendors were generally grouped together according to their trade or wares. Some fairs became well-known for a particular commodity: that of St Bartholomew, for instance, soon gained a reputation for cloth.

The word *fair* means 'holiday' and indeed, fairs were usually held on the saint's day of a local church or priory, with traders congregating to tempt the holiday crowds (see **holiday**, page 39). St Bartholomew's Fair at Smithfield, for instance, opened on 24 August, the Feast of St Bartholomew the Apostle, and ran for three days. *Fair* originated in the plural Latin noun *fēriae*, 'festival, holidays'. In Late Latin the singular form *fēria* was used. This was borrowed into Old French as *feire* and passed from there into Middle English towards the end of the thirteenth century.

Fairs were not only of commercial value, they provided welcome recreation, too. Showmen of all kinds turned up to entertain the crowds:

> *There were jugglers and tumblers, Morris dancers with bells on their shoes, cheap jacks bawling their goods, and quacks who offered cures for every known disease. There were booths where it cost a penny to see a puppet show, and there, surrounded by an admiring crowd, was the same sad performing bear, solemnly dancing to pipe and tabor.*
> (Cynthia Harnett, THE WOOL-PACK, 1951)

Rahere, the former jester, was Lord of St Bartholomew's Fair. He was a reformed character, but never became sanctimonious. Indeed, the prior could sometimes be found at the fair practising his former craft and juggling, to the delight of the crowd.

HOLIDAY

In Saxon times and in the Middle Ages, days were long and hard for craftsmen and peasants alike, who laboured from sunrise to sunset. The regularity of their existence was periodically interrupted by Church feast days which were set aside for religious celebration instead of work. The Old English word for a day of religious observance was *hāligdæg*, literally 'holy day', a compound of *hālig*, 'holy', and *dæg*, 'day'. This became *halidai* or *halliday* in Middle English. Of course a day off work is always welcome, whatever the reason. Holy days were eagerly awaited and were often marked by festivities and fairs. By the fourteenth century, the use of *halliday* simply to denote 'a day off work' was beginning to creep in, and during the sixteenth century was regularly used in this way. *Doo you not knowe that it is a holliday, a day to dance in, and make mery at the Ale house?* writes Barnabe Googe in his translation of Heresbachius's FOURE BOOKES OF HUSBANDRIE (1577). For this reason, since the sixteenth century, an effort has been made to use *holy day* to denote 'a religious festival' and *holiday* for 'a day of leisure'.

1137

ELEANOR SUCCEEDS HER FATHER, WILLIAM X, TO THE DUCHY OF AQUITAINE

••••••

It was not for her beauty, intelligence or energy that Eleanor was sought as a marriage partner but for Aquitaine, her inheritance. This considerable duchy, which comprised the southwest portion of present-day France, was annexed first to France in 1137 when Eleanor married Louis VII, and then to England in 1152 through her marriage to Henry II. Neither relationship was a success (the first ended in divorce) and Eleanor put considerable energy into maintaining a brilliant court of her own at Poitiers.

Eleanor was a cultured woman. She enjoyed the arts, poetry in particular, and invited people of talent, such as the renowned troubadour Bernart de Ventadorn, to Poitiers, where her court became a centre of culture and courtly manners. Aélis de Blois and Marie de Champagne, Eleanor's daughters by Louis VII, shared their mother's love of literature and from the 1160s onwards Marie in particular welcomed outstanding poets to her court at Troyes. The patronage of these women helped to advance the spread of courtly ideals in France.

CHIVALRY, CHIVALROUS

In the late eleventh century, literature began to flourish. The feudal system, now well established in France, and the Crusades (see **1070**, page 19 and **1095**, page 31) provided the stimulus for this awakening. The first excited pride in military prowess and aroused the concepts of honour and loyalty, while the second stimulated faith and Christian patriotism.

In northern France poets began to write *chansons de geste*, epic poems telling of heroic episodes from the reigns of Charlemagne and his successors. The word *chivalry* has its origin in Late Latin *caballārius*, which meant 'horseman', being a derivative of Latin *caballus*, 'horse'. Old French had the word as *chevalier*, 'knight', and then derived *chevalerie* from it to denote 'mounted fighting-men'. The earliest Old French appearance of both these terms was in the CHANSON DE ROLAND, a *chanson de geste* dating back to around 1080, although they were not taken into English until the thirteenth century.

The *chansons de geste* found ready audiences in the town squares but, as feudalism established itself further, the nobility began to emerge as a closed hereditary class and, under the influence of the Church, became more refined in its customs and behaviour. Gradually a code of knightly conduct emerged by which a chevalier was instructed to defend the holy Church against the infidel, to fight bravely for his feudal lord and sovereign, to display courtesy and honesty and to be swift to help the weak and women (see **knight**, page 20). The code also encompassed the concept of courtly love (see **romance**, page 42). This description of a true knight is by the fourteenth-century French poet Eustace Deschamps:

You should lead a new life:
Devoutly keeping watch in prayer,
Fleeing from sin, pride and villainy;
The Church defending,
The widow and orphan helping,
Be bold and protect the people,
Be loyal and valiant, taking nothing from
*   others,*
Thus should a knight rule himself.

He should be humble of heart and always
*   work*
And follow deeds of Chivalry;
He should attend tourneys and joust for his
*   lady love;*
He must keep honour with all
So that he cannot be held to blame.

No cowardice should be found in his doings,
Above all he should uphold the weak,
Thus should a knight rule himself.

All these ideals found expression in the courtly literature of the time. Chrétien de Troyes, for instance, a brilliant protégé of Marie de Champagne, debated them at her court in Troyes. Here he discovered the Celtic tales of King Arthur and his Knights of the Round Table and used their exploits to extol courtly virtues. (The legends had first appeared in French in a verse translation of Geoffrey of Monmouth's HISTORIA REGUM BRITANNIAE (1135) which the Anglo-Norman author, Wace, had dedicated to Eleanor of Aquitaine, Queen consort of England.) Thus the Old French term *chevalerie* also denoted 'the qualities idealised by knighthood', a sense which also passed into English when the word was borrowed in the thirteenth century.

Old French had derived the adjective *chevaleros*, meaning 'valiant like a knight' from *chevalier* towards the end of the twelfth century. It appeared in Middle English as *chevalrous* in the first half of the fourteenth century but its use soon waned as the age of the mounted knight in armour drew to a close. Spenser and Shakespeare used *chivalrous* as a historic term and by the early seventeenth century it was obsolete. Towards the end of the eighteenth century, however, the word reappeared in works dealing with medieval poetry and the spirit of that age. The adjective is now current once more, not only in historical appraisals but also to describe a man 'who displays courteous behaviour, particularly towards women'. However, with women's emancipation advancing apace, it is doubtful how much longer such attentiveness will be extended by one sex and tolerated by the other, so that *chivalrous* may soon be confined to purely historical contexts.

• In the sixteenth century the term *chivalry* to denote 'a company of mounted men-at-arms' was replaced by *cavalry*, a new borrowing from the same root. Late Latin caballārius was taken into Italian as cavaliere, 'horseman'. The Italians derived cavalleria from it to denote 'a company of mounted soldiers'. French borrowed this in the sixteenth century as cavallerie and, from there, it passed into English. In the sixteenth and seventeenth centuries the English form was cavallery, cavalry dating from the eighteenth century. (See **cavalier**, page 18.)

COURT, COURTESY, COURTEOUS

Chivalry demanded courtesy, a show of elegant manners and considerate behaviour towards others. Young boys of good birth were sent away to live in noble households where they acquired the graceful manners and military skills expected of a noble knight (see **knight**, page 20). Such accomplishments were most evident at court, and courtesy and courteous are derivatives of that word.

Latin had the word cohors (formed from Latin cum, 'together' and hort-, as in hortus, 'a garden') to denote 'an enclosure, a courtyard'. The term was also applied to any who might gather in such a yard – a retinue, for instance, or a company of soldiers. (This is the source of the modern English word cohort.) In Late Latin the accusative form cohortem was shortened to cortem and this was borrowed into Old French as cort, 'enclosed yard'. It was here that cort acquired the additional senses of 'a sovereign's retinue' and 'a judicial assembly', apparently from the term's association with Latin cūria early in its history. (Cūria, 'senate house', was used in medieval Latin texts to represent the word cort.) The Old French word was taken into Anglo-Norman as curt and from there, it passed into Middle English as court, with all these various senses.

Meanwhile, in the twelfth century Old French had derived the adjective cortois, curteis from cort to describe a knight whose manners were suited to the refinement of a royal court. According to a twelfth-century text, RONCEVAUX, ideal knights were Beaus et cortois, pleins de chevalerie,

'Handsome and courteous, full of chivalry'. Courteous reached English in the thirteenth century and was applied to many a gentle knight. The young squire in the CANTERBURY TALES (c 1387) had obviously learnt his lessons well, for Chaucer describes him as curteis, lowely and seruysable.

The Old French adjective cortois, curteis soon yielded the noun courtoisie, curtesie to denote 'courtly behaviour' and English acquired courtesy also in the thirteenth century. With the imposition of courtly behaviour came a number of helpful books on etiquette such as the BOKE OF CURTASYE and THE BABEES BOKE. In his BOKE OF NURTURE (1450) Hugh Russell, Duke of Gloucester, instructs the young page in great detail on how to lay a table, adding that he should serve his lord on one knee, bow in response to him and remain standing until told to sit. Russell also frowns at spitting, belching loudly and licking dishes. Such texts were indispensable for those whose behaviour was less than delicate:

> Let not thy privy members be lay'd open to
> be view'd,
> it is most shameful and abhorr'd, detestable
> and rude.

Compare the manners of Chaucer's prioress, obviously a well-bred lady, who would set any aspiring knight a fine example of how to behave at table:

> At mete wel y-taught was she with-alle,
> She leet no morsel from hir lippes falle,
> Ne wette hir fyngres in hir sauce depe.
> Wel koude she carie a morsel and wel kepe,
> That no drope ne fille upon hire brest;
> In curteisie was set ful muchel hir leste.
> Hire over-lippe wyped she so clene,
> That in hir coppe ther was no ferthyng sene
> Of grece, whan she dronken hadde hir
> draughte.

In modern English both courteous and courtesy have lost this dimension of courtly etiquette, retaining only the notion of civility and considerate behaviour. But this expectation of thoughtful conduct now pervades all areas of life, even crowded roads where drivers are constantly reminded that highway courtesy saves lives and the delivery lorries belonging to a well-known high street store bear the message *If driven discourteously call. . .* followed by a telephone number. Courteous behaviour often implies a measure of goodwill. Thus *courtesy* is sometimes found in compounds such as *courtesy title, courtesy card* and *courtesy car,* to denote something to which the recipient is not strictly entitled but which is given as a favour.

• In the early sixteenth century *courtesy* began to be used to denote 'a customary gesture of respect to a social superior'. In the BOKE OF KERUYNGE (1513) the young page was instructed *Whan your souerayne is set . . . make your souerayne curtsey.* About the same time the variants *curtsy* and *curtsey* were beginning to come into use and, by the second half of the century, were often replacing *courtesy* in this context. By the seventeenth century the *curtsey* was understood to be a feminine action of respect involving lowering the body by bending both knees. Men *made legs and bows,* actions which were fraught with potential social embarrassment, as this anecdote written in the late seventeenth century at the expense of the proud courtier Edward de Vere, Earl of Oxford, shows:

> *This Earle of Oxford, making of his low obeisance to Queen Elizabeth, happened to let a Fart, at which he was so abashed and ashamed that he went to Travell, 7 yeares. On his returne the Queen welcomed him home, and sayd, My Lord, I had forgott the Fart.*
> (John Aubrey, BRIEF LIVES, c 1693)

Now what would the BOKE OF CURTASYE have had to say about that?

ROMANCE
The eleventh century saw the rise of the troubadours, minstrel poets who, for two centuries, flourished in Provence and northern Italy. It is not surprising that Eleanor of Aquitaine appreciated the poetry of the region; it was in her blood, for the earliest surviving troubadour poetry we have was written by her grandfather, Guilhem IX of Aquitaine. Much of the poetry's charm (and linguistic legacy) lay in the fact that it was composed in the vernacular rather than the usual Latin. Since Old French used *romanz* to denote the vernacular when making a distinction between it and Latin, the word was also applied to verse or prose narratives written in French by the troubadours and those whom they subsequently influenced. Old French *romanz* was a borrowing of unattested Vulgar Latin *Rōmānicē,* which meant 'in the vernacular' (as against *Latinē,* denoting 'in Latin'). *Rōmānicē* itself had been derived from Latin *Rōmānicus,* 'made in Rome', a derivative of *Rōmānus,* 'Roman', a word from *Rōma,* 'Rome'.

The nobility in the warm Midi region of France enjoyed a calmer and more luxurious lifestyle than in the turbulent and war-torn North, and the women were at leisure to enjoy troubadour company and entertainment. The works of the most gifted troubadours centred around the sweet theme of love, its joys and sorrows, and from this preoccupation there developed the cult of courtly love, which drew its inspiration from divine love. In an age where noble marriages were usually political or economic contracts, as Eleanor of Aquitaine's were, the heart was secretly given elsewhere. A knight sought to achieve perfection through devotion to his lady, who tested and strengthened his worth, valour and love by requiring him to perform certain feats in her service (see Eustace Deschamps in **chivalry**, page 39). Thus chivalry and courtesy were inspired by love:

> *Noble lady, I ask of you*
> *To take me as your servitor;*
> *I'll serve you as I would my lord,*
> *Whatever my reward shall be.*

Look, I am here at your command,
You who are noble, gay and kind.
(Bernart de Ventadorn, mid-12th
century)

Ideally, the lady's married state made her inaccessible, so that her knight was gloriously ennobled by an unconsummated passion. (This, at least, was true in courtly literature, though rarely achieved in real life.)

Eleanor of Aquitaine and her daughters were instrumental in spreading these courtly ideals northwards. Marie de France, famous for her Anglo-Norman LAIS, and Thomas d'Angleterre, who wrote a celebrated prose version of TRISTAN, were both resident at Eleanor's court in England. Marie de Champagne was a patron of the widely influential poet Chrétien de Troyes who explored the nuances of love and the chivalric ideal in his narrative poems of Arthur and his knights and is credited with originating the medieval romance.

The Old French word *romanz, romant* was borrowed into Middle English as *roma(u)ns, roma(u)nce* during the thirteenth century to denote 'a story-poem in the vernacular telling of love and chivalrous exploits'. These strands are still evident in modern English where *romance* refers either to 'a highly fanciful and unrealistic tale' or to 'a love story':

Add to these an amusing collection of bucks,
blades, dandies, rogues, rakes, rapscallions,
dowds and diamonds of the first water and
you begin to taste the flavor of a Regency
Romance. Bright, witty, light-hearted and
customarily chaste, Regency Romances
capture the fragile glitter of a fleeting and
romantic moment in history.
(Elisabeth Fairchild, WHAT THE DEVIL
IS A REGENCY ROMANCE?, 1998)

This last meaning has led to romance being used to denote 'a love affair' or the intensity of emotion experienced in such a relationship:

Publicity has played a large part in 34-year-
old Sophie Rhys-Jones's life, not least
because she met her future husband, Prince
Edward, at a charity event organised by
MacLaurin, the public relations company
that employed her.
Edward was due to play real tennis
against Sue Barker, who unfortunately had
to cancel at the last minute; Sophie stood in
and a royal romance was born.
(RADIO TIMES, 12–18 June 1999)

c 1167

OXFORD UNIVERSITY COMES INTO BEING

• • • • • •

Education in medieval times was undertaken by the Church in monastic or cathedral schools. For ambitious clerics a sound education was the key to ecclesiastical or secular advancement, and students would travel from far afield, or even abroad, to learn from a gifted master. Excellence attracts excellence: an outstanding teacher invariably attracted others of his calibre. In consequence, a town might gradually gain a reputation for intellectual brilliance and become a centre for various schools, offering advanced instruction that exceeded the scope of that in the cathedral schools. These had concentrated on Church life and clerical issues. Now, the university, or *Studium Generale*, as it was called, extended its compass to more general matters, such as medicine, law and the arts.

Paris had been a major centre of learning since the early twelfth century. It gained recognition as a *Studium Generale* some time after 1150 and its schools, which were attached to the Cathedral of Notre-Dame, attracted a large community of English clerics. In 1164, however, Thomas à Becket, the Archbishop of Canterbury, fled to France to escape the English king, Henry II, with whom he was locked in dispute (see **1173**, page 49). In 1167 Henry issued an ordinance requiring the repatriation of all clerics residing in France but possessing revenues in England. Failure to comply would entail forfeiture of those revenues. Becket did not return but the other clerics did. Those from the university at Paris migrated to Oxford, a strategically placed town, where schools to accommodate them were established around the parish church of St Mary. Thus it was that the *Studium Generale* at Oxford came spontaneously into being.

UNIVERSITY

The Latin adjective *ūniversus* means 'whole'. It is a compound of *uni-* (from *ūnus*), 'one', and *versus*, past participle of *vertere*, 'to turn', and its literal sense is, therefore, 'turned into one'. From the adjective Latin derived the noun *ūniversitās*, which meant 'the whole'. Late and medieval Latin used this word, particularly in legal documents, to refer more specifically to 'a society, a corporation', of merchants or craftsmen, for instance. The notion was that of the entire membership being as one. In the twelfth century the new appetite for study led to a migration of students or masters from all over Europe to centres of academic excellence. Scholars and teachers residing abroad would form themselves into a society, a *ūniversitās*, to provide the mutual support and protection they were denied as foreigners. At the renowned law school of Bologna the *ūniversitās* was a student-led body, its German, English and French members undertaking to hire their own tutors locally. In Paris another *ūniversitās* was established, this time a corporation of foreign masters, of whom there were many. Students here paid to attend lectures. The university at Oxford followed the northern European pattern established in Paris, being run by its professors. Medieval Latin *ūniversitās* was borrowed into Old French as *universite* in the early thirteenth century, and from there into Middle English around the turn of the fourteenth century.

DEGREE, GRADUATE

Degree originated in *dēgradus*, 'a step down', an unattested Vulgar Latin word made up of the Latin prefix *dē-*, 'down', and *gradus* 'a step'. It was borrowed into Old French as *degre* and from there directly into Middle English in the first half of the thirteenth century. From its earliest appearance, *degree* acquired a number of figurative applications, all relating to stages in a process or to grade or rank. In the universities of the thirteenth century *degrees* were regarded as 'steps' towards a Mastership and then a Doctorate. The progression was like that of the manual trades where an apprentice proved his abilities, was then licensed to practise his occupation and apply for guild membership, and eventually became a master craftsman. University students were accepted at an early age, some as young as fourteen, the only entrance requirement being proficiency in Latin, the language in which they were taught. Many did not stay more than a couple of years, though four years' study of the liberal arts was required to qualify for a first degree (see **bachelor**, page 21), which was usually examined orally by disputation. After a total of seven years' study, a successful candidate would be awarded the Master's degree and receive a licence to teach the arts. At this stage diversification took place, with students going on to study canon law, civil law, medicine or, most demanding of all, theology. The degree of Doctor of Sacred Theology took a further nine years and was the pinnacle of medieval education.

The notion of an educational step is also reflected in the word *graduate*. From Latin *gradus*, 'a step', came the medieval Latin verb *graduāre*, 'to admit to a university degree', whose past participle *graduātus* gave English *graduate* in the fifteenth century.

• *Degrade* shares the same origins as *degree*. From *dē-* and *gradus* Late ecclesiastical Latin coined the verb *dēgradāre*, which meant 'to deprive someone of rank'. The word came into Middle English in the fourteenth century where it was soon widely used in the sense 'to demote' as a disciplinary measure. In Church contexts, for instance, it meant 'to deprive a priest of his orders'. A knight might be *degraded* for unchivalrous conduct or a university graduate be *degraded* from his degree. At the close of the twentieth century *degrade* is used in military contexts with the sense 'to reduce the enemy's capability':

NATO's goal is to degrade Yugoslav forces' ability to continue their offensive against Kosovar Albanians, alliance officials said in Brussels April 2. Serb forces are beginning to experience fuel shortages, they reported.
(Linda D Kozaryn, AMERICAN FORCES PRESS SERVICE, April 1999)

• Latin *gradus* is also evident in a number of other English words, among them *grade, gradient, retrograde* and *gradual*.

The Latin verb *ingredī*, 'to enter', was formed from the prefix *in-*, 'in', and the verb *gradī*, 'to step', another product of *gradus*. From its present participle *ingrediēns* (stem *ingredient-*) Middle English took *ingredient*, 'something that goes into a (medical) compound or mixture', in the fifteenth century.

STATIONER
As European intellectual activity grew there was a great need for more books. Previously the production of books had been undertaken by monasteries; now lay scribes were set up in workshops to satisfy demand. Nevertheless, hand-copied books were beyond the means of many students and so texts were always read out during lectures and then commented on by the teacher. Copies of books could be bought, or even hired, from the *stationer*, a bookseller authorised by the university to provide those volumes prescribed for the students' study. There is evidence of a stationer at Bologna University in the mid-thirteenth century and at Oxford by 1262.

Medieval Latin had the term *statiōnārius* to distinguish 'a shopkeeper', of whom there were very few (see **c 1350**, page 87), from an itinerant vendor. The word ultimately came from Latin *stāre*, 'to stand' and the derived noun *statiō*, a 'standing still'. Although booksellers in the Middle Ages were itinerant, those licensed by the universities kept permanent shops, hence the application of the medieval Latin term *statiōnārius*. When the word was finally borrowed into Middle English as *staciouner* during the late fourteenth century, it was with the narrower meaning 'bookseller' and not 'shopkeeper'.

Formerly a *stationer* not only sold books but also generally kept a stock of parchment, pens and ink for sale. By the mid-seventeenth century, the stationer's business was beginning to separate into two distinct trades: that of the bookseller who sold texts printed and bound, and that of the *stationer* who dealt in paper, pens, ink and wax. This distinction was complete by the mid-eighteenth century. The collective term *stationery*, which probably developed from *stationary ware(s)*, dates from the 1720s, though the spelling with the letter *e*, which distinguishes it from the adjective *stationary*, was not fixed until the first half of the nineteenth century (see **station**, page 199).

LIBRARY

As universities were established, generous benefactors founded libraries and bestowed gifts of books. The *libraria communis* of Oxford was set up in the 1320s by Bishop Cobham of Worcester. Its precious store of books was chained to prevent theft. Students worked under the eagle eye of an attendant chaplain who ensured that none of the stock was damaged by wet clothing or spilt ink – note-taking was to be in pencil only. Nor were knives permitted in the library, thus removing the temptation to cut out and make off with relevant pages.

The Middle English word *librarie* first appeared in Chaucer's BOETHIUS (c 1374). It was a borrowing of Old French *librairie*, 'library', in use from the early twelfth century onwards. This was derived either from Latin *libraria*, a shortening of the phrase *libraria taberna*, 'a bookseller's shop', or *librarium*, 'a place to store books' (Cicero, 43 BC and Ammianus Marcellinus, AD 400). At the root of these forms is Latin *liber*, 'book', itself a derivation from *liber*, 'bark'. The Greeks and Romans held that, in early times, the inner bark of trees was used as a writing material. The meaning of *library* has always been constant in English. In the Romance languages, however, its cognates have come to denote 'book shop' and derivations from Latin *bibliothēca*, 'collection of books', are used for 'library'.

• *Libel* is derived from Latin *libellus*, 'little book', a diminutive of *liber*, 'book'. In the fourteenth century this was a legal term denoting 'the written complaint of a plaintiff'. In the sixteenth century the term was applied to a scurrilous pamphlet circulated to embarrass someone in the public eye and thus, by the seventeenth century, had come to mean 'a defamatory statement'.

1170

WILLIAM MARSHAL BECOMES A GUARDIAN OF THE YOUNG PRINCE HENRY, HEIR TO THE ENGLISH THRONE

••••••

William Marshal was a landless knight who rose to become *rector regis et regni*, 'governor of the king and of the kingdom'. In his youth his great valour and skill at arms brought him to the attention of Eleanor of Aquitaine, wife of Henry II, who appointed him guardian of her eldest son (see **1137**, page 49 and **knight**, page 20). The Prince died in 1183 but William went on to serve four kings as a soldier and statesman: Henry II, Richard I, John and finally Henry III, to whom he was appointed regent. Each lord he served with unfailing loyalty, courage and wisdom. He was rewarded by being accepted into the Order of the Knights Templars and lies buried in the Temple Church. He was, in the words of Stephen Langton, Archbishop of Canterbury, *the best knight that ever lived.*

MARSHAL

The origin of *marshal* lies in the unattested prehistoric Germanic word *markhaskalkaz.* This compound, made up of the unattested *markhz,* 'horse' (from which English *mare* is derived), and *skalkaz,* 'servant', denoted 'a groom' or 'a stable-hand'. Frankish Latin borrowed this as *mariscalcus* which, under the Frankish kings, came to denote 'master of the horse'. By the time the word had passed into Old French as *mareschal,* the position carried even greater weight. So essential was cavalry to medieval warfare that the *mareschals* were given the additional responsibilities of maintaining order, both in the king's court and his military camp, and of judging matters relating to the laws and practice of chivalry. Eventually, they were recognised as among the chief officers of the court, having charge of the sovereign's military affairs. The Norman and Plantagenet kings also had their marshals. As his name shows, William *Mareschal* (or *Marshal*) was elevated to that post and was one of the marshals in attendance at the coronation of Richard I in 1189. That same year he married Isabella, heiress to Richard FitzGilbert, Earl of Pembroke. After this date the office of *Marshal* was never again held by anyone of lower rank than an earl, thus establishing the title *Earl Marshal.* This is now a hereditary title held by the Dukes of Norfolk.

In the present day, it is military men who mainly use the title: for officers of the very highest rank, the British Army has used the title *Field Marshal* since 1736. In August 1919 George V approved four titles for use in the new service that had shown its worth in the recently ended Great War (*Marshal of the Air, Air-Chief-Marshal, Air-Marshal* and *Air-Vice-Marshal*). The expression *Marshal of the Royal Air Force* came in after the Second World War.

The verb *to marshal* has meant 'to draw up soldiers for battle or parade' since the sixteenth century. The figurative sense 'to arrange in methodical order' (*to marshal one's resources, to marshal one's thoughts*) developed at about the same time. In formal modern English *to marshal* can also mean 'to conduct a person ceremoniously' (*he marshalled him to the door*), a sense which arises from the role of *marshal of the hall,* the person who, in great medieval households, was responsible for the organisation of banquets and ceremonies.

TOURNAMENT

Medieval sources claim that tournaments began around the middle of the eleventh century and were the inspiration of Geoffroi de Preuilly, a French knight. They originally took the form of mock battles, fought in open country with real weapons, and were intended to prepare a knight for the battlefield (see **knight**, page 20). The word *tournament* ultimately stems from Greek *tornos,* which denoted 'a carpenter's compass', and then also 'a turner's wheel'. Latin borrowed this as *tornus,* 'lathe', and from it Vulgar Latin derived the unattested verb *tornidiāre,* which meant 'to wheel, to turn'. Old French took this as *torneier,* 'to tourney, to joust', the allusion being to the contestants' wheeling about to face each other in the fray, and the noun *torneiement* was derived from it. Tournaments were introduced into England in the twelfth century, Middle English borrowing the word *tornement* from Old French in the thirteenth.

Tournaments were widely advertised by heralds and minstrels. Feudal lords, accompanied by their knights and squires, would come from far afield to take part. Some would-be combatants arrived alone and offered their services to a lord for the occasion. Contestants formed themselves into two sides, each knight endeavouring to take captives from the opposition. A captured knight had to pay ransom money or forfeit his horse or armour. The event gave those without land or fortune, like William Marshal, the opportunity to demonstrate their skill at arms and accumulate wealth (see **bachelor**, page 21 and **ransom**, page 55). In one particular tournament Marshal won a total of twelve horses and it was at the tourney that his prowess as a knight was recognised by Eleanor of Aquitaine, who secured his services for her son, Prince Henry, in 1170.

But tournaments aroused heavy opposition. The Church was concerned that the events distracted the Christian knight from his calling as a Crusader, while the kings, particularly Henry III, feared that they might become hotbeds of sedition. Both were dismayed by the casualties and fatalities that inevitably occurred. Gradually tournaments were tamed; weapons were blunted and regulations laid down. Jousting, which relied upon the skill of two practised horsemen facing each other in the lists, replaced battles altogether and events were staged with an increasing air of pageantry. Tournaments were also absorbed into the rituals of courtly love, for a knight could hope to win his lady's favour by fighting for her in the lists (see **romance**, page 42).

Increasingly fanciful and extravagant, tournaments continued into the sixteenth century but finally died out around 1559 when Henry II of France was pierced in the eye and died of his wounds a few days later. The word *tournament* survived, however, occasionally being used to denote 'an encounter', until in the mid-nineteenth century it began to be applied to 'a contest of skill in which an overall winner is determined through a series of elimination games': a *tennis, darts* or *chess tournament*, for instance.

• Greek *tornos*, 'lathe', 'compass', is responsible for other English words through its borrowing into Latin as *tornus*, 'lathe':

Latin *tornus* became *to(u)r* in Old French where it initially meant 'lathe' but also denoted 'a circular movement'. The term was borrowed into Middle English as *tour* in the fourteenth century, its application to 'a journey around and back again' arising in the seventeenth century. How many tour operators since, or their clients, have realised the connection of their holiday journey with a lathe or carpenter's compass?

Latin derived the verb *tornare*, 'to turn in a lathe', from *tornus*. This was taken into Old English as *turnian*, 'to rotate', becoming *turn* in Middle English, its use probably reinforced by Old French *to(u)rner*, which was similarly derived.

CHAMPION

In his youth William Marshal fought in over five hundred tournaments and was truly a *champion*, that is to say 'a fighting man, a man of valour'. The word *champion* goes back to the Latin word *campus* which originally denoted an 'open field' but then developed the senses 'field of battle' and 'tournament arena' where soldiers and gladiators practised and fought. From this, medieval Latin derived the word *campiōnem* to denote 'a combatant' who fought in such an arena. Old French had the word as *champion* and from there it passed into Middle English in the first quarter of the thirteenth century. Besides meaning 'fighting man', champion early came to mean 'one who fights on behalf of another'. In a tournament a knight might be a lady's *champion*, fighting on her behalf and wearing her token in his helmet (see **romance**, page 42). And William Marshal was a *king's champion*, that is 'one who fought for the king'. From 1187 until Henry II's death in 1189, for instance, Marshal fought valiantly alongside his sovereign in France. The figurative sense of 'one who defends a person or cause' emerged in the fourteenth century and is still current:

On his arrival in Philadelphia he [Benjamin Franklin] was chosen a member of the Continental Congress and in 1777 he was despatched to France as a commissioner for the United States. Here he remained till 1785, the favorite of French society; and with such success did he conduct the affairs of his country that when he finally returned he received a place second only to that of Washington as the champion of American independence. (Charles W Eliot, Introductory Notes to THE AUTOBIOGRAPHY OF BENJAMIN FRANKLIN, 1909)

Strong *champions* who fight valiantly often prevail and so, at the very beginning of the nineteenth century, the word was adopted by sports enthusiasts to denote 'a winner, one who has vanquished his opponents', a use which seems to have originated in prize-fighting:

This hero, who justly stiles himself in his advertisement, 'Champion of England', was himself to exhibit all his science. (SPORTING MAGAZINE, 1802)

Nowadays a champion prize-fighter is known as a *champ*, an ugly abbreviation which originated in American usage in the second half of the nineteenth century.

MEDLEY
In English *medley* first denoted 'general hand-to-hand combat between two parties of knights'. According to Grant Uden in his DICTIONARY OF CHIVALRY (1968), medleys were usually friendly contests, although disaster sometimes struck. He cites a bout that took place in 1240 where sixty knights lost their lives, either crushed by falling horses or choked by dust. William Marshal developed the tactic of loitering on the periphery of the action, close to the

crowd of spectators, and then rushing into the medley when the other combatants appeared to be tiring. The source of the word *medley* was Latin *miscēre*, 'to mix'. From it Vulgar Latin formed the frequentative *misculāre*, 'to mix up', from which the unattested noun *misculāta*, 'mixture', was derived. Old French then borrowed the word as *meslee*. Primarily this meant 'mixture' but it was the narrower sense of 'a combat', an allusion to the mingling and mixing of fighting soldiers, that was first taken into English in the fourteenth century, in the shape of *medlee*, a variant of *meslee*. Not until the fifteenth century did English begin to use the word to denote 'a mixture or miscellany'. Today, the main uses are a *musical medley* (of mixed tunes or songs) and a *swimming medley* (of various strokes).

• Old French *medlee* was derived from the verb *medler* (variant of *mesler*), 'to mix'. *Meddle* was borrowed into English in the fourteenth century. It meant 'to mix' but soon picked up the sense 'to involve oneself' with a matter and gradually gained the sense 'to interfere'.

• Old French *meslee* evolved into *mêlée* in modern French and this word was borrowed into English just before the mid-seventeenth century to denote 'a confused struggle or skirmish' – very much the fourteenth-century meaning of *medley*. Nowadays, it is as likely to be used of an affray outside a nightclub or of a jostling crowd outside a court-house.

1173
THOMAS À BECKET IS CANONISED
......

In 1154 the new king, Henry II, following the recommendation of the Archbishop of Canterbury, appointed Thomas à Becket Chancellor. Any hopes the Archbishop nursed that Becket would support the interests of the Church at court were soon dispelled. The new and brilliant Chancellor gave the king his undivided loyalty in all matters and became a close and trusted friend. When the Archbishop of Canterbury died, Henry appointed Becket in his place, hoping for his friend's help to keep the Church in subordination. Instead Becket resigned his chancellorship, transferring his wholehearted loyalty to his new responsibility, the Church. The relationship between Henry and Becket deteriorated from then on as interests of Church and realm clashed.

Who will rid me of this turbulent priest? After eight years of conflict Henry's reckless cry of anger and frustration provoked an unintended response. On 29 December 1170, four of the king's leading knights, *clad, head and body in full armour, everything covered but their eyes, and with naked swords in their hands,* entered the cathedral at Canterbury and struck the archbishop down:

> *Four wounds in all did the saintly archbishop receive, and all of them in the head: the whole crown of his head was lopped off . . . A certain Hugh of Horsea, nicknamed Mauclerk, put his foot on the neck of the fallen martyr and extracted the blood and brains from the hollow of the severed crown with the point of his sword.*
>
> (William FitzStephen, LIFE OF THOMAS BECKET, c 1180)

As soon as news of Becket's death was out, people began to make their way to the martyr's tomb. Healings and miracles were reported and on 12 July 1173 he was canonised by Pope Alexander III, his shrine becoming one of the principal centres of pilgrimage in Europe.

SHRINE

In 1174 King Henry himself, barefoot and dressed in rough wool garments, made a pilgrimage to the martyr's tomb at Canterbury as an act of penance for his involvement in the archbishop's murder. That same year the choir of the Norman cathedral burned down (see **cathedral**, page 24) and in 1175, while rebuilding was underway, a shrine to Becket was also begun.

The Romans kept precious books, documents and letters safe in chests or boxes. The Latin word for such a chest was *scrīnium*. This was borrowed into the Germanic languages, coming into Old English as *scrīn* and developing into *shrin(e)* in Middle English. The word's primary application at the turn of the eleventh century was to the biblical ark of the covenant which contained the two tablets of the law, but it also denoted 'reliquary'. The shrine to St Thomas was no mere casket, however. It was a tomb-like construction containing not only the relics of the saint, placed there on 7 July 1220, but also numerous costly gifts. The whole was richly decorated. A Venetian visitor to the shrine around the turn of the sixteenth century left the following description:

> *The tomb of St Thomas the Martyr excels all belief. Notwithstanding its great size, it is wholly covered with plates of pure gold, yet the*

gold is scarcely seen because it is covered with various precious stones, as sapphires, balasses, diamonds, rubies and emeralds; and wherever the eye turns something more beautiful than the rest is observed. Nor, in addition to these natural beauties, is the skill of art wanting, for in the midst of the gold are the most beautiful sculptured gems, both small and large, as well as such as are in relief, as agates, onyxes, cornelians and cameos; and some cameos are of such size that I am afraid to name it; but everything is far surpassed by a ruby, not larger than a thumb-nail, which is fixed at the right of the altar. The church is somewhat dark, and particularly in the spot where the shrine is placed, and when we went to see it the sun was near setting; nevertheless, I saw that ruby as if I had it in my hand. They say that it was given by a King of France.

Not surprisingly, such a tantalising display of riches proved an overwhelming temptation to Henry VIII when he dissolved the monasteries. In 1538 the treasure adorning the shrine was confiscated and an order given for the bones of Becket to be burnt. It was the end of nearly four centuries as one of Europe's most famous shrines. The saint is still venerated, however, in virtual presence through a website on the Internet.

PILGRIM
The Holy Land, the tombs of Saints Peter and Paul in Rome, those of St James at Santiago de Compostela in Spain and St Thomas à Becket in Canterbury were great centres of medieval pilgrimage. A pilgrim was easily identified by the way he dressed. He wore a rough grey gown and wide-brimmed hat. In his hand he carried a staff and over his shoulder a scrip and bottle containing basic provisions. At each shrine the pilgrim would collect a badge in memory of his visit. That of Compostela was a scallop shell, while the badge of Thomas à Becket bore the saint's likeness.

Pilgrimages to far-flung holy places were not possible for everyone, however, and were undertaken only by the very devout or those seriously expiating their

sins. Shrines of local reputation were important, attracting all kinds of people. The group described by Chaucer, making the relatively short journey from London to Becket's shrine in Canterbury, included a miller, a summoner, a clerk, a yeoman, a merchant, a knight, a monk and a friar.

The word *pilgrim* reflects the notion that the traveller's devotional journey has taken him out of his own neighbourhood or country. It comes from Latin *peregrīnus*, meaning 'stranger, foreigner', and found its way into Middle English by way of Old French *peligrin* around the turn of the thirteenth century. *Peregrīnus* itself was derived from Latin *pereger* which meant 'on a journey, travelling through a (foreign) land', being composed of *per*, 'through', and *ager*, 'land, country'. In English, therefore, *pilgrim* first meant 'traveller, wayfarer' but its particular, and enduring, application to 'a person on a devotional journey' was swift to follow.

CANTER
According to Chaucer, spring was the season of pilgrimage, when the earth stirred to new life after the severity of winter:

Whan that Aprill with his shoures soot [sweet]
The droghte of March hath perced to the roote
And bathed every veyne in swich licour
Of which vertu engendred is the flour . . .
And smale foweles maken melodye,
That slepen al the nyght with open ye . . .
Thanne longen folk to goon on pilgrimages,
And palmeres for to seken straunge strondes [shores],
To ferne halwes [distant shrines], kowthe in sondry londes;
And specially from every shires ende
Of Engelond to Caunterbury they wende,
The hooly blisful martir for to seke,
That hem hath holpen whan that they were seeke [sick].
(Chaucer, THE CANTERBURY TALES, PROLOGUE, c 1387)

Chaucer's pilgrims were a light-hearted crowd in a holiday mood, who ambled along the road to Canterbury gossiping and exchanging stories to entertain each other. English pilgrims, travelling long distances on horseback to visit the shrine of St Thomas à Becket, did not tire either themselves or their horses by galloping, but rode at a comfortable pace which was known as a *Canterbury trot* or *gallop*. Successive generations pruned the term: in the seventeenth century it was sometimes simply referred to as a *Canterbury*, and in the eighteenth it was shortened still further to *canter*.

HOSPITAL

Lodging for weary pilgrims was available along the pilgrimage routes in monasteries, inns or hospices. The GUIDE DU PÉLERIN, a twelfth-century French guidebook for pilgrims, details three great hospices serving the routes to Jerusalem, Rome and Santiago de Compostela. Such foundations belonged to religious orders, and their work involved not only the reception and comfort of pilgrims but also the care of the sick and destitute.

When the word *hospital* arrived in English around the turn of the fourteenth century, it denoted 'a lodging for pilgrims and travellers'. Its earliest recorded use refers to *an hospital arerd of Seint Thomas* in Canterbury. *Hospital* is ultimately derived from Latin *hospes*, which meant 'guest' or 'host'. The stem of this word, *hospit-*, gave the adjective *hospitālis*, 'relating to a guest', from which medieval Latin derived the noun *hospitāle* to denote 'a place where guests are received'. Old French borrowed this as *hospital* and from there it was taken into English. But besides its simple application to a lodging for pilgrims and wayfarers, *hospital* specifically denoted 'hospice', with a wider mission to tend poor and ailing pilgrims. It had thus been applied to the various establishments of the Knights Hospitallers, the crusading order devoted to the reception and defence of pilgrims to the Holy Sepulchre. Pilgrimages, particularly those to distant shrines, were arduous and dangerous undertakings. A pilgrim might

have to endure extreme weather conditions, he might be attacked along the way or pick up a disease of some sort. In the twelfth century the Knights Hospitallers could shelter up to 2,000 poor pilgrims in their monastery in Jerusalem, besides caring for the sick.

The application of *hospital* to an institution providing for the welfare of local people – the elderly or destitute, for instance – began to emerge in the early fifteenth century. Not until the sixteenth century did *hospital* begin to denote specifically 'an establishment providing medical care'. The first mention of *hospital* in this modern sense comes with reference to St Bartholomew's Hospital in London. This hospice had been founded in 1123 by a pilgrim who had safely returned from Rome, having contracted a serious illness while travelling. It was run by a master and his staff of eight monks and four nuns who tended the sick, provided for the needy and took in travellers. In the sixteenth century the institution became a *hospital* in the modern sense when it was refounded by Henry VIII. It then provided 100 beds and was staffed by a physician and three surgeons (see **1133**, page 37).

• *Hospital* is related to a number of other words derived from Latin *hospes*, 'guest, host':

Hospitals and hospices were founded upon the spirit of *hospitality*, 'the kindly reception of guests'. The word came into English in the fourteenth century by way of Latin *hospitālitās* and Old French *hospitalité*. The adjective *hospitable* was borrowed into English in the sixteenth century.

Old French had derived the noun *(h)ostel*, 'a lodging', from medieval Latin *hospitāle* and this was borrowed into English as *hostel* around the middle of the thirteenth century. French *hôtel* was a later form of *(h)ostel*. English borrowed the word as *hotel* and used it to denote 'a higher-class lodging' from the second half of the eighteenth century.

Hospice was borrowed into English in the nineteenth century by way of Latin *hospitium*, 'hospitality', and French *hospice*.

It first denoted 'a lodging for pilgrims' or 'a refuge for the sick or destitute'. The word's application to 'a home for the care of the terminally ill' arose towards the end of the century. The modern *hospice* *movement* was established in the second half of the twentieth century. The movement's first hospice, St Christopher's in London, was founded in 1967 by Cicely Saunders.

c 1186

GIRALDUS CAMBRENSIS WRITES HIS TOPOGRAPHIA HIBERNICA

••••••

Giraldus Cambrensis (Gerald of Wales) was a cleric, the son of a Welsh princess, who nursed a lifelong ambition to become bishop of the ancient see of St David's, Pembrokeshire, and achieve its independence from Canterbury. This dream was not to be, however, for although he was twice nominated to the see, he was twice thwarted. Instead Giraldus gained recognition for his written works.

In 1185 King Henry II sent the youthful Prince John to Ireland in an attempt to reinforce his authority there. Giraldus was among the Prince's party. The journey was a disaster as far as John was concerned, for his immature political conduct provoked unrest and he was soon recalled to his father's side. Giraldus Cambrensis, however, took the opportunity to study the island and produced two books, the TOPOGRAPHIA HIBERNICA (Topography of Ireland, c 1186) and the EXPUGNATIO HIBERNICA (Conquest of Ireland, c 1187). Giraldus was invited to read aloud to the Masters of Oxford the latter volume, with its descriptions of the countryside and its fauna as well as an early history of the country. A subsequent journey around Wales with Archbishop Baldwin of Canterbury, made in order to muster soldiers for the Third Crusade, resulted in an ITINERARY and a DESCRIPTION of that country. An autobiography, written in the early thirteenth century, provided an outlet for his frustrations over the bishopric of St David's.

BARNACLE

Which came first, the chicken or the egg? The barnacle or the barnacle goose? According to observers of wildlife in the Middle Ages, the miraculous goose did not begin life as an egg at all. Some maintained that the bird developed like a fruit on trees growing beside the Irish Sea and fell into the water beneath when mature. Others held that it grew from a substance squeezed from rotting logs along the seashore, which then became encased in a shell, inside which the bird developed. This last explanation was published by Giraldus Cambrensis in his TOPOGRAPHICA HIBERNICA (1186) and was all the more persuasive for being an eyewitness account:

They are like marsh geese, but somewhat smaller, and produced from fir timber tossed along the sea, and are at first like gum; afterwards they hang down by their beaks as from a sea-weed attached to the timber, surrounded by shells, in order to grow more freely. Having thus, in process of time, been clothed with a strong coat of feathers, they either fall into the water or fly freely away into the air. They derive their food and growth from the sap of the wood, or the sea, by a secret and most wonderful process of alimentation. I have frequently, with my own eyes, seen more than a thousand of these small bodies of birds hanging down on the sea-shore from a piece of timber, enclosed in shells and already formed.

The wondrous bird was called a *bernaca* in medieval Latin, a name of uncertain origin which was subsequently taken into Middle English as *bernak*, evolving into *barnakylle* by the fifteenth century.

The mythology surrounding the goose is understandable enough. The birds breed in the Arctic seas and travel south to the coasts of Britain for their winter warmth, so their nesting habits were unknown centuries ago. Giraldus Cambrensis confidently stated that the geese *do not breed and lay eggs like other birds, nor do they ever hatch any eggs, nor do they build nests in any corner of the earth.* Imagination helped to make sense of the sudden appearance of the birds. Close observation of the crustacean from which Cambrensis and others supposed them to have sprung revealed a protruding feathery byssus suggestive of plumage. John Gerard, writing in the sixteenth century, described a rotting tree trunk which he found in the sea encrusted with the shells. Inspecting them he observed *birds covered with soft down, the shell half open, and the birds ready to fall out, which no doubt were the fowls called barnacles* (HERBALL, 1597). Not surprisingly, by the late sixteenth century both the crustaceans and the geese were known as *barnacles*, until the eighteenth century when the birds became known as *barnacle geese.*

It is surprising just how long the belief persisted. Izaak Walton reiterated it in his COMPLEAT ANGLER (1653) and there is evidence to suppose that the story was still generally accepted amongst uneducated people as late as 1870, for PALL MALL magazine for 12 October of that year reported that *The barnacle is supposed by simple people to be developed out of the fishy parasite of the same name.* But to the saints of past centuries the geese were more than an interesting quirk of nature, they were manna from heaven, the provision of the good Lord for his saints. Giraldus explains:

. . . bishops and religious men in some parts of Ireland do not scruple to dine off these birds at a time of fasting, because they are not flesh born of flesh.

On a dark winter's day a nice bit of roast goose went down a treat and the conscience was not even ruffled.

1192

RICHARD THE LIONHEART IS TAKEN HOSTAGE

......

On his way to the Third Crusade, Richard I of England spent the winter in Sicily. There he involved himself in a quarrel over the succession to the Sicilian throne, his intervention helping to prevent

Henry VI, the German king and Holy Roman Emperor, from assuming power. In 1192 Richard was compelled by reports of his brother's treacherous attempts to seize power in England to abandon the Crusade and return home. Shipwrecked in the Adriatic near Venice, he travelled by way of Vienna, disguising himself to escape the notice of Leopold V, King of Austria, with whom he had quarrelled on the ramparts of Acre. Richard's ruse was unsuccessful, however. Leopold arrested the Lionheart in Vienna in December 1192 and imprisoned him in the castle of Dürnstein on the Danube. Some two months later, in February 1193, Leopold handed over his hostage to another of Richard's enemies, Henry VI (see **1095**, page 31).

RANSOM

The price the Holy Roman Emperor demanded for Richard's release was high. The Lionheart was forced not only to relinquish his kingdom to the Emperor and pay homage for its return as a fee, but also to agree to a ransom of 100,000 marks together with a further 50,000 marks in place of knight service in Sicily. The English, who had already been heavily taxed to send their king off on the Third Crusade, were now compelled to pay this huge sum to get him back again. A new tax was levied on all lands, laymen gave a quarter of their chattels (see **chattel**, page 23), the Church surrendered some of its treasures and the Carthusians and other monastic orders tendered the year's revenue from their wool (see **1132**, page 34).

In February 1194 enough of the ransom had been paid to 'buy' Richard back. Indeed, the word *ransom* comes from the Latin verb *redimere* which meant 'to buy back', being a compound of *re-*, 'back, again', and *emere*, 'to buy' (English borrowed the verb, possibly by way of French *rédimer*, as *redeem*, in the fifteenth century). From *redimere*, Latin then derived the noun *redemptiō* to denote 'the action of buying back'. *Redemptiō* found its way into Old French where it circulated in two different forms. It is apparent in *rédemption*, which became *redemption* in English, but much less easily recognisable in *ransoun*, both of which meant 'the act of obtaining a captive's freedom by payment'. *Ransoun*

was borrowed directly into English from Old French in the early thirteenth century, by which time it had developed the extended meaning of 'the sum paid for the release of a captive', its common use today:

'Just what happens in a kidnap case?' asked Reed mildly . . .
'Normally, unless the abductors and their hideout can be quickly established, they make contact and demand a ransom. After that, you try to negotiate the return of the hostage. Investigations continue, of course, to try to locate the whereabouts of the criminals. If that fails, it's down to negotiation.'
(Frederick Forsyth, THE NEGOTIATOR, 1989)

Some of Richard's ransom quite properly found its way into the hands of Leopold V, who very sensibly spent it on extending Vienna and enclosing it with walls.

Ransoms were a common feature of medieval tournaments and warfare, soldiers sparing the lives of their important prisoners to secure a reward (see **tournament**, page 47). The more influential the prisoner, the higher the ransom demanded. The capture of a king was the greatest prize of all, hence the phrase *a king's ransom* to denote 'a large sum of money'. Naturally, in the turmoil of the battlefield it was sometimes difficult to determine which man had captured a noble knight. According to Froissart's contemporary account of the Battle of Poitiers in 1356, by the time the captured

French king, John II, appeared before the Black Prince, up to ten knights and squires were claiming the prize. With a king's ransom at stake, who could blame anyone for joining in? King John himself eventually identified his captor, Denys de Morbeque, who received a modest payment of 2,000 nobles, a mere fraction of the king's ransom which was eventually paid for the return of John to his own kingdom.

1198

THE SHERIFF OF LONDON INTRODUCES MEASURES TO REDUCE THE RISK OF FIRE

••••••

Medieval towns were fortified, encircled by sturdy walls. Inside, space was limited and the houses, particularly of the poor, were huddled together, their upper storeys overhanging the alleyways that separated them. The houses consisted of a timber framework packed with woven reeds which were then plastered with clay. Roofs were thatched. For warmth and comfort, reeds were strewn over the floors. Fire was a constant hazard. Sparks from the fire which burned in a pit in the centre of the room might easily set a thatch or carpet of reeds alight and the blaze would spread swiftly along a row of houses. When the alarm was raised the thatches would be torn off neighbouring properties to prevent the fire spreading, while water was brought from nearby wells or storage tubs to douse the flames.

In 1198 the sheriff of London introduced a number of building regulations designed to reduce the risk of fire. In future, party walls in rows of wooden houses were to be built of stone to a height of 16 feet (5 metres) and a thickness of 3 feet (1 metre), and roofing thatch was to be replaced by stone or tiles.

CURFEW

The *curfew* was a medieval law devised to minimise the risk of fire. The regulation was known in Old French as *covre-feu* (later *couvre-feu*), literally 'cover-fire' (from *couvrir*, 'cover' and *feu*, 'fire'), which gave *coeverfu* in Anglo-Norman and *courfew* or *curfu* in Middle English. Each evening, usually at eight o'clock, a bell would be rung as a signal either to extinguish the fire or to cover the embers with a special lid until morning. In time *couvre-feu* was applied to the bell as well as the regulation. Indeed, in the earliest English references, which date from the thirteenth century, the word is obviously applied to the signal, or to the hour of its ringing.

Using the curfew bell as a means of controlling activity in a town is very long-established. Tradition has it that the curfew was introduced into England by William the Conqueror, who then used the bell to prevent seditious groups meeting under cover of darkness. Whether or not this is true, it is certainly the case that, in medieval towns, the curfew bell became a way of restricting comings and goings by night, in an attempt to preserve order. Edward Rutherford, in his novel LONDON (1997), describes the city settling down for the night:

> *Darkness had fallen. The curfew bell had sounded. The ferry-boats had all withdrawn across the river and tied up on the London side – this was the rule, so that no Southwark thieves could slip across the water into the city. The watch was posted on London Bridge and the city prepared to pass another quiet night under the protection of the king's ordinances.*

From this use comes the present-day meaning of *curfew*, 'an order, usually in times of unrest or danger, obliging people to clear streets and public places and return home by a certain hour':

> *Life under the curfew continued two days. Tourists were trapped in Kathmandu because the airport had closed down. Nepalis suffered, too. A young village woman carrying a load of grass in violation of the curfew was accosted by some soldiers near us. She panicked and ran, whereupon they mindlessly shot and killed her.*

(Thomas Hale, LIVING STONES OF THE HIMALAYAS, 1993)

although, these days, a curfew may also be imposed upon an individual:

> *An electronic tag can enable early release from jail. Just remember not to put the rubbish out after curfew.*
> (THE INDEPENDENT, 10 May 1999)

The medieval curfew bell is still rung in some old English towns. In Midhurst, West Sussex, it sounds at eight o'clock each evening. There is a story that a rider from London was overtaken by nightfall and stranded on the heath. Unable to find his way, he followed the far-off toll of a curfew bell and was brought to Midhurst. Such was his gratitude that he gave a parcel of land, now called the 'Curfew Garden', to provide income for the continued nightly ringing of the bell. Things have moved on, though. Since 1990 the Midhurst curfew has been rung by an electronic system paid for by another benefactor.

1204

CONSTANTINOPLE IS CONQUERED IN THE FOURTH CRUSADE

······

Trade with Asia was greatly stimulated by the Crusades (see **1095**, page 31) and Venice was eager to consolidate and extend her already significant share. The Fourth Crusade provided an opportunity. In return for ships to transport the Crusaders, Venice pressed for an attack on the mighty Byzantine capital, Constantinople, which fell on 13 April 1204. The Latin Empire, which was subsequently established there by the Crusaders, gave the Venetians freedom of the city and trading stations on the Greek mainland, and acknowledged their possession of a number of strategically placed Mediterranean islands, such as Crete and Corfu, which had been wrested from Byzantine control. Venice's commercial prominence in the Mediterranean was assured.

*One of the most precious commodities which passed through Venice after the fall of Constantinople was spices. Although cheap at source, the great distances that Arab traders had to cover with their ships and caravans to procure them and the taxes and tributes demanded en route (not to mention the vagaries of the weather and attacks by robbers) made spices an expensive luxury in Europe. From the thirteenth century the spice trade was monopolised by Venice, who exacted large profits in her role as broker. Eventually, in the late fifteenth century, voyages of discovery were undertaken by Europeans seeking direct access to Eastern markets (see **1492**, page 111).*

SPICE

The medieval diet was monotonous. People ate a limited range of local produce and then, through the long winter months, the supplies they had managed to dry or preserve in brine. Small wonder, then, that when the Crusaders tasted the spices of the Orient on their travels to the Holy Land, they sought to bring them back to Europe. Spices were used in the kitchens of the rich to bring welcome variety and to disguise the taste of food that was no longer quite fresh. Spices were so expensive that they were kept under lock and key. Margaret Paston went to great lengths to secure the best price she could before purchasing her household requirements. On 5 November 1471 she sent a letter from Norfolk to her son John in London which included these instructions:

> *. . . and send me word what price a pound of pepper, cloves, mace, ginger, and cinnamon, almonds, rice, ganingale, saffron, raisins of Corons, greens. Of each of these send me the price, and if that it be better cheap at London than it is here, I shall send you the money to buy with such stuff as I well have.*

The word *spice* first appeared in Middle English around 1225. Its origins lie in Latin *speciēs*. This was a derivative of the verb specere, 'to look' (see **spectacles**, page 69), and denoted first 'appearance' and later 'kind', 'sort' (hence *species* which

was borrowed into English in the sixteenth century). Late Latin used *speciēs* to mean 'goods' or 'wares' of a particular kind. But when the word was taken into Old French as *espice* and from there into English as *spice*, it was used exclusively to denote the aromatic spices of the East.

According to Maistre Chiquart, head chef to the Duke of Savoy in the early fifteenth century, cinnamon, ginger and pepper were classified as major spices, while nutmeg, cloves and mace were minor ones.

CINNAMON

Cinnamon is obtained from the dried inner bark of the cinnamon tree and was brought back from Ceylon (present-day Sri Lanka). Then, as now, the highly specialised task of preparing the harvested tree shoots, stripping away the inner bark and rolling it into quills, was carried out exclusively by the Salagama caste. In the early thirteenth century cinnamon was known in English as *canele*, a word which reflects the fact that cinnamon was sold in sticks. *Canele*, which came into Middle English by way of Old French, was derived from medieval Latin *canella*, a diminutive of *canna*, 'cane' (see **canal**, page 177 and **cannon**, page 81). The spice is known by cognates of this word in the modern Romance languages.

In the ancient world the sweetly scented spice was used by Egyptian embalmers and the Jews burnt it as incense in religious ceremonies. The Hebrew term *quinnāmōn*, a word of non-Semitic origin (Skeat points to the similarity of Malay *kayu manis*, 'cinnamon', literally 'sweet wood'), is responsible for the English word *cinnamon*, which first appeared in the late fourteenth century. *Quinnāmōn* was borrowed into Greek as *kinnamōmon* and then into Latin as *cinnamomum*. From there it passed into Middle French as *cinnamome* and Middle English as *sinamome*. The modern English spelling, however, was influenced by the later Greek and Latin forms, *kinnamon* and *cinnamon* or *cinnamum* respectively.

CLOVE

A banquet recipe for a thick stew dating from the second half of the fourteenth century calls for a large quantity of small birds, such as sparrows and starlings, boiled up in a meat stock flavoured with ground almonds (also known through the Crusades) and spiced with cinnamon and cloves.

Cloves, which are the dried flower-buds of a tropical tree, came from the Indonesian archipelago. *Karuophullon*, the Greek name for the clove, literally means 'nut-leaf', being a compound of *karuon*, 'nut', and *phullon*, 'leaf'. The latinised form *caryophyllum* was borrowed into Old French as *girofle* and from there into English as *gilofre*, and this was the original name of the spice. The French, however, thought that the spice looked rather like a nail and soon began to call it *clou de girofle*, literally 'girofle nail'. This form was taken into Middle English in the early thirteenth century as *clowe of gilofre* or *clowe-gilofre* but was inevitably soon shortened to *clowe* or *cloue*. Thus the name of the spice has its origins in Latin *clāvus*, 'nail', from which the French word *clou* is derived. Meanwhile the discarded *gilofre* was applied to the clove-scented pink and, influenced by *flower*, evolved as *gillyflower*.

GINGER, GINGERBREAD

Like the clove, *ginger* was named for its appearance. The spicy-tasting root is native to southern Asia, where its antler-like shape gave rise to the Sanskrit word *śṛṅgavēram*, from *śṛṅgam*, 'horn,' and *vēra-*, 'body' (that is 'form'). Prakrit took this as *singabēra* which became *ziggiberis* in Greek. The word then passed into Latin as *zinziberi*, from which the Late Latin forms *gingiver* and *gingiber* evolved. The spice was known in late Saxon England, for the word occurs as *gingifer* in an Old English text dating from the turn of the eleventh century. When the term next appears in the context of early thirteenth-century commerce, it is written as *gingivere*, this time either a borrowing of or influenced by Old French *gingivre*.

Preserved ginger, probably used for medicinal purposes, was known as *gingibrātum* in medieval Latin, a term derived from Late Latin *gingiber*. This was borrowed into Old French as *gingebras* and from there into Middle English in the late thirteenth century. But English struggled with the strange-sounding final syllable *-bras*, and by the mid-fourteenth century had substituted a familiar everyday English word *bred*, 'bread'. By the fifteenth century, *gingerbred* no longer denoted 'preserved ginger' but was more appropriately applied to a type of spiced bread sweetened with honey. Such a confection had been made in Paris in the previous century. It was known (and still is) as *pain d'épices*, 'spiced bread'. Curiously, the early English recipe contained grated bread and honey flavoured with a mixture of spices such as saffron and pepper, but no ginger – perhaps ginger was added later so that the bread might finally conform to its name, or perhaps the vital ingredient was omitted in error by a scribe:

> *Take a quart of hony, & seethe it, & skeme it clene; take Safroun, pouder Pepir, & throw ther-on; take grayted Bred, & make it so chargeaunt that it wol be y-lechyd; then take pouder Canelle, & straw ther-on y-now; then make yt square, lyke as thou wolt leche [slice] yt; take when thou lechyst hyt, an caste Box leves a-bouyn, y-stykyd ther-on, on clowys. And if thou wolt haue it Red, coloure it with Saunderys [sandalwood] y-now.*
> (Two Cookery-Books, c 1430)

The medieval taste was for colourful presentation. Food was often dyed brilliant colours, as the recipe above suggests, and details picked out in gold leaf. In Du Fait de Cuisine (1420) Maistre Chiquart specifies 18 pounds (9 kilometres) of gold leaf to decorate dishes for a two-day royal feast. Gingerbread, too, was often highly gilded and this tradition persisted. It gave rise to a number of idioms whose general sense was that things were not quite as they appeared. Written records of the common expression *to take the gilt off the gingerbread*, meaning 'to strip something of its appeal', are surprisingly recent, however, and date from the end of the nineteenth century.

• In the early eighteenth century horse dealers discovered that inserting ginger into a horse's backside made him sprightly and hold his tail well. According to Francis Grose's CLASSICAL DICTIONARY OF THE VULGAR TONGUE (1785), the original term was to *feague* a horse. (Grose adds that, before ginger was thought of, an eel was reputedly used for the same purpose.) Not surprisingly, to *feague* was eventually replaced by a new coinage, *to ginger*, which appeared in print in the first quarter of the nineteenth century. This verb, often with the particularly appropriate addition of *up*, was soon figuratively extended to mean 'to liven up', and in this sense is now a common colloquialism.

• In the eighteenth century cockfighting was extremely popular (see **1849**, page 207). A cock with reddish feathers not unlike the colour of ground ginger was called a *ginger,* so that in the nineteenth century *Ginger* became a common nickname for a person with red hair.

• *Gingerly* has nothing at all to do with the spice or with feaguing horses. When it was first used in the early sixteenth century the adjective meant 'daintily, with tiny steps'. *Gingerly* probably evolved from Old French *gensor*, a comparative form of *gent* which meant 'of noble birth' and hence 'graceful'. This, in turn, was a borrowing of Latin *genitus*, 'well-born', the past participle of *gignere*, 'to bring forth, to beget'.

MACE, NUTMEG
A thirteenth-century encyclopedic work, DE PROPRIETATIBUS RERUM, which was translated into English by John of Trevisa in 1398, states that *the Mace is the flowre, and the Notmygge is the fruyte.* In fact the fragrant nutmeg is the seed of *Myristica fragrans*, a tree native to the Moluccas (Spice Islands) of Indonesia, while mace is the dried aril, or netlike covering, which surrounds it.

According to Chaucer, the aromatic nutmeg was commonly used to flavour ale. By the sixteenth century, in common with all the spices, nutmeg was held to have healing properties; English herbalists advised daily consumption of nutmeg for a hearty constitution, while the renowned Dutch doctor Bernardus Paludanus claimed that *nutmegs fortify the brain and sharpen the memory; they warm the stomach and expel winds* (ITINERARIO, 1598).

The *nutmeg* was named after its aromatic, musky quality, the word being ultimately derived from Latin *nux*, 'nut', and *muscus*, 'musk'. This evolved into the unattested Vulgar Latin form *nuce muscāta*, which was taken into Old French as *nois mug(u)ede*. Anglo-Norman had the unattested variant *nois mugue* (or *muge*), but when this passed into Middle English in the fourteenth century the first element was translated to give *notemugge* or *nutemuge*.

The origins of *mace* are more obscure. The form *macis*, which was borrowed into Middle English from Old French, was mistaken for a plural and *mace* was formed from it as its singular. *Macis* possibly comes from Latin *macir* and Greek *makir*, which was not mace at all but a word for the bark of a spicy Indian root which, like mace, was reddish in colour.

PEPPER
The dried berries of the pepper vine, imported from Indonesia, were enjoyed as a condiment by both the Greeks and the Romans, who borrowed the Sanskrit term *pippalī*, 'berry', as *peperi* and *piper* respectively. Cognates of the Latin word exist in many Old Germanic languages, showing that the spice was introduced to the Germanic peoples along with its Latin name before the fourth century. Old English *pipor* is found in texts dating from around the turn of the eleventh century, as is *pipor corn*, 'peppercorn', to

denote an individual berry (see **corn** in **maize**, page 117). In ancient Greece and Rome tributes were often demanded in pepper. Similarly, in the Middle Ages pepper was so valued that it was worth its weight in silver and town accounts were sometimes kept in it.

• *Pepper* was extended to plants of the genus *capsicum*, which is native to the tropics of America, in the seventeenth century – presumably because a number of them are particularly pungent to the taste, like pepper itself. The word *capsicum* was probably derived from Latin *capsa*, 'box', in the seventeenth century, the allusion being to the hollow fruit.

*Sugar was another valuable commodity for which Venice became a willing broker in the Middle Ages. Until sugar was known in Europe the only sweetening agent was honey. Demand for sugar was high and its scarcity made it extremely expensive. Small wonder, then, that when the Catholic kings finally agreed to support Columbus's voyage to the Indies (see **1492**, page 114), the explorer took sugar cane with him to see if it would thrive elsewhere. Columbus planted the cane on Haiti and its success encouraged the subsequent establishment of lucrative sugar plantations in the New World (see **1627**, page 160).*

SUGAR
Sugar cane probably originated in New Guinea, its cultivation following the migration routes to Southeast Asia and India. In 327 BC one of Alexander the Great's officers reported seeing a kind of reed growing near the River Indus which produced honey without bees. The word *sugar* finds its source in Sanskrit *sakarā*, meaning 'gravel' or 'grit' and hence also 'sugar', because of its gritty crystals. When the cane was introduced into Persia, the Sanskrit term was borrowed as *shakar*. It was the Persians who were responsible for the spread of sugar cane cultivation and refinery through the Arab world. In Arabic the Persian word *shakar* became *sukkar*.

The Crusaders sampled sugar while in the Middle East. One of them, Albert von Aachen, recorded with amazement how the citizens of Tripoli would suck on a kind of cane to extract its sweet flavour. Its intense sweetness conquered palates and won new hearts, prompting Crusaders to take samples home with them. This created demand for the product, a lucrative trade that Venice was happy to facilitate. Arabic *sukkar* was taken into medieval Latin as *succarum*, *zuccarum*, and from there into Italian as *zucchero*. The term finally found its way into English by way of Old French *sukere*, *zuchre* in the late thirteenth century.

CANDY
The Sanskrit word for sugar in larger lumps was *khanda (sakarā)*, 'candied sugar'. *Khanda* originally meant 'fragment', being derived from the root *khand*, 'to break'. The term was borrowed into Persian as *kand* and from there into Arabic as *sukkar quandī*. This found its way into all the European languages, *sugar candy* arriving in English in the late fourteenth century by way of French *sucre candi*. Not until the second half of the eighteenth century did *candy* begin to stand alone. It was used to denote a 'sugar confection' from the early nineteenth century, though *sugar candy* persisted:

> *Handy-pandy, Jack-a-dandy*
> *Loved plum cake and sugar candy;*
> *He bought some in a grocer's shop,*
> *And out he came,*
> *Hop, hop, hop.*

Candy was taken up more widely in American English where today it denotes any sugar- or chocolate-based confection. In modern British English, candy is a type of boiled sweet.

SYRUP
Only a small amount of sugar was traded into Europe in the Middle Ages and it was dispensed or sold through apothecaries or grocers. (Grocers in those days sold goods available through

Mediterranean trade such as dried fruits, spices and sugar – see **grocer**, page 88) Added to liquid, sugar formed a syrup. Syrups were useful for disguising the taste of nasty medicine and, indeed, sugar itself was regarded as medicinal in its own right. *I pray you speak to Master Roger [a physician] for my syrup, for I had never more need thereof, and send it me as hastily as ye can,* wrote the ailing Margaret Paston on 5 February 1472. Syrups were also made up in the kitchen, being excellent for enhancing the flavour or preservation of fruit. The word *syrup,* which appeared in English in the late fourteenth century, is of Arabic origin. Arabic had the verb *shariba*, 'to drink'. From this the noun *sharāb* was derived which denoted 'a beverage' of any kind. The Arabs made heavy use of sugar to sweeten their drinks and so, when *sharāb* was borrowed into European languages, it denoted 'a thick sweet liquid'. The term came into English by way of medieval Latin *siropus* and Old French *sirop*.

MARZIPAN

When the meagre supplies of sugar were not being stirred into syrups they were being made into confectionery. Venice was well placed for shipments of Arab sugar, and European confectionery was first made in the city state around the middle of the fourteenth century. When sugar supplies from the New World started to come into Europe in the sixteenth century, sugar confection became an established art. The rich found the sweetmeats addictive. A visitor to the Elizabethan court had this to say about the queen and her courtly subjects:

> . . . *next came the Queen, in the 65th year of her age (as we were told), very magestic; her face oblong, fair but wrinkled; her eyes small, yet black and pleasant; her nose a little hooked, her lips narrow, and her teeth black (a defect the English seem subject to, from their too great use of sugar)* . . .
> (Paul Hentzner, TRAVELS IN ENGLAND, 1598)

Marzipan, or marchpane as it was then known, was probably one of the confections which contributed to the queen's deteriorating dental health. When she visited Cambridge University the Chancellor, Sir William Cecil, was presented with two pairs of gloves, a marchpane and two sugar loaves. The etymology of *marzipan* is uncertain but a suggestion from Kluyver is recognised at least for its ingenuity, if not for its certainty. He claimed in 1904 that the word derives from Arabic *mawthabān*, which literally means 'seated king'. *Mawthabān* was the name the Arabs gave to a medieval Venetian coin, apparently representing the value of a ten per cent tax, which was embossed with the seated figure of Christ. The Venetians borrowed the Arabic name as *matapan*. When this passed into Italian as *marzapane* it was first applied to a medieval unit of capacity equivalent to a tenth of a load, then to a box of this capacity, then to a fine container of sweetmeats and, finally, to the confections themselves. Marzipan was popular throughout Europe and Italian *marzapane* was borrowed into its languages to produce a number of forms showing slight diversity. English was influenced by these but finally settled on *marchpane* in the sixteenth century.

Marzipan, a sweet paste made of sugar and almonds pounded together, was sometimes made into little cakes and sometimes sculpted into fanciful forms. Three large statues of mythological creatures moulded in marzipan graced the table at the wedding feast of Vincenzo I, Duke of Mantua, in 1581. By the seventeenth century, recipes for the popular confection were being published – for those who could afford the ingredients, of course. The following is quoted in Halliwell and Wright's 1905 edition of Nares' GLOSSARY OF WORDS, PHRASES AND ALLUSIONS:

> To make a marchpane.–*Take two poundes of almonds being blanched, and dryed in a sieve over the fire, beate them in a stone mortar, and when they bee small mixe*

them with two pounde of sugar beeing finely
beaten, adding two or three spoonefuls of
rosewater, and that will keep your almonds
from oiling: when your paste is beaten fine,
drive it thin with a rowling pin, and so lay
it on a bottom of wafers, then raise up a
little edge on the side, and so bake it, then
yce it with rosewater and sugar, then put it
in the oven againe, and when you see your
yce is risen up and drie, then take it out of
the oven and garnish it with pretie concepts,
as birdes and beasts being cast out of
standing moldes. Sticke long comfits upright
in it, cast bisket and carrowaies in it, and so
serve it; guild it before you serve it: you may
also print of this marchpane paste in your

molds for banqueting dishes. And of this
paste our comfit makers at this day make
their letters, knots, armes, escutcheons,
beasts, birds, and other fancies.
(DELIGHTS FOR LADIES, 1608)

In the nineteenth century the confection
was imported from Germany and the
German form *marzipan* entered English,
eventually winning out over *marchpane*.
There is a final twist to the story,
however, for the German word was based
upon an erroneous supposition that Italian
marzapane had been derived from *panis
marcius* or *marci panis*, 'Mark's bread'.

1236

WATER IS FIRST BROUGHT INTO LONDON THROUGH LEAD PIPES

••••••

Commercial activity in Europe had increased markedly from around
the eleventh century and was further stimulated by the Crusades (see
1204, page 57). As a result towns flourished, and by the thirteenth
century they had begun to outgrow their water supplies. When the
situation became critical, provisions had to be brought in from outside
the walls. At Hull, for instance, barrels of sweet water were ferried
across the Humber by boat. In 1236 Gilbert de Sandford, who held
the fief of Tyburn, granted the clear spring waters on his estate to the
City of London 3½ miles (5½ kilometres) away, together with
permission for the necessary lead pipes to be laid across his lands. The
Tyburn waters spilled out into a large stone basin housed in a specially
constructed building at West Cheapside. In later years water was not
the only liquid to gush through London's conduits, however.
According to a contemporary account, when Margaret of Anjou
entered the city in May 1445 for her coronation *the conduits ran wine,
both white and red, for all people that would drink.*

PLUMBER
Several towns in Roman Britain had been
supplied with water by means of
earthenware or lead pipes. In the Middle

Ages monastic orders, also sticklers for
personal hygiene, similarly arranged for a
clean water supply. The monks at
Canterbury, for instance, obtained water

from a spring outside the town walls. The lead piping they laid in 1160 crossed the moat and went through the wall to supply different parts of the monastery. During the fourteenth century a number of monasteries extended their water systems to benefit the hard-pressed towns and cities to which they were attached.

Such enterprises required artisans skilled in using lead. The Romans had called a worker in lead, one who fashioned and laid lead pipes to public baths, fountains and basins, a *plumbārius*, a word derived from *plumbum*, 'lead'. Old French borrowed this as *plommier, plombier* and from there the term passed into Middle English as *plummer, plumber* in the fourteenth century. A BOOK OF ORDINANCES for the trade was published in 1365 and the Worshipful Company of Plumbers was incorporated in 1612.

The word *plumbing* to denote 'the fixtures and fittings of a water system' dates from the nineteenth century. More recently it has become a slang term for 'fillings in teeth' (1955) and a convenient euphemism to denote either 'a toilet' (1950) or, more personally, 'the uro-genital organs' – especially when they misfunction (1960). The phrasal verb to *plumb in*, meaning 'to connect a domestic appliance to the mains water supply' arose in the 1960s with the appearance of automatic washing machines and dishwashers in the home.

• Old French had *plombe* from Latin *plumbum*, 'lead', to denote 'a lead bob or weight'. This was borrowed into Middle English as *plumbe, plombe* towards the turn of the fourteenth century. Lead weights on lines were used by mariners: to *plumb the depths* means 'to sound the depth of water using a lead weight and line'. A *plumb* was also used by masons (see **mason**, page 25) to determine a true vertical (the later compound *plumb-line* is a sixteenth-century coinage), giving rise to the adverbial senses 'straight down' (15th century) and 'precisely' (17th century).

• *Plummet – plomet* in Middle English – was a fourteenth-century borrowing of Old French *plombet*, a diminutive of *plombe*. It denoted 'a plumb bob' used by either mariner or mason. Its use as a verb with the sense 'to drop rapidly' dates from the 1930s.

• *Aplomb*, meaning 'self-assurance, poise', was a nineteenth-century borrowing of French *aplomb*, 'perpendicularity' and hence, figuratively, 'assurance', which was formed from the phrase *à plomb*, 'according to the plumb-line'.

• The verb *to plunge, plungen* in Middle English, was borrowed from Old French *plungier*, 'to dive, to plunge', in the fourteenth century. The French verb was derived from unattested Vulgar Latin *plumbicāre* which meant 'to measure depth with a plumb'.

PIPE

Medieval water pipes were not only made of lead. Wood was also frequently used, especially elm, which was preferred because it was long and straight and particularly resistant to water. Special boring machines were developed to hollow out the elm trunks, giving pipes up to 10 inches (25 centimetres) in diameter and nearly 22 feet (7 metres) in length. The word *pipe* is onomatopoeic, imitative not of gushing water but of bird call. Its origins lie in the Latin verb *pīpāre*, 'to chirp', and describe the repetitive *pi-pi* sound made by young birds. From this came the unattested Common Romance *pīpa* to denote 'a musical pipe', possibly because pipes were used to imitate bird calls for trapping purposes. The Romance word was adopted into prehistoric West Germanic and came into Old English as *pīpe*. The earliest records of the word go back to around the turn of the eleventh century when, although its primary sense was still that of 'a musical instrument', the term was already also being used to denote 'a hollow tube'.

SINK, SEWER

As towns grew, the problems of sewage increased. Medieval streets sloped towards stinking open gutters which received household slops and rubbish. Crows were protected as nature's street-cleaners but rain was a mixed blessing, either bearing the ordure away or turning a blocked drain into a lake of filth. Privies stood over cesspits which were periodically cleansed and emptied by intrepid *gongfarmers* (*gong* was an Old English word for 'a privy' which became obsolete in the sixteenth century, while *farmer*, derived from an Old English verb, meant 'one who cleanses'). Town authorities required that timber-lined cesspits be dug at least 5½ feet (almost 2 metres) from adjoining property, thus offering neighbours a measure of relief from offensive smells and seepage. Those built within a few yards of a well, however, had at least some of their contents recycled – no wonder the population drank mainly wine, ale and small beer (a term for 'weak beer', still found in the expression *It's no small beer*, 'it's not a trifling matter'). Latrines, public and private, were also constructed over streams and rivers, thus completing the contamination of the water supply.

The complaints were endless. In London the River Fleet and the Walbrook were made foul by the privies which emptied into them. Lawrence Wright in his book CLEAN AND DECENT (1960) describes how the monks of White Friars complained to the king and Parliament that the odours of the Fleet overwhelmed the fragrance of their incense. In Nottingham, the Record of 1530 speaks of *a prevye comyng out of the Kynges Jayle in to the hie-wey, vnto the grett noysance of alle the inhabytantes*.

Open drains were sometimes known as *sinks*. The noun was derived from the Old English verb *sincan*, of common Germanic origin, which meant 'to go under water'. Before it was ever a kitchen fixture (a sense which only began to emerge in the sixteenth century), a *sink* was 'a cesspool' (c 1440) and then 'a drain', hence Mother Sawyer's lament over the way the world treats a shrivelled,

poor and ignorant old woman:

Must I for that be made a common sink
For all the filth and rubbish of men's
* tongues*
To fall and run into?
(Rowley, Dekker and Ford, THE WITCH OF EDMONTON, 1621)

The term *sewer* has been current in English since the early fifteenth century. It originated in the unattested verb *exaquāre*, 'to drain', which was composed of the Latin elements *ex-*, 'out', and *aqua*, 'water'. From this Vulgar Latin derived the unattested noun *exaquāria*, 'drainage channel', which found its way into Middle English by way of Anglo-Norman *sewer(e)*. Originally *sewer* denoted 'a ditch for draining marshland', but around the turn of the seventeenth century the commissioners of sewers were also given responsibility for the drainage of wetland towns. The term *sewer* was then carried over from the old to the new area of the commissioners' operations, and applied to 'a waste conduit'. Even then an urban sewer was still an open stream of filth.

A drain empties the effluent from one property. A sewer serves a wider area, and both drains and sewers empty into a *common sewer*, 'a main drain into which most of the area's sewage passes'. This last term became common around 1600, as did the synonym *common shore*. Skinner, an etymologist of later that century, classed *common shore* as a corruption of *common sewer*, through their similarity in spelling and pronunciation. It may well be, however, that it was so named because it emptied its filth out on to the 'shore' of a nearby watercourse to be borne away by the tide.

As early as the fifteenth century Leonardo da Vinci had drawn up plans for underground sewage systems that carried human waste away to nearby rivers discreetly and hygienically but, like all Leonardo's projects of genius, these were disregarded by his uncomprehending contemporaries. The few existing sewers in European towns were not covered over until the eighteenth century and wider provision of sewers not embarked upon until the nineteenth century.

STEW

In recent years of drought, a shocked British public has often been exhorted to bathe with a friend. There is, however, no need to be coy. In medieval times wooden bathtubs were often of a size to admit communal bathing, though the intention was not so much to save water as to economise on the effort required to fill a bath by hand with water, heated over a furnace, and to empty it afterwards. Indeed, bathtime could be turned into quite an occasion, the bathers being served with food and wine and soothed with music.

So public bathing did not perturb the Crusaders, who took to Turkish baths like ducks to water and brought the habit of hot-air baths and sweating rooms home with them. Public *stews*, that is public bath-houses containing hot baths and vapour baths, began to appear in European towns, those in England under the sign of a Turk's Head. Here one could *stew* companionably for, indeed, the verb to *stew* originally meant 'to take a vapour bath' and then by extension, 'to take a hot bath'.

It appears that Vulgar Latin had an unattested verb *estūfāre* which meant 'to take a steam bath'. This was a compound of the prefix *ex-*, 'out of' and the unattested noun *tūfus* 'steam' (from Greek *tuphos*, 'smoke, vapour', from *tuphein*, 'to smoke'). The verb passed into Old French as *estuver*, and from there into Middle English as *stewen* in the fourteenth century.

By the early fifteenth century the verb *to stew* had been adopted by medieval chefs (perhaps originally somewhat tongue-in-cheek after a session at the public stews) with the sense 'to tenderise meat, vegetables or fruit by simmering them in a little liquid'. The earliest recipes are for the stewing of pigeons, partridges and other small birds. The figurative expression *to let someone stew in his own juice,* meaning 'to

allow someone to reap the consequences of his own actions', dates from around the mid-seventeenth century. Surprisingly, it was not until around the middle of the eighteenth century that *stew* was used as a culinary noun to denote 'a dish of meat and vegetables slowly boiled together'. The expression *to be in a stew*, meaning 'to be in an agitated state', arose in the early nineteenth century.

Meanwhile, away from the kitchen, cleanliness was no longer uppermost in the minds of those who frequented the public stews, for they had begun to attract the sort of lady who openly plies her charms, so that by the mid-fourteenth century the term *stew* had become synonymous with 'brothel' (indeed, this sense remained current until at least the 1880s). Many establishments were closed during the first half of the sixteenth century and the business of those that remained was more strictly controlled.

• *Extūfāre* found its way into English as *stew* by way of a Romance language (French) and as *stove* by way of a Germanic borrowing. Old English had *stofa*, 'hot air bath', from Germanic but this fell from use and the modern noun *stove* was borrowed from either Middle Low German or Middle Dutch in the fifteenth century. *Stove* originally meant 'steam room' but during the sixteenth century the term was also applied to the furnace which heated such a room and also to the heating apparatus common in Dutch, German and Scandinavian sitting-rooms. From this latter sense came the modern application of 'an apparatus heated by fuel for the purposes of warmth or cooking'.

SOAP

A courtly dalliance often began with knights and their ladies bathing together. From the beginning of the fourteenth century lovers were able to cleanse each other's bodies with fine soaps imported from the Mediterranean. Of these, soap from Castile, which was based upon olive oil instead of animal fat, was considered superior. Even today, Unilever continue to market Knight's Castile as one of their main personal cleansing bars (i e *soap* in market-speak).

Soap-making was not a new skill, however. Centuries before the arrival of cosmetic soap, household soap had been manufactured by housewives from a mixture of animal fat and lye, obtained from boiled wood ash. The word *soap* can be traced back to the unattested prehistoric Germanic *saipō*, which found its way into many European languages. The Romance tongues acquired it by way of the Latin borrowing *sāpo*. Old English had it from Germanic as *sāpe*, which evolved as *sope* or *saip* in Middle English. The modern spelling *soap* did not appear until the second half of the seventeenth century.

• Soap is not the only cleansing agent available today. The innumerable synthetic preparations available are known as *detergents*. The term is derived from the Latin verb *dētergēre*, 'to wipe away' (from *de-*, 'away', and *tergēre*, 'to wipe'). This verb was borrowed into English as *deterge* in the first half of the seventeenth century for use in medical contexts, with the sense 'to cleanse the body or a wound of infected matter'. Later that century, the noun *detergent* was derived from *dētergent-*, the present participle stem of *dētergēre*, to denote 'a cleansing agent' useful in surgery. Its application to chemical cleansers of any sort arose in the twentieth century.

c 1250

Buttons Are Used to Fasten Clothes

•••••••

The Romans had pushed buttons through corresponding loops to secure clothing, but the method did not ensure a close fit. In the Middle Ages, if a fastener was required, pins, points and laces were used (see **c 1410**, page 103). Not until the thirteenth century was the reinforced buttonhole introduced to Europe, possibly by the Moors. Its impact on fashion was to be dramatic.

Clothes that revealed the curves of the body had been worn in the late eleventh century, the effect achieved by cutting the fabric on the cross and by inconvenient underarm lacing. The thirteenth century saw a return to looser garments, but the introduction of buttons and buttonholes around the middle of the century opened the way for sophisticated tailored garments which were convenient to fasten. By the middle of the following century, tight bodices and tunics, this time with shaped seams, were high fashion (see **c 1350**, page 87).

BUTTON

From their introduction in the thirteenth century, buttons were a fashion statement. They were used not only as fasteners but also for decoration. In the thirteenth century, for instance, ladies began to wear close-fitting *cote-hardies* with tight sleeves buttoned from elbow to wrist. By the fourteenth century a row of buttons also adorned the fronts of their slim-fitting, low-waisted bodices and this abundance of buttons continued into the fifteeth century. Only the wealthy could afford to be fashion-conscious and their buttons were beautifully made of gold, ivory or copper. The word *button*, however, is less distinguished than the finely wrought article it described. It came from the unattested Vulgar Latin verb *bottāre*, meaning 'to thrust, to push forth'. A connected term, *botōne*, carried the sense of something like a bud bursting forth and hence, from resemblance, came to denote 'a button'. *Boton*, the Old French version of this widespread Romance form, first meant 'bud' and then 'button', but when the term was borrowed into English in the first half of the fourteenth century, it simply denoted 'a button'. The word has been used more generally to denote 'a knob' since the early seventeenth century.

• The logically derived term *buttonhole* did not appear until around the middle of the sixteenth century. Shortly afterwards the colloquial phrase *to take someone down a buttonhole* or *to take someone a buttonhole lower* was coined, first appearing in Shakespeare's Love's Labour's Lost (1598). This meant 'to humble someone' and corresponded to the expression *to take someone down a peg,* which arose at the same time and which, alone of the two, is still current in modern English.

• The verb *to buttonhole someone,* meaning 'to detain an unwilling victim in conversation', originated as *to buttonhold* in the first half of the nineteenth century, when it referred to the habit of holding on to a person's button to prevent his departure.

1268

ROGER BACON COMMENTS ON THE OPTICAL USE OF LENSES

••••••

Although Roger Bacon's great work Opus Majus of 1268 contains sketches of convex lenses, accompanied by the earliest known statement on their magnifying properties, he was not the inventor. Convex lenses of polished quartz, used either for starting fire or as magnifying glasses, have been known since ancient times. Strangely, however, there is no evidence to suggest that such lenses were ever used to correct defective sight before the thirteenth century when eyeglasses appeared, apparently coincidentally and simultaneously, in both China and Europe. Their appearance in Italy in 1280 is generally attributed to Alessandro di Spina of Florence who, it is claimed, shamelessly took advantage of his friend, the inventor Salvino degli Armati. In Great Inventions Through History (1991), Gerald Messadié suggests that by 1352 spectacles for the longsighted were probably common enough amongst the wealthy literate to be unremarkable, because in that year Hugues de Provence commissioned a portrait by the Italian painter Tommaso da Modena and sat for it wearing his spectacles. Shortsighted people continued to fumble and stumble their way through life until the early sixteenth century, when concave lenses finally appeared. Pope Leo X was one of the first men to have his myopia corrected: a portrait painted by Raphael in 1517 shows the Pope wearing a pair of concave lenses.

SPECTACLES

The word *spectacles* to denote 'eyeglasses' originated in the Latin verb *spectāre*, the frequentative of *specere*, 'to look' (see **spice**, page 58). A noun, *spectāculum*, was derived from this to denote 'a sight, a show', and this passed into Middle English by way of Old French *spectacle* in the fourteenth century. The Latin senses are still current in English where *spectacle* means either 'an entertainment' or 'an arresting sight', but in the fifteenth century English began to apply *spectacle* to objects that facilitated seeing, such as mirrors, windows or eyeglasses. Of these, only the application to eyeglasses survived. In one of his poems (1415) Thomas Hoccleve writes of *a spectacle which helpeth feeble sighte, Whan a man on the book redith or writ*. In early use the singular, *spectacle*, was used as frequently as the plural to denote 'glasses'. Reference to *a pair of spectacles* dates from the 1420s. A fifteenth-century will includes a *peyre spectaclys of syluir and ouyr gylt* amongst its bequests. The availability of printed material which followed the invention of movable type in the second half of the fifteenth century (see **1474**, page 107), together with the appearance of concave lenses for myopia in the early sixteenth, greatly increased the demand for *spectacles*. A well-known engraving of a sixteenth-century street by Philippe Galle shows a spectacle-maker's workshop where a customer is trying on glasses at random, attempting to find a pair to suit. A Guild of Spectacle Makers was eventually formed which was granted its charter in 1629. It took St Jerome as its patron saint, since a picture painted by Domenico Ghirlandajo in 1480 had depicted the saint with a pair of spectacles on his desk.

GLASSES

The early manufacture of spectacles was costly since lenses were made of precious quartz or beryl. Increasing demand led to experiments with optical glass, most of it produced in Venice and Nuremberg in the sixteenth century. From the early thirteenth century the word *glass* had been widely applied to any object made of the substance, and came to denote 'a container', 'a drinking-vessel' (still in common use), 'an hour-glass', 'a window pane', 'a looking-glass' and, in the sixteenth century, 'a lens'. *Glasses* began to be used to denote 'spectacles' in the second half of the seventeenth century. It was a natural shortening of *glasses of* or *for spectacles,* where *glasses* meant 'lenses'.

Glass evolved from Middle English *glas* and Old English *glæs*. According to one authority, the Old English word sprang from unattested West Germanic *glasam*, a derivative of an unattested Indo-European root *ghel-*, which meant both 'yellow' and 'green'. *Ghel-* was ultimately responsible for a number of colour words in European languages (English *yellow*) and also for terms which mean 'to shine' (English *glare*). Colour and sheen were properties of glass which, when it was made in ancient times, was not clear but coloured.

• The Latin word *lens*, which eventually replaced *glass* in optical use, means 'lentil'. It was brought into English as *lens* in the late seventeenth century. Scientists investigating optics noted that the circular biconvex pieces of glass they were working with were similar in shape to lentils: *A Glass spherically Convex on both sides (usually called a Lens)* (Newton, OPTICKS, 1704).

c 1290

THE MAPPA MUNDI AT HEREFORD IS DRAWN UP

••••••

With the fall of the Roman Empire, European interest in mapmaking dwindled. It was revived in the Middle Ages by monks who, under the watchful eye of a master, turned out large numbers of maps of the known world, intended for the religious instruction of their illiterate flocks. The medieval map that survives in Hereford Cathedral was made under the supervision of Richard of Haldingham and was designed to illustrate the history of the world as described by Orosius, a pupil of St Augustine. The map, which reveals the baffling diversity of the known world and hints at the terrors lurking in the unknown, is given an eternal perspective by the reassuring presence of Christ, in whom all things live, move and have their being. He is depicted at the top of the map in all his risen glory, receiving the penitent into his kingdom on Judgement Day.

MAP

Roman maps had centred the known world around Rome. Similarly, medieval maps drawn by Christian monks showed the earth as a simple circle with Jerusalem at its centre, Asia above, Europe to the left below and Africa to the right. A depiction of this kind was known in medieval Latin as a *mappa mundi*. This literally meant 'cloth or sheet of the world', since the Latin word *mappa* denoted an article made from a square of cloth – a sheet, napkin or tablecloth, for instance. The cloth on which the Hereford *mappa mundi* was painted is a sheet of vellum measuring 64 by 54 inches (162 by 57 cm). The writing, which includes legends such as *Here are strong and fierce camels*, is in black with embellishments in red and gold. Seas and rivers are shown in green or blue (with the exception of the Red Sea which is drawn in red), towns are represented by walls and towers, and mountains by a series of humps. Unexplored territories teem with

mythological creatures and peoples of great diversity: the Phanesii keep warm by wrapping themselves up in their enormous ears while the Sciapod uses his one gigantic foot as a parasol.

During the later Middle Ages, shipping and navigational technology began to improve and voyages of exploration were undertaken. Navigators brought back a wealth of new information for cartographers to interpret. Gradually, more accurate representations of the earth were drawn up which made a nonsense of the *mappa mundi*. But something of the old medieval Latin term was retained by seafarers who, in the first half of the sixteenth century, began to use the abbreviation *map* when referring to one of their sophisticated new charts.

• Latin *mappa* was borrowed into Old French in the altered form *nappe*, 'tablecloth'. English took this as *nape*, 'tablecloth', and then, in the early fifteenth century, added the diminutive suffix -*kin* to form *napkin*, 'a small square of cloth used for wiping the fingers and protecting one's clothes while eating'. Napkins were much needed at the medieval table since forks had not yet been introduced (see **fork**, page 126):

> Laye your knyues, & set your brede, . . .
> your spones, and your napkyns fayre folden
> besyde your brede.
> (BOKE OF KERUYNGE, 1513)

• Towards the middle of the nineteenth century *napkin* began to be applied to the square of absorbent cloth worn by babies. The common abbreviation *nappy* dates from the first half of the twentieth century:

> Mothers and nurses use pseudo-infantile
> forms like pinny (pinafore), nappy (napkin).
> (W E Collinson, CONTEMPORARY
> ENGLISH, 1927)

Old French formed the diminutive *naperon*, 'bib to protect the clothing', from *nappe*. This was borrowed into English in the early fourteenth century. The spelling *apron* began to occur in the second half of the fifteenth century, the initial *n* migrating to the indefinite article, *an apron*.

1296

WILLIAM DE LEYBOURNE IS APPOINTED ADMIRAL OF THE SEA

••••••

In medieval times there was no standing navy. Ships and men, usually from the Cinque Ports, were pressed into service to help defend the kingdom as and when they were needed and fleets were speedily disbanded when hostilities ceased. Merchant ships were transformed into warships by the addition of castles in the stem and stern. These were tower-like structures erected to give the soldiers and archers a better position from which to fight. The seamen were not expected to fight. Their role was to handle the ship and to transport soldiers and knights to engage in face-to-face combat with the enemy, usually on dry land but sometimes on board ship. The master of a vessel had command over its crew, while the fleet came under the authority of an officer known as a 'governor' or 'keeper'. In 1296 Edward I appointed William de Leybourne to a new title, that of *admiral of the English seas* in the Cinque Ports with responsibility for fleets and maritime matters.

ADMIRAL

When Muhammad died in 632 he was succeeded first by his father-in-law, Abu Bakr, and then, in 634, by the Caliph Omar. Omar referred to himself as *amīr-al-mūminīn*, 'commander of the faithful' in Arabic. This became the model for a number of other titles, all beginning with *amīr al-*, 'commander (of) the'; *amīr-al-umarā*, for instance, was 'ruler of rulers'.

During the Crusades, European writers mistakenly treated *amīr-al-* as a single word and borrowed it as such. Old French, for instance, had *amiral*. There was a second mistake of popular etymology: as many Old French words beginning in *am-* were borrowed from Latin terms beginning with *adm-*, Latin *admīrārī*, 'to admire' was believed to be the root, hence the coining of the alternative Old French *admiral* and medieval Latin *admīrālis*.

Middle English also had various alternative forms, largely borrowed from Old French, but eventually *admiral* won out over *amiral*. In Middle English, and in all the Romance languages, the primary meaning of the term was 'emir, prince' or 'infidel commander' in general.

The office of *amīr-al-bahr* or *amīr-al-mā*, 'commander of the sea', was instituted by Moorish administrations in the conquered territories of Spain and Sicily (see **1492**, page 111). (In Spanish this became *almirante de la mar*.) The officers had considerable influence in the maritime affairs of the western Mediterranean. The post was retained by the Norman kings of Sicily following the Christian conquest in the eleventh century, and similar positions were subsequently created by the city-state of Genoa, France (picked up from the Genoese during the Seventh Crusade around 1248) and then in the English Cinque Ports in 1296. Under these influences, the tighter connection of *admiral* with the sea began to grow in English. Subsequently, the office of *Lord Admiral,* who had an administrative role in naval affairs, was created in 1406 by Henry IV. In the course of that century, the earlier general meaning of 'prince, emir' died out, and the simple term *admiral* could now be safely used without the usual qualifications *of the Sea* or *of the Navy* to refer to the most senior naval commanders. (See **marshal**, page 47.)

1300

POPE BONIFACE VIII PROCLAIMS THE FIRST JUBILEE YEAR

••••••

The Middle Ages saw the emergence of powerful princes whose increasing skill and confidence in government aroused inevitable tensions between Church and state. The attempts of Boniface VIII (elected 1294) to reimpose papal supremacy brought the papacy into conflict with the crowns of England and, in particular, France. Taxation was a particular bone of contention. Both Edward I and Philip IV had imposed illegal taxes on the Church to pay for their wars. In 1296 Boniface issued the *Clericis Laicos*, a bull which restricted a monarch's power to tax the clergy. Both kings were swift to retaliate, and Boniface was forced to compromise.

The Pope's declaration of a Jubilee Year in 1300 might be seen as a public relations exercise to restore his image. A plenary indulgence, one that guaranteed admittance into heaven at the very instant of death, was granted to every pilgrim who journeyed to Rome that year, visited certain churches, undertook prescribed fasts and completed a programme of good works. Subsequent Jubilee Years were originally to have taken place every hundred years but this was changed to fifty, thirty-three and then twenty-five years by later popes.

JUBILEE

Jubilee was a year-long period of rest observed every fiftieth year by the ancient Hebrews. Details of it are recorded in the Old Testament book of Leviticus, chapter 25. It was to be a time of favour and grace, of liberty, restoration and rejoicing. During this year land was to lie fallow, property mortaged through financial difficulty was to be returned to its original owner, slaves were to be provided for and given their freedom, and debts were to be cancelled. These commands effectively prevented the economic gap between labourers and landowners from widening by redistributing wealth and providing the poor with a fresh start.

The Year of Jubilee was heralded by blasts on a ram's horn trumpet. The Hebrew term for this instrument was *yōbhēl*, and the celebration took its name from this. When translations of the Old Testament were made into Greek, the word was borrowed as *iōbēlos* and the adjective *iōbēlaios* derived from it. The adjective's subsequent journey into Latin translations was more complex, as the resulting form *jūbilaeus* shows. A direct borrowing from Greek would have given *jōbēlaeus*. However, Latin already had the similar-sounding word *jūbilāre*, 'to shout aloud', and the adjective *jūbilaeus* was a coinage of Christian writers who associated the Jewish jubilee festival with joyous shouting. Originally, the festival was referred to as *jūbilaeus annus,* 'jubilee

year', but by the time the Vulgate translation of the Bible appeared in AD 405, *jūbilaeus* stood alone as a noun and as such was taken into Old French as *jubile* and from there into Middle English.

The Wycliffe Bible translations, which date from the 1380s (see **1382**, page 92), are responsible for establishing the word in English. Apart from the biblical use and that of the Roman Catholic Church, *jubilee* very soon came to mean a 'fiftieth anniversary'. A notable eighteenth-century instance is the great jubilee festival which the actor David Garrick organised at Stratford-upon-Avon in 1769 to commemorate the 150th anniversary of Shakespeare's death. In the nineteenth century two British monarchs enjoyed particularly long reigns. In 1809 a national *jubilee* marked the fiftieth year of the reign of George III, while Queen Victoria called the nation to rejoice at her *jubilee* in 1887 and her *diamond jubilee* (sixty years) in 1897. *Jubilee* in this secular sense is now usually qualified by *silver, golden* or *diamond,* following the German practice of naming silver and golden wedding anniversaries.

Since the sixteenth century *jubilee* has also sometimes denoted 'a period of joyful celebration' or simply 'rejoicing'. This use has doubtless been influenced over the centuries by *jubilation* (14th century) and *jubilant* (17th century), both derived from Latin *jūbilāre*.

1308
Death of the Scottish Theologian Duns Scotus

••••••

Born around 1265 and named after his birthplace, the town of Duns in Scotland, John Duns Scotus was to become an outstanding theologian and philosopher of his age. In his early teens Duns Scotus became a Franciscan, going on to study and lecture at Oxford (see **c 1167**, page 43, and **degree**, page 44). In 1302 he was appointed to the Franciscan chair of theology in Paris but, before his first year was up, the university became embroiled in a quarrel between Philip IV, King of France, and Pope Boniface VIII (see **1300**, page 72). The French king wanted to tax Church property to help finance his wars with England. Duns Scotus declared his support for the Pope and was promptly exiled from France. He returned to Paris in 1304 and lectured there until 1307 when he was appointed professor at Cologne. Some say his hurried departure for Cologne was undertaken for his own safety, his defence of the doctrine of the Immaculate Conception being condemned by many as heretical. Whether this is true or not, Duns Scotus was not much longer for this world: he lived in Cologne for only one year before his death in 1308 while he was still in his early forties.

DUNCE

The medieval school of scholasticism to which Duns Scotus subscribed sought to integrate the philosophy of Aristotle with Christian revelation. Philosophy was described as the servant of theology, a means by which supernatural revelation might be understood. Lectures were based on works of Aristotle, the Bible, the teachings of the early Christian Fathers and the SENTENCES of Peter Lombard. The chosen text would be read out, a point of difficulty (known as a disputed question) raised and different interpretations aired, after which the lecturer would deliver a commentary detailing his own profound conclusions.

John Duns Scotus was a brilliant commentator whose rigorous and intricate analyses challenged the teachings of his Dominican predecessor Thomas Aquinas and earned him the Latin nickname Doctor Subtilis (the 'Subtle Doctor'). His various commentaries on disputed questions became textbooks at the universities. Adherents to Duns Scotus's doctrines became known as *Scotists* or *Dunsmen* and were dominant in university circles until the early sixteenth century when scholasticism began to be challenged by humanism. The rediscovery of Greek and Roman literature, art and civilisation led to the elevation of classical antiquity: the adventurous spirit of speculative and secular enquiry was at odds with scholasticism. *Dunsmen* were censured first by the humanists and then by the reformers, who attacked them initially for the needless complexity of their teaching and then for their unwillingness to embrace the new learning. *Remember ye not*, wrote William Tyndale in defence of the reformation, *how . . . the old barkyng curres, Dunces disciples & lyke draffe called Scotistes, the children of darkenesse, raged in euery pulpit agaynst Greke Latin and Hebrue* (AN ANSWERE UNTO SIR THOMAS MORES DIALOGE, 1530). Thus during the course of the sixteenth century the word *Duns* or

Dunce, which was once simply the name of a little Scottish market town, changed in meaning from 'quibbling sophist' to 'one who is slow at learning': *But now in our age it is growne to be a common prouerbe in derision, to call such a person as is senselesse or without learning a Duns, which is as much as a foole* (Raphael Holinshed, CHRONICLES OF SCOTLAND, 1577-87).

1331

EDWARD III INVITES SEVENTY FLEMISH CLOTH-WORKERS AND THEIR FAMILIES TO SETTLE IN ENGLAND

······

Thousands upon thousands of sheep grazed the English countryside in the Middle Ages and beyond. The trade in surplus wool, just burgeoning in the late Saxon period, expanded apace after the Conquest until wool became the staple upon which the country's wealth depended. Raw wool from England was exported to Europe. Most of it supplied Flemish looms, to be woven into good quality cloth, and this became the principal industry in Flanders. Indeed, English customers who wanted to buy fine cloth often went abroad for it or bought a foreign import. In 1331 Edward III decided to take advantage of ongoing political uncertainties in Flanders to develop a thriving cloth industry at home. He let it be known that Flemish cloth-workers who wanted to come and settle in England would be fairly treated. To stimulate the industry further, he temporarily forbade the export of raw wool. Manufacture grew until, by the mid-fifteenth century, good-quality English cloth was commonly found for sale at trade fairs at home and abroad.

Many terms associated with this ancient industry (such as cloth, dye, spin, weave, wool *and* yarn*) are commonly found in texts of the Saxon period. They are Germanic in origin and have parallel or related terms in the Germanic languages of western Europe and Scandinavia. Others, however, emerged with the growth of the wool industry.*

DRAPER

In the fourteenth century, a man who wove cloth, particularly of wool, was sometimes known as a *draper*. The word came from Anglo-Norman *draper* and Old French *drapier*, a derivative of *drap*, 'cloth'. This, in turn, had evolved from Late Latin *drappus*, 'cloth', whose Celtic source is unknown. Old English already had *weaver* and *webster* (see **spinster**, below) to denote 'one who makes cloth' and so the new term, *draper*, subsequently came to refer to the person who dealt in the finished product. The draper's trade was in woollen cloth and was thus distinguished from that of the mercer, who dealt in costly fabrics such as brocade, silk and velvet.

The related verb *to drape*, which appeared in the fifteenth century, was a borrowing of Old French *draper*, 'to weave woollen cloth'. Its modern meaning appears to have been influenced by *drapery* (from Old French *draperie*). In the fifteenth century this was a collective term for 'cloth', and this is still the case. Indeed, when light worsteds began to appear, they were termed *new draperies* to distinguish them from the old, traditional weaves. Then in the seventeenth century *drapery* began to be specifically applied either to 'the careful arrangement of clothing on figures in works of art' or to 'the clothing or hangings' thus displayed. In a discourse delivered to the students of the Royal Academy of Arts (1771), Sir Joshua Reynolds describes the skill thus: *It requires the nicest judgment to dispose the drapery, so that the folds shall have an easy communication, and gracefully follow each other.* From here, during the nineteenth century, *drapery* came to denote 'loose hangings or coverings' of any sort and the verb *to drape* was revived with the new senses 'to adorn with cloth' and 'to arrange cloth in artistic folds'. The word *drape* is now in vogue among interior designers and in American English *drapes* denote 'curtains' which, these days, fall into place at the press of a button, thanks to the Drape Boss Drapery Controller with its infrared remote:

The lucky owner programmes the timer to open and close drapes, stop them in any intermediate position, and carry out all these wonders of modern civilisation at an adjustable speed.

Who could afford to be without one?

• Also from *drap*, 'cloth,' comes the English variant *drab* which in the sixteenth century denoted a 'type of (woollen) cloth in its natural, undyed, state'. In the late seventeenth century the word also began to be used as an adjective of colour, 'of a dull brownish hue', descriptive of the cloth. This unappealing shade gave rise to the figurative application of 'dull, dreary, uninteresting' in the last quarter of the nineteenth century.

SPINSTER

The unattested Indo-European root *spen-*, 'to draw out, to stretch', is the source of the Old English verb *spinnan* (Middle English *spinnen*), 'to spin', for spinning is the art of drawing out fibres from a tangle of wool or flax and twisting them together to form a yarn. The seventeenth-century phrasal verb *to spin out,* meaning 'to prolong', alludes to the drawing out of a thread. Since the early seventeenth century, *to spin* has also meant 'to whirl round'. According to Skeat, this is an allusion to the rapid motion of the spinning-wheel.

The first written record of the verb occurs around 725 but the agent, *spinster*, does not appear until the second half of the fourteenth century, when cloth was starting to emerge as a boom industry. The form of the word reveals that spinning was women's work: *spinster* is made up of the verb *spin* and the suffix *-ster* which denotes a female agent. Other occupations in the industry were similarly derived. A *kempster*, for instance, was a 'comber of wool' and this, too, was a task undertaken by women. A female weaver was a *webster* but, since weaving for the industry was mostly taken over by men, the feminine form was often simply transferred. So, in the 1362 poll-tax records for the West Riding of Yorkshire, we find Thomas Webester and Johannes Clerke both listed as *webster* when, strictly, it should have been *webbe*.

In medieval times spinning was regarded as a badge of womanhood. Women had always spun for their family's needs and, as the cloth industry grew, they spun extra wool to supply that, too. Spinning and carding could be fitted around their farming and household chores. Formerly it was common practice in official records to list names together with occupations, and so *spinster* is often found appended to the names of women. However, the perceived connection between women and the distaff was so profound that, from the early seventeenth century onwards, *spinster* became a recognised legal term, its appearance after a woman's name no longer denoting livelihood but unmarried status irrespective of social rank. In his GLOSSOGRAPHICA (1656), Thomas Blount says that the term applied to *all unmarried women, from the Viscounts Daughter downward*. By the early eighteenth century *spinster* had started to acquire the derogatory sense of 'old maid' which, by the nineteenth century, was firmly established:

> When the spinster aunt got 'matrimony' the young ladies laughed afresh.
> (Charles Dickens, THE PICKWICK PAPERS, 1837)

In similar vein, in his novel ONE OF OUR CONQUERORS (1891), George Meredith wrote:

> The little dog had qualities to entrance the spinster sex.

Spinsters had become a separate gender.

• From *spinnan*, 'to spin', comes the unattested form *spinthron*. From this evolved Old English *spīthra*, Middle English *spither* and modern English *spider*, literally a 'spinner'. The spider's *web* derives ultimately from the unattested prehistoric Germanic base *web-*, and means 'a woven thing'. In Old English *web* denoted 'a piece of cloth' which was, of course, woven by a *webbe* or *webster*. *Web-* is also the ultimate source of the verb 'to weave'.

• Many English surnames bear witness to the importance of the wool industry since the Middle Ages: *Draper, Dyer, Fuller, Sherman* (from *shearman*, 'one who shears woollen cloth'), *Tucker* ('a fuller'), *Webber, Webster, Weaver*.

LOOM

By the Middle Ages, the upright loom had given way to the horizontal loom. Narrow frames, which produced cloth a yard (just under a metre) wide, were worked by a single weaver rapidly throwing the shuttle from one side to the other. Broad looms, for the production of the high-quality, double-width black cloth known as 'broadcloth', needed a man at each side. The word *loom* comes from Old English *gelōma* which denoted an 'implement or utensil' of any sort. This became *lome* in Middle English, where it was still a general word for 'tool' and, for obvious reasons, in the fifteenth and sixteenth centuries even denoted 'penis' (it still does in modern teen-speak). More especially, from the early fifteenth century *lome*, and sometimes *weblome* (see **webster** in **spinster**, page 76), was applied to the tool of the weaver's trade. This is now the predominant sense of the word, a testimony to the importance of the woollen industry in the centuries that followed.

• The old sense of *loom*, 'utensil', is present in *heirloom*. In the fifteenth century this denoted 'a possession to be disposed of in a will'.

CLOTH

Cloth, the product of the looms, is of unknown Germanic origin. Old English had *clāth*, becoming *cloth* in Middle English. The word meant 'cloth' in general (usually woollen), 'a piece of cloth for a particular purpose', or 'a garment'. Its plural (first *clāthas*, then *clothes*) was early applied to 'all the garments worn by a person', and *clothes* retains this collective sense in modern English.

SHUTTLE

Shuttle goes back to an unattested Old Germanic stem *skut-*, meaning 'to shoot'.

From this Old English derived the noun *scytel*, which meant 'a dart or arrow'. Such missiles are 'shot' at speed, and indeed the verb *to shoot* itself also derives from *skut-*. Although the last written record of *scytel* precedes the Norman Conquest, the term reappeared as *schutylle* in the fourteenth century. This time it occurred in the context of weaving where it denoted the instrument which was 'shot' across the loom to carry the weft thread between those of the warp.

In modern English *shuttle* has been used adjectivally. It generally describes something which, like the weaver's shuttle, shoots backwards and forwards, hence:

Shuttle service (1892) 'a transport service (originally a train) which operates back and forth over a short distance at frequent intervals'

Space shuttle (1969) 'a spacecraft designed to make repeated journeys between earth and a space station'

Shuttle diplomacy (1975) 'negotiations between two nations in dispute made possible through the services of a neutral intermediary who journeys back and forth between them to represent the views of one to the other'

Le Shuttle (1994) 'the train which hurtles back and forth through the Channel Tunnel' (see **tunnel**, page 178). According to the promotional newspaper LE SHUTTLE EXPRESS, the train *has created a seamless link* joining Britain with France and mainland Europe. The name of the service, *Le Shuttle*, in which the French article is tacked on to an English noun, attempts a corresponding linguistic link:

The construction of the Channel Tunnel is a remarkable achievement and some describe it as the 8th wonder of the world . . . It has changed the way we cross the Channel forever because this is the first time since the Ice Age that Britain and the Continent have been joined. Indeed Le Shuttle, our car carrying Channel Tunnel service . . . provides an entirely new form of travel, it is smooth, clean, efficient, innovative, hi-tech, fast – and remains so in all weathers. But, because it's

so fast, people can for the first time just pop over to France as easily as moving from one county to another in the UK.
(LE SHUTTLE EXPRESS, Special Edition, autumn 1997)

ON TENTERHOOKS

A number of processes were involved in manufacturing cloth. First of all the wool was combed to remove dirt and straighten the fibres. It was then ready to be spun into yarn and woven. Next the cloth was trodden or beaten to clean it and cause the fibres to felt and thicken, a process known as fulling. Finally the fabric was stretched on a wooden frame called a *tenter* (possibly from unattested Anglo-Norman or Old French *tentour*, from medieval Latin *tentōrium*, from Latin *tentus*, past participle of *tendere*, 'to stretch'). Here it was secured on rows of bent spikes known as *tenterhooks*, where it was left to dry out without shrinking. The pieces of cloth were all the same size, each one woven to fit the tenters exactly. In the Middle Ages a town where cloth was manufactured was easily recognised by its tenter-fields where the frames stood, row upon row, in the open air.

In the sixteenth century *on the tenter* or *tenterhooks* began to emerge as a figure of speech. Initially it was a person's words or conscience that were *stretched* (that is 'strained') *on the tenters*. Then during the seventeenth century *to be on (the) tenters* was also applied to the emotions with the sense 'to be in a state of disquiet or anxious uncertainty'. The variant *to be on (the) tenterhooks* arose in the eighteenth century and became the preferred form.

• In the early fourteenth century many thousands of sacks of raw wool were sent across annually to Flemish weavers. By the mid-fifteenth century finished cloths made up over fifty per cent of wool exports and supplied many Flemish markets. Not surprisingly, the intensity of trade brought new words into English. From Middle Dutch, English borrowed *nap* (of a fabric), *mart* and *rover*, the latter a reminder that, even in the Channel, precious cargoes of wool were prey to pirates.

FREIGHT, FRAUGHT

Cargoes of wool were carried on small, sturdy, single-masted ships with spacious holds. In the first half of the fourteenth century, Middle English acquired *fraught*, a borrowing of Middle Dutch *vracht*, to denote both 'cargo' and 'the hire of a boat for the transportation of goods'. Later, in the mid-fifteenth century, the variant Dutch form, *vrecht*, was borrowed into English as *freight*. For over two hundred years *fraught* and *freight* were parallel terms in English until *freight* finally won out in the second half of the seventeenth century.

Fraught was not dispensed with entirely, however. The noun had given rise to the verb *fraught* which meant 'to load cargo into a vessel'. The past participle of the verb, also *fraught*, originally described a ship laden with cargo. From the sixteenth century it was extended to refer to anything that was well supplied or equipped. In her diary for 7 November 1786, for instance, Fanny Burney speaks of a *full-fraught pincushion,* while in THALABA (1801) Southey uses the word to describe a pelican's bill *Fraught with the river-stream.* Used figuratively the phrase *fraught with* meant 'charged with'. It could be used to voice optimism or pessimism, thus *fraught with blessings* or *fraught with difficulties.* Gradually, however, the pessimists gained ground. So much so that, in the mid-twentieth century, the adjective *fraught* came to mean 'filled with trouble and anxiety'.

1340

THE AYENBITE OF INWIT APPEARS

••••••

In 1279 a Dominican monk, Frère Loren of Orléans, wrote a devotional manual entitled LES SOMME DES VICES ET DES VERTUES for the French king, Philippe III. The French text was quite well known and possibly influenced Chaucer in his writing of the PARSON'S TALE. In 1340 Dan Michael of Northgate, an English monk from Canterbury, decided upon a translation into the vernacular. Although pedestrian and not without error, the translation provides a fascinating linguistic record of the Kentish dialect at that time:

> Dis boc is ywrite Vor Englisse men thet hi wyte
> How he ssolde ham zelve ssribe
> And maki ham klene ine this libe.
> Dis boc hatte huo Det writ Ayenbite of Inwyt.

REMORSE

The Latin verb *remordēre* means 'to bite back' (from *re-*, 'again, back', and *mordēre*, 'to bite'). Used figuratively it means 'to annoy, to disturb', a pertinent allusion to the way in which painful emotions gnaw away at a person. Medieval Latin derived the noun *remorsus* from this verb and used it in the phrase *remorsus conscientiae*, 'remorse of conscience', which became *remors de conscience* in Old French. Its first recorded use in English occurs in Dan Michael's work. He chose the phrase for the title of his translation although, at first sight, one would be hard pressed to recognise it at all in AYENBITE OF INWIT (1340). Dan Michael's rendering not only provided a perfect translation of the phrase but etymologically mirrored the Latin (and French) terms. *Remorsus,* for instance, was the model for *ayenbite,* where *ayen* meant 'again', and *bite,* 'bite'. *Inwit,* like *conscientia,* meant 'knowledge within oneself, conscience': the words were constructed from Old English *witan* and Latin *scīre* respectively, both of which mean 'to know'. Later in the fourteenth century, English borrowed *remors de conscience* directly from Old French as *remorse of conscience.* Its first recorded appearance was in Chaucer's TROILUS AND CRISEYDE (c 1385) where Pandarus, finding the love-sick Troilus distraught, tries to discover the reason:

Or hastow som remors of conscience,
And art now falle in som devocioun,
And wailest for thi synne and thin offence,
And hast for ferde caught attricioun?

The full phrase survived until the early nineteenth century although, as early as the turn of the fifteenth century, it had been shortened to the single word *remorse.* AYENBITE OF INWIT has enjoyed a certain vogue amongst the self-conscious wordsmiths of the twentieth century, such as Joyce in ULYSSES (1922) and writers for PUNCH and THE LISTENER:

Very probably Bond fans will be able to turn a blind eye to the bites and agenbites of new-Bond's inwit.
(THE LISTENER, March 1968)

1346

EDWARD III USES CANNON AT CRÉCY

• • • • • •

The Chinese invented gunpowder in the ninth century but packed it into fireworks. The English scholar Roger Bacon knew how to prepare the substance as early as 1242, and is sometimes credited with its reinvention, but it was almost certainly introduced into Europe from China, possibly by way of the Arab world. However, it took a good while longer before gunpowder was used to launch projectiles. According to Frederick Wilkinson in his book THE WORLD'S GREAT GUNS (1987) the earliest incontrovertible evidence for gunpowder weapons in Europe appears in the MILEMETE (MILLIMETE) MANUSCRIPT of 1327. These books, written for Edward III by his chaplain, Walter de Milemete, contain two small illustrations of a vase- or bottle-shaped gun, probably about a yard (just under a metre) long, lying horizontally on a raised surface. The gun is loaded with what appears to be an arrow, and armoured knights are igniting the gunpowder charge with a red-hot rod. The device reveals a basic grasp of the mechanics of firearms, and from such rudimentary beginnings true cannon evolved, some of the earliest being employed by Edward III at the Battle of Crécy in 1346.

GUN

The earliest recorded application of *gun* was to the primitive cannon that began to evolve in the early fourteenth century. The unusual etymology of the word advanced by William Skeat, the renowned nineteenth-century professor of Early English, finds strong support, especially with the editors of the OED. It is common for war machines to be given women's names: as recently as the First World War, for instance, the Germans had a powerful gun which they nicknamed *Big Bertha*. But the practice is an old one: *Mad Marjorie* was the name bestowed upon a great cast-iron cannon which came into service in 1430. Skeat suggests that the tradition goes back even further and that large military engines, such as the ballista which was designed to fling missiles in siege warfare, were formerly known by the Scandinavian name *Gunnhildr*. This is a likely choice since its two components *gunnr* and *hildr* both mean 'war'. Evidence that this was the case is not wanting: an item in a munitions account held in Windsor Castle and dating from 1330-31 reads *una magna balista de cornu quae vocatur Domina Gunilda*. When gunpowder cannon were developed, the name was easily applied to those as well. The brief Middle English word *gunne* or *gonne* comes from *Gunna* (*Gunne* in Middle English), a short or 'pet' form of *Gunnhildr*. The term came to be applied to any size of gunpowder weapon, whether a heavy siege cannon or a small hand cannon (which still required two men to fire it), and when small arms began to be developed around the middle of the fifteenth century, it was then extended to include those, too.

CANNON

Metalworking was not very advanced in the fourteenth century, and cannon often exploded because of imperfections in the casting. To remedy this, a way was devised of beating iron bars to shape around a wooden cylinder and then welding them together to form a tube. The joins were then reinforced with metal hoops, one butted against the next. The joins were not perfect, so a second layer of hoops attempted to seal up the gaps. This improvement meant that even bigger guns could be made but they were still potentially dangerous if the welding weakened. In 1460 James II of Scotland was killed when a cannon of this manufacture exploded. Skill in iron casting was not sufficiently developed until 1543, when the first single cast cannon was made at Uckfield, in Sussex. England's superiority here meant that she was able to equip a large navy swiftly and economically (see **deck**, page 122).

The word *cannon* was not applied to heavy guns until the first quarter of the sixteenth century. Even then the word was slow to prevail as the weapons were also known by a great variety of other names, *basilisk, culverin, falcon* and *saker* among them. *Basilisk* seems apt as it was the name of a mythological fire-breathing beast. *Culverin, falcon* and *saker* reveal the custom of bestowing the names of reptiles and birds of prey upon the great guns.

By contrast, the mighty word *cannon* can be traced back to a term denoting a slender 'hollow reed', for this was the meaning of Greek *kanna*. Of Semitic origin, it was borrowed into Latin as *canna*, where the sense 'reed' was extended to denote 'tube, pipe'. *Canna,* complete with its extended meanings, passed from Latin into Italian and other words were derived from it (see **canal**, page 177 and **cinnamon**, page 58). One of these was the augmentative *cannone* which literally meant 'big tube' and which denoted 'a cannon'. This was borrowed into French as *canon* around 1339, and eventually found its way into English almost two centuries later.

1347

THE BLACK DEATH SWEEPS ACROSS EUROPE

······

It is not known for certain where the Black Death originated – infection was probably picked up in the East by traders or sailors returning to Italy – but its progress across Europe was relentless. Bubonic plague reached the port of Melcombe, Dorset, on board a French ship in the summer of 1348 and became endemic. Its victims first experienced a raging fever. Then painful swellings (buboes) appeared in areas such as the groin and armpits, followed by the eruption of blackish blisters. Vomiting and delirium were other unpleasant symptoms. Death occurred within a day or two and came as a happy release. Often the death toll was so high that a few survivors struggled to bury the many dead. Sometimes entire communities perished: the villages of Standelf and Tilgarsley in Oxfordshire, for instance. By the following summer the plague had reached London. One estimate holds that 200 bodies were buried there daily: Spittlecroft churchyard, which was especially consecrated during the epidemic, holds over 50,000 plague victims. By the end of 1349 the plague had spread north to affect the entire country. In all, it is reckoned that about a third of the population of England perished. More localised outbreaks followed, in 1360 and 1379 for instance, which took a further toll.

The plague had a profound effect on feudal society. Land fell vacant because there were insufficient peasants left to work it. Those who survived were now in a position to demand better terms: they took on extra land or negotiated increased payment. If their demands were not met, the peasants ran away from their lord and put themselves in the service of another, so weakening the centuries-old feudal bond.

PESTILENCE, PEST

The name *Black Death*, by which the first terrible outbreak of bubonic plague in Europe is now known, was not contemporary with the event. The phrase, descriptive of the dark pustules which erupt on the victim's body, was first recorded in sixteenth-century Scandinavian chronicles and was then picked up by eighteenth-century German writers. In England the popular children's author Mrs Markham used *Black Death* to describe the catastrophic epidemic of 1348 in a history of England she wrote for schoolchildren (1823), and the term has marked this terrible visitation ever since.

Early writers often referred to the Black Death as *the pestilence* – or sometimes *the first pestilence*, in order to distinguish the catastrophic outbreak of 1348 from later visitations. The Old French word *pestilence* had been borrowed into Middle English at the beginning of the fourteenth century. It came from Latin *pestilentia*, 'highly infectious disease causing great mortality'. The Roman Empire had been no stranger to fatal epidemics with high death tolls. In AD 80, for instance, it is said that thousands perished in Rome. Other epidemics broke out in 167, 169 and 189. Latin *pestilentia* was derived from *pestilens* (stem *pestilent-*), 'unhealthy, infected', an adjective from *pestis*, 'deadly disease'.

The cause of bubonic plague was not known – no one imagined that it was carried by rats and spread by their fleas. Rank smells were commonly thought to be to blame. In 1349 Edward III ordered the Lord Mayor of London to ensure that the city streets were cleansed of all stinking debris and filth so that no one else would die from noisome odours. Over two hundred years later the plague was still thought to be a *corruption or infection of the Air* (Gilbert Skeyne, THE PEST,1568). For this reason the disease remained endemic after 1349 and localised outbreaks were common until the mid-seventeenth century.

In sixteenth-century French the term *peste* was used to denote 'a deadly disease' and more particularly the 'bubonic plague'. It was derived from Latin *pestis*, 'deadly disease', and was borrowed into English in the second half of the sixteenth century. Parish registers, introduced in 1538, show just how frequent localised outbreaks of pestilence were. An inscription under July 1564 in the register for Stratford-upon-Avon reads: *Hic incepit pestis*, 'Here began the plague'. The oath *a pest upon you*, common in French and then English, was not one to be uttered lightly. Modern French retains *peste* for 'a fatal epidemic', where English now uses *plague*. LA PESTE, a novel by Albert Camus (1947), is set against an outbreak of bubonic plague in Algeria. In modern English *pest* now denotes 'a harmful or destructive person or animal', a sense which developed at the beginning of the seventeenth century. Used more colloquially *pest* is simply synonymous with 'nuisance':

In England some players booze a lot. Those who have been out on the town and smell of booze the next morning are the ones I set out after. I chase them during training and won't leave them alone. I'm a pest from the first minute to the last.
(Footballer Dennis Bergkamp, quoted in THE INDEPENDENT, 22 December 1998)

• In spite of its similarity to *pest* in form and meaning, the verb *pester*, 'to annoy with repeated demands', is not derived from it. Rather it comes from the Middle French verb *empestrer* which was borrowed into English in the sixteenth century and the initial syllable dropped. *Empestrer* meant 'to tether a horse with a clog' and hence 'to encumber, to obstruct', being a borrowing of the unattested Vulgar Latin verb *impastōriāre*, 'to hobble a horse'. This was made up of the prefix *in-*, 'in, on', and the unattested noun *pastōria,* 'a clog for restraining grazing horses'. *Pastōria* was, in turn, derived from Latin *pastorius,* 'belonging to a herdsman', a derivative of Latin *pastor,* 'herdsman, shepherd'. In English, too, *pester* originally meant 'to encumber' but as soon as the brand new borrowing *pest* arrived in the language *pester* fell subject to its influence and developed the sense 'to trouble, to plague'.

PLAGUE

The stem *plag-*, 'strike', was responsible for this word. It is the source of Greek *plāgā*, 'stroke, blow'. When it was borrowed into Latin as *plāga,* the term acquired the extended sense of 'injury, wound'. *Plāga* occurs a number of times in the Late Latin of the Vulgate Bible. Indeed, the earliest written records of the word in English, where it appears as *plage,* are in the Wycliffe translations of the Bible (1382), which were taken from the Vulgate (see **1382 & 1388**, page 92).

In the Vulgate the use of *plāga* was extended still further. Sometimes the word denoted 'an affliction', particularly an instance of divine punishment, hence *the ten plagues of Egypt*. The Wycliffe Bible also uses *plage* in this way and the sense is still current: modern English might speak of *a plague of rats*, for instance. This sense was considerably weakened in the early seventeenth century, when *plague* (the *u* was inserted around the middle of the sixteenth century to keep the *g* hard) came to mean 'nuisance, cause of annoyance'. The verb *to plague*, 'to afflict with adversity', was similarly diminished to give the modern colloquial sense 'to torment, to annoy'.

The Vulgate also used *plāga* to denote an 'infectious disease (leprosy)', a sense which passed into English with Wycliffe. Thus, in the sixteenth century *plague* began to be used as a general term for 'a highly infectious disease resulting in a heavy death toll'. The 1552 BOOK OF COMMON PRAYER provided for such epidemics with set prayers to be used *in the tyme of any common plague or sickeness*. But bubonic plague was feared most of all and the term, especially when accompanied by the definite article, was soon more specifically used for this disease.

> *From winter, plague and pestilence,*
> *good Lord, deliver us!*

comes the fervent refrain in Thomas Nashe's masque SUMMER'S LAST WILL AND TESTAMENT (1600). Written during a fearful outbreak of bubonic plague in 1592-3 (though published later), the work reveals sixteenth-century preoccupation with and dread of the disease:

> *Adieu, farewell earth's blisse,*
> *This world uncertaine is,*
> *Fond are lifes lustful joyes,*
> *Death proves them all but toyes,*
> *None from his darts can flye;*
> *I am sick, I must dye:*
> *Lord have mercy on us.*

In later outbreaks the population of York was reduced by a third in 1604, and in 1665 the Great Plague broke out in London. In his diary for 10 June 1665, Samuel Pepys wrote:

> *In the evening home; and there to my great trouble hear that the plague is come into the City . . . To the office to finish my letters and then home to bed, being troubled at the sicknesse, and my head filled also with other business enough; and particularly how to put my things and estate in order, in case it should please God to call me away, which God dispose of to his glory!*

Pepys' diary for the plague years describes the dreariness of the plague-ridden city, the fires lit to cleanse the streets and the air, the curfews, the pest-carts and burials, the sadness over the soaring death toll – and muses over the future of the periwig:

> *Up; and put on my coloured silk suit very fine, and my new periwigg, bought a good while since but durst not wear because the plague was in Westminster when I bought it; and it is a wonder what will be the fashion after the plague is done as to periwiggs, for nobody will dare to buy any haire for fear of the infection, that it had been cut off of the heads of people dead of the plague.*
> (3 September 1665)

This was the last epidemic of bubonic plague to inflict the country. The particular reasons for its sudden disappearance are unknown but new quarantine regulations adopted by European ports were doubtless an important factor.

• The idiom *to avoid like the plague* dates from the first half of the nineteenth century.

• *Token* was the popular term given to the spots which marked the plague victim's body. Written references to this particular use of *token* date from the first half of the seventeenth century but these indicate that it had obviously been part of spoken language for some time. *Token* was ultimately derived from the Germanic base *taik*, 'show, indicate', and therefore means 'sign, mark'.

• The Latin verb *plangere* was also derived from *plag-*, 'strike', the stem which eventually produced *plague*. *Plangere* meant 'to beat noisily' and especially 'to beat the breast or head in grief' and is the source of several English words:

complain (14th century): originally 'to express sorrow' but soon also 'to grumble'. Middle English *compleinen* came from Old French *complaindre,* from Late Latin *complangere,* from Latin *com-,* intensive, and *plangere*.

plaintiff and *plaintive* (14th century): originally the same word, *pleintif,* in Middle English. This was a borrowing of Old French *plaintif,* 'lamenting', from *plainte,* 'lamentation', from Latin *planctus,* past participle of *plangere*. *Plaintive* followed the pattern of other adjectives borrowed from French whose ending was changed from *-if* to *-ive*. *Plaintiff,* originally an adjective used as a noun, retained its *-if* ending by virtue of being borrowed and sustained as a legal term.

c 1350

The Costumes of the Wealthy Become More Flamboyant and Varied

••••••

It was around the middle of the fourteenth century that costume began to reflect the emerging Renaissance movement, with its emphasis on classical heritage and on the personal dignity of the individual. It was rapidly realised that the adornment of the human figure was one way to give a philosophy a physical realisation. For the first time clothes were tailored to reveal the beauty of the human form, a development made possible by the availability of gorgeous textiles imported from Italy and the East and by earlier innovations such as buttons and buttonholes (see **c 1250**, page 67). Garments and accessories of this period were embellished with fur trimming and with jewels.

FUR

Fur, such as beaver, ermine or miniver, was sometimes used to line the cloaks and surcoats of the wealthy in the thirteenth century, but during the fourteenth and fifteenth centuries fur was much in evidence both as a rich trimming on the edges or panels of a garment and as a warm, luxurious lining. This fashionable display even reached the monasteries: Chaucer's worldly monk wore sleeves that were trimmed at the cuff with costly grey fur. In the fifteenth century in particular clothing often became heavy and cumbersome through excessive use of fur. Garments trimmed and lined in this way were described as *furred:*

A burnet cote . . .
Furred with no menivere,
But with a furre rough of here,
Of lambe skinnes
(Chaucer, THE ROMAUNT OF THE ROSE, c 1366)

The origins of *fur* may be traced back to an unattested Indo–European root *pō-* meaning 'protect'. This was responsible for an unattested prehistoric Germanic noun *fōthram,* 'sheath', which was adopted into Old French as *forre,* 'sheath'. From this Old French derived the verb *forrer* meaning 'to sheathe, to encase'. In time this developed the sense 'to line' and in particular 'to line or trim with fur'. Middle English borrowed the verb as *furren* in the fourteenth century and then derived the noun *furre* to denote 'linings and trimmings made of dressed animal pelts'. By the fifteenth century *fur* began to be applied to the soft fine coats of creatures such as stoats and beavers while the animals were still wearing them. In early use, it was also used to denote 'sheep's wool', as the quotation from Chaucer shows.

JEWEL

When the word *jewel* first arrived in English at the end of the thirteenth century, it denoted 'a personal ornament fashioned from gems or precious metals'. In the mid-fourteenth century such costly finery was much in evidence. The heavy belts which encircled the hips of both men and women were set with gold, silver and precious stones, exquisite brooches adorned the men's felt hats, while ladies wore circlets of jewels in their hair. Yet again Chaucer's monk was bang up-to-date, his hood fastened by an elaborate golden brooch fashioned as a love-knot at one end. Indeed, it was not until the late sixteenth century that *jewel* acquired its prevalent modern sense, that of 'a precious stone'.

The origins of *jewel* are somewhat uncertain but the most likely theory traces the word back to Latin *jocus,* 'game, jest'. This became *jeu* in Old French and yielded the derivative *joel,* 'jewel', the sense being 'trinket, plaything'. *Joel* became *juel* in Norman French and *iuel, gewel* in Middle English. An alternative, less favoured, derivation is that the Latin source is not with *jocus* but rather with *gaudium* and then French *joie,* both meaning 'joy, delight'. A jewel would then be 'a little thing of joy and delight', which is a description most owners of precious stones would agree with.

DAMASK, SATIN, VELVET

Many of the exquisite and brightly coloured fabrics used for fashionable costume in the mid-fourteenth century were silk weaves, first introduced by returning Crusaders as early as the eleventh century. By the 1500s, however, luxury fabrics were more widely available for those who could afford them. The terms *damask, satin* and *velvet* all entered English at this time.

Damask, originally a richly patterned silk weave, bore the name of *Damascus* (*Damaske* in Middle English), its city of origin.

Satin, a silk fabric prized for its lustrous sheen, may also be named after its city of export. Present-day *Tsinkiang,* a port in southeastern China, was known as *Tseutung* in the Middle Ages. In Arabic *Tseutung* became *Zaytūn.* The derived term *zaytūnī,* 'of Zaytūn', was applied to the fabric and was subsequently taken into Middle French as *zatanin* and *satin* before being borrowed into Middle English around the middle of the fourteenth century.

Velvet, an Oriental silk fabric with a clipped pile, has its origins in Latin *villus,* 'shaggy hair' (a word akin to *vellus,* 'fleece'). *Villūtus,* a medieval Latin adjective meaning 'shaggy', was derived from this. Old French borrowed the term as *velu* and derived the name *veluotte* from it to denote the sumptuous new fabric with its hairy pile. Middle English borrowed this as *veluet,* in the fourteenth century.

SILK

Silk production had originated in ancient China. Centuries later the secret of sericulture was eventually penetrated by India and Japan. These Asian countries guarded the secret of raw silk for several centuries more until around AD 550 when some silkworms were smuggled into Byzantium. From here sericulture spread with Islam to Spain and Sicily, where it was introduced by the Moors. By the twelfth and thirteenth centuries silk was being produced in the Italian city-states and, from there, imported into the rest of Europe.

Both the Greeks and the Romans had traded western luxuries for silks and the word *silk* came about through this commerce. The Greeks called the eastern traders who provided them with silk *Sēres*, a name which was ultimately derived from the Chinese word *sī*, 'silk'. Some authorities suggest that there were intermediate forms in Mongolian and Manchurian that account for the fuller Greek form. Latin borrowed the Greek name as *Sēres* and from it derived *sēricum*, 'silk', and the adjective *sēricus*, 'silken' (source of English *sericulture* and *serge*). As for the change of the *r* to *l* in the English word, the accepted explanation is that it came about through a borrowing from Latin into the early Slavonic languages. From there it came into Old English.

c 1350

Almost Every Town Now Has a Shop

••••••

In the Middle Ages people lived by agriculture and produced most of their daily requirements themselves. Any surplus produce would be sold at the weekly market in a nearby town and the profit used to buy other necessities (see **market**, page 38). At the market, people sold food they had grown or articles they themselves had made. Only at the great fairs, where many goods were brought from other parts of the country or imported from another, were middlemen tolerated (see **fair**, page 38). As townspeople became more affluent, however, they grew impatient to buy what they wanted at their own convenience instead of waiting for the annual fair to come round. Shops run by people who bought goods from others and sold them on at a profit began to open to satisfy this demand, probably during the thirteenth century. Such enterprise met with opposition from ordinary citizens, wary of being cheated, and also from the craft guilds who resented the fact that someone unskilled should profit by the craftsmanship of another. In spite of this, by the fourteenth century most towns could boast at least one retail outlet.

RETAIL

Retailers were once very unpopular. Making money from the productive efforts of others (fishermen, farmers or craftsmen) was frowned upon. In the early medieval period, such activities had been punishable by a fine or a spell in the pillory. Middlemen were generally suspected of exploiting ordinary citizens who could not afford to buy commodities in bulk at a favourable price but were forced to buy small quantities at a price that reflected the middleman's profit.

This notion of cutting up a commodity for sale in small quantities is reflected in the etymology of *retail*, which came into

Middle English during the fourteenth century when the activity was beginning to gain some acceptance. The term was a borrowing of Old French *retail*, which first denoted 'the action of trimming' and hence 'retail merchandise'. *Retail* was derived from the verb *retailler*, which meant 'to cut off', being composed of the intensive prefix *re-* and the verb *tailler*, 'to cut, to trim'. *Tailler* was derived from the unattested Vulgar Latin verb *tāliāre*, 'to cut', a derivation of the Latin noun *tālea*, meaning 'cutting from a plant'. Curiously, the Old French verb *retailler* was never used in the sense 'to sell in small quantities'. This suggests that the English use of *retail* as a verb may instead be modelled on Italian *retagliare*, which is similarly derived and is used in this way (see also **tally**, page 33).

SHOP

Medieval craftsmen not only made their wares but also sold them directly to the customer. Thus the earliest definition of shop was 'premises (often part of a house) where goods are manufactured and sold'. The word itself goes back to the unattested prehistoric Germanic *skoppan*, which denoted 'a penthouse or lean-to'. By the twelfth century this had found its way into Old French as *eschoppe*, 'stall', by way of Middle Low German *schoppe,* and English then borrowed it from Old French at the end of the thirteenth century.

'Lean-to', 'stall' and 'booth' are all accurate descriptions, for early shops were either tiny wooden structures, erected against the front wall of a house by day and dismantled each night, or simple openings in the wall of a front room, the openings having hinged shutters which were lowered to make a counter top. A fourteenth-century retail business would have been a family concern, the shopkeeper travelling to all the fairs in the district or meeting up with merchants at busy ports while the family minded the shop at home. He would have brought a variety of goods back from his travels, a

different collection each time, so a visit to his shop was one of pot luck. Nor could the customer easily examine the shopkeeper's stock, since his little booth had no space for display and the customer would never have gone inside.

• Retailers gradually gained acceptance and began to prosper during the fourteenth and fifteenth centuries. Although most shops carried a wide variety of goods, those in the great ports were able to specialise rather more. Signs above the door indicated the type of goods within. People were named after their trade (William the spicer) and a number of modern surnames indicate a past connection with retailing: *Spicer, Hosier, Chaucer* and *Mercer* are examples.

GROCER

A merchant who bought and sold in large quantities was known as a *grocer*. The word originated in Late Latin *grossus*, which meant 'large, thick'. From this, medieval Latin derived *grossārius* to denote a 'wholesale dealer', a word which came into Middle English by way of Old French *grossier* and Anglo-Norman *grosser* in the fourteenth century. The Company of Grocers is said to have been incorporated in 1344, when dealers in spices amalgamated with a group of wholesale merchants. From that time on, grocers began to be particularly identified with wholesale trade in spices and other exotic delicacies, so that, just a century after its appearance in English, the term was also being applied to shopkeepers who sold small quantities of spices, dried fruits and sugar directly to the public (see **spice**, **currant**, **sugar**, page 58). It appears, however, that some grocers carried surprising sidelines. In a letter written on 21 September 1472, John Paston asks his brother to purchase a hawk for him, and gives an idea of where one might be found. *There is,* he writes, *a grocer dwelling right over against the Well with two Buckets, a little from Saint Helen's, hath ever hawks to sell.*

1360

EDWARD III ISSUES A ROYAL EDICT PROTECTING HAWKS AND THEIR OWNERS

......

Hawking was introduced into England in Saxon times, but enjoyed a great surge of popularity after the Norman Conquest when it became a favourite pastime. In a letter written on 21 September 1472, John Paston implored his brother in London to buy him a hawk to help him while away the hours which were dragging by:

Now think on me, good lord, for if I have not an hawk I shall wax fat for default of labour, and dead for default of company by my troth. No more, but I pray God send you all your desires, and me my mewed goshawk in haste, or, rather than fail, a soar hawk.

The right to keep the most sought-after hawks was restricted to the privileged classes by law, although the cost and maintenance of such birds were, in any case, prohibitive to all except the rich. The wealthy always took great care to protect their privileges and a number of laws were passed concerning hawking. In 1360 a statute of Edward III declared that if a hawk were found it should be taken to the sheriff, so that he could publish the find throughout the district. The edict also stated that the penalty for stealing a hawk would be two years in prison and compensation to the owner equivalent to the price of the bird.

HAWK, FALCON

Hawk is a general term applied to any of the birds of prey used in falconry, but more particularly it denotes short-winged birds, such as goshawks, which fly close to the ground and take prey in woodland and enclosed country. The term is ultimately derived from an unattested prehistoric Germanic *khabukaz* which came from the root *khab-*, 'to seize'. And, indeed, the true hawk hunts by seizing its prey with its talons then binding to it, forcing it to the ground before fatally puncturing its organs. *Khabukaz* became *he(a)foc* in Old English and *hauk* in Middle English.

Falcon, on the other hand, denotes one of the long-winged birds of prey that soars then swoops upon its quarry. The term came into Middle English as *faucon* in the mid-thirteenth century by way of Old French, which in turn had borrowed it from Late Latin *falcō (stem falcōn-)*. Traditionally *falcō* is held to have derived from Latin *falx* (stem *falc-),* meaning 'sickle', an allusion to the bird's curved talons. However, the presence of related words in German and Dutch point to the possibility that *falcō* was a Late Latin derivation of an unattested prehistoric Germanic word *falkōn*.

Peregrine falcon is a translation of the medieval Latin phrase *falcō peregrinus,* literally 'pilgrim falcon', which arose in the mid-thirteenth century (see **pilgrim**, page 51). It alludes to the fact that the young birds were not taken from their inaccessible nests but captured once they had begun to fly afield.

Some birds of prey, such as the female peregrine falcon, were more highly prized than others and were paraded on the gauntlets of the higher aristocracy. Others were regarded less favourably. A late medieval treatise on hawking found in THE BOKE OF ST ALBANS (1486) contains a list which attempts to pair people of differing social rank with a suitable bird of prey (see **1496**, page 119). The gerfalcon, for example, was deemed fit for the king, the peregrine falcon for an earl, the bastard hawk for a baron and the merlin for a lady. The priest was permitted a sparrowhawk, while the poorer man had to content himself with a tercel. *Tercel (tiercel)* meant 'a third' and was applied to a male goshawk or peregrine falcon because they were approximately a third smaller than the female and were much less powerful in the chase.

MEWS

In the Middle Ages favourite hawks were treated like pampered pets. They were fed upon titbits of choice meat and had perches in the master's dining hall or even his bedroom.

Every summer, hawks moult, shedding their feathers for new plumage. A hawk in this condition is said to be *mewing*, a process which is not complete until the pinion feather has been cast:

Iff an hawke be in mewe yt same sercell [pinion] feder shall be the last feder that she will cast, and tyll that be cast, she is neuer mewed.
(BOKE OF ST ALBANS,1486)

In his request to his brother for a hawk, John Paston insisted on a *mewed hawk,* one which was ready for the hunt. The verb *to mew* came into English in the fourteenth century by way of French *muer*, 'to moult'. This same verb in Old French had the wider sense of 'to change', being a borrowing of Latin *mūtāre*, 'to change'. Since moulting hawks become temperamental and volatile, they were confined in a cage or sometimes a building which was known as a *mew,* where they were tethered well apart to keep them from attacking one another.

In London the mews for the royal hawks were situated at Charing Cross. During the reign of Henry VIII, these buildings were replaced by stabling for the king's horses, although the name *mews* was retained. Thus, in his chronicle of the house of Tudor (c 1548), Edward Hall speaks of *the kynges stable at Charyng crosse otherwise called the Mowse.* By this time the word *mews*, although plural, was being treated as a singular noun. During the first half of the seventeenth century, the continuing royal association between stables and *mews* led to the term being applied to other stabling arranged around a yard or alley which wealthy citizens constructed to house their horses and carriages. A common pattern is for rows of town houses to front on to larger streets, while their backs give out over a mews between them. When such buildings began to fall redundant around the turn of the nineteenth century, they were converted into living accommodation for gentlefolk. Nowadays, they are regarded as city addresses that the smart and fashionable are pleased to live in, probably unaware that their front room was once covered in horse manure.

HAGGARD

Wealthy lords would employ falconers for the training and upkeep of their precious hawks. The easiest bird of prey to train was an eyas, that is a bird taken straight from the nest. Better at the chase but more difficult to tame was a *haggard*, a mature wild bird. In Shakespeare's MUCH ADO ABOUT NOTHING (1599) Hero describes Beatrice as *too disdainful*, adding that *Her spirits are as coy and wilde, As haggards of the rock.*

Haggard did not come into English until the second half of the sixteenth century. It was a borrowing of French *hagard* but the word's origins are uncertain. Attempts have been made to link it with the unattested Germanic *khag-*, source of English *hedge*, an allusion to the bird's wild state. Shortly after its appearance in English, *haggard* was being applied to 'a wild, intractable person', initially a female since it was the female hawk which was most sought after. Again in Shakespeare, Petruchio uses the falconer's craft as an allegory to describe his taming of the intractable Katarina:

> *My faulcon now is sharp, and passing empty,*
> *And 'till she stoop she must not be full-gorg'd,*
> *For then she never looks upon her lure.*
> *Another way I have to man my haggard,*
> *To make her come and know her keeper's call;*
> *That is, to watch her, as we watch those kites*
> *That bate and beat, and will not be obedient.*
> *She eat no meat to-day, nor more shall eat;*
> *Last night she slept not, and to-night she shall not.*
> (THE TAMING OF THE SHREW, c 1592)

By the late seventeenth century, the use of *haggard* to describe 'the wild expression of a person suffering from terror or exhaustion', like a captured hawk being trained, was well established. From here the sense was further stretched to denote 'the drawn, gaunt look of advancing age'. This last was apparently influenced by *hag*, 'an old crone', a word which probably originated in Old English *hoegtesse*, meaning 'witch'.

LURE

The falconer would use a lure to train a bird of prey. The *lure* was a padded weight disguised with feathers to look like a bird. The falconer would bind meat to the lure and train the hawk to feed from it. Then he would swing the baited lure around on a cord, tempting the bird to fly at it. The cord would be gradually lengthened, encouraging the hawk to respond over greater distances. Finally the hawk was loosed to kill for itself and to return to the lure at the falconer's will. *Lure* came into Middle English in the fourteenth century by way of Old French *loirre*, 'bait'. This was probably a borrowing of *lōthr*, an unattested Germanic word meaning 'bait, decoy'. The verb *to lure*, from Old French *loirrer*, meaning 'to call a hawk to the lure', appeared at the same time and was immediately employed figuratively with the sense 'to tempt, to entice'.

Old French had the verb *alurer*, 'to attract'. This was made up of the prefix *a*, 'to', and *leurrer*, a later form of *loirrer*, 'to attract with a lure'. It was borrowed into English in the fifteenth century. The derived nouns *allure* and *allurement* both date back to around the mid-sixteenth century, with the adjective *alluring* appearing in the 1570s.

Shakespeare (see **1616**, *page 153) certainly knew all about falconry (see* **haggard**, *above). To him we owe two current idioms which employ terms of the sport:*

AT ONE FELL SWOOP

Falcons are said to *swoop* when they suddenly fall from a height upon their prey. Shakespeare, using an image from falconry, gave English the expression *at one fell swoop*, meaning 'at a single stroke', in his play MACBETH (1606). Macduff, trying to take in the news of the bloody slaughter of his wife and children utters these words:

> *Oh Hell-Kite! All? What, All my pretty Chickens, and their Damme At one fell swoope?*

PRIDE OF PLACE

Place was a technical term in falconry which denoted 'the peak of a falcon's flight before it closes its wings to stoop (that is, to swoop down on its prey)'. In MACBETH (1606) Shakespeare described this point as *pride of place* in an omen disclosed to Ross by an old man:

> *On Tuesday last,*
> *A falcon, tow'ring in her pride of place*
> *Was by a mousing owl hawk'd at and*
> *   kill'd.*

Pride of place is now commonly used to denote 'an unsurpassed position':

> *Disease-snobbery is only one out of a great*
> *multitude of snobberies, of which now some,*
> *now others take pride of place in general*
> *esteem.*
> (Aldous Huxley, 'Selected Snobberies' in MUSIC AT NIGHT, 1931)

Falconry has left us one last expression which deserves mention:

TO TURN TAIL

Gervase Markham wrote a number of treatises on country matters. One of these, entitled COUNTRY CONTENTMENTS (1611), deals with the pursuits of hunting, hawking and fishing. In it he describes the following behaviour of some hawks:

> *Short winged Hawks . . . will many times*
> *neither kill their Game, nor flie their mark;*
> *but will give it over . . . and (as Faulconers*
> *term it) turn tail to it.*

The term was first recorded in the second half of the sixteenth century. Its idiomatic use with the sense 'to turn and run away' dates from the latter years of that century:

> *A seed of hostility had sprung up in him,*
> *and he wasn't going to turn tail, although he*
> *felt too weak to fight.*
> (L P Hartley, THE HIRELING, 1957)

1382 & 1388

THE FIRST FULL TRANSLATIONS OF THE BIBLE INTO ENGLISH APPEAR

......

In 405 St Jerome completed a new translation of the Bible into Latin. Known as the Vulgate (from Latin *vulgatus*, 'made ordinary or common'), this was the only text available to the medieval Church. Over the centuries some fragments of the Bible were translated into Old English but it was not until the fourteenth century that the first complete translations into English were made.

The project was instigated by John Wycliffe (c 1320–84), a prominent scholar and teacher at Oxford University. He stood against excess and corruption in the Church and went on to denounce some of its principal doctrines, such as transubstantiation and the role of priest as mediator between God and man. Wycliffe was concerned that the Scriptures should be available to everyone in his native tongue – a dangerous idea, since their interpretation would no longer rest solely with Church scholars. To this end he and his followers translated the Vulgate into English. The first version appeared in 1382 and the revised in 1388, after Wycliffe's death.

Wycliffe was condemned by the Church for his views and finally forced to retire to his parish in Lutterworth. His influence extended to Bavaria, however, where his criticisms and teaching were championed by Jan Hus. In 1415 the Council of Constance ordered the execution of Hus and decreed that, after thirty-one years in the ground, Wycliffe's bones should be exhumed, burnt and scattered on the River Swift.

BIBLE

As early as 3000 BC Egyptian manuscripts, and later those of Syria, Palestine and southern Europe, were written on papyrus, a writing material prepared from a large reed-like aquatic plant of this name (see **paper**, page 119). Pasted end to end, sheets of papyrus could be rolled up and stored on rods to make a scroll.

In the first millennium BC large quantities of papyrus were exported to Greece from the Phoenician port of *Byblos* (present-day Jubayl, Lebanon). Greek used the name *byblos* or *biblos* to denote 'papyrus' and, hence, 'a document written on papyrus, a scroll'. Its diminutive form was *biblion*, 'scroll, book'. This was used so frequently that it lost its diminutive force and became the regular term for a 'scroll' or 'book'. The plural of *biblion* was *biblia*. Since the Scriptures are a collection of books, Christian writers referred to them as *ta biblia* in Greek, 'the books'. Although Latin originally borrowed *biblia* as a neuter plural word, ecclesiastical Latin began to treat it as a feminine singular noun. As such it was taken into Old French as *bible* and then into Middle English around the turn of the fourteenth century.

The figurative use of *bible* to denote a 'work of authority' on a particular topic dates back to the turn of the nineteenth century:

The new and illustrated bible of child care that explains clearly how to raise a healthy and happy child from infancy through preschool. (From the cover of Miriam Stoppard, COMPLETE BABY AND CHILD CARE, 1995)

• Different versions or editions of the Bible have been given particular nicknames by book collectors. For instance, the GENEVA BIBLE, which was first published in 1560, was later dubbed the *Breeches Bible* after the quaint-sounding translation of Genesis 3:7 which says that Adam and Eve, suddenly conscious of their nakedness, *sewed figge tree leaues together, and made themselues breeches.* (The Wycliffe translations had also used the same word: *They soweden to gidre leeves of a fige tree, & maden hem brechis.*) Some editions of the GENEVA BIBLE were published in Holland by the Dort press, which had a goose as its emblem, hence the epithet *Goose Bible.*

The *Bug Bible* was also named after an archaic word in its text. Coverdale's Bible translation of 1535 renders Psalm 91:5 as *Thou shalt not nede to be afrayed for eny bugges by night* where *bug* meant 'an imaginary figure of terror, a phantom'. Similarly, the *Bishops' Bible* of 1568 (so called because a large number of bishops worked on this revision of Coverdale's text) became known as the *Treacle Bible* because it uses *treacle* where later versions have *balm*. (This was also a feature of Coverdale's translations.) Jeremiah 8:22, for instance, has *Is there no tryacle in Gilead, is there no phisition there?* The earliest sense of *treacle* was 'salve for relief against venomous bites and malignant diseases' and this was still current in the sixteenth century.

Several editions have been named after printing errors. The *Murderers' Bible* of 1801, for example, confuses *murmurer* with *murderer* (Jude 16) and in an edition of 1823 Rebecca apparently arose with her *camels* instead of her *damsels* (Genesis 24:61), hence *Rebecca's Camels Bible.* Some errors were too grave to be overlooked, however, lest they encouraged loose living. In the seventeenth century, printers Barker and Lucas were fined £300 for carelessly leaving the word *not* out of the seventh commandment, so that it read *Thou shalt commit adultery.* Not surprisingly, the edition was dubbed the *Adulterous* or *Wicked Bible* (1632).

VOLUME

From about the second century BC the use of parchment (cleaned and polished animal skins) became more widespread as a writing material. Unlike papyrus, parchment could be used on both sides and, because it could be folded and bound together between protective wooden boards, was more convenient to use than unwieldy scrolls which always had to be rewound. By about the fourth century AD, folded parchment had all but replaced papyrus in the Roman Empire.

Where Greek had used *biblos* for 'a roll of papyrus', Latin had *volūmen*, a word derived from *volvere*, 'to roll'. Old French borrowed the term as *volume* to denote 'a roll of parchment' and also 'a book'. The earliest recorded uses of *volume* in English are found in the works of John Wycliffe. In his Bible of 1382 he uses the term in its original sense to denote 'roll of papyrus', but in an earlier sermon he laments the fact that his contemporaries *maken gret volyms of newe lawes,* entire books of regulations to replace the concise phylacteries of the Jews.

Volume was often qualified by adjectives such as 'large' or 'great' and by the sixteenth century the term had come to denote the 'dimensions of a book'. This emphasis on size gave rise to the extended sense of 'amount' or 'mass' in general, which dates from the first half of the seventeenth century. Not until the early

nineteenth century did *volume* come to denote the 'loudness of sound':

> *It was before the days of Walkman, and my graduate students used to listen to loud rock music. I retaliated on the other side of the partition by playing classical music, and the volume wars would break out. When I was really desperate I turned to Schoenberg.* (Imre Friedman, quoted in Sara Wheeler, TERRA INCOGNITA, 1996)

(For other words that made their first appearance in English in Wycliffe's Bible, see **jubilee**, page 73 and **plague**, page 83.)

• The Latin verb *volvere*, 'to roll', is also evident in a number of other English words:

convolve (16th century) and *convolute* (17th century): from Latin *convolvere*, 'to roll together'.

convolvulus (16th century): a New Latin name for a genus of plants with twisting stems, commonly known as *bindweed*.

devolve (15th century): from Latin *dēvolvere*, 'to roll down'.

evolve (17th century): from Latin *ēvolvere*, 'to unroll, to roll out'.

involve (14th century): from Latin *involvere*, 'to roll into, to envelop'.

revolve (14th century): from Latin *revolvere*, 'to roll back', and hence *revolution* (14th century [movement], 17th century [politics]) and *revolver* (19th century).

vault (14th century): from Middle English *voute* or *vaute*, from Old French, from Vulgar Latin *volta*, 'a turn' and hence later 'a bend, an arch,' from the past participle of *volvere*, 'to turn'. Thus vault means 'a room with an arched roof'.

voluble (16th century): by turn in the sixteenth century the adjective meant 'capable of rolling with ease about an axis' and then, 'capable of easy movement, gliding', and finally 'given to fluent, ready speech'.

1386

A Mechanical Clock Is Set up in Salisbury Cathedral

••••••

In thirteenth-century London, before the advent of mechanical clocks, a man known as Bartholomo Orologaria noted the time and then struck the hours for the community at St Paul's Cathedral. A record dating back to 1286 required him to be given a loaf of bread every day for performing this duty. It is thought that the development of the mechanical clock took place in the religious houses in the first half of the fourteenth century so that the monks could be reliably summoned to prayer. In England Salisbury Cathedral, founded in 1220, boasted the addition of a mechanical clock in 1386 and this is now the oldest extant clock in the country.

CLOCK

Bartholomo Orologaria was named after his task, for an *orologe* or *horologe* was the term applied to any instrument used for telling the time – a sundial or hourglass, for instance. The Greek word for such a device was *hōrologion* (from *hōrologos*, 'hour-teller', compound of *hōra*, 'hour' and *legein*, 'to speak') and this came into Middle English by way of Latin *hōrologium* and Old French *orloge*. The current English word *horology,* which denotes both 'the science of time-measurement' and 'the art of clock-making', derives from this. Modern French retains *horloge* for 'clock'.

The word *clock* was pressed into service when large mechanical timepieces driven by falling weights, such as the ones at Salisbury and Rouen, were invented in the fourteenth century. *Clock* means 'bell', and these great instruments marked the time, not by hands and a dial, but by striking the hours. The term probably came into English by way of Middle Dutch *klocke*, itself a borrowing of medieval Latin *clocca*, 'bell'. *Clocca* is of Celtic origin and the word is thought to be imitative of the tuneless clatter made by early handbells hammered out of sheet iron rather than the sonorous note of the cast cathedral bell of later date.

The mechanical clock was an invention of great importance. Nevertheless, these early timepieces were not accurate and might lose up to half an hour a day. More reliable by far were the tried and tested services of a good cockerel – Chauntecleer, for instance:

Wel sikerer was his crowyng in his logge
Than is a clokke or an abbey orlogge.
By nature he knew ech ascencioun
Of the equynoxial in thilke toun;
For whan degrees fiftene weren ascended,
Thanne crew he, that it myghte nat been
    amended.
(Chaucer, THE NUN'S PRIEST'S TALE, c 1387)

No mechanical device could ever work by instinct.

• Medieval Latin *clocca* not only denoted a 'bell' but also a 'horseman's cape' because of the garment's bell-like shape. The word was borrowed into Old French as *cloche*. A dialectal variant *cloque* was borrowed into Middle English in the thirteenth century as *cloke,* becoming *cloak* in modern English.

Modern French retains *cloche* for 'bell' and the word has twice been borrowed into English to describe articles that are bell-shaped. The first borrowing was in the last quarter of the nineteenth century, when *cloche* was taken for 'a translucent cover for protecting tender plants and seedlings'. The second was in the first decade of the twentieth century when *cloche hats* first became fashionable.

DIAL

Dial was adapted from medieval Latin *diālis,* 'daily', an adjective derived from Latin *diēs,* meaning 'day'. When the word first appeared in Middle English in the fifteenth century, it denoted a 'sundial' (the compound *sundial* did not appear until the late sixteenth century) and, indeed, throughout the sixteenth and seventeenth centuries *dial* was used quite generally to refer to any kind of timepiece or chronometer:

> *And then he drew a dial from his poke,*
> *And, looking on it with lack-lusre eye,*
> *Says very wisely, 'It is ten o'clock' . . .*
> (Shakespeare, As You Like It, 1600)

The term began to be used for a 'clock face' in the last quarter of the sixteenth century. This usage was firmly established by the mid-eighteenth century, when *dial* was extended to denote the faces of other instruments of measurement, such as a gauge or meter. Although a telephone measures nothing at all, its circular plate bearing letters and numbers was somewhat similar to those on clocks and meters, and so *dial* found an application here, too. Now most telephones are push–button contraptions, but *dial* survives in this context as a verb meaning 'to compose a telephone number' and in combinations such as *dial-a-pizza.*

SPRING

Around the middle of the fifteenth century, some clocks began to be driven by a neater spring-driven mechanism. Indeed, it was the science of horology that first applied *spring* to 'an elastic device of bent or coiled metal'. *Spring* goes back to an Indo-European root which carried the sense of 'swift motion'. When it came into Old English via Germanic, it had the underlying sense of 'leaping' or 'starting forth' and from its earliest appearance the verb *to spring* has meant 'to move with a sudden vigorous bound'. The coil which was introduced into clock mechanisms possessed the property of regaining its shape in an instant if compressed, then released, and was thus called a *spring.* The development of the spring-driven mechanism was a breakthrough which opened the way for the production of practical compact clocks in the early sixteenth century.

• When *spring* was first used as a noun in Old English, it denoted 'a place where water starts forth or rises from the ground'. The vigour and movement of such water sources shows the relation with the original root. From this there flowed a later stream of figurative uses: a general sense of 'source, origin or birth' in the early thirteenth century, for instance; 'the dayspring' or first glow of the dawn at the turn of the fourteenth century; 'the burst of new growth on a plant' in the late thirteenth century; and, in the sixteenth century, 'the spring of the year' when this burgeoning took place.

WATCH

In the early sixteenth century Peter Henlein, a locksmith from Nuremberg, began to produce small portable timepieces which were driven by a mainspring. The clocks could be held in cupped hands, having a mechanism topped by a horizontal dial with a single hand to mark the hours. This advance paved the way for the production of watches, which were also first manufactured in Germany. The word *watch* was ultimately derived from a prehistoric Germanic base carrying the sense 'to be alert, to be awake'. This was responsible for the Old English verb *wæccan* which meant 'to be awake' and therefore 'to keep vigil'. A derivative noun *wæcce*, denoted 'a state of wakefulness' and hence 'an act of vigilance'. In Middle English this word had become *wacche,* still retaining its former senses. By the fourteenth century the term denoted both 'a sentinel' and 'the action of observing and keeping close guard'. *Watch* began to be applied to a timepiece towards the middle of the fifteenth century, when it first denoted 'an alarm clock' – the theme of being alert and wakeful again. It did not refer to a 'small portable timepiece' until the last quarter of the sixteenth century.

c 1390

THE FORM OF CURY, AN EARLY COOKERY BOOK, APPEARS

••••••

The Middle Ages saw a revolution in eating habits. Improved agricultural knowledge and technology brought about the cultivation of better and more nutritious crops. At the same time Crusaders began to bring home exciting new ingredients from the eastern Mediterranean to liven up the dull winter diet of smoked and salted produce (see **spice**, page 58). These factors, together with the increasing refinement of the nobility and, by the fourteenth century, the prosperous merchant and trading class, led to the creation of new recipes for the banqueting table. According to Reay Tannahill (FOOD IN HISTORY, 1973), the earliest cookery books were simply reminders of culinary creativity. They were written for those employed in the kitchens of great households who really could cook and required nothing more than a few notes to jog the memory. For this reason, late medieval recipes are infuriatingly vague about quantities and sketchy over preparation. THE FORM OF CURY is the earliest surviving cookery book written in English. The word *cury* was ultimately derived from Latin *cocus,* 'cook', and meant 'cooked food, a prepared dish'. The book, which appeared in the late fourteenth century, was written for the feasts at the court of Richard II. It contains 196 recipes, many of which are obviously of French inspiration. The production of cookery books increased rapidly with the invention of the printing press in the following century (see **1474**, page 107).

MINCE

Mynce Oynouns and cast ther to Safronn and Salte reads a recipe in THE FORM OF CURY (c 1390). This is the earliest appearance in English of the culinary verb *to mince,* meaning 'to chop finely'. The word can be traced back to Latin *minūtus,* 'small', and is therefore related to the

English adjective *minute*. Latin *minūtus* gave the noun *minūtia*, 'smallness', from which the unattested Vulgar Latin verb *minūtiāre*, 'to cut in small pieces', was derived. This was taken into Old French as *menuisier*, whose thirteenth-century variant *mincier* was borrowed by English cooks in the fourteenth century.

Mince, that staple of modern British carnivorous households, appeared in the nineteenth century as a shortening of *minced meat*. An earlier contraction of *minced meat* had given the compound *mincemeat* in the seventeenth century, a term which also denoted the traditional rich mixture of dried and candied fruits and chopped meat which was used to fill Christmas pies (see **raisin**, page 99). The bloody threat to *mince* the limbs of their victims was used by Shakespearian characters and was perhaps the inspiration behind the late seventeenth-century idiom *to make mincemeat of someone*, meaning 'to destroy a person', as if by chopping him up into little bits. The notion of reducing or minimalising something was behind the phrase *to mince the matter*, which in the seventeenth century meant 'to make light of something'. The expression is now constructed negatively, as in *not to mince matters (one's words)* and has the sense 'to be direct and to the point'.

POACH

The word *poach* comes ultimately from Old French *poche*, 'small sack, bag', and is descriptive of the appearance of an egg cooked by breaking it into boiling water, where the yellow yolk becomes contained in a 'pocket' formed by the firmer white. Indeed, directions in TWO COOKERY-BOOKS (c 1430–50) call eggs cooked in this way *eyron en poche*, 'eggs in bags'. From *poche* Old French derived the verb *pocher*, 'to place in a bag'. The term was then borrowed by French cooks before being taken into English culinary vocabulary. THE FORM OF CURY (c 1390) gives the following scant method for poaching eggs: *Pochee. Take Ayren and breke hem in scaldyng hoot water* . . . The

directions are for medieval cooks who can. Compare these instructions for modern cooks who obviously can't:

Place the fryingpan over a gentle heat and add enough boiling water from the kettle to fill it to 1 inch (2.5 cm). Keep the heat gentle, and very quickly you will see the merest trace of tiny bubbles beginning to form over the base of the pan. Now carefully break the eggs, one at a time, into the water and let them barely simmer, without covering, for just 1 minute. A timer is essential because you cannot guess how long 1 minute is . . .
(Delia Smith, DELIA'S HOW TO COOK, 1998)

Over the centuries the verb *to poach* was confined to the cooking of eggs, but during the nineteenth century, it was applied to the gentle simmering of other delicate foods such as fish or fruit (see also **stew**, page 66).

• The English verb *to poach*, meaning 'to trespass, to trap fish or game illegally', in use since the seventeenth century, may also be derived from French *pocher*, 'to put in a sack, to pocket'.

• The unattested Frankish word *pokka*, 'bag', from which Old French *poche* was ultimately derived, found its way into Old Norman French as *poque, poke*. Anglo-Norman had the word as *poke*, 'bag' (which passed into Middle English and still exists in the expression *a pig in a poke*), and a diminutive *poket*, which was taken into Middle English as *poket*, becoming *pocket* in the sixteenth century. Old Norman French also had the term *pouche*, a parallel to Old French *poche*. This was borrowed into Middle English as *pouche*, 'small sack', in the fourteenth century, becoming *pouch* in the sixteenth.

GRAVY

French recipes feature strongly in early English cookery books: those for *Connynges* (rabbits) *in Grauey* and *Oysters in Gravey* which appear in THE FORM OF

CURY are examples. Indeed, it is an error with an unfamiliar Old French word which has helped to form the English word *gravy*. In Old French cookery books the word *grané* denoted a spiced sauce or dressing made from broth, almond milk and wine or ale, which was used to flavour fish and white meats. The following recipe for *Oysters in Gravey* is a typical example:

> Schyl Oysters and seeth hem in wyne and in hare own broth, cole the broth thrugh a cloth, take almandes blaunched, grynde hem and drawe hem up with the self broth & alye it with floer of Rys and do the oysters therinne, cast in powder of gynger, suger, macys.

THE FORM OF CURY (c 1390)

When the recipes were translated into English the word *grané* was misread as *gravé*. The error arose because of the writing style in medieval manuscripts, where an *n* written hurriedly in a crabbed hand could easily be mistaken for a *u* or a *v* in an unfamiliar word. Hence the various forms, *grauey*, *gravey* and *grave* among them, which appear in late fourteenth- and fifteenth-century English manuscripts. The origin of the Old French word is uncertain, however. A possible etymology derives the word from Old French *grain*, 'grain', the dressing being seasoned with grains of spice. As the culinary arts evolved, the stock and almond milk sauce began to fall from favour, but the word *gravy* was retained and, by the late sixteenth century, was instead applied to 'the juices which run from meat while it is cooking'.

ALMOND, DATE, FIG

A favourite banqueting extravagance of the late Middle Ages was a *train* (see **train**, page 198) of imported fruits and nuts collected on a thread and strewn with batter:

> Trayne roste. Take Dates and figges . . . and then take grete reysons and blanched almondes, and prik them thorgh with a nedel into a threde of a mannys length, . . . rost the treyne abought the fire in the spete; . . . cast the batur on the treyne as he turneth abought the fire.

(TWO COOKERY-BOOKS, c 1430–50)

With the train of Mediterranean produce, a train of unfamiliar words entered English:

Date arrived in the late thirteenth century after a long trek from ancient Greek. The word was borrowed from Old French *date* which, in turn, came from Old Provençal *datil*. The Provençal term was derived from Latin *dactylus*, itself a borrowing of Greek *daktulos*. *Daktulos*, which meant 'finger' or 'toe', had been applied to the fruit of the date palm in ancient times because, to the fanciful Greek imagination, a finger or toe is just what it looked like. Will a box of sticky Christmas dates ever seem the same again? (Actually, don't they look rather more like cockroaches?)

Almond also came from Greek. Greek *amugdalē* was taken into Latin as *amygdala*, which was corrupted to *amandula* in Late Latin. Spanish mistook *amandula* as being of Arabic origin and so, when it borrowed the word, it affixed the full Arabic definite article *al*, resulting in *almendra* (see under **1492**, page 111). Old French *almande* was obviously influenced by the Spanish, for it too gained an *l* in the initial syllable (although it was subsequently dropped again to give *amande* in modern French). English borrowed the Old French word *almande* around the end of the thirteenth century.

The Latin word *fīcus*, 'fig', came from an unknown Mediterranean source. Vulgar Latin derived the unattested form *fīca* from it and this was taken into Old Provençal as *figa*, and from there into Old French as *figue*. The word was borrowed into Middle English as *fige* in the first quarter of the thirteenth century.

RAISIN, CURRANT

The new products and flavours discovered by the Crusaders were used daringly and enthusiastically by cooks in wealthy

European households. Meat was not only jazzed up with spices but with sweet ingredients such as currants, raisins and dates as well. The mince pies we eat at Christmas once contained meat. The suet which lurks in modern mincemeat reminds us of the fact. Here is a recipe from a seventeenth-century publication, Gervase Markham's THE ENGLISH HOUSEWIFE (1623):

> *Take a leg of mutton, and cut the best of the best flesh from the bone, and parboil it well: then put to it three pound of the best mutton suet, and shred it very small: then spread it abroad, and season it with pepper and salt, cloves and mace: then put in good store of currants, great raisins and prunes, clean washed and picked, a few dates sliced, and some orange-pills sliced: then being all well mixed together, put it into a coffin, or into divers coffins, and so bake them: and when they are served up, open the lids and strew store of sugar on the top of the meat, and upon the lid. And in this sort you may also bake beef or veal; only the beef would not be parboiled, and the veal will ask a double quantity of suet.*

The word *raisin* is of Latin origin. Latin had *racēmus* which meant 'a bunch of grapes' and this term passed into Vulgar Latin as unattested *racīmus*. But when Old French borrowed this as *raisin*, it was used to denote a single grape rather than an entire bunch. Middle English acquired the word in the thirteenth century but mostly used it to refer to a *raisin sec*, a grape that had been dried in the sun.

A variety of small seedless grape was grown in the eastern Mediterranean and, through the Crusades, a demand for the sweet dried fruits was created in Europe. The French called them *raisins de Corinthe*, 'grapes of Corinth' after their place of export. This name was taken into Anglo-Norman as *raisins de Corauntz*, becoming *raisins* or *reysons of Coraunce* in Middle English:

> *Lat it seeth togedre with powdor-fort of gynger . . . with raysons of Coraunte*
> (THE FORM OF CURY, c 1390).

The cumbersome term *raisins of Coraunce* was clipped to *coraunce* before the end of the fifteenth century, and the new short form was soon taken as a plural. This did not pose much of a problem since currants are rarely spoken of in the singular. Nevertheless, by the end of the sixteenth century *coren* was tried as a singular form, and when the spelling *currants* emerged in the first half of the seventeenth century, *currant* was later admitted as a singular.

Around the last quarter of the sixteenth century, black and red currant bushes from Northern Europe began to be cultivated in England. But what to call them? The name *currant* was transferred to them by those who were ignorant of their origin and, spying their tiny fruit, believed them to be the plants of origin of the sweet dried currants imported from the Mediterranean. Apothecary John Parkinson knew better. In a book described as *A Garden of Flowers . . . with a Kitchen garden . . . and an Orchard; together with the right orderings, planting and preserving of them, and their uses and vertues,* he attempted to clarify matters:

> *Those berries . . . usually called red currans are not those currans . . . that are sold at the Grocers.*
> (PARADISI IN SOLE, PARADISUS TERRESTRIS, 1629)

How confusing!

c 1400

Tennis Becomes Known in England

••••••

In his CRONICA DI FIRENZE, 'Chronicle of Florence', Donato Velluti tells how, early in the year 1325, some French knights visiting Florence introduced a new game called *tenes* to that city. The game, which involved striking a ball with the palm of the hand, did not apparently catch on there, but it continued to be played in France, where it was known as *jeu de paume,* 'palm game'. Tennis was known in England in the fifteenth century and gained in popularity in the sixteenth. It was, however, a game for royalty and the aristocracy since it required the construction of a special roofed court that only the wealthy could afford. Henry VII and Henry VIII both built courts at various palaces. That at Hampton Court, which became Henry VIII's favourite palace, still exists and is occasionally used by players of the game that is now known as 'real tennis'.

TENNIS

The word *tennis* first appeared in Middle English as *tenetz* around the turn of the fifteenth century. The word is very like the form *tenes* recorded by Donato Velluti in his fourteenth-century chronicle of Florence. It is curious that neither Italian nor English picked up the French name *la paume (jeu de paume* had no mention in English until the eighteenth century) and even more curious that French accounts of the game offer no term from which *tennis* might be derived. The English and Italian names are, however, similar in form to French *tenez*, which means 'take, receive', being the imperative of *tenir*, 'to hold'. Etymologists therefore conclude that *tenez* was a call the server made to his opponent as he struck the ball. The fact that some sort of call was made at this point in the game is borne out by accounts written in Latin.

From royal and aristocratic beginnings tennis gained in popularity throughout the sixteenth century. So much so that in his book THE INSTITUTION OF A YOUNG NOBLE MAN (1607) James Cleland found it necessary to advise moderation. Although

the game was useful for exercise and recreation, the young man of noble blood should take care to avoid exhaustion, disputes with the tennis-keeper (umpire) and the urge to gamble on his skill. But what young man has ever listened to the sage advice of one older and wiser? Besides, by then skill at tennis was considered a necessary accomplishment for a young gentleman's swift integration into university life:

The two marks of his seniority is the bare velvet of his gown and his proficiency at tennis, where when he can once play a set, he is a freshman no more.
(John Earle, MICRO-COSMOGRAPHIE, 1628)

The modern game of *lawn tennis* was devised in the nineteenth century. Credit for this is officially given to Major Walter Clopton Wingfield, a retired British cavalryman, who is said to have mixed elements of racquets, badminton and real tennis for his new game. A book of lawn tennis rules was published by the Major in 1873, and in 1877 the first championship matches took place at Wimbledon. It is Major Wingfield's game that is now known as *tennis*. Those few who keep alive the game that Henry VIII would have recognised play *real tennis*, known in American English as *court tennis*. (For details of a present-day royal who enjoys real tennis, see **romance**, page 42)

• In the early sixteenth century the word *court* was applied to the area used for tennis because it was an enclosed space. For the etymology of the word, see **courtesy**, page 41.

• Tennis has some words in common with other sports. See **bowl** and **umpire**, page 184.

RACKET (RACQUET)
Tennis balls were made of tightly wound cloth and were very hard. In time, rackets were introduced to permit the players greater reach and power. These early rackets were oblong. In his GENERAL HISTORY OF VIRGINIA (1624), Captain John Smith, attempting to describe a beaver, informs his readers that the creature's tail is *somewhat like the forme of a Racket*. The term *racket* goes back to the striking of a ball with the palm. It apparently originated in *rāhat*, a dialectal Arabic word for 'the palm of the hand'. This was borrowed into Italian as *racchetta* before being taken into French as *raquette*. English borrowed the word from French in the early sixteenth century.

   Of course no one imagined that tennis rackets might one day be used as weapons by overheated gentlemen short in temper:

The Earl of Leicester, being very hot and sweating, took the Queen's napkin out of her hand and wiped his face: which the Duke of Norfolk seeing said that he was too saucy, and swore that he would lay his racket about his face. Here upon rose a great trouble, and the Queen offended sore with the Duke.
(Report of a tennis match before Queen Elizabeth, 1565, quoted in Kightly, THE PERPETUAL ALMANACK OF FOLKLORE, 1987)

• *Racket* to denote 'an uproar' also came into English in the sixteenth century but is of English origin and imitative of a disturbance.

FROM PILLAR TO POST
In real tennis, the net was suspended from a post on one side of the court and tied to a pillar which supported the stands at the other. It was a common tactic to wrong-foot or tire an opponent by having him pursue the ball from one side of the court to the other, from the pillar to the post. In the fifteenth century the phrase *from post to pillar* was coined to denote being driven 'from one place of appeal to another' or 'from one difficult situation to another':
He was tost from post to piller, one whyle to hys father . . . anothe whyle to hys frendes, and founde no comfort at them (Hugh Latimer, SEVENTH SERMON BEFORE EDWARD VI, 1549). The idiom was used with a variety of verbs but the most common was *toss*. The reversal of the original word order to give the familiar modern form *from pillar to post* arose around the middle of the sixteenth century, apparently in order to have *post* rhyme with *tost* (tossed):

From piller vnto post
The powr man he was tost.
(VOX POPULI, c 1550, quoted in Hazlitt, ENGLISH PROVERBS AND PROVERBIAL PHRASES, 1869)

• *Bandy* meant 'to hit a ball back and forth' and was one of the verbs sometimes used with the expression *from pillar to post*. *Bandy* came into English in the second half of the sixteenth century, but although it has equivalents in French, Spanish and Italian, its origins are unclear. One theory suggests that it was a borrowing of French *bander*, 'to take sides' – in a dispute or for a game, for instance. From its earliest appearance in English the verb was mostly put to figurative use. This is still the case. The verb means 'to exchange words or blows' (*to bandy words*) or 'to pass around' (*to bandy about*).

c 1410

Wire drawing Is Invented in Nuremberg

······

Before the invention of wire drawing, wire was probably produced by cutting thin strips from metal plates and rounding the edges off with a file. In fifteenth-century Germany a method was devised of inserting pointed iron strips into a tapering die and hauling them through by hand. The worker would position himself so that he could brace his legs against the die apparatus and thus pull all the harder – sitting in a suspended chair was one way of exerting maximum force. The invention of wire drawing greatly speeded up pin production in the fifteenth century.

PIN

People in the Middle Ages, like the ancients before them, used pins to fasten their clothing. Originally fashioned from wood or bone, pins were eventually made of metal, particularly after the invention of wire drawing. A pin is an apparently uncomplicated item, so it is surprising just how much labour was involved to produce one. Metal, initially iron, had to be drawn out to make wire, cut to length, sharpened to a point at one end and ground at the other where the head would be fixed. The head was made from two turns of wire, joined to the shaft and then turned to finish it off. During the fifteenth century France led the field in the production of iron pins from drawn wire and by the sixteenth century had begun to manufacture pins from brass wire. The English, who had never produced enough pins for the home market, imported them from the Continent. Brass pins were brought to England from France in 1540 and it is said that they were first used by Catherine Howard, the wife of Henry VIII. (See c 1250, page 67.)

The word *pin* has its origin in Latin *pinna* or *penna*, which meant 'feather' and also 'pinnacle'. This latter sense was responsible for the word being borrowed into Old English as *pinn* to denote 'a small (pointed) peg' – for fastening parts of a structure together, for instance, or hanging one thing upon another. *Tile pynnes for the new hous* are an item in the church accounts for St Giles in Reading, prepared in 1527. In SYLVA (1664), his book on arboriculture, John Evelyn extols the oak as *excellent for . . . pins and peggs for tyling, &c.* Wooden pegs, termed *pins*, were cylindrical in shape and usually tapered at the end, so that, in the fourteenth century, the word was also applied to the pointed spike which was used to fasten clothing together. Pins assumed such importance in daily life over the centuries, however, that this last application in dress became predominant. Even so, in modern English *pin* is still also used as a technical term in an extended range of specialist areas: in surgery to connect broken bones, in dentistry to fix a crown, in musical instruments to tune the tension of strings, in weapons to set off a hand grenade, in cooking for an instrument to roll out dough, and even in golf for the metal rod and flag that signals the hole.

One could never have enough pins. In THE EVOLUTION OF USEFUL THINGS (1993), Henry Petroski muses over just how many of these essential little articles must have been dropped by fumbling fingers or have worked loose and fallen unnoticed to the floor during the course of the day's activity. Production was so slow that medieval pin-makers could not produce enough of their wares to satisfy demand, and a law was passed stating that pins could only be sold on certain days. Scarcity drove up the price and import duties added to their cost. Women from wealthy families often received an allowance for dress – including the necessary expensive pins. The following is from a record of wills registered at York (1542):

I give my said daughter Margarett my lease of the parsonadge of Kirkdall Churche . . . to buy her pynnes withal.

Thus the term *pin-money* was coined. The idiom continued to denote 'a sum properly settled upon a wife for her various private expenses' until the nineteenth century, when pins ceased to be manufactured by hand. With the advent of mechanisation good-quality pins became readily available. As their price fell, so the idiom was devalued to mean nothing more than 'pocket money'.

NEEDLE

Needles were originally fashioned from bone, horn, thorns or fishbones. In the Middle Ages they were made of iron, and instead of a stamped eye they had a closed hook to hold the thread. The source of *needle* can be traced back to the Indo-European base *nē-*, 'to sew'. This gave the unattested prehistoric Germanic *nēthlō* from which Old English derived *nǽdl* and from which a number of Germanic languages also obtained their words for 'needle'.

Needle-making, thought to have been introduced to Europe by the Moors, was well established in Germany by the second half of the fourteenth century and in the Netherlands in the fifteenth century. During the reign of Elizabeth I efforts were made to cut down on

expensive foreign imports by stimulating domestic manufacture. Pin-making was one industry which was encouraged in this way. Another was needle-making. According to the sixteenth-century chronicler John Stowe:

The making of Spanish needles was first taught in England by Elias Crowse, a German, about the eighth year of queen Elizabeth and in Queen Mary's time there was a negro who made fine Spanish needles in Cheapside, but would never teach his art to any.

Following these slim beginnings, thriving industries were set up, particularly in Whitechapel (London), Hathersage (Buckinghamshire) and Redditch (Worcestershire). The one in Worcestershire became particularly important.

For your own ladies and pale-visag'd maids,
Like Amazons, come tripping after drums
Their thimbles into armed gauntlets change,
Their needles to lances. . .
(Shakespeare, KING JOHN, 1591-8)

• Thimbles, which accompanied needles in the workbox, were originally made of leather. Metal thimbles were not common until the seventeenth century. In EXPERIMENTAL PHILOSOPHY (1664), Henry Power described the eyes of the common fly as being *most neatly dimpled with innumerable little cavities like a small grater or thimble*. Old English had the word *thȳmel*, a derivative of *thūma*, 'thumb', to denote 'a fingerstall', a sheath-like covering to protect an injured thumb or finger. Interestingly, *thȳmel* is recorded just once before apparently disappearing. It emerged from obscurity in the early fifteenth century, some four centuries later, by which time it had come to denote 'a leather sheath worn to protect the finger pushing the needle when sewing'.

1465

ENGLISH PLAYING-CARD MANUFACTURERS CALL FOR RESTRICTIONS ON FOREIGN IMPORTS

· · · · · ·

It is a matter of debate whether playing cards originated in India or China. Nor is it known for certain how they were introduced into Europe, where the earliest references are Italian and date back to around the turn of the fourteenth century. The pastime spread rapidly throughout western Europe in the second half of that century; playing cards were known in Spain in 1371, Switzerland in 1377 and in the Low Countries, Germany and France by 1380. A reference to cards in England dates from around the turn of the fifteenth century.

Playing cards were originally for the amusement of the wealthy, since only the privileged could afford the exquisitely illuminated handmade packs. During the fifteenth century, however, the Germans began to use wood-block printing to mass-produce them. Cards began to percolate down to other levels of society and were also exported. (The invention of the printing press was to make playing cards more affordable still.) By 1465 playing cards had become so popular in England that manufacturers there were calling for restrictions on foreign imports.

CARD

When the word *carde* was borrowed into English around the turn of the fifteenth century it first denoted 'playing card'. All subsequent applications of the word from *visiting card* to *credit card* spring from the original concept of a stiff, rectangular playing card.

The origins of *card* go back to Greek *khartēs*, which meant 'a leaf of papyrus' and beyond that probably to some Egyptian term. Latin adopted the Greek word as *charta*, 'a leaf of papyrus', and this was absorbed into Italian as *carta*, 'leaf of paper'. When card games became popular in Italy, *carta* was more specifically applied to a 'playing card'. With this sense the term was borrowed into French as *carte* during the fourteenth century, and when cards caught on in England the French

term was taken into Middle English as *carde*, the *-t* of *carte* unaccountably changing to a *-d* in the process.

Cards were considered to be a quiet, genteel pastime, quite proper even for a house in mourning. After the death of Margaret Paston in November 1484, her daughter-in-law Margery made enquiries about suitable Christmas entertainment following such a bereavement. This is what she wrote to her husband John on Christmas Eve of that year:

Please it you to wete that I sent your eldest son to my Lady Morley, to have knowledge what sports were used in her house in Christmas next following after the decease of my lord her husband; and she said that there were none disguisings, nor harping, nor luting, nor singing, nor none loud disports;

but playing at the tables, and chess, and cards. Such disports she gave her folks leave to play and none other.

But card games have always involved gambling, even, it seems, amongst royal ladies. Elizabeth of York, Queen of Henry VII, certainly indulged: the money she lost during *hure disporte at cardes this Crismas* is an item in the privy purse accounts for 1502.

The modern pack evolved from the tarot, a set of cards first used in Italy in the fourteenth century for games and then for fortune-telling. The tarot consisted of twenty-two symbolic figure cards and a further fifty-six cards which were divided into four suits. Each suit represented an estate of medieval society (Church, merchants, military and peasantry) and each was ruled by four coat cards *(so called in sixteenth-century English because the figures were robed, and later corrupted to* court card *in view of the personages represented on them). Initially there was no rigid conformity amongst the suit emblems, which varied according to the maker, region or country. Towards the end of the fifteenth century different countries began to standardise their suits. Around 1480 the French, having discarded the figure cards altogether, reduced the court in each suit to three and fixed upon spades, clubs, diamonds and hearts as the four suit marks. Although the English pack conformed visually with the French in the sixteenth century, the fact that cards used in England once carried Italian or Spanish suit emblems has influenced the names of the suits in English.*

DIAMONDS
The old Italian suit which represented the merchant class was marked with coins, *denari* in Italian. The French used a rhomb and the name *carreau*, 'paving tile'. The English adopted the French suit mark but respected the inspiration behind the Italian tarot suit by using the name *diamond*.

The Greek adjective *adamas* meant 'untamable, invincible', being derived from *a*, 'not', and *daman*, 'to tame'. It was later variously used as a name for the hardest known metals or gems. The word passed into Latin as *adamas* and was eventually applied to the 'diamond'. Latin *adamas* (stem *adamant-*) gave the Vulgar Latin variant *adimas* (stem *adimant-*). This became confused with technical terms beginning with *dia-* so that Late Latin had *diamas* (stem *diamant-*), which came into Middle English as *diamaunt* by way of Old French *diamant*. A diamond is a octahedron in form and its plane has the form of a rhomb. Thus the word *diamond* was applied to a figure of this shape, and represented wealth on a playing card.

SPADES
Swords were the Italian symbol of this suit, which represented the army in medieval society. *Spade* is the Italian plural of *spada*, 'broad sword'. The word ultimately derives from Greek *spathē*, meaning 'broad blade of metal or wood', such as the blade of a sword or oar. Latin borrowed this as *spatha*, 'a broad, flat instrument', and hence 'a broad two-edged sword', and from there the word made its way into Italian as *spada*. When the French redesigned the suit marks, they replaced the swords with a symbol which represented the iron head of a pike. (The French name for the suit, *pique*, means 'pike'.) English adopted the French symbol but kept the original Italian name *spade*. This seemed particularly appropriate for the new suit mark, which had the look of a pointed digging spade. And although the Italian name was already plural, English tacked on its own plural ending and called the suit *spades*. To give a final twist to the tale, Italian *spada* and English *spade* are distantly related anyway, for Greek *spathē* was either the source of, or cognate with, the Low German word that gave Old English *spadu* and Middle English *spade*, 'shovel, tool for digging'.

CLUBS
The Italians used batons for this suit, which is held to represent the peasantry. In Spain a stout cudgel was favoured, *basto* in Spanish. When the French

redesigned the medieval pack they chose a trefoil design and called the suit *trèfle*, 'clover'. Some countries adopted the French suit symbol and sensibly translated the matching name; Dutch, for instance, has *klaver*. But English was perverse: remembering that the suit was formerly represented by cudgels it translated the Spanish name *basto* as *club,* from Middle English *clubbe* and Old Norse *klubba*, 'club', and mismatched it with the French trefoil.

ACE
In Roman times an *ās* was the name given to a small copper coin, possibly of Etruscan origin. The same word was also used to denote a 'unit' of weight, measure or coin. When *as* was borrowed into Old French in the twelfth century, it most commonly referred to 'the side of a die marked with a single spot', a meaning it retained when it was taken into Middle English as *aas* around the turn of the fourteenth century. When playing cards became popular in France, *as* was applied to a card bearing one pip. Similarly, in the sixteenth century English used *ace* to denote a one-spot card, the English deck being modelled on the French.

In a game of dice the one-spot had the lowest value and so, in Old French and then in English, *ace* had the figurative sense of 'nothing at all, valuelessness, bad luck'. However, in many card games an ace rates high and this has led to a number of figurative uses with a positive sense: since the late nineteenth century it has been applied to 'a point won in a single stroke in tennis or badminton'; in twentieth-century American colloquial English, and increasingly in British English, *ace* has been used as a noun to denote 'a person who is particularly gifted at something' and also as an adjective to mean 'highly skilled', or 'of superior quality'; and since the First World War *ace* has described 'a fighter-pilot who has shot down at least five enemy planes'.

1474

WILLIAM CAXTON PRINTS THE FIRST BOOK IN ENGLISH

••••••

Although it is disputed, credit for the invention of printing with movable type is generally given to Johannes Gutenberg (c 1439). There is, however, no doubt at all that it was William Caxton who first introduced the printing press to England in 1476.

Caxton, a successful and influential textile merchant, had long been resident in Flanders where he came across some of the early books printed in Germany and the Low Countries. In 1469 he was appointed secretary to the household of Margaret of Burgundy, sister to the English king. Here, observing the nobility's enthusiasm for courtly romances (see **romance**, page 42), Caxton began fully to appreciate the money to be made from a printing press which turned out books of popular appeal. In 1471 Caxton went to Cologne to learn the trade first-hand and, on his return to Bruges, set up a press of his own. The first book he printed was his own translation of a popular French romance, RECUYELL OF THE HYSTORYES OF TROYE by Raoul Fefevre, which he had been working on for some time and which he presented to Margaret of Burgundy. It was the first book ever to be printed in English.

PRINT

Both *print* and *press* are ultimately derived from the same Latin verb, *premere* 'to press'. This was borrowed into Old French as *preindre*. One of its senses was 'to stamp, to press' and the noun *preinte*, formed from its past participle, denoted 'the impression of a stamp, seal or mark'. Both the verb and the noun were borrowed into Middle English in the early fourteenth century, but the verb which Caxton originally used to refer to the printing of books was the related *imprint*. Caxton's preface to THE GAME AND PLAYE OF THE CHESSE (c 1475), a translation of a French allegory published while he was still in Bruges, contains this justification:

> By cause thys sayd book is ful of holsom wysedom . . . I have purposed to enprynte it

while Caxton's first publication from Westminster in 1477 ends with these words:

> Here endeth the book named the dictes or sayengis of the philosophre enprynted by me William Caxton at Westmestre the yere of our lord m.cccc.lxxvij.

This use of *imprint* for the printing of books persisted until the early eighteenth century but already, by the early sixteenth century, *print* was being used in this context.

PRESS

Gutenberg's press was innovative because it used movable type. Early printers took pains to make their books appear handwritten and used a typeface identical to the lettering of the scribes. The lead-alloy letters were made individually in

moulds and then assembled in a frame. This was placed on the lower surface of a wooden press, inked over and covered with the dampened paper. The press was operated by a huge screw which moved the upper surface against the lower so forcing the paper against the inked type.

The word *press* goes back to Latin *premere* 'to press', from whose past participle, *pressum*, the frequentative verb (that is, one denoting repeated action) *pressāre* was formed. This was taken into Old French as *presser*, meaning 'to press', 'to pressurise' and 'to torment'. Middle English acquired it as *pressen* – modern English, *to press* – in the fourteenth century. Old French derived the noun *presse* from *presser*. This first denoted 'the action of pressing' and then 'a pressing machine'. *Press* was borrowed into Middle English in the thirteenth century (well before the verb) when it meant 'a crowd, a throng', a sense which is now archaic. *Press* was first applied to a pressure machine, initially one for cloth and another kind for extracting juice from fruit, in the fourteenth century and to a printing apparatus in the first half of the sixteenth century.

By the second half of the sixteenth century *press* could also denote 'the business containing the printing press': thus the publishing house of Oxford University, established in 1478, eventually became known as Oxford University Press.

During the sixteenth century the state began to wake up to the fact that the written word was powerful and potentially dangerous. An ordinance of 1534 required all manuscripts to be scrutinised and licensed by the Stationers' Company before they could be printed. This opened up a long debate over the desirability of censorship, so that during the seventeenth century phrases such as *liberty* or *freedom of the press* were found. Quite a bit later, at the end of the eighteenth century, another product of the printing process, newspapers and periodicals, began collectively to be referred to as *The Press* or *the press*. Newspapers and broadsheets became more common, and phrases such as *the free press* were widely used. As a result, just as earlier *press* could refer to the printing house, its staff, the printing machinery and the published books, so *press* in this sense came to mean newspapers and all the personnel involved in producing them. Today, the latter sense predominates. The power of the press nowadays resides with newspaper tycoons and press barons rather than with the publishing house (see **mass media**, page 229).

PAMPHLET

By his death in 1491 William Caxton had printed almost a hundred carefully chosen popular titles for the English market, including an edition of Chaucer's CANTERBURY TALES and one of Mallory's MORTE D'ARTHUR. But it was the upheaval of the Reformation and Henry VIII's severance from Rome that fed the English presses and established the industry. Pamphlets, unbound publications just a few pages in length, had been in circulation in England since the first half of the fourteenth century but the controversies of the early sixteenth century fuelled an aggressive pamphlet warfare made possible by the production of cheaper paper and the speed of the printing press.

The word *pamphlet* itself has a curious origin. The late twelfth century had seen the appearance of PAMPHILUS, SEU DE AMORE, 'Pamphilus, or About Love', a light-hearted poem written in Latin all about the amorous escapades of a hero named Pamphilus. The work became so popular in northern Europe that students at the University of Paris had their knuckles rapped for preferring it to their set texts. During the Middle Ages it was common to add the diminutive -*et* to the

titles of short works. THE FABLES OF AESOP, for instance, were affectionately referred to as *Esopet* and the adventures of *Pamphilus* accordingly became known as *Pamphilet* in Old French and *Panflet* in Middle Dutch. It is reasonable to assume that the poem, which also became popular in England, was familiarly known by one of these diminutive forms in English, so that use of the word was then extended to describe other short publications. This had certainly happened before 1344, for Richard de Bury, writing in Anglo-Latin, used the term to denote concise treatises on topics that were far from frivolous, while Thomas Usk includes this prayer in his TESTAMENT OF LOVE (1387), thought to be a plea for clemency written from his prison cell: *Christe . . . graunte of thy goodnes to euery maner reder, full vnderstanding in this leud pamflet to haue.*

Pamphlets were produced throughout the sixteenth century and into the seventeenth, when they were a useful propaganda tool in the Civil War. Only during the later twentieth century have pamphlets mostly lost their proselytising edge and become vehicles to disseminate information.

PUBLISH

The earliest recorded reference to *publish* in the sense 'to issue a book' comes thirty-one years after Caxton's press was set up in Westminster. It is found in Thomas More's DIALOGUE (1528), a controversial volume attacking the writings of the Protestant Bible translator William Tyndale. *I am now driuen*, wrote More, *to this thirde busynes of publishynge and puttynge my boke in printe my selfe.* The verb literally means 'to make something public' and originated in the Latin noun *populus*, 'people'. An adjective, *poplicus*, was derived from this to mean 'of the people', but the term was later altered to *pūblicus* through the influence of *pūber*, which meant 'adult'. *Pūblicus* was borrowed into Old French as *public*, 'public', and, from there, into Middle English in the fifteenth century. A verb *publicare*, 'to make public', was then derived from *pūblicus* and was subsequently borrowed into Old French as *publier* whose stem *publiss-* gave the Middle English verb *publishen* in the fourteenth century. The old sense of 'to make something public knowledge' is still current and is familiar through the Anglican Book of Common Prayer which requires the clergyman to *publish the banns of marriage* to ensure that they are lawful. The prevalent sense today, however, is 'to produce printed material for sale to the public'.

Thomas More's publication pathway was a common one for those who did not enjoy the benefits of patronage. Most printers were publishers and booksellers as well (some, like Caxton, were also authors or translators) and expected to keep all profits from their endeavours. The standard practice had

been to pay off the humble author with a pittance so that all the rights remained with the printer/publisher/bookseller. Alexander Pope, writing in the first half of the eighteenth century, was probably the first to get rich on the proceeds of his literary output. On the other hand, it did mean that authors had to have the purest of motivations to write – no one could accuse them of seeking great financial rewards.

• *Publish* is related to many other English words. A few of them are:
   people (14th century), *popular* (15th century) and *populace* (16th century), all through Latin *populus*, 'people'.
   puberty (14th century) from Latin *pūber*, 'adult'.
   publicity (18th century) from Latin *pūblicus*.

1485

HENRY VII BEGINS HIS REIGN WITH A NAVIGATION ACT

······

A poor king is a feeble king: a wealthy king is strong. When Henry VII came to power, the Crown was impoverished, so Henry sought to make it rich again. Customs duties were one means of swelling the royal purse and the king worked hard to stimulate English commerce. He made trade agreements with the Baltic states and encouraged commercial exchange with Italy in an attempt to break the Venetian stranglehold on the Mediterranean (see **1204**, page 57). The king understood that a shortage of shipping hampered the expansion of English trade. He therefore encouraged the building of merchant ships by introducing a Navigation Act in the first year of his reign. This stated that imported goods had to be carried in English-owned ships manned by predominantly English crews. As a further inducement, customs duties were reduced for ships making their maiden voyage.

DOCK

To further his policies on shipbuilding, Henry founded the nation's first permanent shipyard at Portsmouth. In 1495 he built a dry dock there at the enormous cost of about £193. It is not known whether the construction was of English or foreign design but it greatly facilitated the building and repair of vessels. Henry's dock was largely constructed of wood, and making it watertight was attempted by introducing gravel outside the closed gates to seal them up. Previously ships had simply been hauled through the ooze to rest above the water line, surrounded by a brushwood fence held together with mud. The Middle Dutch word for this muddy bed was *docke*, a term that may have come from the unattested Vulgar Latin *ductia*, 'conduit', from Latin *dūcere*, 'to lead'. It is believed that *dock* was borrowed into English from this Middle Dutch source in the fifteenth century. It was certainly used to refer to Henry's innovation in Portsmouth.

• The *dock* a prisoner stands in during his trial is a borrowing of the Flemish term *dok*, meaning 'hutch, cage, pen', and was probably first used by sixteenth-century English scoundrels as a cant term. It became familiar in the nineteenth century, largely through its occurrence in the works of Dickens.

• From the fourteenth century *dock* denoted 'the fleshy part of an animal's tail', a term which probably originated in unattested Germanic *dukk-*, meaning 'bundle' of straw or thread. Animals' tails are sometimes shortened and the verb *to dock* was derived to describe the action. Thus *to dock* means 'to cut short'.

• There is also a plant *dock* whose name comes from Old English *docce* which is of common Germanic origin.

1492

THE MOORISH KINGDOM OF GRANADA IS FINALLY CONQUERED BY THE SPANISH KINGS

••••••

In 711 a Berber army crossed the Strait of Gibraltar and invaded the Iberian peninsula, sweeping northwards as far as the Pyrenees. Almost immediately the Christian frontier began to press back. Little by little the reconquest was achieved over the centuries until, towards the close of the thirteenth century, only the Moorish kingdom of Granada remained.

In return for recognition and security successive rulers of Granada pledged tribute to the neighbouring Christian kings of Castile, but at the beginning of the fifteenth century the Castilians, who had become restless to complete the reconquest of the peninsula, began to conduct intermittent offensives against the Emirate. The Castilian arm was strengthened in 1469 with the marriage of Isabella I of Castile and Ferdinand V of Aragon, a ceremony which effectively united

Christian Spain. A few years later, when Isabella demanded her customary tribute from the ruler of Granada, he replied with rash but aggressive defiance that his mints *no longer coined gold, but steel.* Six years passed before Ferdinand and Isabella felt strong enough for war. Then in 1482, while the Emirate was weakened by internal power struggles, the Catholic kings began a ten-year campaign which culminated in the surrender of the city of Granada itself on 2 January 1492.

After nearly 800 years of occupation it is surprising that Arabic did not leave a larger mark on the Spanish language. In fact, only a few grammatical prefixes and suffixes were added to the language, and roughly 4000 words, including derivatives and words that became obsolescent on the Moors' departure from Granada (according to Lapesa's Historia de la Lengua Española, *1959). However, Spain did act as a considerable conduit, along with Sicily, for Arabic lexical items to reach the rest of Europe's languages. One obvious linguistic characteristic of the Iberian route is the fusing of the Arabic article* al *with the following stem* (algodón, *'cotton'), whereas the Sicilian path of Arabic influence did not do this* (cotone *in Italian). (See* **admiral**, *page 71.)*

ARTICHOKE

The artichoke is a member of the thistle family and native to southern Europe and the central Mediterranean. According to Pliny the plant, which was prized for the scales and base of its edible flower buds, was once considered the most prestigious herb to grace the Roman banqueting table. It was also widely thought to be medicinal and to cure flagging libido in men. Strange, then, that with so much going for it the artichoke should fall from favour along with the Roman Empire. The plant never plunged into total obscurity, though. The Arabs called the vegetable *al kharshūf, al* being the definite article . It was eaten by the Moors in Spain, where Spanish Arabic evolved the variant form *al kharshōfa* which was then absorbed into Old Spanish as *alcarchofa.* Then, in the fifteenth century, the fortunes of the humble artichoke revived. In southern Italy it became suddenly fashionable to serve a dish of artichokes to one's guests. Italians called the plant *arcicioffo,* a word they borrowed from Old Spanish, but when the vegetable was taken into the north of Italy from the south in the second half of the fifteenth century, *arcicioffo* was corrupted to *arciciocco* and *articiocco* by northern dialects. The delicacy was not introduced into England until the reign of Henry VIII. English wrestled to assimilate the Italian dialectal words. *Archecokk, archichok(e), archy-chock, artochock, artichoak* and *hartichoch* are just a few of the spellings that were attempted. At that time it was believed that the true meaning of a word was often concealed in its form, and some renderings of *artichoke* reveal efforts to arrive at a satisfying etymology hidden within this unfamiliar word: *hortichock* suggests that the plants overran and 'choked' the garden, while *hartichoak* is descriptive of a 'choke' of bristles at the 'heart' of the flower head. (See Minsheu's explanation of **apricot**, below, for a similar attempt to make sense of an unfamiliar word.)

• The Jerusalem artichoke is not a thistle but a species of sunflower with tuberous roots, whose flavour is reminiscent of artichokes. Nor is the plant a native of Palestine: it was brought to Europe in the early seventeenth century from tropical America. Why then *Jerusalem?* The name originally given to the plant in the Italian garden where it was early cultivated and then widely distributed was *Girasole Articiocco,* 'Sunflower Artichoke'. English coped with the difficult foreign term *girasole* by substituting the similar-sounding English word *Jerusalem,* a process known as folk etymology.

APRICOT

Apricots, 'moons of the faithful', are native
to China and their cultivation gradually
spread westwards in ancient times, first to
Persia and then to the Mediterranean. The
Romans originally knew the fruit as
prūnum Armeniacum or *mālum Armeniacum*,
'Armenian plum' or 'Armenian apple',
since they imported the fruit from
Armenia, and thought they originated
there. Over time, however, *mālum
Armeniacum* was replaced by *mālum
praecoquum*, 'early ripening apple'. This
name, often simply shortened to
praecoquum, arose because the velvety fruit
of the apricot tree matures earlier than that
of the peach, to which it is related. The
adjective *praecoquus* was a variant of *praecox*,
which was used of fruit to mean 'ripened
prematurely'. *Praecox* in turn was a
derivative of *praecoquere*, 'to cook
beforehand', a compound of *prae-*, 'before',
and *coquere*, 'to cook'.

Praecoquum was borrowed into Late
Greek as *praikokion*, and from there into
Arabic as *al birqūq*, 'the apricot', *al* being
the definite article. The Moors in Spain
developed the variant *al borcoq(ue)* and this
was eventually responsible for Spanish
albaricoque, Portuguese *albricoque* and
Catalan *albercoc* or *abercoc*. The earliest
English form *abrecock* was probably
borrowed from Catalan in the sixteenth
century. Before long, however, it fell
subject to French influence, adopting the
final *t* of the French word *abricot*, itself a
borrowing from Catalan. About the same
time a *p* began to replace the *b* in the initial
syllable. This aberration may be accounted
for by attempts to discover the word's
meaning concealed within its form (see
artichoke, above). One theory, which was
explained by the lexicographer John
Minsheu in THE GUIDE INTO THE
TONGUES (1617), had the word derived
from the phrase *in aprīco coctus*, 'ripened in a
sunny place'. Ironically, the correct
etymology had been published in English
some twenty-nine years earlier by Henry
Lyte in his translation of the CRUYDEBOEK
(1554), a herbal by the Flemish physician
and botanist Rembert Dodoens:

*There be two kindes of peaches . . . The
other kindes are soner ripe, wherefore they be
called abrecox or aprecox.*
(Lyte, translation of Dodoens, 1578).

The herbal, regarded as the standard
authoritative work in the Netherlands,
France and England, was obviously not on
Minsheu's bookshelf.

COTTON

Cotton, originally brought from India,
was used in ancient Egypt, Rome and
Greece but was not widely known in
Europe until much later. The Moors first
introduced cotton cultivation into the
hospitable climate of southern Spain in
the ninth century and Granada, Cordoba
and Seville became centres of cotton
production. The crop was known as *qutn*
in Arabic. Spanish Arabic had the dialectal
form *qoton* which passed into Old Spanish
as *coton* (later superseded by *algodón*) and
from there into other European
languages. Middle English borrowed the
word from French *coton* in the fourteenth
century. *Cotton* did not at first apply to
finished cloth, however, but to the
downy plant substance in its unspun state.
Throughout Europe in the Middle Ages
cotton was in demand for wadding. A
gambeson, a tunic worn for comfort
beneath a coat of mail, might be padded
with it (a now obsolete synonym *acton*
comes from *algodón*), or a mattress or
cushion stuffed with it:

*Let your nightcap be of scarlet, and this, I do
advertise you, to cause to be made of a good
thick quilt of coton, or else of pure flocks or
of clean wiil, and let the covering of it be of
white fustian, and lay it on the featherbed
that you do lie on . . .*
(Andrew Boorde, DIETARY OF
HEALTH, 1542)

Some cotton cloth was woven, however.
References to it date from the fifteenth
century in English and in the fifteenth and
sixteenth centuries *cotton* also denoted 'a
candle wick'.

BLUE BLOOD

Not only was the Iberian peninsula occupied by the Moors, it also had a large Jewish population. Inevitably, relationships forged between the races over a long period produced many citizens of mixed blood. It was the proud boast of some of the ancient aristocratic families of Castile that their family lines had never been thus contaminated. Proof of their racial purity was evident in the fairness of their skin through which the veins showed blue. They were said to be of *sangre azul*, 'blue blood'. Those whose ancestors had consorted with the Moors had darker complexions which did not show off the blueness of the veins. The expression *blue blood* to denote 'a person of aristocratic birth' was borrowed into English in the nineteenth century:

If there was really no alternative to removing Lord Cranborne, a wiser head might have allowed him to resign. This would have protected his dignity in the eyes of those sensitive Lords for whom the word 'sacking' is deeply offensive. The 'dismissal' of the Tories' principal hereditary peer leaves too much messy blue blood over too much crimson carpet.
(THE INDEPENDENT, 5 December 1998)

1492

CHRISTOPHER COLUMBUS SAILS WEST AND DISCOVERS THE WEST INDIES

••••••

One of the results of the Crusades was to introduce the countries of western Europe to the riches of the Orient, among them luxurious fabrics, gems and spices. The trade routes were plied by Arab merchants and Venice prospered as broker for these goods (see **1204**, page 57). Western countries began to search for alternative routes so that they could trade directly with the East and transport larger cargoes by sea. The Portuguese were the first to begin exploration in the early fifteenth century. They gradually ventured the length of the West African coast with a view to reaching Asia by sailing round Africa. However, a Genoese sailor, Christopher Columbus, was convinced that, since the earth was spherical, the most direct route would be a westerly one. Basing his calculations on erroneous estimations from the works of Ptolemy and Marco Polo, Columbus proposed an exploratory voyage first to King John II of Portugal in 1484 and then to Queen Isabella in Spain. It was Isabella who eventually agreed to finance an expedition and Columbus set sail on 3 August 1492.

Altogether Columbus made four voyages, during which he discovered many of the West Indian islands, explored some of the South American and Central American coastline and established the first European colony in the New World on the island of Hispaniola.

INDIAN

The name *India* comes ultimately from Sanskrit *sindhu* which meant 'river', specifically the Indus and the region through which it flowed. Over time the Persians and Greeks began to apply the name (*hind* in Persian and *India* – from *Indos* – in Greek) to all the territory which lay to the east of the Indus. This concept was taken up by Latin which had *India* from Greek. Even in the Middle Ages the same hazy definition of *India* prevailed. Columbus set sail from the Spanish port of Palos on 3 August 1492 and eventually reached land on 12 October. Although he had discovered the Bahamas, he believed the islands to be the outer reaches of *India*. They were accordingly referred to as *las Indias*, 'the Indies', and their inhabitants as *Indios*, 'Indians'. Columbus's error remains: the islands of the Caribbean are still called the *West Indies* and the native peoples of the Americas *Indians*.

The plural *Indies* is due to the varied history of adoption into English of the Latin *India*. The Old English form was exactly the same as the Latin; the Middle English borrowing via French was *Inde*; an early sixteenth-century revision from the Latin produced *Indy* (and hence the plural *Indies*); the current shape of the word dates to the end of the sixteenth century, and probably testifies to the influence of Spanish and Portuguese.

CANNIBAL

The native Indians Columbus initially made contact with were the Tainos, distant relatives of the Arawaks of South America. In his JOURNAL he described them *as the best people in the world and above all the gentlest*. Not all the natives were friendly, however – at least, not according to the JOURNAL. Around the beginning of the fifteenth century another people, the Caribs, had migrated to the islands and settled those of the Lesser Antilles. (*Caribbean* is derived from their name.) Columbus found out about them when he landed in Cuba on 27 October 1492.

The Taino there called them *Caniba*. This excited Columbus, who thought the name signified that the people, *canibales* as he then called them, were subjects of the Grand Khan, and he took it as confirmation that he was, indeed, in Asia. In fact *Caniba* was a variant of *Carib*, an Arawakan term which was akin to *Calina, Calinago* and *Galibi*, names by which the Carib referred to themselves and which signified 'valiant men'. According to Kirkpatrick Sale in his book THE CONQUEST OF PARADISE (1992), although Columbus could scarcely communicate with the Taino and had met no Caribs, he put together a picture of Carib ferocity and cannibalism which he shared with the credulous sailors who accompanied him on his voyages. No evidence, either then or since, has supported this view. However, the myth apparently enabled Columbus to justify brutality towards and subsequent enslavement of the native peoples, who were obviously less than human. In the end, any peaceable Indian carrying a club was a fierce Carib savage looking for his next human meal.

The Spaniards back home needed little convincing that the ferocious 'valiant men' devoured their human enemies. Horror stories about the *canibales*, the man-eating Caribs of the Indies, were soon current throughout Europe and satisfied long-held expectations that such barbarism existed at the earth's extremities. In the sixteenth century there were even erroneous attempts to derive *cannibal* from Spanish *can* and Latin *canis*, 'dog', an allusion to the animal appetite of this people. In Shakespeare, tales of *cannibals that each other eat* were amongst the stories Othello told to Desdemona (OTHELLO, 1604) and the name of *Caliban*, the deformed savage in THE TEMPEST (1611), was apparently modelled on *carib-an*.

Later in the seventeenth century, a troop of soldiers in the English Civil War (see **1642**, page 163) used the fearful reputation of the *cannibals* as a rallying cry. A journeyman serving with the Parliamentarian army sent this report to his master on action seen on 22 August 1642:

> *This night our soldiers wearied out and quartered themselves about the time for food and lodging, but before we could eat or drink an alarum cried 'Arm, arm, the enemy is coming', and in half an hour all our soldiers were cannibals in arms, ready to encounter the enemy, crying out 'a dish of cavaliers to supper'.*

By the eighteenth century the reputation of the *Cannibals* was so well established that the word was no longer applied as a proper noun, but simply denoted 'one who eats human flesh.'

CANOE

The Caribbean peoples were skilled navigators. Their craft were made from massive hollowed-out trunks of the silk-cotton tree, some large enough to transport up to 150 people. According to Columbus's JOURNAL the craft were *all in one piece, and wonderfully made.* The Arawakan language had *canoa*, a word of Carib origin, for such a dugout vessel. This term passed into Spanish through the records made by Columbus, and from there into other European languages. *Canoa* was current in English as late as the eighteenth century but several modified forms also appeared, among them *canow*, *caano*, and *canoo*.

As new lands and peoples were discovered *canoe* was also applied to native paddle-propelled craft of different construction, the birch bark canoes of some of the North American Indians, for instance. Later explorers penetrated the vastness of North America by canoe. One such was the Frenchman La Salle, who navigated the Mississippi river to the Gulf of Mexico in 1682. *Canoe*, to denote a light boat used for sport and recreation, dates back to the late eighteenth century and in 1866 Scotsman John MacGregor established canoeing as a sport.

HAMMOCK

The airiness and cleanliness of Taino houses impressed the Europeans. The people slept in *hamacas*, hanging beds which Columbus, in his JOURNAL, described as *nets of cotton*. By the seventeenth century, these practical beds were being used by sailors on board ship. (By the early eighteenth century regulations demanded that sailors' hammocks should be hung 14 inches (36 centimetres) apart.) The Taino word *hamaca* was taken into Spanish and from there into English in the mid-sixteenth century. The spelling *hammock* did not prevail until the nineteenth century.

HURRICANE

Taino houses were constructed of strong staves planted close together. They were circular, built to withstand the violent cyclones to which the region was prone. A Carib word for such a tempest was *huracan*. This was picked up by the Spanish and was the form used by Oviedo, who was commissioned to chronicle the history of the Indies (HISTORIA DE LAS INDIAS) in 1535. The word first appeared in English in the mid-sixteenth century as *haurachana*. At the same time, however, English also adopted the form *furacano*. This came from an earlier Spanish borrowing of an alternative Carib form *furacan*. Its subsequent use in English was influenced by Portuguese *furação*. English juggled with a variety of forms based on these two borrowings for a century or so until *hurricane* became increasingly frequent and finally prevailed in the second half of the seventeenth century.

MAIZE

The word *maize* came into English in the mid-sixteenth century through Spanish *maiz*, a borrowing probably of Taino *mahiz*. This New World plant was grown as a staple throughout the Americas. By the time Columbus observed its cultivation for the first time in the West Indies, maize had already been bred to the point where it could not survive in the wild. The Tainos grew maize on their *conucos*, low mounds where a selection of interdependent crops was cultivated. Root crops, such as cassava, prevented the soil from washing away, while tall leafy plants, like maize, shaded others and helped retain moisture.

• In English the word *corn* may be variously applied to the main cereal crop of a region, so that sometimes it may denote barley and sometimes wheat or rye. In the early seventeenth century English settlers in North America found the Indians there cultivating maize and, being unfamiliar with the plant, called it *Indian corn*. The term was soon shortened to *corn*, which then became the American English word for 'maize'. *Corn* is an Old English word with cognates in other Germanic languages. These come from an unattested prehistoric Germanic *kurnom*, 'grain of cereal', which can be traced back to *grnom*, 'worn-down particle', a derivative of the unattested Indo-European root *ger-*, 'to wear down'. *Grnom* is also the source of Latin *grānum*, 'a grain, a seed', from which English gets *grain*.

POTATO

One of the crops that the Taino grew on their *conucos* (see **maize**, above) was the *batata* or sweet potato. *Patata* was a Spanish variant of this Taino word and when the plant became more widely known in Europe, *patata* was assimilated into some of the languages. English took the word as *potato* in the second half of the sixteenth century. Sweet potatoes were much enjoyed. When John Hawkins, the Elizabethan naval commander, tasted them he thought them *the most delicate rootes that may be eaten*, adding that they *doe far exceede our passeneps or carets* (VOYAGE TO FLORIDA, 1565). Apart from being delicious the potatoes were thought to be aphrodisiac and were therefore doubly irresistible. William Harrison called them *venerous roots . . . brought out of Spaine, Portingale, and the Indies* ('Description of England', in CHRONICLES OF HOLINSHED, 1587). And in Shakespeare's THE MERRY WIVES OF WINDSOR (1598) Falstaff, eager to arouse the affections of Mistress Ford, cries *Let the sky rain potatoes*.

In 1530 the Spaniard Pizarro set about the conquest of Peru. One of the staples grown by the Incas in the Peruvian Andes was a plant with edible tubers which was first described in 1553 by Pedro de Cieza de Leon in his CRÓNICA DE PERU. The Spaniards confused this plant with the more familiar sweet potato, to which it is in fact unrelated, and referred to it as *patata*. Tubers were taken back to Spain, where the plant was grown as a curiosity in the 1570s. The potato gradually became known in Europe, possibly reaching England independently in 1586, but in all these countries it was simply regarded as an ornamental plant – people thought it was poisonous because it is a nightshade. Nevertheless, by the late seventeenth century, the nutritional value of the potato was recognised in England, where the plant was commonly grown in gardens, while in Ireland it had become the staple crop. The French and Prussians needed more convincing, however. In the second half of the eighteenth century Antoine-Augustin Parmentier wrote pamphlets promoting the potato and assuaging fears that it caused leprosy. Parmentier's efforts are recognised in French cuisine where *Parmentier* indicates that a dish contains potatoes. In Prussia potatoes were grown as food and fodder by order of Frederick the Great. By the close of the century the staple of the Incas had become a staple of Europe.

TOBACCO

During his first voyage, Columbus observed the Taino custom of making a rough roll of dried leaves from a certain plant, kindling the end and inhaling the smoke. (In fact this practice was not exclusive to the Taino and had probably originated with the Mayans at least 1,500 years earlier.) The Spanish probably recorded the word *tabaco* from the Taino and applied it to the plant, although the Indians themselves may have used the term to refer to the roll of leaves or even, if the Spanish chronicler Oviedo is to be believed, to a pipe. It is ironic that Columbus dismissed as weeds what was soon to become one of the modern world's greatest cash crops. Nevertheless, the Spanish eventually took *tabaco* back to Spain where its use caught on, partly because the plant was rumoured to have medicinal properties. Before long the Spanish were setting up tobacco plantations in the Indies and by the second half of the sixteenth century samples of the herb were finding their way into the courts of Europe.

Europeans smoked their tobacco in pipes and the English court, too, began to experiment with pipe-smoking. In his DESCRIPTION OF ENGLAND (in CHRONICLES OF HOLINSHED, 1587), which details contemporary life and customs, William Harrison wrote:

> *In these daies the taking-in of the smoke of the Indian herbe called Tabaco, by an instrument formed like a litle ladell, wherby it passeth from the mouth into the hed & stomach, is gretlie taken-vp & vsed in England.*

The word *tabaco* which Harrison used was a direct borrowing from Spanish. This and the variant spelling *tabacco* began to lose ground to the modern form *tobacco* from the early seventeenth century. Indeed the modern spelling is found in a pamphlet, A COUNTERBLASTE TO TOBACCO, published in 1604 by none other than King James I, who detested the herb and argued forcefully against it. In spite of this royal condemnation, the entire economy of the new Virginian colony of Jamestown was soon established on tobacco. The king could not afford to restrict imports and see the colony fail, so shipments increased year by year and England gradually became dependent on the 'pernicious weed':

> *Pernicious weed! whose scent the fair annoys,*
> *Unfriendly to society's chief joys,*
> *The worst effect is banishing for hours*
> *The sex whose presence civilizes ours.*
> (William Cowper, CONVERSATION, 1782)

• In 1560 Jean Nicot, the French Ambassador to Portugal, sent some tobacco seeds to Catherine de Medicis, the Queen Consort and Regent of France. The French gave the tobacco plant the New Latin name *herba nicotiana* in Nicot's honour. (All plants of this genus are now labelled *nicotiana*.) The French derivative *nicotine*, to denote the poisonous alkaloid obtained from dry tobacco leaves and used as an insecticide, was borrowed into English in the early nineteenth century.

1495
THE FIRST PAPER MILL IN ENGLAND IS BUILT

••••••

The manufacture of paper from cellulose pulp was invented by the Chinese but was a closely guarded secret for hundreds of years. The process was finally made known to the Arabs at Samarkand by Chinese marauders who had been taken prisoner. It was the Moors who introduced paper-making to Europe with the establishment of a paper mill in Spain in the middle of the twelfth century (see **1492**, page 111). From there the craft spread to Italy and, during the fourteenth century, to France and Germany.

When movable type was invented towards the middle of the fifteenth century, the need for paper greatly increased (see **1474**, page 107). Caxton printed on imported paper when he established his press at Westminster in 1477. There is no evidence at all of paper-making in England until 1495, when an edition of Bartholomaeus Anglicus's work DE PROPRIETATIBUS RERUM was issued by Caxton's successor, Wynkyn de Worde. A note at the end of the book commends its thin paper, made in England by John Tate.

PAPER

In ancient times a kind of paper was manufactured from the stems of a tall reed which was particularly abundant in the Nile delta. The pithy inner stem of the plant would be cut into pieces measuring about 20 inches (50 centimetres), sliced lengthways and placed vertically on a hard surface. More strips would then be laid horizontally over these and the whole would then be beaten with a mallet and pressed with weights until it fused together into a sheet that could be trimmed and rubbed smooth with stones. These sheets could then be pasted together to make a scroll (see **bible**, page 93 and **volume**, page 94). The Greeks called the reed *papūros* (presumably from an Egyptian word) and this was borrowed into Latin as *papȳrus* where it denoted not only the reed but also the 'paper' made from it. When paper-making became widely known, the word was then applied to the new writing material which in Europe was manufactured principally from flax and hemp. In Old French the Latin word had become *papier* and this passed into Middle English in the first half of the fourteenth century by way of Anglo-Norman *papir*.

1496

WYNKYN DE WORDE PUBLISHES AN EDITION OF THE BOKE OF ST ALBANS

••••••

The first edition of THE BOKE OF ST ALBANS was published in 1486. It contained a collection of treatises on heraldry, hawking and hunting. A fanciful invention of the eighteenth century attributed the last of these to a certain Juliana Berners, said to be the abbess of Sopwell near St Albans. In fact the treatise was almost certainly by Dame Juliana Barnes, the lady of a manor of that name near St Albans. The book proved so popular that in 1496 Wynkyn de Worde, Caxton's successor at Westminster (see **1474**, page 107), published a second edition, this time containing a treatise on *fysshynge with an angle*.

ANGLING

Fishing as a game sport was known in ancient times: wealthy Romans fished in ponds constructed and stocked for this purpose. But enthusiasm for angling waned and was not rekindled until the late Middle Ages. THE TREATYSE OF FYSSHYNGE WITH AN ANGLE is evidence of renewed interest. The treatise offers practical advice on the making of hooks, rods, lines of plaited horsehair and artificial flies (*Ye muste furst lume to mak . . . your rod, your lynys . . . & your hokes*). It also gives information on the feeding habits of various fish. Its author tempts the reader to try the sport, lyrically comparing the restfulness of a day spent in fresh air and fragrant meadows with the exertion and exhaustion of hunting.

The word *angle* in the treatise's title originally meant 'fishing hook' but was later extended to denote 'a rod and line'. It developed from Old English *angul*, a word with a number of Germanic cognates whose ultimate source was the unattested Indo-European root *ank-*, 'to bend'. (This root was also responsible for Latin *angulus*, 'corner', from which English borrowed *angle* in the fourteenth century.) THE BOKE OF ST ALBANS contains the first uses of the verb *to angle* and the verbal noun *angling* (*Fysshynge, cally'd Anglynge wyth a rodde*). Figurative use of the verb with the senses 'to try to procure something by crafty or devious means' and 'to elicit comment' arose in the late sixteenth century.

• There was a district in Schleswig that was shaped like a fishing hook. The Germanic tribe who lived there consequently named it *Angul* and they themselves became known as *Angles*. In the fifth century AD the Angles were amongst the Germanic tribes which migrated to England. The name of these invaders lives on in *England*, which is from *Engla land*, 'land of the Angles'.

BAIT

THE TREATYSE OF FYSSHYNGE WITH AN ANGLE gave plenty of good advice on *how ye shall make your baytes brede where ye shall fynde them: and how ye shall kepe theym*. The noun *bait* came into Middle English around the turn of the fourteenth century, influenced by two related sources. The first of these was the two Old Norse nouns *beit*, 'pasture', and *beita*, 'fish bait'. The second was the Old Norse verb *beita* (a separate word) which meant 'to cause to bite', being a causal form of *bita*, 'to bite'. This verb developed two strands of meaning in English. The sense that influenced the noun *bait* was 'to cause a creature to bite for its own nourishment', in other words 'to feed and water an animal': *While that [he] rest him, And bayte his Dromedarie or his hors* (from an English translation, c 1400, of Sir John Mandeville's description of a journey in the East, written in Anglo-Norman around 1356). The second strand was 'to cause one creature to bite another', more specifically 'to set dogs on to an animal', a sense which is evident in the sport of bear-baiting and which has given rise to the figurative sense of 'to harass or torment (verbally)' in modern English:

They were certainly not intimidated by authority, as Sid was, and they regarded the baiting of policement as something of a harmless sport. It was all part of the game. The police hassled them, they made it as difficult as possible for the police. Everyone respected that stance.
(Garry Kilworth, A MIDSUMMER'S NIGHTMARE, 1996)

1509

ALEXANDER BARCLAY'S THE SHIP
OF FOOLS APPEARS

••••••

In 1494 the German poet, Sebastian Brant, published DAS NARRENSCHIFF, a satirical poem which tells of fools from all walks of life who board a ship bound for Narragonia, the Land of Fools. The passengers, who exemplify every kind of human vice and folly known to contemporary society, are mercilessly ridiculed. The allegory met with great success and was widely translated from the original Swabian dialect. Most of these translations were not exact but were adaptations devised to reveal and reprove follies and abuses particular to the societies for which they were written. Alexander Barclay's popular adaptation, which he called THE SHIP OF FOOLS, gives a vivid account of English life in the early sixteenth century.

SATIRE

Although the concept of *satire* is evident in the fourteenth-century works of Langland and Chaucer, it is Alexander Barclay who makes the earliest recorded use of the word in English, referring to his SHIP OF FOOLS as *this satyre*. According to ancient Roman grammarians, the origins of the word itself are more culinary than literary. The term *lanx satura* meant 'full dish' (from *lanx*, 'dish', and *satura*, feminine form of *satur*, 'full of food, replete', cognate of *satis*, 'enough') and was applied to a bowl filled with various kinds of fruit or a dish containing a mixture of ingredients. It was often simply shortened to *satura*, meaning 'medley, mixture', and *satira*, a later form of this, was accordingly used to denote a verse composition which dealt with an assortment of topics. In classical literature *satira* developed specifically into a poem which exposed a whole range of follies and excesses in society. The satirical

works of Horace gently ridicule human folly, while those of Juvenal angrily attack the corruptions of Roman society.

The misapprehension that *satira* was derived from Greek *saturos*, 'satyr', was common in the Renaissance, and since satyrs were crude and licentious, some writers accordingly produced unrefined and offensive work.

• Latin *satis* is found in other English words such as *sate*, *satiate*, *satisfy* (from Latin *satisfacere*, from *satis*, 'enough', and *facere*, 'to do') and *saturate*.

• The adjective *sad* originally meant 'full, sated' and therefore 'tired, weary'. It comes from Old English *sæd*, a derivative of an unattested prehistoric Germanic *sathaz*, 'satiated', which shares the same root as Latin *satis*, 'enough'. The sense 'sorrowful, mournful' developed in the late fourteenth century from these earlier expressions of weariness.

1512

HENRY VIII FOUNDS THE ROYAL DOCKYARD AT WOOLWICH

••••••

Henry VIII's fascination with ships had begun when he was a boy, his enthusiasm doubtless fuelled by stories of Portuguese and Spanish expeditions to the New World (see **1492**, page 111). In 1497 and 1498 his father, Henry VII, had also commissioned exploratory voyages to find a northwest passage to Asia. From the beginning of the sixteenth century mighty ships were being developed in southern Europe to open up and defend the territories of the New World.

At the same time, the political map of Europe was changing. Across the Channel, France now had influence over the seaports of Brittany, while Spain was set to control the maritime prowess of the Netherlands (see **1568**, page 131). There was also a growing recognition amongst nation states of the value of permanent military forces which could be called upon immediately and knew what they were about. Henry VII had already gathered a small war fleet of five ships, but the time had come to expand English sea power and consolidate the country's position in Europe. While he was content to leave commerce to the merchants, Henry VIII began to build a fleet of warships paid for with money from the dissolved monasteries. His flagship, the *Henry Grâce à Dieu*, was built at the new naval dockyard at Woolwich in 1514.

NAVY

The term *navy* was not new to English in the sixteenth century. It appeared in the first half of the fourteenth century as a borrowing of Old French *navie*, 'fleet', from Latin *nāvis*, 'ship'. Originally, it denoted simply 'a number of ships' or, more specifically, 'a fleet of ships, particularly one summoned for war' (see **1296**, page 71). Not until Henry VIII wisely set about creating a permanent battle fleet, together with an effective naval administration, did *navy* gain its modern sense of 'the whole battle fleet of a nation, together with its crews, officers and maintenance'. The king eventually achieved a fleet of up to eighty-five warships. Of these forty-six were built in English shipyards while the remainder were either prizes or bought. A state paper from the reign of Henry VIII (1540) declared that *the nauy . . . is . . . a great defence and surete of this realme in tyme of warre, as well to offende as defende,* a sentiment which was reinforced four centuries later by the great military leader, Viscount Montgomery: *In all history, the nation which has had control of the seas has, in the end, prevailed.*

DECK

In Middle Dutch the word *dec* meant 'a covering' of some sort. More specifically it could refer to 'a cloak' or 'a roof'. The word with its general sense of 'a covering' was borrowed into English in the second half of the fifteenth century. It is possible that sailors sometimes used the word to denote 'a tarpaulin', a protective canvas used to cover a load or a boat. But 'deck' in its nautical sense belongs to the period of intensive shipbuilding at the beginning of the sixteenth century.

Light guns had been used on board English ships since around the mid-fourteenth century, placed in the castles stem and stern. In Henry VIII's reign heavy muzzle-loading cannon were developed which could inflict considerable damage (see **cannon**, page 81). The king determined to carry these cannon aboard ship and since they were too heavy for the castles (see **1296**, page 71), had them mounted low in the ship, their muzzles protruding through gun-ports. For the first time ships could fire broadside. One of the first ships to be armed in this way was the *Henry Grâce à Dieu,* which carried a total of 186 small and great guns. The *deck* was understood to be a 'roof' offering cover to the guns and gunners or sailors and supplies beneath. As ship design evolved during the sixteenth century, more *decks* were added but the notion of a *deck* as a 'floor' was still undeveloped: *In a broad Bay, out of danger of their shot . . . we vntyed our Targets that couered vs as a Deck* (John Smith, GENERAL HISTORY OF VIRGINIA, 1624). As one man's roof is another man's floor, it wasn't too long before the early sense of 'covering' was lost.

Curiously, the nautical application of the Dutch word seems to have been uniquely English; it did not occur in Dutch for another 160 years. The word did not remain purely nautical, however. Already, by the close of the sixteenth century, *deck* was being used for a stack of playing cards, the allusion possibly being to a ship with several decks. From the second half of the nineteenth century, *deck* started to be applied more generally to denote 'a floor or platform' of any kind. It was used, for instance, to describe the platform of a landing stage, and at the end of the century denoted the upper floor of a bus or tram. Nowadays, estate agents use it to describe a wooden platform functioning like a patio; audio enthusiasts buy *tape decks* as a part of their sound system.

• A familiar Christmas carol invites us to *deck the hall with boughs of holly.* The verb *to deck,* meaning 'to adorn', comes from Middle Dutch *dekken,* 'to cover', and was borrowed into English in the early sixteenth century. Its use with *out* (*all decked out for a night on the town*) arose in the mid-eighteenth century.

• *Deck* and *thatch* share a common, if remote, ancestor. The unattested Indo-European root *teg-* led to their presumed Germanic descendants *thak-* and *thakjan.* Old English used *thack* principally as a noun, meaning 'roof' and also its straw covering. It became obsolete in the former sense, and was superseded by *thatch* in the latter.

1516

A JEWISH GHETTO IS FOUNDED IN VENICE

••••••

The Jewish race rejected Christ and crucified him. This view was at the heart of the medieval Church's intolerance of the Jews. Since the Church was an autonomous institution enjoying the loyalty of the people, it could impose its views. Persecution of the Jews was common throughout Europe from the twelfth century onwards. In England in 1190, for instance, 500 Jews who were cornered in York castle cut one another's throats to avoid worse torture at the hands of a mob outside. Jews were banished from England altogether in 1290 and did not return until 1655 when Oliver Cromwell permitted their re-entry. Similar horrific persecution took place in France, Germany, Spain and Italy, setting up a chain of almost constant Jewish migration. Cruel oppression and their own fervent religious observance naturally drove Jewish populations to live together in tight communities, but many authorities also insisted upon segregation. In 1516 an enclave for the segregation of Jews was established in Venice, and other cities then followed the Venetian pattern.

GHETTO

The Jewish section in Venice was established on an island, formerly the site of an iron foundry. The Italian word for 'foundry' is *getto* and the name *ghetto* may well have been derived from this. An alternative suggestion is that, since Jewish quarters were set apart from the cities, *ghetto* was a shortening of Italian *borghetto*, a diminutive of *borgo*, which meant 'suburb (outside the city wall)'. After 1516 other ghettos were set up following the Venetian pattern. That of Rome dates from 1555. The ghettos were enclosed by walls, access through the gate was strictly regulated and the inhabitants were obliged to keep curfews. Since the ghettos could not spread beyond their walls, the inhabitants built upwards so that conditions became cramped and insanitary. Nevertheless, within their limits the settlements were autonomous.

The first appearance of *ghetto* in English comes in CRUDITIES (1611), Thomas Coryat's description of his European travels. Later in the seventeenth century the English diarist, John Evelyn, was privileged to visit the ghettos in both Rome and Padua, where he was invited to be present at a circumcision and a wedding. Conditions in the ghettos were miserable. Evelyn describes how *the Jews in Rome all wear yellow hats, live only upon brokage and usury, very poor and despicable, beyond what they are in other territories of Princes where they are permitted* (15 January 1645). When, during the nineteenth century, ghettos were gradually abolished in western Europe, the last to go was that of Rome in 1870.

Tragically, Nazi policies in the 1930s revived the term *ghetto* with the purpose of segregating Jews. However, the term itself had always remained current, and in the late nineteenth century, it began to be used to denote 'a run-down, overpopulated city quarter where a predominantly minority group lives, isolated from mainstream society by social or economic constraint':

It is both a cliché and a truism that the overwhelming majority of sporting heroes come from the wrong side of the tracks. Boxing, as endlessly recorded, always offered a way out of the ghetto. It made the fighters mean. They were scrapping for much more than just a trophy – they were slugging it out to put food on the table.
(Simon Kinnersley in THE TIMES MAGAZINE, 22 May 1999)

In present-day English, *ghetto* may be given a figurative twist and applied to 'a segregated area or group bearing a particular distinguishing characteristic':

We are mostly adjusted now to the significance of a poet's sexuality in any assessment of his work, though there is an argument against categorisation of gays in a literary ghetto.
(review of ARTHUR RIMBAUD by Benjamin Ivry in THE TIMES, 29 April 1999)

c 1518

TABLE FORKS ARE REGULARLY USED IN ITALY

......

Delicate table manners have long preoccupied the Italians. As early as 1290 Fra Bonvicino da Riva offered diners the following advice:

Let thy fingers be clean. Thou must not put either thy fingers into thine ears, or thy hands on thy head. The man who is eating must not be cleaning by scraping his fingers at any foul part.

The good friar's advice will seem doubly sound when it is understood that, in the Middle Ages, people used just their knives and fingers to eat with. Since each platter of food was intended to be shared with a fellow guest, who dabbled freely among the contents, and diners were expected to slice chunks off the communal joint with their knives while holding it steady with their hands, the presence of a neighbour who picked his nose or cleaned his gums at table might prove unsettling to the digestion.

Table forks were introduced into Italy from Greece probably around the turn of the twelfth century but only began to find acceptance during the fourteenth century (stimulated perhaps by the misgivings of writers such as Fra Bonvicino). By the sixteenth century their use was *de rigueur* for elegant dining, French merchant Jacques le Saige remarking in 1518 how the Venetians always took up their food on silver forks.

FORK

Although visitors to Italy were enthusiastic about forks, the utensil's progress to the tables of Europe was slow. English travellers in the early seventeenth century reported on Italian table etiquette with astonishment:

At Venice each person was served (besides his knife and spoon) with a fork to hold the meat while he cuts it, for there they deem it ill manners that one should touch it with his hand.
(Fynes Moryson, ITINERARY, 1617)

On his return from a journey around France, Italy, Switzerland and Germany, Thomas Coryat made a similar observation:

I observed a custom in all those Italian cities and towns through which I passed that is not used in any other country that I saw in my travels . . . The Italian and also most strangers that are commorant in Italy do always at their meals use a little fork when they cut their meat. For while with their knife which they hold in one hand, they cut the meat out of the dish, they fasten their fork which they hold in their other hand upon the same dish, so that whatsoever he be that sitting in the company of any others at meal, should unadvisedly touch the dish of meat with his fingers from which all at the table so cut, he will give occasion of offence unto the company as having transgressed the laws of good manners. . .
(CRUDITIES HASTILY GOBBLED UP IN FIVE MONTHS, 1611)

Coryat was impressed by Italian hygiene:

The reason of this their curiosity is, because the Italian cannot by any means indure to have his dish touched with fingers, seeing all men's fingers are not alike clean

and went on to adopt the practice for himself:

I myself thought to imitate the Italian fashion by the forked cutting of meat . . . oftentimes in England since I came home.

But Coryat was considered effeminate and the table fork did not catch on. That is not to say that forks were unknown outside Italy before the sixteenth century – silver forks, for instance, are occasionally mentioned in English inventories and wills dating back to the fourteenth century and were apparently used for spearing sticky sweetmeats such as syrupy pears or green ginger – but it did not occur to anyone to put them to regular use at table.

The word *fork* came from Latin *furca*, which was applied to a variety of two-pronged objects, such as an agricultural fork, a forked stick, a yoke or a gallows. *Furca* was extensively borrowed into Romance and Germanic languages, where its principal sense was 'pitchfork'; as such it was taken into Old English as *forca*, becoming *forke* in Middle English. *Fork* was first applied to 'a pronged implement used for eating' around the second half of the fifteenth century but it was not until the early eighteenth century, when English society finally revolted against messy fingers and the personal habits of fellow diners, that this sense became common.

The expression *fingers were made before forks* is commonly used when fiddling about with a knife and fork becomes so frustrating that the diner picks the troublesome morsel up with his fingers instead. Not surprisingly, it dates from the first half of the eighteenth century, when refined eating was still in its infancy in England. It first appears in Swift's POLITE CONVERSATION (1738): *They say fingers were made before forks, and hands before knives.* It is modelled upon an earlier saying, *God made hands before knives,* which dates back at least to the sixteenth century.

1519
Cortés Enters Tenochtitlan
......

Fiery comets, the appearance in the night sky of an ear of corn running with blood, the sudden and inexplicable flooding of Tenochtitlan, a man with two heads roaming the city streets – according to León-Portilla, sinister signs such as these had started to appear years before the Spaniards set foot in the Aztec capital and foreshadowed certain catastrophe. There is a report that the Aztec emperor himself had had a vision of soldiers approaching Tenochtitlan riding animals like deer. Certainly Montezuma was mindful of the promised return from exile of the fair, bearded god Quetzalcoatl. Not surprisingly, therefore, when Montezuma received news that a small army of fair-skinned warriors from across the sea was progressing through his empire, some of them on horseback, he was filled with foreboding. His dismay increased when his seers began to prophesy that he would be overthrown and the warriors would rule.

When Cortés and his small force entered the capital on 8 November 1519, Montezuma welcomed him as Quetzalcoatl. Cortés later recorded the event in a letter to the Spanish king, Charles I:

> *We were received by Montezuma with about two hundred chiefs, all barefooted and dressed in a kind of very rich livery. They approached in two processions along the walls of the street, which is very broad and straight and very beautiful. Montezuma came in the middle of the street . . . As we approached each other I descended from my horse and was about to embrace him, but the two lords in attendance intervened so that I should not touch him, and then they, and he also, made the ceremony of kissing the ground . . . we continued on through the streets until we came to a large and handsome house, which he had prepared for our reception.*

The welcome did not last. Cortés sought to control the empire and protect his small army by holding Montezuma hostage, but the Aztec priests began to resent Spanish opposition to their human sacrifices and the people to resent the insatiable Spanish thirst for gold, which was demanded as an ongoing tribute. Rebellion finally broke out following an unprovoked massacre of Aztec worshippers at a religious festival. Montezuma was sent out to reason with his people but was stoned in the attempt and wounded. Three days later the emperor died (possibly at the hands of his captors who had no more use for him now that he had lost authority) and the Spanish were forced to flee. The following year they returned with reinforcements and an impressive battle strategy and, after a three-month siege, the mighty Aztec capital of Tenochtitlan finally fell to Spain.

CHOCOLATE

The Aztecs were a warrior people and the aggressors in many wars of conquest. The victorious Aztecs did not occupy new territory but demanded regular and onerous tributes with menaces from defeated leaders. (Indeed, a number of tribes within the Aztec Empire collaborated with Cortés in its downfall to free themselves from this burden.) Items demanded as tributes included decorated cloaks and tunics, ceremonial feathers, bird skins, tiger skins, amber and jade and baskets of cocoa beans.

The Maya were the first to exploit cocoa beans, which they used as currency. They also made them into a spicy drink which was used in some of their religious ceremonies. It was Mayan merchants who introduced the cocoa bean to the Aztecs and taught them to prepare *xocolatl*, literally 'bitter water', the name being a compound of Nahuatl *xococ*, 'bitter', and *atl*, 'water'. However, since the dry climate around Tenochtitlan prohibited the cultivation of cocoa, the Aztecs were forced to procure the precious beans from further afield as tribute. According to the Franciscan priest Bernardino de Sahagún, who arrived in Mexico in 1529, *xocolatl was the drink of nobles, of rulers* (HISTORIA GENERAL DE LAS COSAS DE NUEVA ESPAÑA). And in his VERDADERA HISTORIA DE LA CONQUISTA DE LA NUEVA ESPAÑA, Bernal Díaz, who accompanied Cortés to Mexico, wrote how Montezuma was served *in cups of pure gold a drink made from the cocoa-plant which they said he took before visiting his wives*, adding that it was always served *with great reverence*.

When Cortés eventually returned to Spain in 1528, he took a supply of *xocolatl* with him. The Spanish court loved the foamy beverage which they called *chocolate*, a borrowing of the Nahuatl term. For almost a hundred years *chocolate* was a well-kept secret. Supplies of cocoa were meagre and the court did not want to share its little luxury with the rest of Europe. Then in 1615 Philip II of Spain married his daughter, Anne of Austria, to Louis XIII of France. Unable, or unwilling, to forgo her cup of chocolate, Anne took supplies with her, and before long the beverage was all the rage with the French court, who called it *chocolat*. The drink caught on in England, probably introduced from France, around the mid-seventeenth century and was known as *chocolate*. By this time supplies of cocoa beans were more plentiful, so chocolate not only became popular at Charles II's court, but was available at a price in chocolate- and coffee-houses as well. Best of all, not only was chocolate delicious, it was also rumoured to be good for you:

The Confection made of Cacao called Chocolate or Chocoletto, which may be had in divers places in London at reasonable rates, is of wonderful efficacy for the procreation of children . . . and besides that it preserves health, for it makes such as take it often to become fat and corpulent, fair and amiable.
(William Coles, ADAM IN EDEN, 1657)

VANILLA

To make chocolate, the Aztecs first roasted dried cocoa beans in earthenware pots and then ground them to a paste with various flavourings upon a heated stone. The paste was then patted into little cakes and left to dry. When needed, the cakes were crumbled into hot water and whipped to a froth with a whisk. For a long time chocolate was prepared and then exported in this form. When English and Dutch pirates in search of treasure came across this unpromising cargo on Spanish ships they called it 'sheeps' shit' and discarded it in disgust. In his study of the Aztec people, HISTORIA GENERAL DE LAS COSAS DE NUEVA ESPAÑA, Bernardino de Sahagún records some of the ingredients that were mixed into the chocolate product. They included chilli water, powdered aromatic flowers, wild bee honey and vanilla.

The aromatic vanilla flavouring the Aztecs used came from the pods of a tropical orchid. Since the shape of the pod reminded the Spanish conquistadors of the scabbard they each wore, they named it *vainilla*, literally 'little sheath', a diminutive of *vaina*, 'sheath'. The word *vanilla* was borrowed into English in the mid-seventeenth century when the pleasures of chocolate were first introduced.

Vanilla has an unlikely doublet, however. Spanish *vaina* was derived from Latin *vāgīna* which meant 'sheath, scabbard' but which the Romans also used in a jocular fashion for the 'female genital canal'. *Vagina*, stripped of its ancient jokiness, was borrowed from Latin into English as a serious anatomical term in the last quarter of the seventeenth century.

• The word *chilli* was borrowed by the Spanish from the Aztecs as *chile* or *chili*. Again, this word made its appearance in England in the 1660s. *Chilatl*, or 'chilli water', was another ingredient in chocolate paste. The chocolate consumed in the Spanish court was a modified recipe, however, as the drink was too bitter for European taste. The chilli water was omitted, but sugar and Eastern spices such as cinnamon and nutmeg were added instead.

TURKEY

The Ottoman Empire originated in the Asian part of Turkey (Anatolia) around the turn of the fourteenth century and gradually expanded until, by 1520, it

controlled most of the regions surrounding the Mediterranean Sea. During the sixteenth century these dominions were commonly referred to as 'Turkish' lands. And so, when the African guinea fowl began to be imported into England by way of Turkish territory, the English called the exotic bird *turkey cock*. Later in the same century, when the bird was brought from Guinea in West Africa by the Portuguese, it was also sometimes referred to as a *Guinea fowl*.

During the conquest of Mexico, Cortés and his men had feasted on a completely different type of fowl which had been domesticated by the Aztecs and other Central American tribes. The Aztecs called the hefty bird *huexolotl*, a name imitative of its gobbling cry. Some of these fowls were sent back to Spain immediately after the conquest, and their domestication proved so successful that, by the middle of the sixteenth century, the birds were known throughout Europe. The English, thoroughly bewildered by the assortment of foreign table-fowl now on offer, called the American bird *turkey cock*, too. Whether the English were ignorant of the New World origin of the bird or whether they were under the impression that the not dissimilar African and American birds were related species, is not known. Eventually, however, the birds were distinguished one from the other. *Guinea fowl* was thought appropriate for the African bird while the American fowl erroneously retained the name *turkey cock*, a label that was eventually reduced to *turkey*.

• Curiously, although wild turkeys were also common in the eastern part of North America, they were of a different species which was not easy to domesticate. For this reason the early North American colonists began to import birds from Europe, so that the world's stock of domesticated turkeys originates from those bred by the Aztecs in the sixteenth century. The turkey began to feature in American idiom during the nineteenth and twentieth centuries. Anything or anyone considered third rate, inept or stupid might be called a *turkey*, an allusion to the doltish, timorous nature of the domesticated bird. The creature is also reputedly easy to capture, so that *turkey* might mean 'an easy task' or 'easy money'.

• The origin of the early nineteenth-century expression *to talk turkey*, meaning 'to talk frankly', is usually explained by an anecdote in which a white man goes hunting with an Indian. When the time comes to divide their catch the white man, thinking to outwit his companion, says, 'Either you can have the buzzard and I'll take the turkey, or I'll have the turkey and the buzzard's yours.' To which the Indian replies, 'You never talked turkey to me!' Possibly the expression *cold turkey* to denote 'total, rather than gradual, withdrawal from an addictive substance in order to effect a cure', in use amongst drug addicts from around 1920, emerged from the sense of *turkey* as 'plain facts, the bottom line'.

TOMATO

Amongst the crops grown by the Aztecs was a pulpy fruit which they called *tomatl*. The Spaniards borrowed this word as *tomate* and took plants back with them to Spain. The tomato plant was suited to the warm, sunny climate of southern Europe where the fruit was cultivated to be eaten. Northern Europeans were more cautious. Not only was the tomato plant more difficult to raise in chillier climes but it was also identified with the poisonous deadly nightshade. In these countries it was grown as a curiosity and therefore rare.

Strangely, once the Spaniards had introduced the *tomate* to Europe, it became known by different names. The Italian coinage *pomodoro*, 'apple of gold', is seen by some as an indication that the original Aztec plants produced a different golden-coloured fruit from their bright red modern descendants, while the French term *pomme d'amour*, 'apple of love', alludes to its supposed capacity to excite passion. However, these two names sound remarkably similar which suggests that they could well be corruptions of a common term. The proposed expression is *pomme des Mours*, 'apple of the Moors', a name given in the sixteenth century to the aubergine by virtue of its popularity in Moorish cuisine. It is suggested that the tomato was early identified as a species of aubergine and therefore received the label *pomme des Mours*. At this point folk etymology, which replaces one word with a similar-sounding familiar alternative, set to work. The ripening tomatoes might be described as 'golden', hence Italian *pomodoro*, while medicinal or aphrodisiacal properties were often attributed to New World produce (see **potato**, page 117), giving rise to French *pomme d'amour*.

In England in the late sixteenth century the tomato was first known as *love-apple*, a translation of the French. (German similarly had *liebesapfel*.) The borrowing of *tomate* from Spanish first occurred in a translation into English of a history of the Indies made in about 1604. After this there were no further uses until the second half of the eighteenth century when *tomate* began to appear in travel texts along with the alternative form *tomato*, the final *o* probably intended to give the word a common Spanish ending.

But the English are a cautious race, and in spite of its two-hundred-year-old reputation as a philtre, the tomato remained a fruit to be eaten principally by foreigners. The supplement to CHAMBERS CYCLOPEDIA (1753) defined the *Tomato . . . or love-apple* as *a fruit . . . eaten either stewed or raw by the Spaniards and Italians and by the Jew families in England.* Indeed, it was not until the twentieth century that tomatoes gained popularity in Britain and were considered a common food.

AVOCADO

The avocado pear was widely cultivated by the Aztecs who named it *ahuacatl*, 'testicle', after its shape. The Spanish had a go at assimilating the word and ended up with *aguacate*. This form was still unacceptable, however. It soon fell subject to folk etymology and was nonsensically replaced by the more familiar term *avocado*, meaning 'advocate'. Unlike the tomato, the avocado was not seriously cultivated in Europe but was known through travel in tropical America. In this context the word came into English in the late seventeenth century as *avogato*, *avocato* or *avocado pear*, the final element added because the fruit is about the size and shape of a large pear. Yet again folk etymology was active and English corruptly substituted *alligator pear*, the alternative term apparently suggesting itself because the trees were often found growing in places where alligators lurked. Then, around the turn of the twentieth century, it was discovered that avocado trees were easy to propagate by grafting. Eventually, orchards were planted worldwide in countries with suitable climates so that the fruit became readily available. Since it was marketed as *avocado*, the quainter *alligator pear*, though still occasionally used, fell from favour.

1568

WILLIAM THE SILENT LEADS THE DUTCH REVOLT AGAINST SPANISH RULE

......

In 1506 the Netherlands, a collection of disparate provinces, were inherited by Charles, Duke of Burgundy (the future Holy Roman Emperor Charles V). Charles was brought up in the Flemish court and regarded the Netherlands as his home, but in 1516 he succeeded his maternal grandfather to the Spanish throne, thus binding his homeland to Spain.

Throughout his reign Charles made attempts to effect a more centralised administration in the Netherlands but the states were jealous of their individual freedoms and resisted. They were also thriving commercially and did not want their wealth squandered abroad. Many foreigners came to the Netherlands to trade, bringing with them Reformation doctrines which were readily received. When Catholic Charles sought to suppress this growing Calvinism, it fuelled further unrest.

In 1555 Charles resigned first the Netherlands and then, in 1556, Spain and its territories to his son, Philip. Philip II of Spain was a deeply religious man who had only known the Spanish court and had no great affection for the Netherlands. He was more determined than his father to quench Calvinism. In 1567 Philip sent troops into the Netherlands to stamp out the smouldering Dutch revolt. In 1568, unified by discontent and their Calvinist faith, the Dutch rallied to William of Orange to resist Spanish rule (see also **1609**, page 151).

BELEAGUER

In England Queen Elizabeth kept a watchful eye on events in the Netherlands, wary of the threat a powerful Spanish army posed to her Protestant realm. She found ways to encourage the rebels without becoming directly involved and tried to persuade Philip to withdraw his troops. When the Dutch leader, William of Orange, was assassinated at the instigation of the Spanish king in 1584, she was finally compelled to commit herself. In 1585 Elizabeth sent a force of 6,000 men to the Netherlands under the leadership of the Earl of Leicester.

The struggle in the Netherlands was often characterised by long sieges rather than battles and the Dutch word *belegeren*, 'to besiege', was on everyone's lips. Literally it means 'to camp round', coming from *be-*, 'about', and *leger*, 'camp'. It was borrowed into English as *beleaguer* at about this time and retains much of the same sense today:

Officers from the Wiltshire and other forces had gathered in strength to the north, south, east and west. There was an unofficial order to beleaguer New Age travellers and keep them away from Stonehenge. Many had already reached their destination, of course, in earlier days, but now the time had come to close the doors on further travellers.
(Garry Kilworth, A MIDSUMMER'S NIGHTMARE, 1996)

The term was also put to almost immediate figurative use to mean ' harass, put under pressure', and this too is still current:

But my heart sank. The people looked beleaguered. Their singing quavered and whined in the void. A few acolytes in pale violet drifted back and forth like disconsolate angels and in the balcony a little choir set up a shrill, heartbreaking chant, whose verses lifted and died away like an old, repeated grief. Beneath them where a verse should have come, the people seemed to let out a deep, collective sigh.
(Colin Thubron, THE LOST HEART OF ASIA, 1994)

• Dutch *leger* meant 'bed' and hence 'camp' and is ultimately related to English *lair* (Old English *leger*) and *lie*. Indeed the unattested Indo–European root *legh-* from which these words sprang is ultimately responsible for a host of words in the Germanic languages which have the underlying notion of 'to lie down'. *Lair* itself has had a number of meanings connected with 'lying' in its long history. From Saxon times until the nineteenth century it denoted 'a grave'(a sense still current in Scotland) and also 'a bed', and in Middle English also meant 'fornication'. Its use for 'a wild animal's den' dates from the sixteenth century. More recently *lair* has been used informally to denote 'a hideout'.

1569

THE FIRST LOTTERY IN ENGLAND IS ORGANISED

••••••

The first public lottery in England was under the patronage of Elizabeth I. The Queen, wary of Spanish presence in the Netherlands (see **1568**, page 131) and of the potential threat to her own Protestant realm, was anxious to repair the English ports and strengthen their defences. She decided upon a lottery to raise money for the scheme. The idea was not new; lotteries were popular with the Roman emperors. In the fifteenth century, town lotteries had been held in Flanders and in the first half of the sixteenth century lotteries were held both in France and in a number of Italian cities to pay for public works. The royal charter drawn up for the first English lottery stated that *the number of Lots shall be Foure hundreth thousand, and no moe: and euery Lot shall be the summe of Tenne shillings sterling onely, and no more.* The draw for *a great number of good Prices, aswel of redy Money as of Plate* took place at the western door of St Paul's Cathedral.

From then on lotteries financed many worthy projects. With the approval of James I, for instance, lottery revenue helped the Virginia Company provide for the settlement of Jamestown (see **1607**, page 142). During the reign of Charles II, lotteries were planned by the Master of the Mint. After the razzmatazz of candlelit processions and entertainers, an expectant crowd would gather for the grand draw where a stake of £10 could reap a £1000 reward.

Over time, however, lotteries fell open to fraud and this, combined with the growing insistence that they encouraged gambling, led to their being discontinued in 1826.

LOTTERY

Casting the lot settles disputes and keeps strong opponents apart. This biblical axiom comes from the Old Testament book of Proverbs (18:18). Most of the book dates back to the tenth century BC and this verse is by no means the earliest reference to casting lots, the ancient practice of settling disagreements or distributing possessions by the random selection of a specially marked object from a pool of similar objects. Proverbs 16:33 reads: *The lot is cast into the lap, but its every decision is from the Lord.* Here it is thought that the lots may have been small pebbles thrown into an arbiter's lap and concealed beneath a fold in his robe until drawn.

The Germanic peoples employed a similar system for decision-making and the unattested prehistoric Germanic root *khlut-* is responsible for a number of words in Germanic and Romance languages that relate to the practice. Middle Dutch, for instance, gained the word *lot* which denoted 'an object used in chance selection'. During the fifteenth century a number of towns in the allied regions of Flanders and Burgundy offered citizens the opportunity of buying lots which, if drawn, would entitle the holders to valuable prizes. Profits would go towards the building of fortifications or to poor relief. Such schemes were known as a *loterijes* in Middle Dutch, a word derived from *lot*. The word was borrowed into English in the sixteenth century when it was first applied to the *very rich Lotterie generall* of Elizabeth's reign.

• Old English derived *hlot* from *khlut-* to denote 'an object used in arbitration by chance', and this became *lot* in Middle English. The word in this sense is present in a number of expressions, still current, which date back to the Middle Ages: *to throw in one's lot with* and *to fall to the lot of*, for instance. During the eighteenth century *lot* began to be used to denote 'a number of similar or associated people or things' and, by the early nineteenth century, the word was being used colloquially and expansively to refer to 'a large number or quantity'.

1588

THE POPULATION OF PARIS ERECT BARRICADES AGAINST THEIR KING

For a period of thirty-six years, from 1562 to 1598, the stability and prosperity of France were blighted by the Wars of Religion. The Huguenots, French Calvinists, were demanding the same religious freedom that Catholics enjoyed. The House of Guise championed the Catholic cause while the Huguenot leadership eventually fell to Henry of Navarre.

In 1576 the French king, Henry III, signed a peace which accorded full religious liberty to the Huguenots. In response the Duke of Guise and other strict Catholics formed a Holy League with a view to having the treaty revoked. In 1585 the death of the Duke of Anjou obliged Henry III, who was childless, to recognise Protestant Henry of Navarre as his heir, and the League's activities intensified. In 1585, backed by the King of Spain and the Church, it succeeded in forcing the King to repeal the terms of the peace.

Guise now had the upper hand and pressed for further advantage. In 1588 he entered Paris, although he had been forbidden by the king. The Parisians welcomed him, erecting barricades to prevent any loyal subjects from supporting their sovereign. Henry III fled and was forced to declare the Duke Lieutenant-General of France. Guise was now in a position to exert a strong influence on state policy. A few months later the Duke was assassinated at the instigation of the desperate king but the following year Henry himself was murdered by a monk who believed himself to be on a divine mission. Henry of Navarre, as the new King of France, fought on to overcome the League and achieved religious tolerance and peace under the Edict of Nantes of 1598 (see **1685**, page 168).

BARRICADE
On 12 May 1588 the Duke of Guise entered Paris and the population rose against their king. The people used huge casks (*barrique* in French, a borrowing of Spanish *barrica*, 'barrel'), weighted with earth and paving stones, to block the streets and isolate the king from any loyal support. Consequently the event was referred to as *la journée des barricades*. Within two years the episode was recorded in a posthumous edition of Foxe's ACTES AND MONUMENTS (more popularly known as the BOOK OF MARTYRS) as *the day of the Barricadoes*. This is the first record of *barricade* in English. The spelling *barricado* reflects the fact that, when French words ending in -*ade* were borrowed into

English, they were assumed to be of Spanish, Portuguese or Italian origin and were usually given the ending *-ado*.

Shakespeare was amongst the first to make a verb of the new noun. In ALL'S WELL THAT ENDS WELL (1603), Helena asks the rogue Parolles *Man is enemie to virginitie, how may we barracado it against him? Barricado* remained current into the nineteenth century. *Barricade* appeared towards the middle of the seventeenth century either as a direct borrowing from French or in an attempt to assimilate *barricado* to the French spelling:

We barricaded the town, and at every passage placed our ordnance and watched it all night, our soldiers content to lie on bare stones.
(Letter from a journeyman serving with the Parliamentarians in the English Civil War to his master in London, dated 22 August 1642).

From one Civil War to another – George Orwell in HOMAGE TO CATALONIA (1938) records this scene:

The Barcelona streets are paved with square cobbles, easily built up into a wall, and under the cobbles a kind of shingle that is good for filling sandbags. The building of those barricades was a strange and wonderful sight; I would have given something to be able to photograph it. With the kind of passionate energy that Spaniards display when they have definitely decided to begin upon any job of work, long lines of men, women, and quite small children were tearing up the cobblestones, hauling them along in a hand-cart that had been found somewhere, and staggering to and fro under heavy sacks of sand. . . In a couple of hours the barricades were head-high, with riflemen posted at the loopholes, and behind one barricade a fire was burning and men were frying eggs.

• Spanish *barrica*, 'cask', is related to English *barrel* which came into English by way of Old French *baril* in the early fourteenth century. The Spanish and Old French words are probably derived from unattested Late Latin *barra*, 'bar, rod', a reference to the staves from which the casks were constructed.

Barra, a word of unknown origin, had passed into Spanish, Portuguese and Italian as *barra*, and into Old French as *barre*. It is present in other English words borrowed from these languages:
bar (12th century): a borrowing of Old French *barre*
barrier (14th century): originally 'a stockade to block an enemy's passage', from Anglo-Norman *barrere*, from Old French *barriere*, from *barre*
embarrass (17th century): from French *embarrasser*, 'to hamper, to disconcert', from Spanish *embarazar*, from Italian *imbarazzare*, from *imbarrare*, 'to confine (with bars)' hence 'to impede', from Latin *im*, 'in', and Late Latin *barra*, 'bar'.

1589

WILLIAM LEE INVENTS THE FIRST KNITTING MACHINE

•••••••

The first knitting machine was invented by a clergyman, William Lee, who allegedly embarked upon the project because the lady who held his affections paid more attention to her knitting than to him. Lee's stocking frame produced a flat stocking which had to be sewn up by hand at the back. In 1589 Lee presented Elizabeth I with a pair of woollen stockings and a request for a patent on his invention. Instead of agreeing, the Queen challenged him to knit stockings of silk. (She herself had worn silk stockings provided by her silk-woman, Mrs Montague, since 1560.) However, when Lee eventually reappeared at court with a pair of fine silk stockings for his sovereign, the Queen again refused his patent on the grounds that the machine was a threat to the livelihood of some of her subjects. Lee found a more sympathetic patron in the French king, Henry IV, and set up business across the Channel in Rouen. It was William Lee's brother who, in spite of vehement protests from the hand-knitters, eventually succeeded in establishing the knitting industry in England in the early seventeenth century. Lee's original design was so cleverly devised that its principles remain to this day the basis of modern knitting machines.

KNIT

Knitting is an ancient craft brought into Western Europe in medieval times, probably from the Middle East. During the late Middle Ages the skill was perfected on the Continent and hand-knitted garments were often worn.

Knit and *knot* are close cousins. The Old Germanic stem *knutt-*, 'knot, knob', gave Old English *cnotta* and Middle English *knot(te)*, 'knot'. One might expect a derived verb *to knot*; however, this did not appear in English until the sixteenth century. Instead Old English had the verb *cnyttan*, 'to fasten with a knot', which also sprang from *knutt-* by way of unattested Old Germanic *knuttjan*. This became *knitten* in Middle English and eventually the modern word *knit*, but still with the sense 'to tie a knot'. Thus, in Tyndale's translation of the New Testament (1525), Peter's vision in Acts 10:11 is described as *a greate shete knytt at the iiij. corners.* While, to continue the biblical theme, Samuel Hieron urges the reader: *Look to the first marriage that euer was; the Lorde Himselfe knit the knot* (WORKES, 1607).

Nets in particular were made by twisting and knotting lengths of twine to make a mesh. The first written record of

nets being *knitted* dates back to the thirteenth century. Although knitting with needles does not involve tying knots at all, the resulting fabric has the general look of a net and so, when knitting began to flourish in England in the first half of the sixteenth century, the verb *to knit* was also applied to this method of fashioning bonnets and hose. With the appearance in English of the new verb *to knot* and the growing popularity of knitting, *knit* soon became chiefly confined to this context. *Knitting* as a noun denoting 'knitted work' dates back to the eighteenth century.

STOCKING

In the Middle Ages men wore an all-in-one garment called a hose, which covered the lower part of the body and the legs. After about 1520 the fashion was for hose cut off at the knee to make two garments. These were known as the *upper stocks*, resembling knee breeches, and the *netherstocks*, which were like fitted stockings. The latter were often simply referred to as *stocks*. This word appears to be a humorous allusion to the instrument of punishment known as the *stocks* in which the guilty person was held by the legs in a wooden frame. The *stocks* themselves were named after the two upright posts in the frame (from Middle English *stok*, 'post, stake' and Old English *stoc*, 'tree trunk'). Knitted *stocks* gave a close, flattering fit and the Reverend Lee's stocking-frame could produce them in a fraction of the time taken by a hand knitter. The earliest written record of *stocking*, a derivative of *stock*, dates back to 1583, not long before Lee's invention. The phrase *in stocking feet* is applicable to men and women alike, a reminder that, until the twentieth century, *stockings* were worn by both (see **bluestocking**, page 176).

• The meanings of English *stock* are so diverse that it seems improbable that they all stem from a single word. Nevertheless, that is the case. The unattested prehistoric Germanic word *stukkaz* gave the Old English word *stoc*, 'tree trunk, stump of a tree', and a number of related words in other Germanic languages.

Stock was figuratively used from the fourteenth century to mean 'the original member of a family line, a line of descent, a breed'. We might speak today of a person coming from *good stock* or *farming stock*, for instance.

Since a tree trunk is a hefty piece of wood, *stock* denoted a number of objects which were load bearing; a gun carriage, for example. Many of these uses are now obsolete, but the idea of a sound foundation, together with that of a living tree trunk from which new life springs, may have been the notion behind the use of *stock* in a variety of contexts to mean a 'fund or store', from the fifteenth century onwards:

The modern use for a 'tradesman's store of merchandise' arose in the seventeenth century. The related phrase *to take stock*, 'to make an inventory', dates from the eighteenth century and was figuratively applied with the sense 'to evaluate' in the first half of the nineteenth

Stock to denote 'cattle' dates from the sixteenth century. It is an obvious extension of the word in its sense of 'store' but is doubtless also influenced by the earlier meaning 'breed'

Broth which is used as a base for soup or gravy has been called *stock* since the eighteenth century. Again, this use has the notion of 'store' since, in the best kitchens, the stock pot was always on the hob.

• The original notion of a tree trunk and its characteristics also lingers in other words and compounds:

The adjective *stocky*, used to describe a sturdy plant in the early seventeenth century, was applied to a solidly built, thickset animal or person in the 1670s.

In the sixteenth century, *stock* was used in a large number of compounds such as *jesting-stock*, *talking-stock* and *torturing-stock*. The notion here was probably that, like a wooden stump, the person to whom they were applied was devoid of feeling. Indeed, *stock* denoted a 'senseless, stupid person' from the early fourteenth century. Of these compounds *laughing-stock* remains current.

The phrase *(to stand) stock still*, that is 'as still as a stock or log', has been in use since the fifteenth century.

1597

The Essays, or Counsels, Civill and Morall of Francis Bacon Are First Published

••••••

Francis Bacon (1561-1626) was a philosopher and statesman who rose to be Lord Chancellor under James l. His political career ended in 1621 when he admitted to having taken bribes from plaintiffs while he was a judge. He then went into retirement and applied himself entirely to his philosophical and scientific studies and to writing. Bacon's works are prolific and mainly philosophical. His Essays are his best-known contribution to literature and treat a variety of subjects: matters of state, personal and public mores, religion and philosophy. The first printing contained only ten essays. There were to be two further editions, in 1612 and 1625, which contained thirty-eight and fifty-eight essays respectively.

ESSAY

Francis Bacon introduced the *essay* as a literary genre into the English language. Neither the concept nor the coinage were Bacon's, however, but were borrowed from French moralist Michel de Montaigne (1533-92). In 1571, after an early career in government, Montaigne retired to his family estate where he devoted himself to writing. The result of his labour was three volumes of compositions in which he used his own circumstances, thoughts, feelings and emotions as a vehicle for exploring a wide variety of subjects. He called these personal literary ramblings Essais. The French word *essai* meant 'an attempt, an effort'. Montaigne's use of the term indicated that he was simply making an unpolished attempt to capture his thoughts on paper.

The origins of French *essai* can be traced back to the Latin word *exigere*. This verb meant 'to weigh', and hence 'to examine, to test', and it influenced the formation of the Late Latin noun *exagium*, 'a weighing, a trial, an examination'. Old French borrowed *exagium* as *assai* and the variant *essai* to mean 'a test or trial of someone or something' and hence 'an attempt (to prove oneself)'. English adopted *assay* in the fourteenth century, eschewing *essay* until the late sixteenth century when *essai* had begun to prevail in French. In English, too, *essay* became the established form (although, unlike French, English retained *assay* when referring to the 'qualitative analysis of a precious metal'). While *essay* to denote 'an endeavour' has a rather formal ring in modern English, thanks to Montaigne and Bacon the word now also describes an established literary genre and, on a less august level, commonly trips off the tongue of schoolchildren and students who attempt to express their thoughts with pen and paper in academic compositions.

1599

EDMUND SPENSER, THE ELIZABETHAN POET, DIES

• • • • • •

Spenser was a pupil of the Merchant Taylor's school, which had been founded in 1561 to educate the children of tradesmen. Here he came under the influence of Richard Mulcaster, the school's headmaster. Mulcaster was among those who argued forcefully for education in the mother tongue rather than Latin:

> *For is it not in dede a mervellous bondage, to becom servants to one tung for learning sake . . . whereas we may have the verie same treasur in our own tung? our own bearing the joyfull title of our libertie and fredom, the Latin tung remembring us of our thraldom and bondage?*

Spenser, too, loved the English language and his poetry is enriched by words from Middle English, in particular those used by Chaucer. Terms thus revived by Spenser and his contemporaries were known as *Chaucerisms* in the sixteenth century (see also **1616**, page 153). When Spenser died, he was buried in Westminster Abbey close to Chaucer, the poet he esteemed so much:

> *In the South crosse-aisle of Westminster abbey, next the Dore, is this Inscription: Heare lies (expecting the second comeing of our Saviour Christ Jesus) the body of Edmund Spencer, the Prince of Poets of his tyme, whose divine spirit needs no other witnesse, then the workes which he left behind him.*
> (John Aubrey, BRIEF LIVES, c 1693)

DRIZZLE, SHADE, SUNSHINE

It is a wonder how the English would ever have indulged their preoccupation with the weather without some of the words that were salvaged from Middle English during the sixteenth century by Spenser and his contemporaries. The word *drizzle*, for instance, was not in use before the mid-sixteenth century. It is probably a frequentative of a rare Middle English verb *dresen*, 'to fall', which came from Old English *drēosan*, and appears in Spenser's THE SHEPHEARDES CALENDER (1579) as *drizzling*. Shade, on the other hand, was more commonly found in Middle English, where it existed as *schade* (from Old English *sceadu*). The word disappeared around the early fifteenth century but was revived during the second half of the sixteenth. Spenser was responsible for the adjective *shady* which he used in THE SHEPHEARDES CALENDER . *Shadow*, which is basically the same word as *shade*, comes from *sceaduwe*, a variant form of *sceadu*. Its increasing use in the time of Spenser was doubtless strengthened by the resounding phrase of Psalm 23, in versions of the Old Testament from Coverdale's Bible of 1535: *the valley of the shadow of death*.

But what need is there of shade without *sunshine*? The noun *sunne* and the verb *sine* were constantly placed together in phrases such as *ere* or *while the sun shines* and Middle English *sunnesine* probably evolved as a compound of these two parts of speech. (*Sunrise* similarly comes from ambiguous grammatical constructions in *before the sun rise*, etc). The word, rarely found in Middle English, was used by Coverdale in his translation of the Bible (1535). *Sunshine* then appeared in THE SHEPHEARDES CALENDER , this time as an adjective to mean 'sunny':

All in a sunneshine day, as did befall

a particular use that was picked up by Shakespeare, who used it figuratively:

God save King Henry . . .
And send him many years of Sunne-shine days.
(RICHARD II, Act 4, scene i, 1595)

Later, in THE FAERIE QUEENE (the first three books of which appeared in 1590), Spenser coined the adjective *sunshiny*, which remains current.

BLATANT
In the second three books of THE FAERIE QUEENE (1596) Spenser personifies calumny as a monster with a thousand tongues, offspring of Envie and Detraction:

Unto themselves they gotten had
A monster which the blatant beast men call,
A dreadful feend of gods and men ydrad.

Sir Calidor comes across the *blatant beast* befouling the church. He defeats the monster and binds it with chains, but the beast breaks free again.

It is not known what inspired the epithet *blatant beast*. Some etymologists have suggested that Spenser had an archaic form of *bleating* in mind; sixteenth-century Scottish had *blaitand*. The objection to this is that it does not adequately convey the sense that Spenser intended. Others suggest that he derived the name from the imitative Latin verb *blatīre*, 'to babble, to blab'.

Spenser's poem was immediately successful and there are frequent references to the *blatant beast* in other writers from the turn of the seventeenth century onwards. Within sixty years *blatant* had entered English as a free-standing adjective, for Thomas Blount defined the term as *babling, twatling* in his GLOSSOGRAPHIA, a dictionary of difficult words compiled in 1656. *Blatant*, then, was being figuratively applied to people who were offensively noisy or were clamorous in expressing their opinions. Then, towards the end of the nineteenth century, the word underwent a shift in meaning when it no longer confined itself to an assault on the hearing but became an adjective critical of shameless acts or attitudes that were glaringly obvious to the eye:

She stood, slightly out of breath, and looked, with something that encompassed both rage and despair, at the blatant, unmistakable evidence of Dale's relentless purpose.
(Joanna Trollope, OTHER PEOPLE'S CHILDREN, 1998)

COSSET
Cosset makes its début in THE SHEPHEARDES CALENDER (1579), where Spenser uses the word to denote 'a hand-reared lamb'. It is unclear where the poet found inspiration for the term. Skeat points to its phonetic affinity with Old English *cotsæta*, 'cottager', and the derived Anglo-Norman forms *coscet* and *cozet*, which are found in the Domesday Book. Applied to a lamb, the sense would be a 'lamb that is reared in a cottage or by a cottager'. This theory is strengthened by similarly derived words for hand-reared

lambs in both Italian and German. Against the suggestion is the lack of evidence. There is no record of *cozet* ever referring to a lamb and the word does not recur after its appearance in the Domesday Book. The secret rests with Spenser. Nevertheless, such was the popularity of THE SHEPHEARDES CALENDER that the term soon became current and remains so, although it is not often heard in modern non-agricultural society. The derived verb *to cosset*, meaning 'to indulge, to pamper', is much more familiar.

He won't like it, you know, if you have the flu.
   Really. . .?
   You see, most people are naturally sympathetic towards illness. They're kind to people with high temperatures. They even cosset them. But not him! He runs a mile. Sneeze once and he'll be off! In the opposite direction!
(John Mortimer, A VOYAGE ROUND MY FATHER, 1970)

The verb first appeared in the mid-seventeenth century but was not much used in written English until the mid-nineteenth century.

1600

WILLIAM GILBERT PUBLISHES HIS TREATISE DE MAGNETE

......

William Gilbert was born in Colchester in 1544 and was educated at St John's College, Cambridge. In 1573 he moved to London where he practised medicine and, in 1601, he was appointed physician to Elizabeth I and then to her successor James I. It is not for his medical skill or work at court that Gilbert is remembered, however, but for his outstanding scientific research detailed in his principal work DE MAGNETE which was published in 1600 and which is regarded as the first major scientific work to be written in England. Although his work was written in Latin and was not translated until 1893, it was widely read, laid the foundations for understanding of electricity and magnetism, and was a precursor to the modern theory of gravity.

ELECTRICITY
The ancient Greeks liked to collect amber which they used for decorative purposes. It is probable that, as early as 600 BC, the Greek philosopher Thales of Miletus was aware that the resin had the power to attract pieces of light material, such as feathers, hair or bits of straw, when it was rubbed with fur. The Greek word for 'amber' was *elektron* and this became *ēlectrum* in Latin – a term, incidentally, which was also sometimes used in Middle English to refer to the resin.

It had been supposed since ancient times that amber alone possessed this almost magical quality. William Gilbert's treatise DE MAGNETE demonstrated that substances other than amber were capable of developing frictional electricity and he derived the modern Latin adjective, *ēlectricus* from *ēlectrum* to describe the force that such substances exert after rubbing. Both the adjective *electrick* and the derived noun *electricity*, used originally to denote 'the power of certain frictionally stimulated substances to attract light bodies', appeared in English in Sir Thomas Browne's PSEUDOXIA EPIDEMICA of 1646. Over the centuries, as *electricity* was better understood, the term was gradually widened in scope. The figurative use of the term to denote 'intensity of feeling' or 'state of keen excitement' dates from the end of the eighteenth century.

MAGNET

Another phenomenon known to the ancient Greeks was the magnetic property of the loadstone (magnetic oxide of iron). In the twelfth century sailors in the Mediterranean began to use the mineral in navigation when it was realised that the loadstone always pointed north-south when freely suspended. (The word *loadstone* literally means *way-stone*; *loadstar* means 'star (the North Star) that points the way'.) The ancient Greeks mined magnetic oxide of iron at Magnesia, a city in Asia Minor. They called it *Magnēs lithos*, 'stone of Magnesia', which was then shortened to *magnēs* . The word was taken into Latin as *magnēs* and from its stem, *magnēt-*, Old French had *magnete*, 'loadstone' which was borrowed into Middle English around the mid-fifteenth century, with the sense only of 'magnetite ore'.

William Gilbert's famous treatise DE MAGNETE, MAGNETICISQUE CORPORIBUS, ET DE MAGNO MAGNETE TELLURE translates as 'On the Magnet and Magnetic Bodies, and on That Great Magnet the Earth' and is his most impressive work. He found he could make magnets by stroking iron bars with a loadstone or by placing them along the earth's magnetic field and hammering them. He also discovered, by noting that a compass needle always points north-south and dips downward, that the earth itself behaved like a great bar magnet. Indeed, it was Gilbert who coined the term *magnetic pole*, the word *pole* coming from Latin *polus*, a borrowing of Greek *polos*, 'the axis of a sphere'. The terms *magnet* and *magnetic*, in the senses common today, made the transition from Latin into English not long after his death in 1603.

1605

A PLOT TO BLOW UP THE HOUSES OF PARLIAMENT AND THE KING IS UNCOVERED

••••••

The story of the Gunpowder Plot is a familiar one. When James I came to the throne, the Catholics hoped he would grant them a degree of religious freedom. This was not to be. Instead, following his chief adviser, Robert Cecil, the King adopted a policy of repression. In 1604 a small group of angry Catholic conspirators, led by Robert Catesby, met together to plan the destruction of the King and his Parliament. To this end they rented a house whose cellar ran under the House of Lords. By March 1605 thirty-six barrels of gunpowder had been stowed beneath the parliamentary chamber in readiness for the State Opening of Parliament the following November. But one of the conspirators began to weaken and sent a message to his brother-in-law, a peer of the realm, warning him not to attend the ceremony. Cecil and the Council were alerted and, early on the morning of 5 November, guards were sent to the cellar where the plot was uncovered.

GUY

Guy Fawkes was born into a distinguished Protestant family but became a zealous convert to Roman Catholicism. In 1593 his enthusiasm for his new faith led him to join the Spanish forces engaged in religious and political conflict in the Netherlands (see **1568**, page 131 and **1609**, page 151). The story goes that Robert Catesby approached Guy Fawkes about the Gunpowder Plot because he needed the military expertise of someone who could work with explosives but who would not be easily recognised. When guards were sent to the cellar beneath the Palace of Westminster in the early hours of 5 November 1605, it was Guy Fawkes who was caught red-handed with lengths of fuse on his person (see **train**, page 198). Later, under torture, Fawkes revealed the names of his fellow conspirators, who were all arrested, tried and executed.

The conspiracy also allegedly involved a wider group of Catholic gentlemen. One of these, Sir Everard Digby, was charged with preparing an uprising in the Midlands to coincide with the London explosion. In BRIEF LIVES (c 1693), John Aubrey had this to say about *a most gallant gentleman*:

'Twas his ill fate to suffer in the Powder-plott. When his heart was pluct out by the Executioner (who, secundum formam, cryed, Here is the heart of a Treytor!) it is credibly reported, he replied, Thou liest!

It may well be true that not only Digby but all the conspirators were innocent. Contemporary opinion was not wholly convinced by Robert Cecil's discovery of the plot. An Italian gentleman, visiting England at the time, commented:

Those that have practical experience of the way in which things are done hold it is certain that there has been foul play and that some of the Council secretly spun a web to entangle these poor gentlemen.

There is a fair amount of evidence to support this view. But whether Guy Fawkes was a victim or true conspirator, the dramatic role he allegedly played in the Gunpowder Plot brought him to notoriety. From then on, 5 November was marked by the lighting of bonfires to celebrate the deliverance of the King and Parliament, a practice which continues today. In his diary for 5 November 1664 Samuel Pepys writes how he was inconvenienced on his way back from the theatre, *the coach being forced to go round by London Wall home because of the bonfires, the day being mightily observed in the City.* While on 5 November 1685 John Evelyn records how he was too ill to go to church, to his great sorrow, *it being the first Gunpowder Conspiracy anniversary that had been kept now these eighty years under a prince of the Roman religion [James II].* An ominous addition to the entry reads: *Bonfires were forbidden on this day; what does this portend!*

As part of the festivities an effigy of Guy Fawkes was paraded around the streets before being burnt on the blazing bonfire. (Indeed in Lewes, Sussex, a figure of the Pope is also burnt to this day.) At the beginning of the nineteenth century these figures, dressed in a mis-matched assortment of old clothing, were referred to as *guys*, a sense which is still current during the annual celebrations on 5 November. By the 1830s the use of the term had been extended to denote 'a person of grotesque appearance', in particular one who was bizarrely dressed and looked a fright. A weakening of this latter sense probably influenced the American English generalisation of *guy* to mean 'man, fellow', a slang usage which arose around the middle of the nineteenth century. Although still colloquial, it can now refer to the nicest of icons, such as tennis star Tim

Henman, without a hint of the grotesque:

> *So where does a nice guy like Our Tim, the son of an Oxford solicitor, Tony, whose family is steeped in tennis tradition . . . fit into this dog-eat-dog era?*
> (Simon Kinnersley in THE TIMES MAGAZINE, 22 May 1999)

1607

SUCCESSFUL ENGLISH SETTLEMENT OF NORTH AMERICA BEGINS

......

In 1584 Sir Walter Raleigh had obtained permission to establish a colony in North America. The fleet set sail in 1585 under the command of Sir Richard Grenville, who had this to say about seeking fortune in the New World:

> *Who seeks the way to win renown*
> *Or flies with wings of high desire;*
> *Who seeks to wear the laurel crown,*
> *Or hath the mind that would aspire;*
> *Tell him his native soil eschew,*
> *Tell him go range and seek anew.*
> *To pass the seas some think a toil,*
> *Some think it strange abroad to roam,*
> *Some think it grief to leave their soil,*
> *Their parents, kinsfolk, and their home.*
> *Think so who list, I like it not,*
> *I must abroad to try my lot.*
> (quoted in Jones, THE EARLY MODERN WORLD, 1979)

In spite of the adventurous spirit of these first English colonists, the venture on Roanoke Island, Virginia, failed. Raleigh later sold his patent to a group who, in 1606, formed themselves into the Virginia Company. The following year, three ships carrying settlers and supplies sailed for Virginia. On 14 May 1607, Jamestown was founded on a marshy peninsula in the James River, named after the Stuart king,

James I. Here the settlers suffered great hardships: many died of disease, they bickered amongst themselves and grew apathetic towards their own welfare. They did not plan or cultivate and almost starved. The colony was saved by the arrival in 1610 of Lord De La Warr (Delaware) who brought timely supplies and established order.

Many words which are now familiar in English come from native dialects of Algonquian origin and were first recorded by the early settlers in North America in the first half of the seventeenth century. These include moccasin *(from Narragansett* mohkussin*)*, pow-wow *(from Narragansett* powwaw *and Natick* pauwau, *'medicine man' – the sense behind the word being 'he uses divination, he dreams'), and* wigwam *(from Abnaki* wīkwām, *literally 'their house'). Amongst this vocabulary are the names of animals which the colonists came across for the first time and for which they borrowed the Native American words:*

MOOSE

This animal was hunted by tribes in the northern forests. Captain John Smith, one of the original leaders at Jamestown, wrote accounts of the colony and life in Virginia, in which he defined the creature as *Moos, a beast bigger than a stagge. Moos* was from Natick dialect and probably derived from *moosu*, 'he trims, he shaves', a reference to the way the animal rips the bark and lower branches from trees while feeding.

RACOON

The animal was hunted for its meat and fur. It is not known for certain which Algonquian dialect the word *racoon* was taken from. In TRUE RELATION (1608), an account of the early settlement in Virginia, Captain John Smith records the term first as *rahaugcum* and then as *raugroughcum* which give a fair impression of the difficulty of transcribing the native word *ärähkun* (from *ärähkunem*, 'he scratches with his hands'). Not surprisingly, the English soon simplified it to *racoon* and, for the people back home, the settlers described the animal as being rather like a badger or the size of a fox and with a bushy tail.

The British public had to wait another two hundred years or so to see the creature for themselves, however. In the eighteenth century, American Indians, teepees and assorted wildlife were often a feature of shows and pleasure gardens (see **tattoo**, page 180). Thomas Turner, a shopkeeper in the Sussex village of East Hoathly, regularly kept a diary. His entry for 6 October 1758 stands out from descriptions of the daily round. *This day*, he wrote, *entertained my family at 3d expense with the sight of a racoon*.

• Racoon hunters in the American West trained coon dogs to flush out their nocturnal quarry. Often the dogs would chase the creature into a tree and then remain there barking until the huntsmen arrived, unaware that the cunning racoon had made its way to an adjacent tree in the dark. From this comes the common idiom *to bark up the wrong tree*, 'to pursue an erroneous line of enquiry', which dates from around 1830.

SKUNK

The Native Americans often named animals after their distinctive habits. The skunk is, of course, notorious for its defence of squirting a foul-smelling liquid from glands under its tail whenever it is alarmed. The Abnaki dialect had *segākw*. Its unattested Proto-Algonquian origin may have been *shekākwa*, a compound formed from the unattested *shek*, 'to urinate', and *ākw*, 'small animal'. English first had the word as *squnck*. The spelling *skunk* dates from the turn of the eighteenth century.

• Skunks were prized for their distinctive fur, which could, to a certain extent, be deodorised. Nevertheless, skinning a skunk was not a pleasant task, hence the nineteenth-century American proverb of independence and responsibility *let every man skin his own skunk*.

The use of *skunk* in colloquial American English to denote 'a detestable person' (a term which is sometimes used in an affable way) dates from around 1840.

TERRAPIN

Besides hunting wild game and raising crops, the Indians feasted upon creatures taken from the lakes and rivers: fish, clams and freshwater turtles, *turepé* in Abenaki and *tulpe* in Delaware. The settlers, too, fished in the creeks. The Reverend Alexander Whitaker (under whose teaching Pocahontas was converted to Christianity) wrote of finding pike, carp, eel, crayfish and *torope* on the end of his fishing-hook (GOOD NEWES FROM VIRGINIA,1613). The little turtles were plentiful, and the colonists soon began to call them *terrapines*, a corruption of the dialect term with an unaccountable *-ine* ending. Today Chesapeake Bay, close to which Jamestown was founded, is still renowned for its shellfish and tasty diamondback terrapin.

• In their accounts, North American settlers writing in the second half of the seventeenth century defined the *terrapine* as a small 'tortoise' or a 'turtle'. The differentiation between *tortoise* as a land reptile and *turtle* as a marine species was only just beginning to emerge at that time.

The popular Late Latin name for a *tortoise* was *tortūca*. This term is thought to have derived from the adjective *tortus*, 'twisted, crooked' (past participle of *torquēre*, 'to twist'), and to refer to the twisted feet of the land tortoises found in southern Europe. Middle English not only borrowed Late Latin *tortūca* but also its French derivative *tortue*. These two borrowings resulted in a host of Middle English variants, among them *tortuca, tortuce, tortu(e)*, and *tortose*. However, the modern term *tortoise*, which dates from the late 1560s, was probably a

development from Late Latin rather than French. To add to the confusion, for a short while in the sixteenth century the Spanish form *tortuga* was also current, brought back by adventurers following the discovery of different species in the New World.

Many of these newly discovered species were what we would call *turtles* today. In the sixteenth and early seventeenth centuries they were simply *tortoises* or *tortoises of the sea*. John Davies of Kidwelly was careful to distinguish between *Land-Tortoises, Sea-Tortoises,* and *Fresh-water Tortoises, which are different figures* (HISTORY OF THE CARIBBEE ISLANDS, 1666). The word *turtle* was applied to the marine creatures by English seamen and adventurers from around the mid-seventeenth century. It apparently originated as a corruption of the French *tortue*, 'tortoise', and was then assimilated to the already existing but totally unconnected word *turtle*, 'turtle-dove' (from Old English *turtle*, from Latin *turtur*, 'turtle-dove', imitative of the bird's cooing). The word was still regarded very much as a seaman's term throughout the first half of the eighteenth century but became more widely accepted when turtle began to feature as a delicacy on eighteenth-century menus.

The Indians were initially friendly towards the settlers and helped them survive, but as the Europeans sought to impose the structures and culture of the Old World upon the New, they began to resist. In 1622, for instance, a confederacy of Indian tribes from the coastlands of Virginia attempted to annihilate the colonists at Jamestown. This was the first of the Indian Wars, a long series of battles and skirmishes lasting more than two and a half centuries, during which white settlers gradually pushed back their frontiers and gained supremacy of North America.

BURY THE HATCHET

The *hatchet* to which the idiom refers is, of course, a tomahawk (from Renape *tāmāhāk*, from *tāmāham*, 'he cuts'). This was a kind of axe with a head of stone or bone which Indians of the northeast and Great Lakes used as an agricultural tool and also in hunting and warfare. When trade with Europeans was established, metal axe heads were supplied. The idiomatic expression *to bury the hatchet*, 'to settle one's differences, to forgive', has its origins in a native peace custom where a tomahawk was ceremonially buried to symbolise an end to hostilities. In 1680 Samuel Sewall, writing from Boston to his brother Stephen back in England, had this to say about negotiations between Major John Pynchon and the restive Mohawk tribe:

> *I writt to you in one of ye Mishchief ye Mohawks did: which occasioned Major Pynchon's goeing to Albany where meeting with ye Sachem [chief] they came to an agreement and buried two Axes in ye Ground; one for English another for themselves; which ceremony to them is more significant and binding than all Articles of Peace the Hatchet being a principal weapon with them. Are not to come in a hostile way on this side Hudson's River. But ye came out of place.*

Subsequent references to the peace ceremony are plentiful throughout the Indian Wars. The idiomatic use of *bury the hatchet* in American English dates from the last quarter of the nineteenth century.

Nevertheless, the land the colonists struggled to control was a beautiful one:

INDIAN SUMMER

In the autumn of each year, around mid-October, the weather in the northern American states turns mild and the atmosphere smoky and hazy. This seasonal gentleness was recorded from the late eighteenth century as the *Indian summer*. According to a sermon published in 1812 by James Freeman, minister of the First Episcopal Church in Boston,

Massachusetts, the natives believed the stillness to be a blessing sent by their god Cautantowwit, but a certain Joseph Doddridge had a more jaundiced view of the season:

> *The smokey time commenced and lasted for a considerable number of days. This was the Indian summer, because it afforded the Indians another opportunity of visiting the settlements with their destructive warfare.* (NOTES ON THE SETTLEMENT AND INDIAN WARS IN WESTERN VIRGINIA AND PENNSYLVANIA FROM THE YEAR 1762 UNTIL THE YEAR 1783, 1824)

There is a misconception that an *Indian summer* comes from Indian rather than North American weather patterns. Whatever the attribution in the popular mind, there is undoubtedly sincere gratitude for a last few days of sunny weather, coming unseasonably late in the autumn, that delays the onset of winter.

In 1830 Thomas de Quincey used *Indian summer* to describe 'a period of joyful wellbeing and tranquillity late in life before death finally closes in', a figurative use which has been taken up by many other writers since then:

> *Meanwhile she was quite content that Sebastian should become tanned in the rays of Sylvia's Indian summer.* (Victoria Sackville-West, THE EDWARDIANS, 1930)

In INDIAN SUMMER OF A FORSYTE (1918), an interlude between the first two volumes of THE FORSYTE SAGA, John Galsworthy describes the relationship between the elderly Jolyon Forsyte and Irene, the young estranged wife of his nephew Soames. Although their relationship is purely that of an affectionate uncle and niece, the company and friendship of a beautiful woman brighten the last weeks of Old Jolyon's life – making it an *Indian summer*, in fact.

1608

THE POET JOHN MILTON IS BORN

••••••

John Milton was born into a well-to-do family who encouraged his undoubted abilities. When he left Christ's College, Cambridge, Milton wavered over an earlier intention to enter the established Church, with which he was increasingly at odds. Still undecided, he spent the years between 1632 and 1637 at his father's home. Here he undertook a rigorous programme of private study to equip himself for a career as either a clergyman or a poet. Returning to England in 1639 after touring France and Italy, Milton's interests began to take a political turn. As unrest turned to civil war, (see **1642**, page 163) Milton took up his pen as a pamphleteer, eloquently and audaciously arguing for religious, civil and political freedoms:

> *Whatever he wrote against Monarchie was out of no animosity to the King's person, or owt of any faction or interest, but out of a pure Zeale to the Liberty of Mankind, which he thought would be greater under a fre state than under a Monarchiall government. His being so conversant in Livy and the Roman authors, and the greatness he saw donne by the Roman commonwealth, and the vertue of their great Commanders induc't him to.*
> (John Aubrey, BRIEF LIVES, c 1693)

In 1649 Cromwell appointed Milton Secretary to the Council of State, to translate foreign correspondence and to publicise the views of the Commonwealth at home and abroad. The Restoration (1660) brought this chapter of his life to a depressing end. Now totally blind, he retired to live with his third wife and the three daughters of his first, unhappy marriage. With their help he finally embarked upon the epic poem he had always longed to write: PARADISE LOST was published in 1667 and PARADISE REGAINED in 1671. His last published poem, SAMSON AGONISTES, also appeared in 1671. Milton died in 1674.

TRIP THE LIGHT FANTASTIC
This idiom, now humorously used for 'to dance', was extracted in the nineteenth century from two lines in Milton's poem L'ALLEGRO (1632). The poet begins by invoking the goddess Mirth and urging her to enter dancing with her companion, Liberty:

> *Come, and trip it as ye go*
> *On the light fantastic toe;*

Milton's particular use of *fantastic* to describe the fanciful movements of the nymph's dance is quite singular and caught the imagination of later writers. The poet and critic Joseph Warton, who thought Milton sublime, wrote of *fantastic-footed Joy* (ON APPROACH OF SUMMER, c 1790). Disraeli was not so reverent. From him comes the jocular description of Mr St Ledger who *prided himself . . . on his light fantastic toe* (VIVIAN GREY, 1826).

EVERY CLOUD HAS A SILVER LINING

The first scene of Milton's masque COMUS (1634) is set in a wild wood. A virtuous lady is making a journey accompanied by her two brothers. They leave her to look for berries but fail to return and so, at nightfall, she finds herself lost and alone in the wood. As she summons Faith and Hope to accompany her and expresses confidence that the Supreme Good will guard her, she is rewarded by an encouraging sign:

Was I deceived, or did a sable cloud
Turn forth her silver lining on the night?
I did not err, there does a sable cloud
Turn forth her silver lining on the night,
And cast a gleam over this tufted grove.

The Lady's bright sign became a proverb of encouragement in the nineteenth century. Dickens turned his attention to it in BLEAK HOUSE (1852): *I turn my silver lining outward like Milton's cloud.* A little later Samuel Smiles, the industrious advocate of self-help, stiffened the resolve of his readership with the exhortation, *While we see the cloud, let us not shut our eyes to the silver lining* (CHARACTER, 1871), a lesson which was well learnt by Ellen Thorneycroft Fowler:

Though outwardly a gloomy shroud,
The inner half of every cloud
Is bright and shining:
I therefore turn my clouds about
And always wear them inside out
To show the lining.

(THE WISDOM OF FOLLY, c 1900, quoted in STEVENSON'S BOOK OF PROVERBS, MAXIMS AND FAMILIAR PHRASES, 1947)

SENSUOUS

Middle English had the word *sensual* (from Late Latin *sensuālis*, from Latin *sensus*, 'perception, feeling', from *sentīre*, 'to feel'). Its original meaning was 'belonging to or affecting the senses'. Soon, however, the term gained pejorative overtones when it was widely used to refer to base appetites: *He was gyuen to all sensuall luste of his body* (Robert Fabyan, THE CONCORDANCE OF CHRONICLES, 1516). In his pamphlets Milton had occasion to use the word in its strict sense. Wishing to present his argument precisely and avoid unhelpful connotations, he eschewed *sensual* in favour of *sensuous*, a word of his own coinage. The term first appeared in OF REFORMATION TOUCHING CHURCH DISCIPLINE (1641) and then in OF EDUCATION (1644). Milton's nice distinction did not catch on immediately, however. We owe its place in modern English to Coleridge who, in an essay on criticism published in 1814, wrote: *Thus, to express in one word what belongs to the senses, or the recipient and more passive faculty of the soul, I have reintroduced the word sensuous . . . used by Milton.*

Used correctly, *sensuous* has proved a fortunate coinage. In this article from THE INDEPENDENT (26 April 1999) the word is used effectively to describe the eye-catching and colourful GSW tower in Berlin, designed by British architects Sauerbruch and Hutton:

'Sensuous' is a word Louisa Hutton uses a lot to describe this interchange of ceramics with concrete and glass: this play upon rough with smooth, mirrored with polished, clear with opaque.

But, as is common with words which are similar to each other, *sensual* and *sensuous* are often confused and used interchangeably, particularly by writers for the popular market:

> . . . *Madonna, sensuous blonde hair flying, red lips pouting and silk dress clinging to her ample curves, had fashioned herself into Monroe's mirror image.*
> (DAILY MAIL, 19 July 1999)

. . . a tendency followed even by more careful authors:

> [*The eighteenth-century botanist Sir Joseph Banks was] full of the juices of life, standing six feet tall and weighing in at about 13 stone (182 pounds), with dark liquid eyes and a mouth that a romance novelist of today probably would describe as sensuous.*
> (T H Watkins, 'The Greening of the Empire: Sir Joseph Banks', in NATIONAL GEOGRAPHIC, November 1996)

Could it be that Milton's adjective is poised to become a mere synonym of *sensual*?

PANDEMONIUM

Satan makes his appearance in Book I of Milton's epic poem PARADISE LOST (1667). Awakening his host of fallen angels, Satan tells them the disturbing news circulating in Heaven that a new world is to be created. At *Pandaemonium*, his capital, Satan convenes a council to consider a course of action. Milton first describes *Pandaemonium* as *the high Capital of Satan and his Peers*, and then as the *citie and proud seate of Lucifer*. The poet fashioned the name from Greek *pan-*, 'all', and *daimōn*, 'spirit, demon' and it therefore means 'dwelling place of all the demons'.

Milton's epic was so much admired that by the mid-eighteenth century *Pandemonium* had become a synonym for 'hell' and by the end of that century represented more generally 'a place notorious for wickedness': *We found ourselves in that dreary pandaemonium, . . . a Gin-shop* (Bulwer Lytton, PELHAM, 1828).

The final shift in meaning took place in the second half of the nineteenth century,

when writers began to use *pandemonium* to describe the chaos and furore which commonly characterises such a disreputable gathering. Today *pandemonium* is applied to any scene of disarray, confusion or devastation:

> *Father Sheehan rushed to Belfast's Royal Victoria Hospital after the [Omagh] bombing and found pandemonium. Father Paul Byrne, the hospital chaplain, asked him to say the last rites for the dying.*
> (THE TIMES, 27 March 1999)

As for PARADISE LOST as a whole, although the epic undoubtedly influenced the work of later poets, some critics have judged it worthy but dull. Dr Johnson liked to have the last word:

> PARADISE LOST *is one of the books which the reader admires and lays down, and forgets to take up again. Its perusal is a duty rather than a pleasure.*
> (Samuel Johnson, THE LIVES OF THE ENGLISH POETS, 1779–81)

• English has drawn many other words and phrases from Milton's works, besides those described above. From his contemplative poem IL PENSEROSO (c 1631), for instance, comes the earliest mention of the familiar idiom *there's more to this than meets the eye* (meaning 'this has greater significance than is immediately apparent') – except that Milton alludes to the skill of great bards who have sung

> *Of forests, and enchantments drear, Where more is meant than meets the ear.*

The person moving to a new town or job who speaks of going to *pastures new* is quoting from the final optimistic line of LYCIDAS (1637), an elegy written upon the untimely death of his friend, Edward King, who was on board a ship which sank while crossing to Ireland. The little adjectival phrase *in the making*, 'in development, becoming realised', is also from Milton's pen and comes from his pamphlet AREOPAGITICA (1644): *Opinion in good men is but knowledge in the making.*

• Thomas Hobson (1544-1631) was a carrier who kept a livery stable at Cambridge. His customers were never permitted to choose their own horses but were obliged to hire Hobson's choice, which was always the animal which stood closest to the stable door. In this way Hobson was able to ensure that all his horses were fairly ridden and none was overworked. This system of hiring out horses has given English the idiom *Hobson's choice*, meaning 'no choice at all'. In the spring of 1630 plague broke out in Cambridge and the inhabitants were forbidden to travel. It was rumoured that enforced inactivity caused the carrier's death in January 1631. Milton was among the many students who wrote affectionate verse in his memory:

*Here lies old Hobson, Death hath broke
  his girt,
And here alas, hath laid him in the
  dirt . . .
'Twas such a shifter, that if truth were
  known,
Death was half glad when he had got him
  down . . .
But lately finding him so long at home,
And thinking now his journey's end was
  come,
And that he had ta'en up his latest inn,
In the kind office of a chamberlain
Show'd him his room where he must
  lodge that night,
Pull'd off his boots, and took away the
  light:
If any asked for him, it shall be said,
Hobson has supp'd, and's newly gone to
  bed.*

1609

HOLLAND BECOMES EFFECTIVELY INDEPENDENT FROM SPAIN

••••••

In the sixteenth century, the Netherlands became part of the vast Hapsburg empire and was ruled by Spain (see **1568**, page 131). During the Reformation the Calvinist population came into long and violent conflict with its Catholic rulers until, in 1609, Spain was finally forced to recognise the independence of the northern provinces (modern Holland).

The Reformation created a climate for new forms of artistic expression. Unlike the Catholic Church, which commissioned works of sacred art to adorn its buildings, the Protestant faith did not favour sacred representation. Since the mid-sixteenth century, therefore, Dutch artists had begun to identify popular taste and explore alternative subjects, such as scenes of daily life, portraits, still life and landscape. As the Dutch prospered, both at home and with their new colonies, newly created wealth was often spent on paintings.

Eventually, collecting art became a fashion bordering on obsession. In his diary for 13 August 1641, John Evelyn marvelled at it:

> *We arrived late at Rotterdam, where was their annual mart or fair, so furnished with pictures (especially landscapes and drolleries, as they call those clownish representations), that I was amazed. Some of these I bought, and sent into England . . . it is an ordinary thing to find a common farmer lay out two or three thousand pounds in this commodity. Their houses are full of them, and they vend them at their fairs to very great gains.*

Although this trend encouraged mediocre talent, it also provided for artists of genius. The eminence of the Dutch school is responsible for three English linguistic borrowings in the seventeenth century.

EASEL

Dutch artists used the word *ezel* to describe the wooden frame they used to hold a canvas while they were working on it. The term literally means 'donkey', the allusion being to a beast of burden carrying a load. The word was used in the same way that English later used *horse* to denote 'a supportive wooden frame' – in the compound *clothes-horse*, for example. *Easel* was borrowed into English in the first half of the seventeenth century.

ETCH

Although etching was known in the early sixteenth century, it became widespread in the seventeenth. To make an etching, a copper plate was coated with acid–resistant wax or resin. The drawing was scratched into the resin with a needle until the metal beneath showed through. The plate was then submerged in acid which corroded away the exposed copper lines, so that the design was 'eaten' into the metal. Prints could be made from the plate as soon as the resin ground had been cleaned off. Etching became a favourite technique of the Dutch master Rembrandt because it offered a greater range of tone than woodcut or engraving, the variation depending on how long any part of the design was exposed to the acid bath.

The English verb to *etch*, which dates from the 1630s, comes from Dutch *etsen*.

This was a borrowing of German *ätzen* which meant 'to etch, to corrode', but which was originally a causal verb meaning 'to feed, to make to eat'. *Ätzen* itself ultimately came from unattested prehistoric Germanic *atjan*, the causative of *etan*, 'to eat' (and source of the English verb *to eat*).

Etching to denote 'a copy from an etched plate' is an eighteenth-century derivative of the verb *to etch*.

LANDSCAPE

Dutch landscape painting had begun to emerge during the second half of the sixteenth century, but in the seventeenth century it developed and flourished. The Hague, Leiden and Haarlem were important centres for the genre, producing artists such as Jan van Goyen and Jacob van Ruisdael. The Dutch word for the genre was *landschap*, which originally meant 'province, tract of land'. English borrowed the word as a specialised painters' term for 'a picture depicting natural inland scenery':

> *There is a painting by Asher Brown Durand called KINDRED SPIRITS, which is often reproduced in books when the subject turns to the American landscape in the nineteenth century. . . Painted in 1849, it shows two men standing on a rock ledge in the Catskills in one of those sublime lost world settings that look as if they would take an*

expedition to reach. . . Below them, in a shadowy chasm, a stream dashes through a jumble of boulders. Beyond, glimpsed through a canopy of leaves, is a long view of gorgeously forbidding blue mountains. To right and left, jostling into frame, are disorderly ranks of trees which immediately vanish into consuming darkness
(Bill Bryson, A WALK IN THE WOODS, 1997)

Not until the first half of the eighteenth century was the word also applied to 'a view over the countryside':

Looking around her now, Morgana grieved at the bareness of the landscape. England had been stripped clean of woodland and forest. Only a few scrubby spinneys decorated the ridges. She wondered if Scotland and Wales had suffered the same deforestation, and hoped they were still tree-bearing lands.
(Garry Kilworth, A MIDSUMMER'S NIGHTMARE, 1996)

The Dutch spelling *landschap* was sometimes used in English texts throughout the seventeenth and eighteenth centuries, but the word had first appeared in English as *landskip* in the late 1590s. This corruption, which prevailed until the end of the nineteenth century, arose in part because Dutch *sch* is close in pronunciation to English *sk*. The modern English form *landscape,* which also reflects this pronunciation, dates from the early seventeenth century.

In the second half of the eighteenth century, *scape* began to appear as a back-formation of *landscape* to denote 'a view of scenery of any kind'. In a letter written in 1773, English clergyman and naturalist Gilbert White uses *scapes* when referring to views over Plumpton Plain, near Lewes in Sussex. Within a few years words such as *seascape, prison-scape* and *cloud-scape* began to appear. The late nineteenth century added *townscape* and the twentieth century *moonscape.*

1616

WILLIAM SHAKESPEARE DIES

······

The birth of William Shakespeare is traditionally celebrated on 23 April, although the only announcement of his arrival in the world is the record of his baptism at Stratford parish church on 26 April 1564. As the son of a glover, an established tradesman, he enjoyed a sound education, probably at the local grammar school. Although married at eighteen to a woman eight years his senior who bore him three children, Shakespeare spent much of his working life in London, away from his family in Stratford. It is not known how he became established in the theatre, but by 1592 he was already known as a playwright. According to John Aubrey in BRIEF LIVES (c 1693):

He began early to make essayes at Dramatique Poetry, which at that time was very lowe; and his Playes tooke well.

Shakespeare was also a skilful actor and, soon after 1594, became a leading member of the Lord Chamberlain's Men, a troupe of actors amongst whom he built his successful career. If the traditional date of his birth is correct, Shakespeare died on his fifty-second birthday, 23 April 1616. The monument to him at Holy Trinity, Stratford reads:

Reader for Jesus' Sake forbear
To dig the dust enclosed here:
Blessed be he
that spares these Stones,
And cursed be he
that moves my bones.

*The printing press, the spread of popular education and a vigorous spirit of enquiry were just some of the important factors that facilitated and promoted the use of European vernacular languages during the Renaissance. But, when compared with Latin and Greek, with their polished grammars and copious vocabularies, the vernacular languages seemed clumsy and impoverished. Those who wrote in English enriched their vocabulary by borrowing from Latin and Greek ('inkhorn' terms), by adopting foreign words encountered through travel or by reviving Old English words that had fallen into disuse ('chaucerisms') (see **1599**, page 139). Each method attracted its critics. Shakespeare's vocabulary store was immense, not only because he moulded or extended existing words (using the noun* petition *as a verb; coining* employer *from* employ; *attaching prefixes and suffixes to achieve economy of expression, as in* misquote, reword *and* marketable*), but because he readily and daringly employed hundreds of words which had only recently come into modern English, some of which make their first recorded appearance in his works. These include: from Latin and Greek* tranquil, obscene, critical, dire, meditate, vast, apostrophe *and* catastrophe; *from existing English stock* jaded, foregone *and* doom *(see **domesday**, page 30); and from the Romance languages* alligator, mutiny, pedant *(see also **barricade**, page 134 and **cavalier**, page 163 – this last used by Shakespeare in the sense of 'a spirited courtly gentleman who is trained at arms').*

An aspect of Shakespeare's genius was his knack of creating memorable phrases which have become idiomatic:

CRUEL TO BE KIND

The King of Denmark has died. Claudius, his brother, has succeeded him and has married his widow, Gertrude. The ghost of the old king appears to Hamlet, his son. He tells Hamlet that he was murdered by Claudius and charges him with avenging his death. Hamlet breaks the news of his uncle's treachery to Gertrude and pleads with her to withdraw her affection from Claudius, saying *I must be cruel only to be kind* (HAMLET, Act 3 scene iv, c 1601). *To be cruel to be kind* is now proverbial and means 'to do something which appears heartless in order to achieve the long-term good':

I know you'll think me hard and worldly, I'm only being cruel to be kind. Love can't live on five pounds a week. It would be criminal to put it to such a test. You do understand, don't you?
(W Somerset Maugham, THE BREAD WINNER, 1930)

NOT BUDGE AN INCH

THE TAMING OF THE SHREW (c 1592) opens with an altercation between an alehouse keeper and Christopher Sly, a tinker whose family *came in with Richard the Conqueror*. The hostess wants Sly to pay for the glasses he has broken and goes off to find the constable while Sly mutters, *I'll answer him by law. I'll not budge an inch; let him come, and kindly.*

The word *budge* was brand new to English in the 1590s, and Shakespeare used it in several of his plays. It was a borrowing of Old French *bouger*, 'to move from one's place, to disturb oneself'. This, in turn, came from the unattested Vulgar Latin *bullicāre*, 'to bubble up', a frequentative of Latin *bullīre*, 'to boil'. In English, *budge* (originally *bouge*) did not simply mean 'to move, to stir' but implied a certain stubbornness or standing firm. This implication is heavily underlined by the defiant Sly when he swears he'll not budge *an inch*. Idiomatic use of Sly's statement, in more figurative senses, began during the first half of the nineteenth century. Then during the first half of the twentieth century *budge* began to be used colloquially to mean 'to change one's mind', again with negative implications of stubbornness, and the idiom followed suit:

> *You're as obstinate as a mule . . . you don't intend to budge an inch, do you?*
> (Noël Coward, PRIVATE LIVES, 1930)

PAINT (GILD) THE LILY

Here once again we sit, once again crown'd, states King John with satisfaction (KING JOHN, Act 4, scene ii, c 1591). But, according to his barons, this was one coronation too many. Pembroke calls it *superfluous*, telling the King that he was *crowned before, and that high royalty was ne'er pluck'd off*, while Salisbury is poetically outspoken:

> *Therefore, to be possess'd with double pomp,*
> *To gild refined gold, to paint the lily,*
> *To throw a perfume on the violet,*
> *To smooth the ice, or add anothe hue*
> *Unto the rainbow . . .*
> *Is wasteful and ridiculous excess.*

Not until the early nineteenth century, however, was the phrase *to paint the lily* picked out as an idiom with the sense 'to

apply unnecessary ornamentation, to over-embellish'. But familiar texts are usually only half-remembered and before long, Shakespeare's charming figure was being misquoted as *to gild the lily*, an error that has now been completely absorbed into the language:

> *The end result [of the new-look BBC Six O'Clock News] is a triumph of elegance and simplicity over graphic design for graphic design's sake, Lambie-Nairn claims. 'We didn't want to over-gild the lily. And we had to ensure everything we did was in character . . .'*
> (DAILY EXPRESS, 11 May 1999)

TOO MUCH OF A GOOD THING

> *As a surfeit of the sweetest things*
> *The deepest loathing to the stomach brings.*
> A MIDSUMMER-NIGHT'S DREAM
> (c 1595)

In AS YOU LIKE IT (1599), fair Rosalind has been banished from court and now lives in the Forest of Arden disguised as a countryman. Here she meets up with Orlando, a young nobleman with whom she fell in love at court. Discovering her love to be reciprocated, Rosalind, still disguised, encourages Orlando to imagine that she is Rosalind and to woo her:

> ORLANDO: *And wilt thou have me?*
> ROSALIND: *Ay, and twenty such.*
> ORLANDO: *What sayest thou?*
> ROSALIND: *Are you not good?*
> ORLANDO: *I hope so.*
> ROSALIND: *Why then, can one desire too much of a good thing?*
> (Act 4, scene i)

It seems, in answer to Rosalind's question, that one can, for the phrase *too much of a good thing* has become idiomatic and is used in the negative sense of 'something enjoyable marred by excess' – long holidays that begin to drag, or one's favourite pudding for dinner every night, for example. Although its use is recorded from the early nineteenth century, the expression had probably been part of everyday speech much longer for, in 1809, Sydney Smith almost apologised for using what he classed as *a very colloquial phrase.*

Other Shakespearian idioms in modern use are expressions which already existed in Shakespeare's day but which the playwright reworded:

EVERY INCH (A KING)

In open countrsyide outside Dover, the Earl of Gloucester and his son Edgar come upon a madman *fantastically dressed with weeds.* The madman is none other than King Lear, whose wits have been turned by the callousness of his daughters. Lear rants and Gloucester, who has been blinded, recognises his voice:

> *The trick of that voice I do remember well. Is't not the King?*

to which Lear replies:

> *Ay, every inch a king. When I do stare, see how the subject quakes.*
> (KING LEAR, Act 4, scene vi, 1604–5)

Every inch, meaning 'every bit' has been idiomatic since the fifteenth century, and remains so in modern English (*every inch of him*). But this particular twist of Shakespeare's, combining the idiom with a title (modern English substitutes a state or profession), has become proverbial in its own right, having the sense of 'in every respect':

> *The portrait showed him as a handsome, conscientious-looking man in his late forties, every inch a company president.*
> (Christopher Isherwood, THE WORLD IN THE EVENING, 1954)

TO EAT OUT OF HOUSE AND HOME

The scene is a London street. Suddenly Mistress Quickly, the hostess of the Boar's Head Tavern, Eastcheap, appears accompanied by two officers. Mistress

Quickly has appealed for the arrest of Sir John Falstaff for debt, bewailing that *He hath eaten me out of house and home; he hath put all my substance into that fat belly of his* (SECOND PART OF KING HENRY IV, Act 2, scene i, 1597).

Shakespeare was, in fact, rewording a current expression, *to eat out of house and harbour* (*harbour* meaning 'shelter, abode'), which had been in use since at least the turn of the fifteenth century. Shakespeare's version won out. His SECOND PART OF KING HENRY IV dates from around 1597. Within three years the amended expression had been borrowed by another playwright, John Day, and by the second half of the seventeenth century was the acknowledged form: *They would eat me out of house and home, as the saying is* (Thomas Shadwell, THE SULLEN LOVERS, 1668).

THERE'S THE RUB

In the second half of the sixteenth century, *rub* was a bowling term. Bowlers, having loosed a bowl that rolled too quickly, might run after it crying *rub, rub, rub* in an attempt to influence its speed. A bowl was said *to rub* when its course was hindered or diverted by an obstacle, and *a rub* itself was 'an encumbrance' of some sort that prevented the bowl's sure flight. From around 1590 the noun began to be applied figuratively to 'an obstacle or problem of a non-material kind': *They are well inclined to marry, but one rub or other is ever in the way* (Robert Burton, THE ANATOMY OF MELANCHOLY, 1621). This new figurative sense was the one employed by Shakespeare in Act 3, scene i of HAMLET (1601), where the Prince, overcome by sorrows, considers suicide, but shrinks back in fearful contemplation of an unknown afterlife – and *there's the rub*:

> *. . . To die, to sleep;*
> *To sleep, perchance to dream. Ay, there's the rub;*
> *For in that sleep of death what dreams may come,*
> *When we have shuffled off this mortal coil,*
> *Must give us pause.*

The phrase has been quoted since the early eighteenth century and is now idiomatic, with the sense 'there's the drawback, there's the difficulty':

When the girl's family learned about the letters, they took immediate steps to retrieve them. But there was the rub. The man to whom they'd been written no longer had them. They had just been stolen from him.
(Ellery Queen, 'A Question of Honour' in QUEEN'S BUREAU OF INVESTIGATION, 1955)

IT'S GREEK TO ME

There are, in Rome, those who want to see ambitious Caesar crowned king and those who love freedom and oppose it. Cassius and Brutus, who are amongst the latter, noting Caesar's crestfallen appearance, ask Casca the reason for it. Casca tells how Caesar was offered a crown three times but three times refused, because the common crowd was hostile to it. Cassius presses Casca for every detail and Casca answers to the best of his ability:

CASSIUS: *Did Cicero say anything?*
CASCA: *Ay, he spoke in Greek.*
CASSIUS: *To what effect?*
CASCA: *Nay, an I tell you that, I'll ne'er look you i' th' face again. But those that understood him smil'd at one another, and shook their heads; but for mine own part, it was Greek to me.*
(JULIUS CAESAR, Act 1, scene ii, 1599)

The remark *it was Greek to me* is both a statement of fact and a comment on the intelligibility of what was said to a non-speaker. Casca's difficulty of not having Greek was a problem known in medieval times, when the language was not widely known and European scholars coming across Greek script would comment *Graecum est, non potest legi* (It is Greek, it cannot be read). This convention was early used by Italian Francesco Accursius who famously annotated the texts of Roman law in the first half of the thirteenth century. There was a renewed study of Greek in the Renaissance, to the extent that words began to be introduced direct from that source in the period, rather than following an indirect route via Latin or French. However, a continuing unease with Greek surfaced in English in a prose comedy which predated JULIUS CAESAR by some thirty-three years. George Gascoigne's SUPPOSES (1566) was a translation of I SUPPOSITI (1509) by Italian poet and playwright Ludovico Ariosto and contained the comment, *The gear is Greek to me.* Shakespeare certainly knew Gascoigne's play, for it was the inspiration for his own TAMING OF THE SHREW (c 1592). Shakespeare was probably also aware that the Greeks themselves had run into linguistic difficulties. They had found Hebrew a bit of a challenge and had the idiom *It's Hebrew to me* to denote 'unintelligible speech'. Thus there is probably more to Casca's witty comment *it was Greek to me* than is at first apparent.

Shakespeare's line was picked up by other writers almost immediately, the first being Thomas Dekker who, within a year of the first performance of JULIUS CAESAR, used *It's Greek to him* with the same double meaning in PATIENT GRISSIL (1600). In modern English *it's Greek to me* is used not only to denote 'unintelligible speech' or 'twaddle' but also 'incomprehensible concepts or ideas':

He had been teaching Greek for half a century; yet it was Greek to him that art has been the greatest factor in raising mankind from its old savage state.
(John Galsworthy, CASTLES IN SPAIN, 1927)

TOWER OF STRENGTH

On the eve of the Battle of Bosworth, Richard III prepares to face Henry Tudor, Earl of Richmond, who is challenging him for the crown. Richard is encouraged to learn that the enemy numbers just six or seven thousand; his forces are treble that number and, what is more, they are inspired by the institution they serve:

Besides, the King's name is a tower of
   strength,
Which they upon the adverse faction want.
(RICHARD III, Act 3, scene iii, 1591)

In January 1549, the Church of England had received its first prayer book. The book, composed by Archbishop Cranmer, was written in glorious English prose and was intended for use in worship by every Englishman. In the Bible, God and his name are often compared to a strong tower (*The name of the Lord is a strong tower*, Proverbs 18:10) and Cranmer used this biblical figure in his Book of Common Prayer, where, in the Solemnisation of Matrimony, we find the supplication *O lorde . . . Bee unto them a tower of strength*. Although Mary Tudor abolished all Protestant reform and reimposed Catholicism, the prayer book was restored by her successor, Elizabeth I. The offices of the prayer book would have been familiar to Shakespeare, who transferred the figure *a tower of strength* from the Lord's name to that of the sovereign in RICHARD III. In 1852 Tennyson applied the phrase to the Duke of Wellington in an ode written on the Duke's death. After this, the expression was in frequent idiomatic use to denote 'a strong, reliable person':

> *The night-nurse was immensely capable and she never failed in an emergency. The dressers, often inexperienced or nervous, found her a tower of strength.*
> (W S Maugham, OF HUMAN BONDAGE, 1915)

(See also **at one fell swoop**, page 91, **pride of place**, page 91 and **green**, page 253.)

1622

POPE GREGORY XV SETS UP THE SACRED CONGREGATION FOR THE PROPAGATION OF THE FAITH

······

The exploration and colonisation of hitherto unknown lands in the sixteenth century challenged the Roman Catholic Church to make the true faith known to indigenous peoples. From the end of the fifteenth and through the sixteenth centuries, this was done by patronage, whereby the Pope entrusted the Catholic crowns of Spain and Portugal with the responsibility for converting native peoples to Christianity, organising dioceses in the colonies and selecting priests to serve in them. In the seventeenth century it was felt that this sacred commission was not always being adequately fulfilled. In 1622 Pope Gregory XV established the *Sacra Congregatio de Propaganda Fide* to remedy matters. This small body of cardinals was charged with all the missionary responsibilities formerly assigned to patronage and with the defence of the Catholic faith in regions prey to heretics.

PROPAGANDA

The modern Latin title *Sacra Congregatio de Propaganda Fide*, 'Sacred Congregation for Propagating the Faith', was soon reduced to the more manageable *propaganda*. The word itself has its roots in horticulture, being the feminine gerundive of the Latin verb *prōpāgāre*, 'to propagate'. (The English verb *to propagate* obviously comes from the same source.) Plants are propagated by means of slips or layers, and this is evident in the origins of *prōpāgāre* which comes from *prōpāgo*, meaning 'shoot, slip' and more specifically 'layer of a vine'. This in turn derives from *prō-*, 'forth,' and *pāg-*, root of *pangere*, 'to fasten', and hence 'to peg down (vine) layers for increase'.

It took very nearly a century after the establishment of the Sacred Congregation before *propaganda* appeared in English, rather than Latin, referring to the Catholic organisation and its work. By the end of the eighteenth century, however, the name *propaganda* was being applied to 'a society or movement of any firm persuasion which makes a concerted effort to spread its particular doctrine'. Since such organisations tended to be subversive, the term became a disparaging one. The following definition is supplied by William Brande in his DICTIONARY OF SCIENCE, LITERATURE AND ART (1842):

> *Derived from this celebrated society [the Congregatio de Propaganda Fide] the name propaganda is applied in modern political language as a term of reproach to secret associations for the spread of opinions and principles which are viewed by most governments with horror and aversion.*

By the early 1900s *propaganda* had come to mean 'a systematic programme of information intended to disseminate or discredit a doctrine or cause'. Before long the term could denote not only the systematic programme, but the means of delivery (such as a *propaganda leaflet*) and the ideas themselves that it contains:

> *White propaganda, the truth; gray, a composition of half-truths and distortions; or black, a pack of lies.*
> (A J Russell, POUR HEMLOCK, 1976)

In BRAVE NEW WORLD REVISITED (1958), Aldous Huxley makes this nice distinction between philosophy and the workings of *propaganda*:

> *Philosophy teaches us to feel uncertain about the things that seem to us self-evident. Propaganda, on the other hand, teaches us to accept as self-evident matters about which it would be reasonable to suspend our judgement.*

So ubiquitous is propaganda today that it has spawned a host of phrases: *propaganda machine, campaign, chief, poster, war* and many others.

MISSIONARY

In 1627, on the recommendation of the newly formed *Propaganda*, Pope Urban VIII founded a training college for missionary candidates, with a view to improving the quality of overseas mission. According to J A De Jong, writing in THE HISTORY OF CHRISTIANITY (1977), the initiative came in response to an enquiry into patronage which listed amongst its criticisms the ill-treatment of indigenous peoples, competition between religious orders and a tendency to press for political advantage to the detriment of the gospel. The zealous overhaul given to Catholic overseas evangelisation in the seventeenth century was responsible for *missionary*.

The word *mission* came into English at the very end of the sixteenth century. It probably arrived by way of French *mission*, which, in turn, came from Latin *missiō*, 'a sending', from *mittere* (stem *miss-*), 'to send, to let go'. Although it initially meant 'a sending' in general, *mission* was most often applied to the 'sending' of a person to perform a particular service. It was early used, for instance, for the 'sending' of Jesuit priests abroad. By the 1620s the word had continued its secular and religious development and might refer to 'a foreign delegation or embassy' or to 'a group of people sent overseas to convert the heathen'.

Missionary is a deriviative of *mission* and appeared in English around the mid-seventeenth century. In 1656 it was included in Thomas Blount's GLOSSOGRAPHIA, a dictionary of difficult or new words, where it was defined as: *persons sent; commonly spoken of Priests sent to unbeleeving Countries to convert the people to Christian Faith.* In the eighteenth century, Ephraim Chambers noted in his CYCLOPAEDIA (1728) that *The Romanists reproach the Protestants, that their ministers have no mission.* This was not, in fact, true but Protestant evangelisation was initially tied up with the trading companies and military expansion in the colonies, and was not as centralised as the Catholic effort. As the evangelistic fervour grew in the 'Great Awakening' of the early 1740s in America and in the wider Protestant revival in the second half of the century, so the term *missionary* spread beyond its earlier Catholic contexts.

Although *missionary* was used from the late seventeenth to the early nineteenth centuries to denote 'an envoy on a political mission', this use was sporadic and has not survived. *Mission*, however, has continued to develop. Its use for 'a commission, the business upon which an envoy is sent' dates from the 1670s. This sense was extended in the first half of the

twentieth century, by way of American English, to refer to 'a military assignment' and, by the same route, is also used to denote 'the expedition of a spacecraft'. *Mission* to mean 'a calling, a vocation' dates from the turn of the nineteenth century.

• Latin *mittere* is also evident in a number of other English words, amongst them *admit (admission), commit, dismiss, emit, omit, submit, transmit:*

mass (Old English): from Latin *missa*, 'dismissal'. Possibly an allusion to the words of dismissal at the conclusion of the service, *Ite, missa est.*

mess (12th century): in Late Latin *mittere* not only meant 'to send' but also 'to put'. Hence the Late Latin noun *missus* (past participle of *mittere*), 'placement, course of a meal'. This was borrowed into Old French as *mes*, 'a serving, a course', and then directly into Middle English. In the fifteenth century *mess* also denoted 'liquid food, pap', and in the nineteenth century 'a mixture', hence *to be in a mess* and *to make a mess of.*

message (13th century): from Old French, from Vulgar Latin *missāticum*, 'a sent' communication'.

missile (17th century): from Latin *missilis*, 'missile weapon', literally 'capable of being sent' (from Latin *missus*, past participle of *mittere*, 'to send', and *-ilis*, 'capable of').

1627

ENGLISH COLONISTS ESTABLISH A SETTLEMENT ON BARBADOS

......

The earliest European visitors to the small island of Barbados may have been the Spaniards in search of slave labour in the sixteenth century. They stripped the island of its native population but did not stay. Then in 1625 an English ship returning home from the Caribbean happened upon Barbados, which was uninhabited, and annexed it to the Crown. Settlement of the island began two years later. The colony's future was uncertain for a number of years while proprietorial rights were disputed back in England. Once these were established, the colonists sought to make their fortune, abandoning the cultivation of tobacco and cotton and turning the land over to sugar cane instead around 1640.

RUM, GROG, GROGGY

There was heavy demand for sugar in seventeenth-century Europe where the commodity was in short supply (see **sugar**, page 61). Europeans began to take sugar cane cuttings to the Americas and the West Indies where the crops thrived in the humid tropical climate and fertile soil. Barbados came to sugar production early and fortunes were made on her plantations.

When sugar is produced, a residue known as molasses remains. Rather than let this syrup go to waste, someone back in the seventeenth century had a go at distilling it. The result was rum. The liquor was certainly known on Barbados by 1650, just a few years after sugar cane cultivation was introduced to the island, and probably originated there. The fiery spirit was popularly called *kill devil*. It was certainly much stronger than brandy and was described in one contemporary account as *a hott, hellish and terrible liquor* (DESCRIPTION OF BARBADOS, c 1651). The etymology of the word *rum*, however, is obscure. It may be a shortened form of *rumbullion* or *rumbustion*, but the origin of these terms is equally mysterious. A Devonshire dialect used *rumbullion* to denote 'a great uproar', which is certainly the effect a few glasses of the spirit would produce in a company, but there is no telling evidence of a link. From English the word *rum* soon passed into other European and Scandinavian languages. (For the history and etymology of other distilled spirits, see **gin**, page 173).

Rum was much enjoyed during the eighteenth century when it was often mixed with sugar, water and nutmeg to make a liquor called *bumboo* or *bumbo*. An entry in the diary of Thomas Turner, a shopkeeper from East Hoathly, describes a regular intoxicating evening in the Sussex village:

We smoked a pipe or two and then went down to Jones's where we drank one bowl of punch and two mugs of bumboo . . . I spent 12d and came home again in liquor.
(28 March 1756)

Tampering with the fiery liquor was not always acceptable, however. In the eighteenth century, British sailors were permitted a daily allowance of rum, a privilege which persisted until 1970. In 1740 Admiral Edward Vernon issued the order that the sailors' rum should be diluted with water to prevent drunkenness. The admiral habitually wore a cloak made of *grogram* (corruption of French *grosgrain*, 'coarse grain'), a stiffened fabric woven from silk, mohair or wool, or a mix of these, and named after its coarse texture. This garment earned Vernon the nickname *Old Grog*. Following his unpopular order, the name *grog* was transferred to the sailors' rum and water mixture. The following ditty was penned by a Mr Trotter on board the *Berwick* in 1781:

A mighty bowl on deck he drew,
And filled it to the brink;
Such drank the Burford's gallant crew,
And such the gods shall drink,
The sacred robe which Vernon wore
Was drenched with the same;
And hence his virtues guard our shore,
And grog derives its name.

A sailor who managed to get drunk despite the water content in his tipple was described as *groggy*. In an issue of the

GENTLEMAN'S MAGAZINE for 1770, *groggy* was twenty-fifth in a list entitled *Eighty names for having drunk too much*. In the first half of the nineteenth century, the adjective was taken up by farriers to describe a horse which tottered drunkenly because of an infirmity in its forelegs. This use was soon extended to rheumatic human beings and to those who, having come out badly in a fight, staggered about as if intoxicated or infirm. In present-day English the word has now broadened out to mean 'dazed' or 'semi-conscious', from taking drugs, for instance, or on awakening from deep sleep.

PINEAPPLE

Pineapple is a compound word whose etymological sense is 'edible fruit of the pine tree'. In the fourteenth century, *pineapple* denoted 'a pine cone'. The word is made up of *pine* (from Old English *pin* and Old French *pin*, from Latin *pīnus*, 'pine tree') and *apple* (from Old English *æppel*). In past centuries the word *apple* not only referred specifically to an 'apple' but was also widely applied to various other fruit and some vegetables. It appears as the second element of *pineapple* because pine cones contain edible kernels whose pungent taste added spice to early recipes. Sometimes *pineapple* denoted the pine nuts themselves rather than the whole cone.

When the Spanish explored the West Indies and South America, they found an abundance of a delicious but unfamiliar fruit which they dubbed *piña*, 'pine cone', because its appearance put them in mind of the fir cones back home. (Columbus was apparently the first European to taste pineapple while on Guadeloupe in 1493.)

English travellers to the region in the sixteenth century borrowed the Spanish term, transcribing it as *pina* or *pinna*. Raleigh, for instance, found *great abundance of Pinas* in Guiana, and he extolled them as *the princesse of fruits that grow under the sun* (DISCOVERIE OF GUIANA, 1596). However, it was not until the second half of the seventeenth century, about the time that the first pineapples were brought to England, that English adopted or translated the Spanish analogy and began to refer to the fruit as either *pine* or *pineapple*. According to John Evelyn's diary, these first pineapples were a gift for Cromwell in 1657. The Protector must have been pleased with the presentation for, after the Civil War (see **1642**, page 163), he had been concerned to keep a firm hold on the colonies that were so vital to English trade and prosperity. Nevertheless, Royalist emigration to Barbados following the Puritan victory in the wars ensured a Restoration welcome for Charles II on the island, and what was good enough for Cromwell was good enough for Charles. John Evelyn's diary records how, on 9 August 1661, His Majesty was ceremoniously presented with *the famous Queen Pine brought from Barbadoes*.

During the eighteenth century the pineapple was cultivated under glass as a curiosity. According to Bernard de Mandeville's commentary on his FABLE OF THE BEES (1714), *the first ananas, or pine-apple, that was brought to perfection in England, grew in [Sir M Decker's garden] at Richmond*. Not until the second half of the nineteenth century were ships able to bring cargoes of the fruit to Britain in reasonable condition.

1642

THE FIRST BATTLE IN THE ENGLISH CIVIL WAR IS FOUGHT

······

Charles I was a refined, courteous man but one who remained aloof from his subjects. Wedded to an unshakable belief that he ruled by divine right, he led by example, seeing little need to explain himself to a parliament he mistrusted and misunderstood. Costly wars with France and Spain put him under growing financial pressure which, to parliament's displeasure, he sought to ease through forced loans and arbitrary taxation. Furthermore, Charles's fervent attempts to impose Anglicanism on the country put him at odds with the Puritan majority in the House of Commons. Between June 1625 and March 1629 the King had dissolved no fewer than four assemblies and for the following eleven years ruled personally without calling a parliament at all.

Ever a devout Anglican, in 1637 Charles sought to impose the liturgy upon his Scottish subjects. Presbyterian resistance resulted in two wars obliging the bankrupt and defeated crown to call on parliament yet again. The Long Parliament, which met in November 1640, was determined to re-establish parliamentary authority. The king's two chief ministers were impeached and executed while Charles himself was forced to agree to bills prohibiting the methods of government and taxation he had employed over the past eleven years and declaring that Parliament could only be dissolved with its own agreement.

Charles was visiting Scotland in August 1641 when news broke of a rebellion in Ireland. Parliamentary leaders, anxious that any army raised to quash it should not be used against them, tried to wrest military command from the king's control by means of a militia bill. Charles, fearing Parliament's next target would be his Catholic queen, appeared in the House of Commons with 400 armed men and tried to arrest five of its prominent members. The attempt failed. Charles fled to the north to raise support and civil war broke out in October 1642.

CAVALIER

During the Civil War members of the Parliamentary party came to be referred to as *Roundheads*. The name, initially one of ridicule, was a reference to the custom Puritan men had of wearing their hair cut close. Its origin is disputed. In his HISTORICAL COLLECTIONS OF PRIVATE PASSAGES OF STATE (1692), John Rushworth claims that during a particularly riotous parliamentary exchange in December 1641, a demobilised army officer, David Hide, swinging his sword aloft, threatened to *cut the Throat of those Round-headed Dogs that bawled against Bishops*. But another seventeenth-century writer, Richard Baxter, says that the term arose from an innocent question posed by Queen Henrietta Maria at the trial of chief minister Thomas Wentworth in the spring of 1641. Pointing out the Parliamentary leader John Pym, the queen asked the identity of the roundheaded man. Whatever the origin of the name *Roundhead*, its date, 1641, is undisputed.

Sneering and ridicule are, of course, characteristics of all good rows and the Puritans were not above a spot of name-calling themselves. How they despised the flamboyant appearance of their opponents with their long curling locks and lace collars and cuffs. By 1641 the Parliamentary party had taken to calling the Royalists *Cavaliers*. The word was a relatively new borrowing which had come into English in the late sixteenth century. It originated in Latin *caballus*, 'horse', from which Late Latin derived *caballārius* to denote 'a horseman' (see **cavalry** in **chivalry, chivalrous,** page 40). In Italian this became *cavaliere*, 'a knight', and from there was borrowed into French as *cavalier* in the sixteenth century. When English first acquired the term it possessed all the associations of honour and gallantry expected of a gentleman accomplished in arms and horsemanship. Within a few years, *cavalier* began to be used pejoratively to denote 'a swaggering, blustering fellow'. The Puritans seized the term and applied it to those on the king's side who, full of bravado, clamoured for war. The astrologer William Lilly had this to say about the situation at Christmas 1641:

The Courtiers againe, wearing long Haire and locks, and always Sworded, at last were called by these men [the Puritans] Cavaliers; and so after this broken language had been used a while, all that adhered unto the Parlament were termed Round-heads; all

that tooke part or appeared for his Majestie, Cavaliers, few of the vulgar knowing the sence of the word Cavalier.
(MONARCHY OR NO MONARCHY IN ENGLAND, 1651)

The Roundheads' pejorative use of the term *cavalier* has left a legacy in contemporary English. The word began to be used as an adjective meaning 'haughty, offhand' just after the middle of the seventeenth century, which is its meaning today. Its senses now extend to 'casual, careless':

On her visits, Aunt Ursula can disapprove of me and my mother at one fell swoop, since we share not only a house but a disgracefully cavalier attitude towards housework.
(Sue Limb, OUT ON A LIMB, 1992)

On the other hand, *Roundhead* is purely a historical term. The Cavaliers were more successful linguistically in deriding the Puritans, in that from about 1600 *puritan* and *puritanical* were increasingly used disparagingly, and still are.

KEEP YOUR POWDER DRY
The first battle of the Civil War took place at Edgehill on 23 October 1642. On the side of the Parliamentarians was a troop of cavalry from Huntingdon, Cambridge, whose Puritan captain, Oliver Cromwell, was to emerge as an outstanding military leader. Cromwell recognised that religious fervour and good discipline produced soldiers zealous for victory. These principles of faith and practicality are evident in this famous exhortation to his regiment as it crossed a stream before engaging the Royalists at Edgehill: *Put your trust in God, my boys, and keep your powder dry*. Nowadays *keep your powder dry* is idiomatic and means 'be fully prepared for prompt action, wait for the best moment to take decisive action', and has become an expression favoured by financial advisers publishing on the Internet:

Be prepared for a long haul and keep your powder dry. Don't ramp up your business

operations in anticipation of a financing.
(Dean Dexter, 'Entrepreneurship: The
Complete Small Business', in NEW
HAMPSHIRE ONLINE EDITIONS, 1996)

*Leave your current [investment] positions
but don't add to them. In other words,
keep your powder dry to buy if and when
there is a down turn.*
(SGT. SHERMAN'S BOOK OF TALES,
1998)

Politicians thinking of running for the
Presidency also like to keep their options
open:

*By late 1997, Rove was in steady contact
with operatives in key states, asking veterans
whom to call, whom to meet, how to make
approaches and what they were hearing. His
line to them was the same: 'Keep your
powder dry.' It was too early to ask for
commitment, but with those four words, the
Bush team froze dozens of fund raisers and
organizers in place so no other candidate
could win them over.*
(TIME, 21 June 1999)

PLUNDER
The Thirty Years' War (1618-48) was a
bitter political and religious struggle of
German origin that eventually involved
most of the countries of western Europe.
Although intermittent, battles were fierce
and besieged towns were often pillaged
and their inhabitants massacred. The
German verb *plündern*, 'to loot', was in
common use throughout the war.
Plündern was a derivation of the noun
plunder which referred to 'lumber,
household bits and pieces'. The verb,
therefore, literally meant 'to rob a
household of absolutely everything, its
worthless articles included'. In 1630 the
Swedish King Gustavus Adolphus joined
the conflict in an effort to lend aid to the
German Protestant princes while securing
Swedish interests in the Baltic. English
soldiers who joined the Swedish forces
picked up the word *plündern* as *plunder* and
the term became current in English
accounts of the war. A report in the

SWEDISH INTELLIGENCER (1632) notes
how *the Swedish Dragoones . . . plundered
the Townes of Wurtbach and Waldsee, neere
unto Weingarten.*

It was, however, the outbreak of the
Civil War in England and, in particular,
the conduct of the Royalist troops, which
made the new term commonplace. As
early as November 1642 complaint was
made against the king's army who *after they
had possessed themselves of [Braintford] . . .
plundered it without any respect of persons.*
William Prynne was swift to condemn *all
violence, plunder, rapine, and disorders in
Souldiers.* He praised the restraint and
discipline of the Parliamentarians who
*never yet approved the plundering (or in plain
English, robbing) of any man, by any of their
forces, they having plundered no places taken by
assault,* whereas the Royalists had *miserably
plundered all the Kingdom almost* (THE
SOVERAIGNE POWER OF PARLIAMENTS,
1643). Prynne could be accused of a
certain bias. He was, after all, a well-
known Puritan pamphleteer – but a
courageous one, having before the war
been fined, imprisoned, branded and
deprived of both ears for his
outspokenness. Accusations were levelled
against the troops led by the dashing and
brilliant Prince Rupert in particular. *Many
Townes and Villages he plundered,* wrote
Parliamentarian Thomas May, in
HISTORY OF THE LONG PARLIAMENT,
1647, going on to define *plundered* as
robbed and adding *at that time first was the
word plunder used in England, being borne in
Germany.*

WARTS AND ALL
As the Civil War progressed, so did the
military and political stature of Oliver
Cromwell. After the war Cromwell was
amongst those who signed the king's
death warrant in 1649. He was responsible
for the subsequent creation of the
Commonwealth and became Lord
Protector in 1653.

Oliver Cromwell was by no means as
fanatical or dour as different portraits of
him might suggest. He was, by nature,
forceful and decisive but not vindictive or

intolerant. His Christian faith inspired his discipline and sense of duty. He was a loving family man who enjoyed hunting, music, a glass of sherry, a pipe of tobacco, the company of friends and family, and practical jokes – at the marriage of one of his daughters he is said to have smeared the chairs of certain respected guests with something sticky. And Cromwell was certainly not vain. He had brown hair, greenish eyes, a large and very red nose set off by a ruddy complexion, and a number of blemishes. Indeed, it is these imperfections that gave rise to the modern expression *warts and all* which is commonly used to mean 'without attempting to conceal flaws and defects'. During the Commonwealth, the well-known painter, Peter Lely, was invited to paint a portrait of Cromwell. This is how Horace Walpole, writing just over a hundred years later, reported Cromwell's instructions to the artist:

> *Mr Lely, I desire you would use all your skill to paint my picture truly like me, and not flatter me at all; but remark all these roughnesses, pimples, warts and everything as you see me, otherwise I will never pay a farthing for it.*
> (ANECDOTES OF PAINTING IN ENGLAND, 1762)

Lely was true to his commission. He painted Cromwell with puritanical severity, *warts and all*.

c 1662

SKATING BECOMES POPULAR IN ENGLAND

• • • • • •

Skating in northern Europe began in an age when winter's grip was icy and the canals, lakes and rivers froze hard. During the Middle Ages the people of the Netherlands made the most of bitter winters by skating upon the canals, a pastime which was sometimes copied by Londoners. Stow's SURVAY OF LONDON (1598) carries the following account:

> *When the great fenne or moore (which watereth the walles of the citie on the north side) is frozen, many young men play upon the yce: – some stryding as wide as they may, doe slide swiftly, some tye bones to their feete, and under their heeles, and shoving themselves by a little picked staffe doe slide as swiftly as a birde flyeth in the air, or an arrow out of a crosse-bow.*

This is by no means the earliest description. William FitzStephen, writing in the late twelfth century, also made mention of the activity, but it was not until the arrival of a new style of skate from Holland, around 1662, that ice-skating started to become a popular sport.

SKATE

Skating on blunt blades made from animal shinbones persisted in the Netherlands until towards the middle of the seventeenth century, when steel blades were introduced. These were fixed to a wooden sole and secured to the wearer's boots with straps and a screw. The skates, which afforded swifter and more stylish progress, were introduced into England in the early 1660s. Two celebrated diarists of the time, Samuel Pepys and John Evelyn, both happened to pass through St James's Park on 1 December 1662. There, on the canal, a number of gentlemen with skates were performing *after the manner of the Hollanders*, entertaining the royal family with a demonstration of the new sport. *I first in my life*, wrote Pepys, *did see people sliding with their skeates*, adding that he thought it *a very pretty art*. Evelyn, too, was impressed, remarking upon *the strange and wonderful dexterity of the sliders* and going on to exclaim *with what swiftness they pass, how suddenly they stop in full career upon the ice*.

And so, in the 1660s, *skate* was borrowed into English from Dutch. It is not by origin a Dutch word, however, but goes back to the unattested Frankish *skakkja*, 'shank', from unattested *skakan*, 'to run swiftly'. In Old French this became *eschasse* and denoted 'a stilt'. *Eschasse* was modified to *escase* in Old Northern French and this dialect form was then borrowed into both English and Middle Dutch. In sixteenth-century English it became *scatch*, 'stilt', but is now no longer used. In Middle Dutch it became *schaetse* and its meaning mysteriously changed from 'stilt' to 'skate'. Although it is impossible to account for this shift in sense with any

certainty, the nineteenth-century etymologist H Wedgwood offers the comment that both stilts and skates are contrivances for lengthening the stride. Middle Dutch *schaetse* evolved into modern Dutch *schaats*, 'a skate', with *schaatsen* as its plural form. However, when *schaats* was borrowed into English as *scates* in the 1660s the final *s* was immediately misunderstood to be a plural ending, the error being compounded by the fact that skates necessarily come in pairs. Thus a singular was formed by simply lopping off the final *s*.

• Over the next two centuries, skating was enjoyed more and more both in Europe and North America, where it was introduced in the 1740s by British soldiers. Its popularity increased during the nineteenth century, when skate design was considerably improved. These common idioms date from the late nineteenth and early twentieth centuries:

To get one's skates on (19th century): 'to hurry along'. Originally a military expression.

To skate on thin ice (19th century): 'to behave rashly'. Foolhardy behaviour on thin ice was not uncommon as this snippet from the YORK COURANT for 5 January 1748 shows:

It is estimated that no less than a dozen persons have lost their lives this last week, by unadvisedly skating upon thin ice, which broke and drowned them: whereof five expired at one time, within the sight of some fifty spectators in St James's Park.

To skate over or *round a subject* (20th century): 'to avoid mentioning a sensitive or difficult subject'.

1685

THE EDICT OF NANTES IS REVOKED

••••••

The Edict of Nantes of 1598 brought the French Wars of Religion to an end by granting the Huguenots certain important political and religious freedoms (see **1588**, page 134). Under Henry IV the Huguenots had prospered but Henry's successors, who wanted an absolute monarchy, felt threatened by Huguenot power and a new wave of persecution began. In 1629, following a dangerous Huguenot revolt, Cardinal de Richelieu declared void the political clauses of the edict. Fifty-six years later, during the reign of Louis XIV, the edict was revoked altogether. Cruel persecution ensued. John Evelyn, upon hearing the news, gave vent to his anger through the pages of his diary:

The French tyrant [Louis XIV] *abrogated the Edict of Nantes . . .*
without any cause; on a sudden demolishing all their [Huguenot]
churches, banishing, imprisoning, and sending to the galleys all the
ministers; plundering the common people, and exposing them to all sorts
of barbarous usage by soldiers sent to ruin and prey on them; taking away
their children; forcing people to the Mass, and then executing them as
relapsers; they burned their libraries, pillaged their goods, eat up their
fields and substance, banished or sent the people to the galleys, and seized
on their estates.
(3 November 1685)

REFUGEE

Following the Revocation of the Edict of Nantes in 1685 and the ensuing persecution, hundreds of thousands of Huguenots fled France and sought refuge in sympathetic Protestant countries. Switzerland, Germany, Denmark, the Netherlands and the American colonies accepted them. Many also came to England where, to John Evelyn's shame, *they found least encouragement* while *great collections were made for them in foreign places, more hospitable and Christian to appearance* (3 November 1685).

The term *refugee* in English dates from this great exodus of Huguenots from France. It is a borrowing of French *réfugié* which is the past participle of *réfugier*, 'to take shelter'. Indeed, the earliest English spelling was *refugie* but, within a year or two, it had been anglicised to *refugee* and this form was soon prevalent. In his diary for 24 April 1687, Evelyn, a staunch Anglican, records how *at Greenwich, at the conclusion of the Church-service, there was a French sermon preached . . . to a congregation of about 100 French Refugees*. The verb *réfugier* was derived from *refuge*, an Old French noun meaning 'refuge, shelter' (source of English *refuge* in the fourteenth century). *Refuge*, in turn, came from Latin *refugium*, a derivative of *refugere*, 'to flee back', which was formed from re-, 'back', and fugere, 'to flee'. Until the second half of the eighteenth century, refugee almost always denoted a Huguenot. However, in 1783, when the North American colonies gained their independence from Britain by the Treaty of Paris, the term was applied to loyalists who fled America in large numbers to settle in Canada. This liberated the word for future application to any person who flees to another country to avoid political or religious persecution.

1707

THE SECRET FORMULA FOR THE MANUFACTURE OF PORCELAIN IS DISCOVERED

······

During the fourteenth century, examples of Chinese porcelain began to find their way into Europe where their whiteness and fine translucent appearance was much admired. In 1557 the Portuguese established a regular trade route with China based on Macao and began to import eastern luxuries. Porcelain was eagerly sought after in Europe; individual pieces were treasured like jewels, carefully mounted and displayed. Since the import of porcelain was costly and its manufacture a Chinese secret, Europeans experimented to discover the formula. In Florence in 1575 the Medici factory succeeded in producing a soft-paste porcelain from white clay and glass frit, but the process was beset by problems. More successful soft-paste wares were produced in France in the late seventeenth century but, in spite of the best efforts of skilled European potters, the secret for making true porcelain was not discovered until the early eighteenth century.

Johann Böttger and Ehrenfried von Tschirnhaus, working under the patronage of Augustus II, Elector of Saxony and King of Poland, hit upon the formula in about 1707 after a deposit of clay similar to Chinese kaolin was found in Saxony. A royal porcelain factory was subsequently set up at Meissen near Dresden in 1710. The discovery spawned a breed of men known as arcanists (from Latin arcanum, 'secret'), who set out to sell the formula to other European royal houses and Böttger himself was detained by Augustus to protect the discovery

PORCELAIN, CHINA
Italian had the word porcellana to denote 'a cowrie shell' ('Venus shell'). The term was curiously derived from porcella which meant 'little sow', being a diminutive of porca, 'sow', from Latin porcus, 'pig'. Apparently, in the fertile imaginations of the medieval Italians, the shape of the

shell's orifice was reminiscent of a sow's vulva. The word occurs in IL MILIONE (1298), Marco Polo's late thirteenth-century account of his seventeen-year sojourn in Asia. In the work he likened the lustrous sheen of some earthenware he had seen to the glossy shell, describing it as *alla porcella*, 'in the style of a cowrie shell'. IL MILIONE was written in Franco-Italian, a strange compound language that was in vogue during the thirteenth and fourteenth centuries, and through this popular work the term *porcellana* was taken into Old French as *porcelaine*, 'cowrie shell'.

When fine Chinese earthenware began to find its way into Europe, the Italians accordingly called it *porcellana*. The meaning of the existing French word *porcelaine*, 'cowrie shell', was similarly extended and the term was also borrowed into a number of other European and Scandinavian languages, coming into English by way of French in the sixteenth century.

Porcelain is not the only word in English for this type of translucent, resonant earthenware: there is also *china*. In the seventeenth century, *chinaware* literally meant 'earthenware from China'. Before long the term was shortened to *china* and then gradually became synonymous with *porcelain,* indicating the name of the material irrespective of its country of origin. This was hastened probably by the influence of a Persian term widespread in the East: *chīnī*, 'porcelain'. This expression, probably picked up by merchants in India, was known in seventeenth-century England, and may also account for the wide variety of spellings for *china* that were common at the time: *chiney, chany, cheenie,* etc.

• The secret ingredient in porcelain is *kaolin*. This is a pure white clay consisting of decomposed granite. Chinese supplies came from a mountain in the northern Chinese province of Jiangxi, hence the Mandarin Chinese name for the material, *gaō ling*, from *gaō*, 'high', and *ling*, 'hill'. A French missionary priest, Father d'Entrecolles, writing about the manufacture of porcelain in China in 1712, rendered the Chinese word as *kaolin* in French and the term was soon after borrowed into English.

1731

THE POET WILLIAM COWPER IS BORN

••••••

William Cowper, a rector's son from Great Berkhampstead, Hertfordshire, battled with depression for most of his adult life. He sought solace in the evangelical Christian faith which he shared with the Unwins, friends with whom he lodged. After Mr Unwin's death, Mrs Unwin and Cowper moved to Olney. Here they were befriended by John Newton, the eminent evangelical preacher, who engaged Cowper's help in writing the OLNEY HYMNS (1779). Before they were completed Cowper suffered another bout of severe depression and attempted suicide. It was Mary Unwin who suggested that he should write poetry to keep his melancholy at bay: his satires

were published in 1782; his humorous ballad THE DIVERTING
HISTORY OF JOHN GILPIN was begun in the same year; and THE
TASK appeared in 1785. Mrs Unwin became ill in 1791 and died in
1796, leaving Cowper depressed and inconsolable until his own death
on 25 April 1800.

GOD MOVES IN A MYSTERIOUS WAY

This is the first line of one of the
contributions Cowper made to the
OLNEY HYMNS (1779). The hymn speaks
of the way omnipotent God uses testing
circumstances to shower mercy and
blessings upon his children:

> *God moves in a mysterious way,*
> *His wonders to perform;*
> *He plants his footsteps in the sea,*
> *And rides upon the storm.*

The first line has become proverbial and is
quoted by those who have faith and those
who have none on a variety of occasions.
When something that was doomed
unexpectedly turns out well, for instance,
or divine intervention is hoped for:

> *Paul made soothing noises and said he*
> *would get Peter to ring me. I was certainly*
> *getting my share of Apostolic attention.*
> *Maybe if Peter was stumped I'd get a call*
> *from the Almighty Himself, maybe a Fax.*
> *God'll fix it, I thought, on my knees. After*
> *all, he moves in a mysterious way . . .*
> (Sue Limb, OUT ON A LIMB, 1992)

or even when one is simply stumped for
an adequate answer:

> *The next day, we were allowed to inspect*
> *the appendix itself in a glass bottle. It was a*
> *longish black wormy-looking thing, and I*
> *said, 'Do I have one of those inside me,*
> *Nanny?'*
> *'Everybody has one,' Nanny answered.*
> *'What's it for?' I asked.*
> *'God works in his mysterious ways,' she*
> *said, which was her stock reply whenever she*
> *didn't know the answer.*
> (Roald Dahl, BOY, 1984)

THE WORSE FOR WEAR

THE DIVERTING HISTORY OF JOHN
GILPIN (1785) tells of a man, John
Gilpin, and his wife of *twice ten tedious*
years who plan to celebrate their
wedding anniversary at the Bell at
Edmonton. John is late starting out for
the party and his borrowed horse, which
has strong homing instincts, carries him
at full gallop not to the Bell but to
Ware, where his master lives. Having
lost his hat and wig along the route,
Gilpin is forced to borrow from the
horse's owner:

> *. . . straight he came with hat and wig;*
> *A wig that flow'd behind,*
> *A hat not much the worse for wear,*
> *Each comely in its kind.*

This is the earliest mention of the
phrase *the worse for wear* which is now
idiomatic and means 'battered from
much use'. It still retains notions of
'run down' and 'shabby', which have
been reinforced since the middle of the
sixteenth century by a similar phrase
worse for the wearing. The principal
meaning today is 'inebriated, drunk',
its meaning also reinforced by a
nineteenth-century phrase *to be the*
worse for liquor.

Inspiration for THE TASK *(1785) came from*
Cowper's friend Lady Austen, who
challenged him to write a poem in blank
verse. When Cowper asked for a subject, she
helpfully suggested the sofa. That, then, was
Cowper's set task. The poem, which runs
into six books, opens with a salutation to
the sofa but its main theme is the benefits of
rural life to man's total well-being. It has
contributed the following to the stock of current
English expressions:

VARIETY IS THE SPICE OF LIFE

Book II of THE TASK, entitled THE
TIME-PIECE, contains a passage where
Cowper reflects upon ever-changing
fashion and the compulsion always to
have something different:

Variety's the very spice of life,
That gives it all its flavour. We have run
Through every change that fancy at the
   loom,
Exhausted, has had genius to supply.

Cowper's line *variety's the (very) spice of life*
has become proverbial in English, but the
idea was not a new one. When Dr
Samuel Johnson wrote that *The great source*
of pleasure is variety (LIVES OF THE POETS:
BUTLER, 1779), he was merely expressing
a sentiment first aired by ancient Greek
and Roman writers and frequently
reiterated since then: by Aphra Behn, for
instance, who wrote that *Variety is the soul*
of pleasure (THE ROVER, 1680), or John
Gay who claimed that *Variety's the source*
of joy below (TO BERNARD LINTOT,
1715). Cowper's genius simply lay in
couching an old sentiment in imaginative
and highly evocative terms.

THE CUP THAT CHEERS

Book IV of THE TASK is entitled THE
WINTER EVENING. The poet describes
the pleasures of shutting out the dark and
cold and settling down for the evening:

Now stir the fire, and close the shutters fast,
Let fall the curtains, wheel the sofa round,
And, while the bubbling and loud-hissing
   urn
Throws up a steamy column, and the cups,
That cheer but not inebriate, wait on each,
So let us welcome peaceful evening in.

Cowper's poem betrays familiarity with
the philosophical works of George
Berkeley, Bishop of Cloyne, who wrote
in the first half of the eighteenth century.
Whilst in America Berkeley had learnt
about the benefits of tar-water, a remedy
which he later found to be effective in the
treatment of dysentery amongst the poor
of Cloyne. Encouraged, he applied tar-
water to a variety of ailments, mild and
chronic, in both man and beast and
discovered it to be widely efficacious. In
1744 Berkeley published SIRIS, a blend of
metaphysics and medicine. The work
became very popular, chiefly for its
exposition on tar-water, which Berkeley
proclaimed to be *of a nature so mild and*
benign and proportioned to the human
constitution, as to warm without heating, to
cheer but not inebriate. As a result, tar-water
became a sovereign remedy during the
eighteenth century and well into the
nineteenth. Cowper's borrowed
description *the cups, that cheer but not*
inebriate does not, of course, refer to tar-
water but to comforting cups of tea – a
simple, wholesome pleasure.

1736

THE FIRST 'GIN ACT' IS PASSED

••••••

Gin was first distilled in Holland in the seventeenth century where
it soon became a popular drink. It was brought to England by
soldiers returning from the Netherlands and became popular
amongst the poorer classes in the early eighteenth century because
it was so cheap to produce. For no more than a penny, a man,
woman or child could temporarily obliterate the miseries of

poverty, a message dinned into them by the well-known contemporary jingle: *Drunk for a penny, dead drunk for two pennies, clean straw for nothing.*

By the 1720s, gin consumption had become a frightening social evil. The vice and destitution it caused were shockingly depicted by William Hogarth's political engraving of a teeming London slum scene entitled 'Gin Lane' (1751), where only the gin house and the pawnbroker prosper. It is estimated that, in the capital alone, there were over seven thousand outlets selling gin. In a petition against spirituous liquors presented to the House of Commons in 1735, the Justices of the Peace for Middlesex complained that most of the gin was not sold under licence but from the premises of ordinary tradesmen, and demanded action. In 1736 legislation was passed which placed a duty of five shillings a gallon on the drink in an attempt to curb sales. Although its proper title was probably something very legal and parliamentary, it is always popularly known as the 'Gin Act'.

GIN

In the seventeenth century, at the University of Leiden in the Netherlands, a professor of medicine, Franciscus Sylvius, concocted a cheap diuretic draught by distilling juniper berries, potent for this purpose, with spirits. This pleasant medicine was appreciated by patients throughout the land who convinced themselves of its efficacy and called for a repeat prescription.

Before long the draught was no longer regarded as a medicine but was imbibed simply for pleasure. The Dutch called the spirit *genever*, meaning 'juniper', a word which had been previously borrowed into Middle Dutch from Old French *genevre*, itself a derivation from Latin *jūniperus*, 'juniper'. When English soldiers were introduced to the intoxicating liquor and took it home with them, the Dutch word *genever* was corrupted to *geneva* through confusion with the name of the Swiss town (and for this reason often appears with a capital G). Before long *geneva* had been shortened to *gin*, evidence of the spirit's growing popularity:

The infamous Liquor, the name of which deriv'd from Juniper-Berries in Dutch, is now, by frequent use . . . from a word of

midling length shrunk into a Monosyllable, Intoxicating Gin
(Mandeville, FABLE OF THE BEES, 1714)

The Reverend James Townley was born in the same year that Mandeville's work was published. By the time Townley had reached adulthood, the adjectives *intoxicating* and *infamous* were too tame to describe the evils of gin drinking, as this lament from his pen shows:

Gin, cursed Fiend, with Fury fraught,
Makes human Race a Prey,
It enters by a deadly Draught,
And steals our life Away.

Another respected clergyman added his voice to those tormented by the intoxicated condition of the country's poor. In 1743 John Wesley advocated temperance, insisting that his followers abstain from *drunkenness, buying or selling spirituous liquors, or drinking them, except in cases of extreme necessity*, in other words, medicinal use.

It was the influence of men like Wesley and further Acts of increasing severity that eventually brought the problem under control by the end of the century.

• *Geneva* had been preceded by yet another ardent spirit from Holland. *Brandewijn*, literally 'burnt wine' (wine that had been heated to distil it), was produced there in the sixteenth century. There is a story, which may or may not be true, that a sixteenth-century Dutch shipowner hit upon the idea of heating wine, thinking to condense it for transportation and then add water at the destination. But people thought the distilled wine tasted good just the way it was and the demand for it grew. It was imported into England in the first quarter of the seventeenth century, when it was known as *brandwine* or *brandewine*. By 1657 popular usage had reduced the word to *brandy,* while official documents had the fuller *brandy wine*, the term by now erroneously understood to be a compound of *brandy* and *wine.*

More expensive than home-produced gin, brandy never became the constant tipple of the masses but certainly pickled the better-off. In a letter to Anthony Wood, written in 1689, John Aubrey describes his visit to Mr Rushworth who had *quite lost his memory with drinking Brandy*, adding that *his Landlady wiped his nose like a child.*

1745

'GOD SAVE THE KING' IS FIRST PERFORMED

······

In 1745 Charles Stuart, the Young Pretender, crossed from France to Scotland to restore the Catholic Stuart kings to the British throne. In Scotland he soon raised an army and prepared to invade England, gathering support from English Jacobites as he went. In September 1745 in the Drury Lane Theatre, London, the curtain had just fallen after a performance of Ben Jonson's comedy THE ALCHEMIST. Suddenly it rose again to reveal the cast of the play singing a patriotic hymn, 'God Save Great George Our King' (the king was George II, a Protestant Hanoverian). The scenario was repeated time and again in London's theatres until the prayer was heard. Charles failed to get further south than Derby and the following year was routed at the Battle of Culloden. He spent the rest of his life in exile.

Traditionally 'God Save Great George Our King' is attributed to the songwriter, dramatist and poet Henry Carey, but its authorship is uncertain. Indeed the tune, whose timing is suggestive of a dance, may be much older than the words. In 1746 Handel introduced the hymn into his 'Occasional Oratorio', which dealt with the Jacobite defeat of the previous year. From then on the music came to symbolise Britain and was frequently included in royal ceremonial occasions. From this repeated patriotic use it became the oldest national anthem.

ANTHEM

'God Save the King' was popularly described as a national *anthem* as early as 1825 although, as Engel later wrote in his INTRODUCTION TO THE STUDY OF NATIONAL MUSIC (1866), *Anthem is musically an inappropriate title for this tune*. The fitting term would have been *hymn*.

The word *anthem* originated in Greek *antiphōnos*, 'sounding in response' (from *anti*, 'contrary, against', and *phōnē*, 'voice, sound'). Late ecclesiastical Latin adapted this as *antiphona* and it was then assimilated into Old English as *antefn*, a term which referred to 'words sung as a response in a liturgy'.

Antefn gradually evolved in English becoming *antemn*, *antem* and finally, in the sixteenth century, *anthem*. By this time the word was being applied to 'a religious choral composition' which was either sung unaccompanied by a choir ('full anthem') or by solo voices and a chorus singing alternately with instrumental accompaniment ('verse anthem'). These works, composed in English for the Anglican Church, were somewhat similar to the Roman Catholic motets which were sung in Latin. As the *anthem* developed, the need was felt for a term to describe its original sense of 'a sung liturgical response' and so, in the sixteenth century, the ecclesiastical Latin word *antiphona* was reborrowed into English as *antiphon*.

From the end of the sixteenth century onwards *anthem* had, from time to time, been used poetically in secular contexts to denote 'a song of praise'. And so it was that, by the close of the first quarter of the nineteenth century, the term came to be inappropriately applied to 'God Save the King' when the decision was made to adopt it as a national hymn. Thereafter, besides its strict musical sense, *anthem* denoted 'a patriotic song symbolic of a nation'.

Of course, these days it is not only one's country which is deemed worthy of an outpouring of praise and loyalty. Every Saturday in the season, the stands of football stadiums the length and breadth of the country ring with the *anthems* of adoring fans urging their teams on to victory.

• 'God Save the King' is technically a *hymn*. The ancient Greeks had the word *humnos* to denote 'a song of praise' which was raised to the gods or to national heroes. In the Greek translation of the Old Testament *humnos* was used to render a number of Hebrew words which meant 'a song of praise to God'. Consequently the word was borrowed as *hymnus* by Christian translators and writers in Latin. From their texts the term passed into Old French as *ymne* and from there into Middle English as *imne*, the latinised form *hymn* emerging in the sixteenth century. Hymns are now an essential ingredient of Christian praise and worship, and great care is taken in their selection, as the following extract from a church service sheet shows:

> *Hymn 43: 'Great God, what do I see here?'*
> *Preacher: The Rev. Horace Blodgett*
> *Hymn 47: 'Hark! an awful voice is sounding'*
> (CLASSIC CHURCH BULLETIN 'BLOOPERS', 1999)

In the sixteenth century *hymn* also began to be used outside Christian contexts in its original Greek sense, so that it came to mean 'a song of praise to a god, a hero or a country' – a more fitting term than *anthem* for 'a national patriotic song', but not one that prevailed.

1750

MRS VESEY BEGINS HER FAMOUS LITERARY GATHERINGS

●●●●●●

Card-playing and gossip were the main entertainments offered at soirées in eighteenth-century England. Mrs Vesey, the vivacious wife of an Irish MP, found herself bored with this endless round of trivia and irritated by the general notion that women were the foolish sex. She decided to invite to her home men and women of wit and learning for evenings of intelligent conversation and debate. Pedantry was frowned upon, gossip was taboo and refreshments were light – only coffee, tea and lemonade were served. Her gatherings were so successful that other like-minded society hostesses followed suit, most notably Mrs Boscawen and Mrs Montagu, whom Dr Johnson described as 'Queen of the Blues'. Besides Johnson and Boswell, the actor David Garrick, novelist Samuel Richardson, writer and politician Horace Walpole and artist Sir Joshua Reynolds were regular guests.

BLUESTOCKING

A number of those who attended the assemblies at the houses of Mrs Vesey, Mrs Boscawen and Mrs Montagu were either too poor or too unworldly to care for the niceties of sophisticated society. One of these was Mrs Elizabeth Carter, a woman of high intellect but feeble fashion sense. Another was the poet Benjamin Stillingfleet, who became a regular member of the circle and habitually turned up to their evenings in his blue woollen stockings. Worsted stockings were cosy, homely, everyday attire. Black silk stockings were required for full dress. It is said to be Admiral Boscawen who, eyeing Stillingfleet, laughingly dubbed the select group *The Blue Stocking Society*, implying that they were improperly turned out for a society gathering. The quip caught on. Ladies who met thus for stimulating conversation were called *Blue Stockingers* or *Blue Stocking Ladies* and, by the end of the century, *Blue Stockings*. During the nineteenth century the term was contemptuously applied to any lady who had or affected scholarship and this same note of ridicule still accompanies the word today:

Ecudation, Ecudation And Ecudation

[sic] *It's absolutely essential that your father stumps up for a good school. After all, it's all very well having a bunch of GCSEs, but if you don't want to end up a hairy-armpitted bluestocking, you have to know how to use your cutlery! Besides, the right school will set you up with a whole host of nice friends for life.*
(THE INDEPENDENT, 4 May 1999)

(For more about **stocking** see **1589**, page 136.)

1761

CONSTRUCTION OF THE BRIDGEWATER CANAL IS COMPLETED

••••••

Coal from the Duke of Bridgewater's mines at Worsely had to be transported ten miles overland to supply the thriving textile industry in Manchester. In 1759 the Duke consulted James Brindley, a self-taught engineer in his employ, with a view to constructing a canal between his coalfields and Manchester. The enterprise was immediately successful. In Manchester the cost of coal was halved from seven pence (3p) to three pence halfpenny. Work to extend the canal from Manchester to Liverpool was begun in 1766 and an entire network of inland waterways was soon under construction linking four major rivers: the Trent, the Mersey, the Severn and the Thames.

CANAL

Latin *canna*, from which English gets the word *cane*, meant 'reed' or 'cane' (see **cannon**, page 81 and **cinnamon**, page 58). A derivative, *canālis*, which denoted 'pipe' or 'channel', was taken into Old French as *chanel*. Later French reworked this word, either from the original Latin or from Italian *canale*, and came up with the form *canal*. This was borrowed into English in the sixteenth century, where it denoted 'a waterpipe' and 'a water course' in general. In seventeenth-century France a long narrow artificial stretch of water was sometimes used to ornament a park or garden. The French applied the word *canal* to such a feature and this use was reflected in English. The long strip of water in St James's Park was one such. Charles II, apparently under advice from the notable French landscape designer André le Nôtre, had the water feature constructed from several existing pools when the park was redesigned. Afterwards, the king could often be seen strolling by the canal and was even known to swim in it. His subjects too enjoyed the water. In winter they skated

on it (see **skate**, page 166) and in summer were refreshed by it. In his diary for 15 July 1666, Samuel Pepys records how one stifling summer's day he *walked through the Park, and there, it being mighty hot and I weary, lay down by the canal, upon the grass, and slept awhile.*

The seventeenth century also saw the construction of important artificial watercourses to facilitate the transportation of goods, particularly in France. Yet again the French used the term *canal* and once more the use was reflected in English. As industry grew the need for direct transportation became pressing in Europe. Inland waterways answered that need. During the eighteenth and early nineteenth centuries, many countries developed a network of canals, the one in England beginning with the Bridgewater canal, and their importance did not begin to wane until the coming of the railway era (see **1825**, page 198).

• Middle English had borrowed the Old French word *chanel* around the turn of the fourteenth century. It eventually became *channel* in modern English. The words *channel* and *canal* are thus doublets – that is, two words of the same derivation but having developed separate senses.

TUNNEL

When the Duke of Bridgewater asked James Brindley to construct a canal for him he had in mind a simple channel whose water level would be regulated wherever necessary by locks. Instead, Brindley proposed a canal that reduced the number of locks by requiring an *aqueduct* (from Latin *acquae ductus*, combination of *aqua*, 'water', and *ducere*, 'to lead') to span a valley, and a navigable tunnel. A major tunnel had already been constructed for the Canal du Midi in France (1666–81) but Brindley's canal tunnel was the first to be excavated in England for transport. Surprisingly, the word *tunnel* has distant connections with the wine industry. Medieval Latin had the word *tunna* to denote 'a cask (for wine)'. This found its way into Old French as *tonne*, 'barrel', from which a diminutive *tonel*, meaning 'cask', was subsequently formed. However, when *tonel* was borrowed into English towards the middle of the fifteenth century, it was not used to denote a barrel of any sort but was applied to a net for trapping partridges. The mouth of the net was wide and led to a pipe-like passage which was supported along its length by hoops and became narrower at the end. Partridges were decoyed into this trap to be captured by the huntsman who, at least by the seventeenth century, was cunningly concealed behind a wooden screen made to look like a grazing animal. *To take Partridges with the Tonnell . . . there must a man be placed behind a Cow or a Horse, of wood, or of osier, painted in . . . the fashion of a Cow or a Horse,* read the instructions in Gervase Markham's COUNTRY FARME (1616). This practice gave rise to the expression *stalking horse*, originally used to describe 'a screen for concealment in the shape of an animal', now meaning 'a distraction, diversion, decoy'.

By the early sixteenth century the shape of the net had suggested the application of *tunnel* to 'the hearth and flue of a chimney'. Sir Walter Scott in his novel ROB ROY (1818) illustrates this application well:

> *The fire . . . roared, blazed, and ascended, half in smoke, half in flame, up a huge tunnel, with an opening wide enough to accommodate a stone seat within its ample vault.*

Both this use and that of the partridge trap remained current until the beginning of the nineteenth century. Given its application to the long dark shaft of a chimney, *tunnel* seemed an appropriate term for 'an underground passage' and is first used in a letter describing Mr Brindley's skills in driving a large tunnel through a hill. Other canals were subsequently routed through tunnels and later so were railways and roads. Ironically, although *tunnel* originated as a borrowing from French, that language turned to English in the second half of the nineteenth century and borrowed it back, this time with the sense 'underground passage'. In 1987–91 a great tunnel was built beneath the English Channel to link Britain with the French continent. The scheme was first mooted to Napoleon in 1802 by French engineer Albert Mathieu-Favier, who was obviously impressed by the tunnels on the inland waterways and thought on a grand scale. Known in English as the *Channel Tunnel*, this Anglo-Norman feat of engineering has since been dubbed the *Chunnel* (see **shuttle**, page 77).

• Although *tunnel* was never connected to the wine industry in English, the link is maintained in two other English words, *tun* and *ton*. Both words come from the same ultimate, but uncertain, source. The latter is found in an Anglo-Saxon glossary of 725; the former follows an independent route via medieval Latin *tunna*, 'a large wine barrel', and was taken into Old English first as *tunne*. In Middle English the variant *tonne* developed, which was used as a measure of capacity, being the amount of space taken up by a regular *tun* of wine. The volume of freight a ship could carry was thus measured in *tonnes*. But large barrels are also very heavy when full and so, by the end of the fifteenth century, the term was also being used for a unit of weight. Until the second half of the seventeenth century the spellings *tun* and *ton* were used interchangeably but thereafter were distinguished one from the other, *tun* being used for 'barrel' and *ton* for weights and measures. There remains some variation, however; *tonne* is still found as an alternative for *ton*, and as its metric equivalent.

1765

The First Public Restaurant Is Opened in Paris

••••••

The opening of the first restaurant is credited to a certain Monsieur Boulanger, a Parisian soup-seller, who in 1765 opened an establishment offering customers a selection of wholesome soups and meals. This was something of a novelty. Eighteenth-century diners were not accustomed to being offered a choice when forced to eat out, and simply took what the innkeeper had decided to serve up that day. Nevertheless, it was another seventeen years before the illustrious Grande Taverne de Londres was opened in Paris to cater for more sophisticated and expensive tastes.

RESTAURANT

Monsieur Boulanger called his wholesome soups *restaurants*, 'restoratives', broths to revive flagging energy levels, and the word was painted on a board hanging above the door of his establishment to attract passing trade. *Restaurant* was the present participle of the verb *restaurer*, 'to restore', which Monsieur Boulanger used as a noun. *Restaurer*, in turn, came from Old French *restorer*, a borrowing of Latin *restaurāre*, 'to restore, to repair'. After the French Revolution (1789–99) many excellent chefs, who had previously been employed by the aristocracy, set up their own businesses and restaurants proliferated. By 1804 Paris alone had more than 500 such establishments. During the first half of the nineteenth century the word *restaurant* was borrowed into the many languages of Europe and Scandinavia to denote 'eating place', arriving in English in the 1820s.

1768

JAMES COOK SAILS FOR THE PACIFIC OCEAN IN THE ENDEAVOUR ON THE FIRST OF HIS THREE VOYAGES

......

In 1768 the Royal Society and the Admiralty appointed James Cook to command a scientific expedition bound for the Pacific. Cook, who had been previously engaged in charting the coasts of Newfoundland and Labrador, was to carry a team of astronomers and botanists to Tahiti to observe the planet Venus crossing the sun, then on into the Pacific in search of the southern continent, *Terra Australis* (Latin meaning 'southern land'). Contemporary scientific opinion held that a substantial southern land mass had to exist, to counterbalance those of Europe and Asia in the Northern Hemisphere.

On 26 August 1768 Cook left England on board the *Endeavour*. After working in Tahiti, the expedition sailed on southwards to New Zealand. Cook charted both islands before sailing west, eventually fetching up on the east coast of Australia at Botany Bay. The *Endeavour* arrived back in England on 13 July 1771. Since this first voyage had neither established nor disproved the existence of a southern continent, Cook made a second expedition from 1772 to 1775. After skirting the Antarctic ice mass and further exploring the southern Pacific he concluded that *Terra Australis* did not exist.

Cook's third expedition, begun in 1776, was an attempt to find a Northwest Passage around Alaska, starting from the Pacific. In 1778 Cook reached the Arctic Ocean by way of the Bering Strait but could find no passage through the ice. The expedition sailed back to Hawaii where Cook was killed while trying to recover a stolen cutter from the Polynesian inhabitants.

The journals written by James Cook during his voyages have furnished English with several words:

TATTOO

Tahiti had been charted and claimed for England two years before Cook landed there in 1769. Apart from observing planetary movement, the expedition spent about three months studying the island, its flora and fauna and the way of life of its inhabitants. Cook found the Tahitians a civilised and attractive people: he admired their friendly, considerate manner, their dazzling smiles and graceful movements and the fact that they kept themselves scrupulously clean by bathing three times a day. In his journal for July 1769, Cook also describes how *both sexes paint their Bodys, Tattow, as it is called in their Language. This is done by inlaying the Colour of Black under their skins, in such a manner as to be indelible.* He goes on to say that it is *a painful operation, especially the Tattowing their Buttocks, it is performed but once in their Life times. Tattow* was Cook's rendition of the Tahitian term *tatau*, which also existed in several other Polynesian languages. The words were derived from a common Polynesian *ta*, 'to strike', a reference to the puncturing of the skin *with small instruments made of bone, cut into short teeth.*

Cook was to see finer and much more elaborate examples of tattooing when he landed in New Zealand in October of that year. Expedition artists sketched the decorated Maoris and tattooing began to catch on amongst British sailors. During the late eighteenth and the nineteenth centuries, tattooed Polynesians and American Indians were often paraded as curiosities at entertainments in Europe and America. Interest in body art, particularly amongst sailors, grew and tattoo parlours were eventually established in all the major world ports during the nineteenth century. By this time Cook's rendering *tattow*, which had remained current until the early nineteenth century, had been replaced by *tattoo*, a corruption of the general Polynesian term.

KANGAROO

The amazement experienced by James Cook and his crew when they first encountered a six-foot kangaroo can hardly be imagined. Joseph Banks was a botanist on board the *Endeavour*. An entry in the ship's journal records how Banks's greyhound was seen in pursuit of two animals which *greatly outstripped him in speed, bounding forward on two legs instead of running on four.* Banks himself was lost for words: *What to liken him to I could not tell. Nothing certainly that I have seen at all resembles him.* Sketches were made and the first published edition of Cook's VOYAGES was later embellished by an engraving of the creature taken from a beautiful oil painting by George Stubbs.

According to Rex and Thea Rienits in their book THE VOYAGES OF CAPTAIN COOK (1968), Stubbs had never seen a kangaroo but based his work on sketches and on a skin that Banks brought home with him on the *Endeavour*. How the artist must have marvelled at his creation. But what was this strange animal's name? In his journal for 4 August 1770, Cook says that the natives called the creature *kangooroo*, and this statement is supported by Joseph Banks. However, in early reports from the first penal colony which was set up in 1788 at Port Jackson (later Sydney), writers say that the natives called the creature *patagorong* or *patagaran* and were ignorant of the word *kangaroo*. During the first half of the nineteenth century there was much debate as to whether *kangaroo* was a native word or not. Some called it a 'barbarism', while others claimed to have heard it from the natives themselves. It might, of course, have been a local name or one that had simply fallen from regular use. One theory, for which there is no evidence, is that a crew member, pointing out the animal and asking what it was, received the reply *kangaroo*, 'I don't understand', in a native dialect, and took this for the name.

• Strangely, the term *kangaroo court* to describe 'an unofficial court with no legal standing' seems to have arisen not in Australia but in America around the mid-nineteenth century. The allusion to the *kangaroo* is difficult to fathom. That has not stopped enthusiasts from proposing an answer. Some say that, since the term appeared in 1849, the date of the Californian gold rush, it may have originally described self-appointed tribunals which judged those who 'jumped in' to claim the prospecting rights of others. The fact that the earliest record is traced to Texas, not California, stands against this theory. Mock courts were also a feature in American county jails of the period, where hardened inmates 'tried' new prisoners to exact money from them. *Kangaroo court* may, therefore, be a popular allusion to Australia's infamy as a penal colony and at the same time to one of its well-known animal curiosities (see **1788**, page 189). Others claim that the origin is in the Australian prisoners' belief that they had no more say in what happened to them than a kangaroo. Unfortunately, all the textual evidence is American, and nothing has been found from Australian written records. A figurative explanation is that the term may have been applied to illegal courts, swiftly set up to mete out rough-and-ready on-the-spot justice, as a result of comparing the irregular practices of such a body with the leaps of a kangaroo.

There is, in short, no conclusive evidence of anything other than lively imaginations – of somebody somewhere who first used the phrase, and of etymologists ever since.

TABOO

During his third voyage Cook called in at Tonga. The journal he kept of his brief sojourn there in 1777, published in A Voyage to the Pacific Ocean (1776–80), introduced the word *taboo* to the English language. The Tongan word, which Cook spelled as *taboo*, was *tabu*, a form which is common in several other Polynesian languages. Variants include Maori *tapu* and Hawaiian *kapu*.

Taboos were common amongst the Polynesian peoples, being the unwritten code of law by which their societies were organised. *Taboo* was a system of prohibitions which effectively maintained a rigid caste system, set objects or practices apart for sacred use, and forbade harmful behaviour. Disobedience was punishable by death.

When anything is forbidden to be eat, or made use of, wrote Cook, *they say, that it is taboo*. Short poles, *taboo staves*, were set up to remind people of the rules and the consequences of disobedience. Some taboos were permanent; others were declared as and when they were deemed necessary. Lands or fishing territories could be placed under taboo for a season to aid their recovery and conserve them for the future, for instance. Sometimes, however, the imposition of taboo seemed quite arbitrary. At Tonga, Cook remarked that, of the group he was with, *not one of them would sit down, or eat a bit of any thing*. When Cook expressed his surprise he was told that they were all taboo. *Why they were laid under such restraints, at present, was not explained*, he added.

For the next fifty years or so *taboo* cropped up in English in accounts of Polynesian society but then, during the 1830s, it began to be used figuratively in English to denote 'a behaviour or practice which is prohibited by social custom'. In linguistics a *taboo word* or *expression* describes a term which is regarded as socially offensive – a strong swearword, for instance, or a term of racial abuse.

1774

THE RULES OF CRICKET ARE LAID DOWN

••••••

When lessons for the day were over, John Denwick and his schoolfriends from the free school of Guildford would run outside to a favoured piece of ground *and play there at Creckett and other plaies*. John's remembrance of his schooldays in the closing years of Henry

VIII's reign is recorded in a document dated 1598 and is the earliest known reference to cricket. Origins of the game are obscure. One theory assumes that cricket developed from a country pastime in which a stone or knob of wood was rolled at a sheep-pen hurdle, this target being defended by a youth armed with a shepherd's crook. Another says that it evolved from the earlier club-ball, where the batsman guarded a hole in the ground with a stout stick. During the seventeenth century cricket grew in popularity in southern England, and references to it are more plentiful. County rivalries emerged in 1709 with a game between Kent and Surrey. Such important matches attracted large unruly crowds, and heavy betting on the result was common. In the eighteenth century a considerable number of new clubs was formed, usually under the patronage of local gentry, and a definitive set of rules became necessary to regularise play. These were drawn up in 1774 by a committee of noblemen and gentlemen, among them the Duke of Dorset and Sir Horace Mann.

CRICKET

The exact origins of the sixteenth-century name *cricket* are very uncertain. The best explanation delves into a fifteenth-century French text, where the term *criquet* refers to a stick to be aimed at in a game of bowls, rather like the stumps in cricket. French *criquet* may in turn derive from a Middle Flemish term *krick*, 'crutch'.

Through the centuries cricket has remained an English curiosity. The game is still largely restricted to Britain and some of the former British colonies, all of whom regularly thrash the home country. Few English people really understand the rules, and those who do are sometimes a little smug. In an interview for THE INDEPENDENT (12 July 1999), journalist Deborah Ross asked Dr Vernon Coleman if there was anything in life that pleased him. There was. Dr Coleman apparently enjoys a good book, a nice bit of countryside and *cricket, because it confuses the Americans.*

Written records of basic cricket vocabulary date from the eighteenth century when many clubs were formed and attempts were made to standardise the game. Words such as fielder, bat *and* bowl *were subsequently adopted by other team bat-and-ball games, finding their way into the vocabulary of rounders and from there into baseball.*

BAT

An illustration of a cricket match from the early eighteenth century shows a batsman wielding a long stick with a curved end, rather like that used in hockey but ending in a broader blade. The subsequent change to the modern shape was dictated by the evolution of bowling styles. The early term, *cricket-staff*, which dates from at least the beginning of the seventeenth century, was usurped by *bat* in the early eighteenth. The sixth edition of Phillips' NEW WORLD OF ENGLISH WORDS (1706) defines the new term as *a kind of Club to strike a Ball with, at the Play call'd Cricket*. *Bat* was a particular application of a current word which meant 'staff' or 'club'. This term had originally come into late Old English as *batt*. Its ultimate origins may lie in a Celtic source responsible for the Latin verb *battuere*, 'to beat' (see **battery**, page 194). Almost certainly it was influenced by the Old French word *batte*, 'cudgel', from *battre*, 'to beat' (itself from Latin *battuere*).

BOWL

Latin *bulla* meant 'bubble', a term which was also extended to other rounded objects. It was borrowed into French as *boule* where it first meant 'sphere, ball' and was then applied to the balls used in the popular game of bowling. Middle English borrowed *boule*, together with its various meanings, directly from French in the fifteenth century. In English the sense 'round thing, sphere' did not survive beyond the eighteenth century and so *bowl* became exclusively a sporting term. Originally, the ball was rolled along the ground in cricket. The action was like that used in the game of *bowls*, and the verb is borrowed from this sport.

As cricket became more competitive, the way in which the ball was delivered developed. Already before 1800 underhand bowling above the ground was permitted. Around 1825 a round-arm delivery, one made by sweeping the arm outward, was introduced amidst cries of protest that the ball was being thrown. Overarm bowling was brought in around 1860, again giving rise to much criticism and debate. At the close of the nineteenth century all three styles were permitted although overarm bowling was the more usual. Even though the ball has not been literally *bowled* since the late seventeenth century and the modern action can deliver the ball above the ground at around 100 mph (160 kph), the verb *to bowl* has been retained.

UMPIRE

In the Middle English poem PIERS PLOWMAN (William Langland, 1362), Clement the cobbler and Hikke the hackney-man engage in a game of barter. Clement offers his cloak to Hikke in return for the latter's hood and the pair call upon Robyn the ropemaker to act as *noumpere* and judge the fairness of the exchange. *Noumpere* is the original form of *umpire* and is first recorded in Langland's poem. It is derived from Old French *nonper* or *nomper*, which meant 'not equal, peerless', being a compound of *non-* 'not'

and *per* 'equal, peer' (from Latin *par*, 'equal'). The underlying sense then is 'one who is not paired but set apart, and therefore in a position to arbitrate'. The word was not long in Middle English before *a noumpere* began to appear as *an oumpere*, the initial *n* being mistaken as part of the indefinite article. A variety of spellings followed until the word finally settled at *umpire* sometime during the seventeenth century.

Although modern English uses *umpire* principally in sporting contexts, it was originally widely used to mean 'arbitrator, impartial judge'. The word's sporting debut came in 1714 when Sir Thomas Parkyns was called upon to act as *umpire* not in a cricket match but in a wrestling bout.

As cricket increased in popularity in the nineteenth century, it engendered a number of idiomatic expressions which have entered everyday speech:

BAT ON A STICKY WICKET

In the second half of the nineteenth century the term *sticky wicket* was applied to a wicket that had become spongy through rain. A skilful bowler was able to exploit this, thus presenting the batsman with particular difficulties. Bowlers like dampness in the air and on the pitch. By the mid-twentieth century the phrase *to bat* or *be on a sticky wicket* was being used figuratively with the sense 'to be faced with a difficult situation.' Nowadays only amateur batsmen contend with real sticky wickets: in professional cricket the wicket is covered to protect it from rain.

HAT TRICK

In the second half of the nineteenth century a bowler who succeeded in taking three wickets with three consecutive balls could expect a reward, usually a new hat. The feat therefore came to be known as *the hat trick*. The term is now applied to a triple victory in other sports or pursuits.

HIT FOR SIX

When a batsman hits the ball clear over the boundary, he has *hit it for six*, that is, he scores six runs at the bowler's expense. Thus the bowler has been *hit for six* – a demoralising experience for him. This cricketing phrase has been used figuratively since the 1930s, with the sense of one person demolishing the arguments of another: *The Chancellor hit the Leader of the Opposition for six.* Latterly it has also been used more generally to mean 'overwhelmed': *Her death hit me for six.*

NOT CRICKET

The phrase *it is not cricket* occurred time and again in cricketing handbooks from the second half of the nineteenth century. The words effectively censured improper play and unsportsmanlike attitudes. *Do not ask the umpire unless you think the batsman is out*, states THE CRICKETERS' COMPANION (1867), *it is not cricket to keep asking the umpire questions*. By the turn of the twentieth century the phrase had caught on figuratively to denote 'dishonourable, unfair conduct':

> *TWO BIRDIES? IT'S JUST NOT CRICKET*
> *The cricket World Cup has witnessed some weird things in its 24-year history, but yesterday hit all previous oddities for six. Not one, but two pigeons were killed by the ball.*
> (THE TIMES, 5 June 1999)

OFF ONE'S OWN BAT

The phrase *off his own bat* to refer to a batsman's personal score dates from the mid-eighteenth century. It was used figuratively with the sense 'through one's own efforts' soon after.

1786

JONAS HANWAY, THE FIRST TO CARRY AN UMBRELLA IN LONDON, DIES

......

There is plentiful evidence that umbrellas were used in ancient times in China, India, Persia and Egypt to shade illustrious people from the sun's rays. Umbrellas appear on early chinaware, for instance, and are depicted in carvings found at the ancient Persian capital of Persepolis. Although the Greeks had them, and then the Romans, the use of umbrellas did not survive into the Middle Ages. Not until the sixteenth century did the Popes readopt them, as much as a mark of prestige as for the protection they afforded against the sun. But what was good for Popes was proper for gentlefolk, also. In his Italian-English dictionary WORLDE OF WORDES (1598), John Florio described the Italian umbrella, still unknown in England, thus:

> *a little shadow, a little round thing that women bare in their hands to shadow them . . . also, a kind of round thing like a round skreene that gentlemen use in Italie in time of sommer.*

Gradually the use of umbrellas began to catch on in Europe where they were recognised as useful not only against the sun but also against the rain. The French carried umbrellas in the seventeenth century and, by the eighteenth century, the rest of Europe had begun to follow suit.

The arrival of the umbrella in England was not a happy event, however. Inclement weather usually meant plenty of trade for hackney-coachmen and sedan-chairmen, but a citizen with an umbrella might be tempted to walk rather than ride. In an account of his life (1778), a footman named John Macdonald wrote of how he brought a fine silk umbrella back from Spain but was intimidated each time he used it by people calling out *Frenchman! Why don't you get a coach?* Macdonald *persisted for three months, till they took no further notice of this novelty. Foreigners began to use theirs; and then the English.* John Macdonald was obviously a man of determination and courage. Nevertheless it is not he but his contemporary, a Mr Jonas Hanway, who is usually credited with regularly carrying an umbrella and with popularising its use in London.

UMBRELLA, PARASOL

Umbrellas were originally used as sunshades and this is reflected in the word's etymology. In Italy, where the umbrella's renaissance took place, the object was known as an *ombrella* or *ombrello* (the gender of the word was apparently in dispute). This literally means 'little shade' being a diminutive of Italian *ombra*, 'shade', itself a derivative of Latin *umbra*. Writers of travel books introduced the word into English as *umbrella* (or, with the masculine ending, as *umbrello*) in the early seventeenth century. In a lively account of his travels around Italy, Thomas Coryat made a valiant stab at describing an umbrella, bringing the word to English notice at the same time:

> *Many of them doe carry other fine things . . . which they commonly call in the Italian tongue 'umbrellaes' . . . These are made of leather something answerable to the forme of a little caunopy and hooped in the inside with divers little wooden hoopes that extend the umbrella in a pretty large compasse.*
> (CRUDITIES, 1611)

But the intrepid traveller Fynes Moryson had it on good authority that these new-fangled things were not such a good idea:

> *In hot regions, to avoid the beams of the Sun, in some places (as in Italy) they carry Umbrels, or things like a little Canopy over their heads: but a learned Physician told me, that the use of them was dangerous, because they gather the heat into a pyramidal point, and thence cast it down perpendicularly upon the head.*
> (ITINERARY, 1617)

In spite of the grave reservations of Moryson and his learned friend, umbrellas eventually found their way to England in the eighteenth century. The English had rather more need of shelter from the rain than shade from the sun and used their *umbrellas* in wet weather with a total disregard for the word's shady etymology. And so, in his poem TRIVIA OR THE ART OF WALKING THE STREETS OF LONDON (1716), John Gay describes:

> *Good houswives who underneath*
> *   th'umbrella's oily shed,*
> *Safe thro' the wet on clinking pattens tread.*

The date of this poem, and a similar but even earlier reference by Swift, rather casts doubt on Jonah Hanway's claim to fame. Possibly Mr Hanway made it respectable for a gentleman to be seen carrying an umbrella. Whatever the facts, by the early eighteenth century the fate of the word was sealed. In spite of its sunny beginnings, *umbrella* was destined to be connected with drizzle and downpours.

Meanwhile, in the seventeenth century English had plundered French vocabulary and found *parasol* to denote 'a portable sunshade'. The French in their turn had taken the word from the Italians who, in the sixteenth century, had coined the compound *parasole* from *para-*, meaning 'defend' or 'shield' (the imperative of the verb *parare*, 'to defend, to shelter' from Latin *parāre*, 'to make ready') and *sole*, meaning 'sun' (from Latin *sōl*, 'sun'). Literally, then, *parasol* means 'protect from the sun'.

• Latin *umbra* is also the source of the common idiom *to take umbrage*. *Umbra* had given the adjective *umbrāticus*, meaning 'belonging to shade, shadowy'. From this Vulgar Latin derived the unattested noun *umbrāticum* which was taken into Old French as *umbrage* and from there into English in the fifteenth century. In Old French and then in English *umbrage* first meant 'shade, shadow', a sense which now survives only in poetic language. During the seventeenth century French picked up the notion of 'shadow' for figurative application and used the word to denote 'suspicion'. English followed suit. The phrase *to take umbrage*, meaning 'to take offence' arose in the late seventeenth century.

1788

Robert Barker Exhibits the First Panorama

······

In 1796 a Scottish painter, Robert Barker, was granted a patent for a pictorial entertainment which he described as *La Nature à coup d'Oeil* (Nature at a Glance). The invention took the form of a huge cylinder, about 60 feet (18 metres) in diameter, which had a continuous painted scene covering its inner surface. Spectators, who stood on a platform in the centre, were able to feel part of a scene which faded to the horizon and, by slowly turning, see it unfold before them. Robert Barker's first panorama, a view over Edinburgh, was put on display in the city itself in 1788 and exhibited in London the following year.

Barker's innovation soon led to much more sophisticated developments, including the clever use of lighting, sound effects and sheer lengths (John Banvard produced a panorama 1,200 feet (370 metres) long that showed the landscape along the course of the Mississippi River). In due time, and with the influence of the diorama and stereopticon among others, the panorama led to cinerama, in which several movie projectors synchronise the projection on to a very wide curved screen.

PANORAMA

Robert Barker followed his cityscape of
Edinburgh with another of London. But
he did not only exhibit city views. The
medium was just as effective for scenes of
action and Barker also presented a lifelike
battle from the Napoleonic Wars.
Effective use was made of lighting to
bring the scenes to life. Although he had
called his invention *La Nature à coup
d'Oeil* when submitting it for patent,
Barker soon hit upon *panorama* as a more
suitable name for publicising his work. He
coined the word from the Greek prefix
pan-, meaning 'all' and *horāma*, meaning
'sight, view', a derivative of the verb
horān, 'to see'. Barker's invention soon
became very popular. Other talented
artists, at home and abroad, also tried their
hand at panoramas so that, by the turn of
the nineteenth century, the amusement
merited mention in the supplement to the
illustrious ENCYCLOPEDIA BRITANNICA
(1801): *Panorama, a word . . . employed of
late to denote a painting . . . which represents
an entire view of any country, city or other
natural objects, as they appear to a person
standing in any situation, and turning quite
round.*

Such was the excitement generated by
the *panorama* that, from the early
nineteenth century, the term was also
being applied to the sort of far-reaching
uninterrupted view one might gain from
the summit of a hill or from a rooftop.

*Below lay a panorama in brilliant sunshine.
Through Taylor's telescope they could pick
out every detail. 'The country, covered with
wheat, barley, peas, beans, etc'. . . The
streams winding between the fields. . .*

*Farm houses with their fruit trees. . .
Beyond these lay the magnificent Yangtze,
fifteen to twenty miles broad. . . Over the
river on the sacred hills of the southern
shore, sunlight touched the gold of temples.
Distance blended all that was harsh or cruel
or ugly into a tapestry of loveliness.*
(J Pollock, HUDSON AND MARIA,
1962)

At the same time *panorama* was also
being used figuratively to denote 'a
comprehensive presentation of a subject
or sequence of events'. This latter use is
well illustrated by BBC Television
which, in 1953, chose *Panorama* as the
title of a current affairs programme which
still presents each week an in-depth
report on a topic of concern.

The adjective *panoramic* was derived
around 1813 and was applied to a camera
in the 1870s. Towards the end of the
century a *panoramic camera* became known
as a *panoram*. By the early twenty century
panoram was also being used as a verb:

*We are before the Erie cut, and as the
camera 'panorams' around, we get a
glimpse of our splendid Eleventh Avenue
Stable in Jersey City.*
(WELLS FARGO MESSENGER, October
1915)

But the term was far too long for the
hectic world of the motion picture
industry. By 1930 the word had been
shortened yet again and the abbreviation
to pan was in use with the sense 'to move
a camera round to follow action or to
give a panoramic effect'.

1788

CAPTAIN ARTHUR PHILLIP ESTABLISHES A PENAL COLONY IN AUSTRALIA

••••••

James Cook's claim to eastern Australia for Britain was fortuitous, even though the country itself was generally considered inhospitable and of little economic value (see **1768**, page 180). British interest was twofold. Firstly, the territory would provide a valuable base for economic activity in East Asia and the Pacific. More pressingly, Australia was needed as a penal colony. The early years of the Industrial Revolution in Britain were marked by great social upheaval and a subsequent increase in crime. Prisons were severely over-crowded, a problem that was further exacerbated in 1783, when American independence put an end to the transportation of convicts to those former colonies. Australia provided the solution. In May 1787 British naval commander Captain Arthur Phillip left Portsmouth with eleven ships to found a penal colony on Australia's east coast. About a thousand people accompanied him, of whom 759 were convicts. Phillip arrived at Botany Bay in January 1788 and established the settlement at nearby Port Jackson. He named it Sydney after Lord Thomas Townshend Sydney, the British minister to whom he was responsible. This event is now commemorated annually with a public holiday on 26 January, Australia Day.

Some of the words borrowed into English from native Australian dialects come from the settlement's early history when the colonists learnt about survival and explored the region with the help of the Aborigine people. These words include dingo, koala, wallaby, *and* wombat. *Others are:*

COOEE

This was a call the Aborigines used to summon one another from a distance. The initial syllable was stressed and drawn-out while the last was high-pitched and sharp. First noted in 1790, it was soon in general use throughout the colony and was rapidly picked up by newcomers. The call gave rise to the Australian phrase *within a cooee of,* meaning 'nearby, within

calling distance'. In his SLANG DICTIONARY of 1864, Hotten defines *cooey* as an *Australian-bush call,* adding *now not infrequently heard in the streets of London.* PALL MALL GAZETTE for 3 January 1889 tells of two Australian squatters who *on a visit to the mother country lost themselves in a London fog, and were only reunited after a series of shrill and vigorous 'coo-e's'.*

BOOMERANG

This Aboriginal missile consists of a curved piece of wood which, when it is thrown, rotates in the air. Some boomerangs are made to return to the thrower. These are up to 30 inches (76 centimetres) in length and are used mainly for sport. A slightly larger non-return boomerang with a gentler curve is used for hunting and fighting. In 1798 the Judge Advocate of the Sydney colony made a collection of local vocabulary. Under the heading 'names of clubs' he mentions *wo-mur-rāng*. A later vocabulary from the Botany Bay region has *būmarin*. These two words may well have referred to the weapon, in which case they were further modified by the colonists to give *boomerang*. Alternatively *boomerang*, which was confirmed as *the Port Jackson term* by Captain King in an official survey written in 1827, was a straightforward borrowing of the native term from one of the Aboriginal languages current at the time.

The missile's unusual flight and its ability to return to its starting-point led to the development of a figurative use in the late nineteenth century. *Boomerang* began to describe an 'action or statement that rebounds unfavourably on the instigator' and the verb *to boomerang*, in use since about 1880, meant not only 'to fly back to the point of departure' but also, figuratively, 'to backfire':

> *The drug industry is highly sensitive, particularly in the big US healthcare market, to price pressure from buyers. A build-up in stock by wholesalers could give buyers a weapon that may boomerang on manufacturers.*
> (THE TIMES, 11 January 1999)

ABORIGINES

Captain Cook and those responsible for the original settlement of Australia called the indigenous people 'natives' and later 'Australians' (the latter being derived from *Terra Australis* and widely applied to the natives of Australasia and Polynesia before the annexing of the island-continent of Australia for Britain). *Aboriginēs*, the name these people are commonly known by today, was the term the Romans applied to earlier inhabitants of their land. It may even have originated as the name of a particular tribe, which then underwent the mysterious process of folk etymology,

to emerge as if it had been derived from Latin *ab orīgine*, 'from the beginning'. When *Aboriginēs* was borrowed from Latin into English in the sixteenth century, it carried the same meaning, 'predecessors of the ancient Romans', but from the seventeenth century was extended to refer to 'the original inhabitants of a (European) country'. By the second half of the eighteenth century the native inhabitants of countries colonised by Europeans were also called *aborigines*, hence the specific application to the indigenous population of Australia which started to develop in the mid-nineteenth century. This is its only use today. The word was at first only plural. For the singular, there have been several variants: *aboriginal* was the preferred form for a long time, and still is among conservative speakers; although strictly incorrect etymologically, the singular *aborigine* arose around the mid-nineteenth century and is the popular choice today. Latin *ab orīgine* is the preposition *ab*, 'from', plus the ablative of *orīgō* (stem *orīgin-*) which means 'beginning', being derived from the verb *orīrī*, 'to arise'.

• Related words which have found their way into English are *original* (12th century) and *origin* (14th century).

The verb *orīrī* has also spawned:

abort (16th century): originally 'to miscarry'. From Latin *abortare*, from *abortus*, past principle of *aborīrī*, 'to miscarry', from *ab-*, 'away', and *orīrī*, 'to arise'.

orient (12th century): Middle English, from Old French, from Latin *oriēns* (stem *orient-*), 'rising' and hence 'rising sun', present participle of *orīrī*, 'to arise'.

SQUATTER

Sheep were imported into Australia to help sustain the settlements there and, indeed, the Australian climate proved more favourable to grazing than agriculture. Coincidentally, by the beginning of the nineteenth century supplies of wool to the British cloth industry had become critical. Enterprising colonists recognised a potential market and sheep farmers began to occupy illegally large tracts of unallocated pasture. These pastoralists (an Australian word for 'sheep or cattle farmer') soon became known as *squatters.*

The word *squatter* was imported from that other land of frontiers, the American West. It was derived from the verb *to squat,* which ultimately goes back to the Latin verb *cogere,* 'to drive together'. The past principle of *cogere* was *coāctus* from which Vulgar Latin derived the unattested verb *coactīre,* 'to press together'. This gave rise to Old French *esquatir* (from the intensive prefix *es-* and *quatir,* 'to flatten') which passed into Middle English as *squatten,* 'to press flat, to crush', at the end of the thirteenth century. Around the beginning of the fifteenth century *squatten* was applied to both the attitude of an animal which presses itself close to the ground to stalk or hide and the posture of a crouching person. Since squatting is hardly a comfortable position of

permanence, American English derived the term *squatter* in the late eighteenth century to mean 'a person who claims land for which he has no legal title'. The use of *squatter* to denote 'one who lives in an unoccupied building illegally' arose in England in the second half of the nineteenth century:

> *On the Corniche [in Beirut] apartments commonly sell for £1 million, while the road out to Damascus is still lined with ruins, some of which have been repossessed by squatter families or, more bizarrely, by car showrooms.*
> (THE TIMES, 13 March 1999)

In Australia the *squatters* became so powerful through the success of their wool-growing that by 1840 the authorities were forced to regularise their situation and in modern Australian English the term now denotes 'a large-scale sheep farmer'.

1791

LUIGI GALVANI PUBLISHES HIS FINDINGS ON 'ANIMAL ELECTRICITY'

······

Luigi Galvani was born in Bologna, Italy, in 1737. He studied medicine at the University of Bologna and was later appointed professor of anatomy there. A chance observation made while carrying out research on the anatomy of the frog was eventually to lead to the invention of the electrical battery (see **1800**, page 193).

GALVANISE

In his laboratory one day Luigi Galvani noticed that the frog's leg he was dissecting had jerked when he touched the nerve with his scalpel. At the same time an assistant reported a spark from an electrostatic machine. Galvani carried out many other investigations and was able to demonstrate that the convulsions were

the result of electrical action. Galvani also experimented by impaling frogs on brass hooks and hanging them on an iron railing. He discovered that the legs of a freshly killed frog twitched when they were brought into contact with two different metals. In the eighteenth century electricity was understood to be like a fluid (hence the term *electric current,* as if electricity flowed like a river). Galvani concluded that an electric fluid, which he called 'animal electricity', was present in animal nerve tissue.

Galvani's theory of 'animal electricity' was disputed by Alessandro Volta, who demonstrated that the reaction was a chemical one (see **1800**, page 193). Nevertheless his name lives on in the verb *to galvanise*. The verb came into English through French *galvaniser* in the early nineteenth century when the discoveries of Luigi Galvani were being put to medical use – to stimulate paralysed limbs, for instance, or attempt resuscitation. *Galvanise a frog, don't galvanise a tiger*, warned Sydney Smith (WORKS, 1825). Later in the century Galvani's work led to attempts to stimulate the brains of wounded soldiers after the Battle of Sedan in 1870. Not surprisingly, by the middle of the century *galvanise* was being used figuratively to mean 'rouse into life or action':

With his blue eyes blazing, the red-bearded admiral tapped his huge finger on Percy's chest. 'Fleming, if you are ever given food like this again, you are to pick up the telephone, ring HQ and ask for me personally . . . Do you understand?'

'Oh yes, sir,' said Percy. 'I do!'. . .

And after a brief private word with the station chief, the Admiral was off to galvanize and put heart into some other unsuspecting outpost.

(Edward Rutherfurd, LONDON, 1998)

From around the end of the 1830s, *to galvanise* also meant 'to plate with metal through galvanic action', and so, when it was discovered that coating iron with zinc prevented it from rusting, the term *galvanised iron* was used even though it was rarely produced by galvanism.

Galvani and Volta may have disagreed professionally, but they had great mutual respect. It was Volta who coined the expression *galvanism*.

1795

MUNGO PARK BEGINS HIS EXPEDITION TO THE NIGER RIVER

••••••

Early in his career the young Scottish surgeon Mungo Park took a post on board a ship trading in the East Indies. The botanical studies of Sumatra he made while travelling brought him to the attention of the African Association of London. At that time the Association was anxious to conduct explorations into the hitherto unknown African interior and Park was engaged to trace the course of the Niger River. He was just twenty-three years old.

Park began his hazardous expedition to the Niger in June 1795. Recurrent bouts of fever and four months' captivity by a local chief, from whom he eventually managed to escape, were amongst the hardships he endured on his perilous journey. Park finally reached the mighty Niger River at Ségou on 20 July 1796 and began to follow the river downstream. Sadly, his supplies were too meagre to allow him to continue and he was forced to return.

In 1805 Park went back to Africa, this time intending to reach the mouth of the Niger by canoe. Tragically, the expedition went missing. Not until 1812 was it discovered that the party had been attacked near the rapids at Bussa where Park had drowned.

MUMBO JUMBO

Once back in Britain after his two-year expedition of the African interior, Mungo Park set about writing an account of his expedition. TRAVELS IN THE INTERIOR DISTRICTS OF AFRICA appeared in 1799. It captured popular imagination and was an immediate best-seller. In one part of his vivid narrative, Park tells of a hideous idol known amongst the tribes of the Niger as *Mumbo Jumbo*. This demon was a great favourite amongst the men of the region who would invoke him to terrorise their women into submission. Park described *Mumbo Jumbo* as *a strange bugbear . . . much employed by the Pagan natives in keeping their women in subjection.* With the publication and success of Park's book, Mumbo Jumbo's secret was out. During the first half of the nineteenth century he was mentioned by other writers and, by around the middle of the century, his jingle of a name had come to denote 'an object of senseless homage'. In modern English *mumbo jumbo* is used to describe 'language intended to bewilder or baffle, meaningless jargon'. The Internet is full of cries for help from people setting up computer systems who don't understand *all the technical mumbo jumbo*. Or the term might be applied to a 'nonsensical ritual':

> . . . *I've seen that rubbish in your dugout. The wee carved figures, cards and candle ends. Chuck it out. Trust to preparation and good leadership. Trust your men . . . Cut out the mumbo-jumbo and believe in yourself.*

(Sebastian Faulks, BIRDSONG, 1993)
These uses emerged at the end of the nineteenth century. Mumbo Jumbo still retains some of his mystery, however. In spite of the best efforts of etymologists who have studied the languages of the Niger region, no one has yet been able to work out where the demon's name originally came from, or what it means.

1800

ALESSANDRO VOLTA INVENTS THE BATTERY

• • • • • •

The Italian physicist Alessandro Volta was not convinced by Luigi Galvani's theory of 'animal electricity' (see **1791**, page 191). He thought chemical reaction was a more likely explanation for the twitching frogs' legs. He demonstrated that Galvani had created a simple electric cell, the frogs providing the necessary moisture between electrodes of dissimilar metals. Volta used this principle to construct the first battery, which he detailed in a paper to the Royal Society, London, in 1800. It consisted of a collection of cells piled one on top of the other. Each cell comprised two metal discs, one zinc and one copper, separated by a pasteboard pad moistened with a salt solution. The electric current flowed along a wire connecting the top and bottom discs in the pile. A reliable current of electricity which could be used for practical purposes was now available.

BATTERY

Volta's invention is known as 'Volta's pile', a reference to the stack of cells the physicist used. The Romance languages have retained the word *pile* for 'battery' (French *pile*, Italian *pila*, Spanish *pila*, Portuguese *pilha*) but English immediately employed *battery*.

The Old French term *batterie*, 'beating', was derived from *bat(t)re*, 'to beat', from Latin *battuere*, 'to beat'. It was borrowed into English as *battery* in the sixteenth century. In legal terms it denoted 'an illegal assault with repeated blows' and this sense remains in the term *assault and battery*. In war the word, first in French and then in English, also denoted the 'bombardment of heavy artillery' upon a target and was then applied to a 'collection of pieces or units of artillery strategically deployed for combined action'. Eighteenth-century scientists took this latter concept and applied it to an apparatus made up of several Leyden jars linked together for greater effect, calling it a *battery*. (A Leyden jar was a vessel used to store static electricity.) Benjamin Franklin was amongst the first to use the word in this sense, just two years after the invention of the Leyden jar in 1746. In 1800 Alessandro Volta notified the Royal Society of his work on the electrochemical 'pile', but when Sir Humphrey Davy described this arrangement of cells the following year, he eschewed the term adopted by Continental Europe and used *battery* instead. Strictly, *battery* should still be used for an arrangement of two or more cells, but modern usage applies the term to a single cell (see **cell**, page 36).

• It is thought that a Celtic source may have been responsible for the Latin verb *battuere*, 'to beat', a theory which finds support in the Gaulish term *andabata*, 'a gladiator', one who fought in a helmet without eye openings for the amusement of the crowd. Whatever its ultimate origin, *battuere* plays a part in the history of a number of other English words:

Battle from Old French *bataille*, from Vulgar Latin *battālia*, alteration of Late Latin *battuālia*, 'gladiatorial exercises'.

Battalion Old Italian took the Vulgar Latin word *battālia* as *battaglia*, 'battle, company of soldiers'. Soon the augmentative prefix *-one* was added to give *battaglione*, 'battalion'. This was borrowed into French as *battaillion* and from there into English as *battalion* in the late sixteenth century.

Batter from Middle English *bateren*, from Anglo-Norman *baterer*, from Old French *bat(t)re*, from Latin *battuere*, 'to beat'. *Batter*, 'a beaten mixture of egg, milk and flour', came into English by way of Anglo-Norman *batour* and Old French *bateure*, 'the action of beating, threshing grain', a derivative of *bat(t)re*, 'to beat'.

Battuere is also evident in the English verbs *combat*, *abate* and *debate* (see **bat**, page 183).

1819

BARON CAGNIARD DE LA TOUR INVENTS THE SIREN

······

In 1819 Charles Cagniard de la Tour invented an acoustic device which produced a musical sound of definite pitch when a jet of compressed air or steam was forced against evenly spaced perforations around the edge of a rapidly rotating disc. The instrument could be used for calculating the number of vibrations in any note by multiplying the number of holes by the number of revolutions per second: *It has been ascertained by means of the siren that the wings of the mosquito move at the rate of 15,000 times a second* (J Knight, PRACTICAL DICTIONARY OF MECHANICS, 1874–77).

SIREN

The Sirens of Greek mythology were two sisters, part women and part bird, who sat upon their islands bewitching sailors with their wondrously sweet singing and enticing them to their deaths. The Greek hero, Odysseus, forewarned by the sorceress Circe, stopped the ears of his crew with wax. He bound himself to the mast of his ship so that he could enjoy the loveliness of the Sirens' song but was restrained until he was beyond its power. The Argonauts, too, sailed clear unharmed, being accompanied by Orpheus, whose singing transcended that of the Sirens.

Greek *Seiren* appeared in Middle English as *serein* or *siren* in the first half of the fourteenth century by way of Old French *sereine*, Late Latin *Sirena* and Latin *Sīren*. Here it originally denoted one of these creatures of classical mythology and was also often confused with the mermaid of northern folklore. In the late sixteenth century the term was figuratively applied to 'a dangerously alluring woman, a temptress', a sense which is still current. Then, in 1819, *siren* was applied to the acoustic instrument invented by Charles

Cagniard de la Tour, who may have named it after its capacity of being sonorous in water – although, according to the ENCYCLOPAEDIA METROPOLITANA (1830), the notes it produced were also mellifluous, *clear and sweet, like the human voice*. Later in the nineteenth century, larger-scale instruments of similar construction were used on steamships to give warning signals and then, in the twentieth century, *siren* was applied more generally to any instrument that produced a sustained blast of sound to alert people to danger: an air-raid signal, for instance, or the warning device carried on speeding emergency vehicles:

One afternoon I was at home, the siren having sounded, and I saw a German bomber circle the lighthouse half a mile away and drop a bomb on Larder's caravan camp. A Mrs Read suffered a fractured arm and leg when the caravan she and her husband shared was flattened by the explosion.

(Wartime account by a nine-year-old boy, in Westall, CHILDREN OF THE BLITZ, 1985)

1820

GIDEON MANTELL FINDS A NUMBER OF LARGE FOSSILISED TEETH IN TILGATE FOREST

••••••

It is quite probable that the mythological Chinese dragon, the national emblem which is revered as a deity in Taoism, arose from discoveries of dinosaur fossils over two thousand years ago. Throughout more recent history, as successive generations dug and quarried the earth, dinosaur remains, like other fossils, inevitably came to light and were discarded in ignorance, explained away by folklore or superstition, or given a biblical interpretation. In 1770 the fossilised jaws of *Mosasaurus*, a huge marine lizard, were dug out of a Dutch chalk mine near Maastricht. Could this be an example of a creature now extinct? The question was not properly investigated until the early 1820s, when a number of strange fossilised bones were dug up in different sites in southern England and scrutinised by enthusiastic amateurs. Gradually, the realisation began to dawn that the earth was once home to creatures that were quite different from any existing animal.

DINOSAUR

Gideon Mantell was a doctor who enjoyed collecting fossils in his spare time. In 1820, on an outing to Tilgate Forest in Sussex, he came across several large teeth and some leg bones embedded in the sandstone. Mantell was intrigued by the fossils and worked hard to identify them. In 1825 he published a description of his find and his conclusion that the remains were those of a large fossil reptile. He named the creature *Iguanodon*, 'Iguana tooth', because he imagined it must have looked rather like an iguana. In 1834 a better idea of the size and appearance of the creature was formed when the partial remains of a similar reptile were found near Maidstone. Meanwhile another fossil collector, clergyman William Buckland, had found a jawbone with some teeth belonging to a different kind of reptile, and a specimen

of yet another type was found in the Weald in 1832. Interest in such fossils began to spread to the Continent, where more discoveries were made. In 1841 the eminent scientist Sir Richard Owen, who had been studying the various finds, wrote a paper for the British Association for the Advancement of Science. He concluded that all the specimens belonged to a group of large extinct reptiles. He classed them as *Dinosauria*, more popularly *dinosaurs*, a term he coined from the Greek words *deinos*, 'terrible', and *sauros*, 'lizard'. This recognition sparked an increasingly zealous quest in Europe and North America for other dinosaur remains.

It is a popular misconception that dinosaurs were simply ponderous, cretinous creatures, ill-adapted for survival. In the middle of the twentieth century, this view gave rise to *dinosaur* being used figuratively to describe 'someone or something that has been unable to keep pace with change':

Cathedral choirs are, despite their excellence, musical dinosaurs, just as the cathedrals themselves are musical museums. No major composer this century has written more than a handful of works for church use in any denomination.
(Alan Kennedy in a letter to THE INDEPENDENT, 20 May 1999)

• Paleontologists named the dinosaurs they studied after their appearance and coined descriptive words from Greek:

Horned dinosaurs are known as *ceratopians*. The herbivorous three-horned monster found in North America was called *triceratops*, literally 'three-horned face', a combination of *tri*, 'three', and *keras* (stem *kerat-*), 'horn', and *ōps*, 'face'.

Dinosaurs capable of flight were named *pterosaurs*. The term was coined from *ptero-* (from *pteron*, 'feather, wing'), an element used in combination with another word to indicate the presence of feathers or a wing, and *sauros*, 'lizard'.

Pterodactyl uses *ptero-* with *dactulos*, which means 'finger'. The creature had finger-like claws on the tips of its wings.

Armour-plated dinosaurs were erroneously called *stegosaurs*, that is 'roof lizards'. The plates on their backs were originally thought to lie flat and overlap, like roofing-tiles, hence the combination of *stegos*, 'roof', and *sauros*, 'lizard'. In fact the plates stood on end in two rows that ran the length of the dinosaur's back and it is now thought that, instead of protecting the creature's backbone, the plates, which carried an abundant blood-supply, were a means of controlling body temperature.

The *tyrannosaur* or *tyrannosaurus* was a huge carnivorous dinosaur whose fossilised remains have been discovered in North America and eastern Asia. Its fearsome size, muscular back, legs and neck, and its serrated teeth enabled it to prey on large animals. It was a tyrant, as its name suggests, *tyranno-* being the combining form of *tyrannos*, 'tyrant'.

FOSSIL

When *fossil* came into English in the seventeenth century, it was used both as an adjective and a noun and simply denoted '(something) dug out of the earth', a rock or mineral for instance. This sense is still evident in the term *fossil fuel*, which has been in use since the mid-nineteenth century. *Fossil* was a borrowing of French *fossile*, which was derived from Latin *fossilis*, meaning 'dug up', from *fossus*, past participle of *fodere*, 'to dig'. Soon after its appearance in English *fossil* was also applied to the petrified remains of animals and plants, since these too were dug from the earth. Aristotle and, much later, Leonardo da Vinci had been familiar with fossil shells, recognising evidence of a different sea level at one time, but it was not until the eighteenth century that this early interest began to pick up. As geological principles were worked out and their significance widely appreciated, *fossil* lost its original sense, 'dug up', and was exclusively applied to 'the remnant or impression of a life-form from a previous age hardened in the earth'.

From around the mid-eighteenth century, *fossil* was used figuratively to describe 'a person or thing that is old-fashioned or incapable of keeping up with progress'. *Dinosaur* was to develop an identical sense a century later.

1825

THE STOCKTON AND DARLINGTON RAILWAY IS COMPLETED

••••••

In the early nineteenth century much of London's coal came from the mines at Darlington in Co Durham. As output increased, the need for more efficient transportation between the coalfield and the port of Stockton-on-Tees became evident. In 1821 Parliament agreed to the building of a railway link between the two centres. The original intention was to use horses to haul the wagons but the planners' attention was drawn towards the work of George Stephenson, a mine mechanic who had built several efficient steam locomotives. It was eventually decided to employ horse and steam power. The railway, which opened on 27 September 1825, mostly carried freight but was also licensed to transport passengers.

TRAIN

The noun *train* has its origins in the Latin verb *trahere*, 'to pull'. An unattested variant *tragere* gave rise to the unattested Vulgar Latin verb *tragināre*. This was taken into Old French as *tra(h)iner*, 'to pull, to drag', and the verb gave rise to the noun *train* which developed a range of senses, all with the underlying notion of 'something that is dragged along'.

When the word was first borrowed into Middle English in the fourteenth century as *trayne*, it meant 'delay', the implication being 'time dragged out'. This sense became obsolete in the second half of the sixteenth century.

In the fifteenth century *trayne* denoted 'that part of a dress or robe that trails along the ground behind the wearer'. The wearing of a *train* was originally a statement of social rank. The nobility could be very sniffy about etiquette and it was not unusual for quarrels to arise over who amongst them was entitled to a train-bearer and who was not. A BOOK OF PRECEDENCE written around the turn of the seventeenth century cleared the matter up for once and for all:

A Baronesse may haue no trayne borne; but haueing a goune with a trayne, she ought to beare it her selfe.

Later, short *trains* became a fashion statement but had to be pinned up for dancing lest they were trodden on or became entangled in the lady's legs. *Trains* these days are more or less confined to robes and gowns worn for ceremonial occasions and weddings.

Also from the fifteenth century comes the sense 'a retinue, a group of attendants' which, like a long robe, trailed in the wake of a person of importance. Funerals are still attended by a *train of mourners* and attractive girls by a *train of admirers*. This notion of 'a sequence of persons, animals, things or ideas' is evident in *mule train, train of events* and *train of thought*. The concept doubtless influenced the new sense of *train*, 'a string of wagons coupled together', which first appeared in English in the early 1820s. At first the locomotive was considered separate from the train of trucks, like a queen and her retinue. A contemporary account of the opening of the Stockton and Darlington railway in 1825 describes how *the engine started off with this immense train of carriages.* Within ten years, however, *train* denoted not just the carriages but also the locomotive that pulled them.

ENGINE

In his SECOND NUN'S TALE (c 1386) Chaucer tells us that *A man hath sapiences thre, Memorie, engin and intellect also.* The word *engin* was borrowed into English from Old French *engin* in the fourteenth century with the sense 'innate aptitude' or 'genius'. Old French had taken *engin* from Latin *ingenium*. This term was derived from the prefix *in-* and the root *gen*, 'to procreate, to generate', and meant 'inborn skill, talent placed in one from birth'. Sometimes this native wit might be abused and channelled into deceit and trickery, so that *engin* also denoted 'plot' or 'wile', evidence of native cunning. Before long the word was being applied to more substantial products of innate ability, when it began to denote 'a mechanism or device'. Thus, from the fourteenth century onwards, *engin* might refer to anything from a machine used in warfare (*an engin of war*) or an instrument of punishment or torture, to a microscope or pair of scissors.

During the seventeenth century *engine* was applied to increasingly complicated mechanisms such as watches or air-pumps. Steam-engines, developed during the course of the eighteenth century, became so important to industry that by the early nineteenth century 'steam-engine' had become the prevailing sense of the word. Following the success of steam locomotives on the Stockton and Darlington railway, a locomotive freight and passenger service linking Liverpool and Manchester was proposed. Several mechanical engineers tendered their locomotive designs and in 1829 the Rainhill trials were held to find the best. The winner was Stephenson's Rocket which succeeded in completing the course, at times reaching a speed of twenty-nine miles an hour. The great age of rail travel had begun. *Engine* now also denoted 'steam locomotive', a machine

capable of generating motion. Consequently, with the development of the motor car in the second half of the nineteenth century, the term was easily applied to the *internal-combustion engine* which made motor transport possible (see **1885**, page 220).

From being a key term of the mechanical revolution, the word has found its place in the electronic world of the present day. There can be hardly a user of the Internet who has not employed a *search engine* to find information from the millions of web sites around the world.

STATION

The Latin noun *statiō* (stem *statiōn-*) was derived from *stāre*, 'to stand', and means 'a standing, a standing still'. The word soon developed a range of senses. It could, for instance, denote 'a dwelling' or 'a residence'. In military language *statiō* meant 'a station' or 'a post' and in post-Classical Latin it also meant 'a job or position', particularly in a government office. The term was borrowed into Old French as *station* and, from there, into Middle English where, over time, this useful word was employed in a variety of contexts reflecting those of Latin.

Then during the late sixteenth century a new sense, which was unrelated to any previously employed in Latin, began to emerge, that of 'a temporary stopping-place on a journey'. This concept was further developed two hundred years later in the United States where *station* came to denote 'a regular stopping-place along a coach route' so that horses could be changed and refreshments taken. When railway construction began in England in the nineteenth century the stopping-places along the track where people boarded or left the train were called *stations*. The earliest mention of the word occurs in a report on the Liverpool and Manchester Railway (1830) which states that the railway *will cost above £800,000 including the charge for stations and depots at each end* (see **stationer**, page 45).

1827

Friction Matches Are Invented by British Chemist John Walker

••••••

How easy it is to take for granted something as small and inexpensive as matches, yet the path to their invention was strewn with safety hazards, and its completion gave the world instant portable fire. From the late eighteenth century onwards, chemists wrestled with the problem of producing instantaneous fire. One early invention had consisted of a closed glass tube containing a strip of thick paper impregnated with wax and tipped with phosphorus. When the tip of the tube was snapped off, the phosphorus ignited on contact with the air. Another invention had consisted of a small bottle containing partly oxidised phosphorous into which strips of wood dipped in sulphur were inserted. In 1828 Samuel Jones invented the 'promethean match'. A glass bead filled with sulphuric acid was coated with an inflammable mix of potassium chlorate, gum arabic and sugar and then wrapped in paper. When the bead was cracked with pliers or the teeth, the paper caught alight – along with the facial hair of the user! The first friction match, however, was invented by an English chemist, John Walker, who rubbed wood sticks tipped with a mixture of potassium chloride and antimony sulphide between sheets of sandpaper to produce an explosion of sparks and a lungful of pungent fumes. Nevertheless, although the matches were unpleasant to use and of a rather inconvenient size, being one yard (just under a metre) long, Walker was obviously working along the right lines. His basic idea was taken up, improved upon and has been in use ever since.

MATCH

In the fourteenth century *match* simply denoted 'the wick of a lamp or candle'. The word was borrowed from Old French *mieche*, itself a borrowing of Latin *myxa* which denoted 'the spout of a lamp'. On a larger scale, from the mid-sixteenth century *matches* were also being used by the military. These were lengths of cord or hempen rope which, being especially treated to burn at a consistent rate, were used to ignite firearms or gunpowder. On 5 November 1605, the notorious Guy Fawkes was discovered red-handed placing explosives in the cellar beneath the House of Lords in London (see **1605**, page 142). According to a speech delivered by James I just after the discovery, when Guy Fawkes was seized and searched, his captors *found three matches . . . ready upon him.*

In domestic contexts during the mid-sixteenth century *match* began also to refer to 'a piece of cord or spill of wood dipped in melted sulphur' which could be set alight by a spark from the flint and steel of a tinder box and used to light a candle or a fire. These articles were known as *brimstone matches*, *brimstone* being the popular name for sulphur. Brimstone matches and tinders were the only convenient means available for producing and transferring flame until the end of the eighteenth century, when a growing interest in chemistry resulted in a flurry of fire-producing inventions. The term *light* rather than *match* was applied to many of these new devices: John Walker called his invention a *friction light*. Then in 1828 Samuel Jones invented his *promethean match*, and the term *match* was subsequently applied to any of the chemically charged wood splints used to produce fire, whether by contact with sulphuric acid or through friction.

• Match to denote 'a marriage' or even 'a sporting contest' is unrelated to the sense described above. Rather, it comes from Old English *gemoecca*, a word of Germanic origin, which denoted 'mate, equal'. This became *macche* in Middle English and developed a range of senses with the underlying notion of 'a counterpart, a person or thing corresponding to or similar to another'.

1827

NICÉPHORE NIEPCE TAKES THE FIRST PHOTOGRAPH

······

The French inventor Nicéphore Niepce possessed plenty of ingenuity but little artistic skill. Although he greatly enjoyed making lithographic prints (it was a fashionable hobby in the early years of the nineteenth century in France), it was his son who did the artwork. When the boy was obliged to do his military service, Niepce was unable to pursue his hobby. Undaunted, he continued a series of experiments (begun in 1793) to find ways of registering images permanently on a surface.

His renewed attempts, from 1813, were to use sunlight to copy engravings. A chosen engraving was given an application of oil. It was then placed on a pewter plate which had been treated with a range of photosensitive compounds. Exposure to a few hours of sunlight gradually hardened the compound under the light parts of the engraving, while that beneath the darker ink stayed soft enough to rinse off. What remained was a copy of the engraving. In succeeding years, he turned to the *camera obscura*, trying to fix the image on paper with silver chloride, then with a kind of bitumen on glass.

In 1826-7 a major achievement in photographic history was realised when Niepce succeeded in permanently fixing the view of his house's courtyard on to a pewter plate, again with bitumen. In this process, any plate so produced could then be etched, and prints made from it. Niepce's fame rests not only on producing the first permanent photograph, as we know it, but also on developing a way of reproducing it. Perhaps his wealthy background allowed him to disregard the possibilities of commercial exploitation of his discovery, and even the scrutiny of his fellow scientists. He insisted on secrecy, for example, after telling the British Royal Society of his discovery in 1827. Eventually, in 1829, he agreed to collaboration with the younger Daguerre, who had already established a reputation as a scene painter, and by 1826 was turning his attention to recording images through the action of sunlight. The working partnership brought little improvement in results before the death of Niepce in 1833, though experimentation with iodine and copper plate coated with silver made possible an important accidental discovery of 1835. Daguerre found mercury vapour cut down exposure time enormously; after two more years of experimenting, he was able to fix permanently the image so produced.

It was Daguerre who ultimately made the money, by selling the rights to the French Government in 1839, and claimed the fame – the invention (called the daguerreotype) incorporated his name, in contravention of the contract he had signed with his partner. Niepce's son, who agreed to these arrangements, was perhaps mollified by the substantial pension he received. Daguerre, who began his career as a tax man, went on to become an officer of the Legion of Honour.

CAMERA

The ancients knew that, if light is allowed to filter through a tiny hole into a darkened room, images of outside objects and views appear reversed and upside-down on the opposite wall. From such a chamber the safe observation of a solar eclipse was made possible or an artist might make an accurate tracing of a projected object or view. The addition of a lens in the late sixteenth century sharpened the image, and the use of a mirror turned it the right way up. But the optical principle did not need a room to be effective. Scaled-down versions in boxes worked just as well. In eighteenth-century English, the term for such apparatus, whether a room or box, was *camera obscura,* which was coined from Latin and literally meant 'dark chamber'. Human laziness (or, alternatively, the principle of least effort) being what it is,

the phrase was often shortened to *camera* from its earliest appearance in the language. Development of the apparatus into a photographic device in the nineteenth century began when Nicéphore Niepce placed a light-sensitive plate inside to produce the first photograph, a view of his courtyard at Gras from an upstairs window. As enthusiasm for photography grew, so the full phrase *camera obscura* decreased until, by the middle of the century, *camera* sufficed.

• The Latin word *camera* (variant *camara*) originally meant 'vaulted chamber', being a borrowing of Greek *kamarā* which denoted 'anything with an arched cover', an 'arched room', for instance. In Late Latin the notion of 'vault' began to disappear and *camera* was used more generally to denote 'room'. The term was taken into Old French as *chambre* and from there was borrowed directly into Middle English in the thirteenth century. The spelling *chamber* dates from the sixteenth century.

• While French adopted and adapted Latin *camera*, Spanish borrowed its variant, *camara*, to denote 'room'. (Present-day Spanish is *cámara*, meaning 'room, hall, chamber'.) From this *camarada* was derived, which originally meant 'roomful' and then came to denote 'room-mate', particularly in military circles, and hence, 'companion'. The word was borrowed into French as *camarade* and from there into English as *comrade*.

PHOTOGRAPH

Niepce called his method of capturing permanent images by the action of light on chemically treated surfaces *heliography* – 'sun drawing'. Following his inspiration and experiments, others were prompted to improve the process. Louis Daguerre, who painted scenery for a type of *son-et-lumière* entertainment he staged in Paris, regularly made use of a *camera obscura* for his work. He produced a positive photographic image on a metal plate by using mercury vapours. After a period of trial and error, by 1837 he managed to fix the image with a strong solution of common table salt. Modest to a fault, Daguerre called his process the *daguerreotype*. Meanwhile an English scientist, William Fox Talbot, frustrated because he was unable to sketch the stunning Italian landscapes he saw while on holiday, thought of using chemically prepared paper and a *camera obscura* to capture them. He eventually managed to produce a paper negative from which any number of prints could be made. Talbot named his process *photogenic drawing* and, in January 1839, made known his discovery to the Royal Society. In March 1839 Sir John Herschel, who had made profitable suggestions to help Talbot with his experiments, also wrote a paper for the Royal Society outlining *the application of the Chemical Rays of light to the purpose of Pictorial Representation*. Herschel called the process

photography. The term was coined from Greek *phōto-*, stem of *phos*, meaning 'light', and *-graphia*, 'writing', from *graphein*, 'to write'. It is suggested that Herschel may have taken inspiration from both Talbot and Niepce by combining the more scientifically accurate elements of their proposed terms. The paper also introduced the words *photograph* and *photographic*. These gained immediate acceptance, even in France where they appeared in official papers (including a document discussing Daguerre's government pension) within two months.

The Victorians were captivated by photography, and none more so than the Queen herself. From her pen we have the earliest mention of the abbreviation *photo*:

I send you. . . a wonderful photo: of the Queen of Naples.
(LETTER, 28 November 1860)

FILM

Old English had the word *filmen* to denote 'a fine natural membrane'. This might be the skin of an egg, for instance, or the membrane covering the eye or the brain, or the stem of a plant. During the sixteenth century use of this word was extended to describe a thin skin of any material at all. In the nineteenth century pioneers of photography accordingly applied the term *film* to the thin coating of light-sensitive emulsion that they spread on photographic plates or paper. In 1888 American George Eastman produced his first Kodak push-button camera which held a whole roll of sensitive paper, enough for a hundred exposures. The following year the paper was replaced by film on transparent nitrocellulose, an invention of the Reverend Goodwin. With these innovations *film* no longer simply denoted the light-sensitive coating but was applied to the entire product which became known as 'flexible film' as opposed to dry plates.

Around the time that the Kodak camera appeared, photographers began to explore the possibility of using a series of rapidly presented photographs to convey the idea of motion. Thomas Edison proposed capturing a sequence on a light-sensitive drum but his assistant, Englishman William Dickson, hit upon the idea of using Eastman's Kodak film, perforated at the edge to keep it straight as it fed through the Kinetograph camera and then the Kinetoscope viewer. This was the advent of silent movies. These were originally known as *moving pictures* (the shortened Americanism *movie* dates from around 1912). Surprisingly, the phrase remained current until as late as the 1950s when it finally lost out to *film*, used to denote 'a moving picture' from the beginning of the twentieth century.

• Edison and Dickson's Kinetograph and Kinetoscope were soon superseded in 1895 by the *Cinématographe*, a combined camera and projector invented by Auguste and Louis Lumière. On 3 October 1986 Queen Victoria, who was always amused by the latest technology, described in her journal how *We were all photographed . . . by the new cinematograph process, which makes moving pictures by winding off a reel of films.* The word was coined from Greek *kinēma* (stem *kinēmat-*), meaning 'motion', a derivative of *kinein*, 'to move'. Within two months the *cinematograph* was being exhibited at halls in London and amazing audiences with scenes of stormy seascapes and views of the busy Thames from Waterloo Bridge. *Cinématographe* proved far too cumbersome for the French who, before the end of the century, had clipped the term to *cinéma*. English followed suit around 1909.

1828

STANISLAV BAUDRY STARTS HIS OMNIBUS SERVICES IN PARIS

······

When philosopher and mathematician Blaise Pascal financed a limited public transport scheme in Paris in the second half of the seventeenth century, the king and government were not amused. If common folk were permitted to sit alongside their more illustrious compatriots, they might start to think too highly of themselves. Not until the 1820s was the scheme revived.

During the early nineteenth century stage-coaches conveyed passengers from the outskirts of large European cities to their centres. In the French town of Nantes, Stanislav Baudry decided to operate a similar service from the town centre to his bath-house in the suburbs for the convenience of his clients. Soon, however, Monsieur Baudry realised that many of his passengers were not bath-house customers at all, but simply in need of transport out of town. Inspiration struck. Not only would he run stopping transport services to the town centre and back, but he would redesign the coaches so that passengers could climb on and off with ease. The enterprise was so successful that Baudry soon graduated to the capital, where he was granted ten routes. And so it was that in 1828 Baudry's horse-drawn omnibuses made their first appearance on the streets of Paris.

BUS

The success of Baudry's enterprise excited immediate interest abroad. George Shillibeer, an English coach-builder, proposed a similar service for London. In a memorandum to the Chairman of the Board of Stamps dated 3 April 1829 he expressed his intention thus:

I am . . . engaged in building 2 Vehicles after the manner of the recently established French Omnibus, which when completed I purpose starting on the Paddington road.

Shillibeer's service, which ran from Paddington station to the City, began to operate on 4 July that year, its route determined by the prerogatives already granted to hackney carriages.

Shillibeer's memorandum is the first recorded use of *omnibus* in English. There is a story that the original conveyance was named after a shop in Nantes which stood at the end of its route. Apparently the store, which was run by a Monsieur Omnes, had the slogan 'Omnes omnibus' (Omnes for everybody) displayed in its window. It is certainly possible that Stanislav Baudry was influenced by such a slogan when he called his conveyance the *voiture omnibus*, 'vehicle for everybody' (the Latin word *omnibus*, 'for all', being the dative plural of *omnis*, 'all').

Shillibeer's conveyances could carry twenty passengers and were pulled by three horses harnessed side by side. They were soon a familiar sight in the capital and, before long, the rather cumbersome term *omnibus* had been clipped to a more acceptable length: *buss* appeared in 1832 and *'bus* around 1845. Sticklers for correctness battled on with the more ponderous *omnibus*, however; the common figurative expression *to miss the bus*, meaning 'to miss an opportunity', began its existence as *to miss the omnibus* during the 1880s. But *bus* has long since ousted the more formal *omnibus*.

The vehicles also kept pace with automotive developments (exchanging the pollution of knee-high horse dung in the city streets for the noxious emissions from the internal combustion engine) with the appearance of the steam omnibus and the motor-bus (see **1885**, page 220).

TRAM

Broadway was the route of the first American omnibus in 1831. But bus journeys in America were to be endured rather than enjoyed, passengers often alighting bruised and shaken from their rough ride over one of the many unpaved roads in the rapidly expanding city. Almost immediately a solution was found. In 1832 John Stephenson, inspired by the railways, introduced the streetcar, designed to run on rails. Not only did the track ensure a comfortable ride for the passengers, but less effort was required from the horses pulling the conveyance and so heavier loads were possible. The cost of line installation and maintenance was too expensive, however, and it was another twenty years or so before many American cities were prepared for the financial outlay. At the same time European cities began to show interest, with London finally approving the system in the 1870s.

Although Britain adopted the streetcar, it did not adopt the name. Instead an existing term, *tram*, was pressed into service. Appearing in Scotland around the turn of the sixteenth century, *tram* originally denoted the 'shaft of a barrow', the word being a borrowing of Middle Low German *trame*, 'beam'. From the first quarter of the sixteenth century, *tram* was applied to the frame or sledge used for transporting baskets of ore in various mining districts of England. Later, when these *trams* were mounted on small wheels and rolled along parallel wooden rails for ease of movement, *tram* was also applied to such a rail, either because it was made of wooden beams (going back in sense to its Middle Low German origin) or because a compound such as *tram-track* was understood. The compound *tram-way* was used in mining contexts from around 1825 and when, in the 1860s, the British began to contemplate a streetcar scheme in London, *tram-way* seemed a logical term to choose. The vehicles themselves were then called *tram-cars*, a compound which was soon shortened to *tram* (see **car**, page 220).

1848

GOLD IS DISCOVERED AT SUTTER'S MILL, NORTHERN CALIFORNIA

••••••

On 24 January 1848 James Wilson Marshall was at work building a sawmill when he discovered gold. He and the landowner, Swiss émigré John Augustus Sutter, secretly entered into a mining partnership but news of the find soon leaked out. Immediately, people from all over California converged on the region. By 1849 news had spread abroad and people from all walks of life arrived in the state hoping to get rich quick. California's population grew seven-fold in two years. The new arrivals were known as *forty-niners*, a reference to the year they settled in California. Most of them were American citizens, but their number also included many hopefuls from as far afield as Europe, South America, Australia and China.

PAN OUT

An earlier gold-find in Georgia in the late 1830s had given rise to the verb *to pan*, meaning 'to wash gravel in a pan in order to extract the gold'. (The noun *pan*, 'wide, shallow vessel', from which it was derived can be traced back to the unattested West Germanic *panna*, a possible borrowing of Latin *patina* from Greek *patane*, 'pan, dish'.) However, the find at Sutter's sawmill provoked the wildest gold rush in North America. Veins there were said *to pan well* or *poorly* according to their yield. Mark Twain observed that *Here's hoping your dirt'll pan out gay* was a customary salutation in the Californian mining camps (LETTERS FROM HAWAII, 1866). This turn of phrase was figuratively applied in the 1860s when *to pan out* was used independently of gold mining contexts with the sense 'to yield a result, to work out', a sense which is still current:

'We will not be pursuing the project any further,' said a spokesman for United News. 'We will continue working with Warner Brothers on other projects. But this deal did not pan out and threatened to become expensive, so we decided to put it aside.'

(THE SUNDAY TIMES, 15 November 1988)

Warner Brothers would have recognised *pan* in another sense (see **panorama**, page 188).

STRIKE IT RICH

The original meaning of the verb *to strike* in Old English was 'to touch lightly'. (*To streak* and *to stroke* are relatives, the latter still retaining the original sense of 'to touch lightly'.) The modern sense 'to hit with force' began to emerge towards the end of the thirteenth century. When mining fever hit the United States, *to strike* quickly acquired the sense 'to hit bedrock': to come to the layer of solid rock beneath looser ground where the largest quantities of gold were to be found. The expression *to strike it rich* arose in the Californian mining fields in the 1850s whenever a particularly bountiful seam of ore was found close to this rocky layer.

The term *bedrock* was also coined at this time, its figurative use to mean either 'the lowest level' or 'basic principles' dating back to the 1860s:

I asked her about the recent murders.
  She gave a grimace. 'It's awful.
Everyone's really upset about it, because
trust is such a kind of bedrock part of hiking
the AT [Appalachian Trail], you know? I
thru-hiked myself in 1987, so I know how
much you come to rely on the goodness of
strangers. . .'
(Bill Bryson, A WALK IN THE WOODS,
1997)

JEANS, DENIM, LEVIS

In the 1850s a Bavarian immigrant called
Levi Strauss arrived in San Francisco
hoping to sell supplies to the miners. He
had with him several rolls of cotton
canvas intended for tents. Instead, Strauss
identified a ready market for stout canvas
trousers and overalls suitable for the
rugged conditions in the goldfields – in
other words, what later came to be called
denim jeans or *Levis*.

The word *jean* originally denoted a type
of heavy, twilled cotton fabric, or fustian.
It was a shortening of the sixteenth-
century English term *Jene* or *Geane fustian*,
an indication that the fabric was originally
manufactured in the Italian city of Genoa,
whose name in Middle English was
variously rendered as *Geane, Jene, Jayne* or
Jane (from medieval Latin *Janua*). Before
Strauss's arrival on the mining workwear
scene in the mid-nineteenth century, the
word *jeans* was already in recent use in
England to describe hardwearing trousers
made from this type of cloth.

Later, Strauss replaced the tent canvas
with another type of durable fabric called
denim, which he dyed blue. Again the
name of the original place of manufacture,
this time Nîmes in France, is hidden in
the word, for *denim* is a shortening of *serge
de Nîmes*. Nevertheless, it was not until
the twentieth century that *denims* came to
denote 'overalls or trousers made of
denim' or that Strauss's hardwearing
denim trousers came to be classed as *jeans*.
By this time the garments were worn by
workmen throughout the United States
and had become indispensable wear for
American cowboys who, in the 1920s,
began to call them *Levis's* or *Levis* after
their manufacturer.

1849

COCKFIGHTING IS MADE ILLEGAL IN GREAT BRITAIN

······

Cockfighting originated in Asia and later became popular with the
ancient Greeks and then the Romans. In spite of vigorous opposition
from the Church, it became a favourite pastime in the markets and
fairs of medieval Europe. According to William FitzStephen,
cockfighting was the traditional Shrove Tuesday amusement of
schoolboys in twelfth-century England: in the North schoolmasters
received a payment known as the *cockpenny* for arranging the
Shrovetide fights. From the early sixteenth century, cockfighting
gradually became a favourite sport of royalty and the privileged classes.
The Puritans disapproved of gambling and Cromwell prohibited
cockfighting in 1653, but Charles II, who was always out for a good

time, reversed the Puritan rule and erected an indoor cockpit at Whitehall. In eighteenth-century England, people of all classes indulged their enjoyment of blood sports, cockfighting in particular. Not all fights took place in permanent cockpits: many were local tavern affairs. Thomas Turner, a shopkeeper of East Hoathly, Sussex, gives a matter-of-fact account of such an occasion in his diary for 2 May 1764:

> *This day was fought a main of cocks, at our public-house, between the gentlemen of East Grinstead and the gentlemen of East Hothly, for half-a-guinea a battle and two guineas the odd battle, which was won by the gentlemen of East Grinstead, they winning five battles out of six fought in the main. I believe there was a great deal of money sported on both sides.*

Heavy gambling and drinking marked all cockfights, no matter where they were held. César de Saussure, who visited England during the mid-eighteenth century, was amazed by the spectacle and astounded at the sums wagered:

> *At Whitehall Cockpit . . . where the spectators are mostly persons of a certain rank, the noise is much less; but would you believe that at this place several hundred pounds are sometimes lost and won?*
> (A FOREIGN VIEW OF ENGLAND IN THE REIGNS OF GEORGE I AND GEORGE II, 1902)

Not until the late eighteenth century did moralists again begin to raise their voices in protest. This time they augmented their objections to gambling with concerns about cruelty and the depravity of human nature. Nevertheless, public displays of cockfighting were not declared illegal until the middle of the following century and private meetings persisted for a long time after.

Although cockfighting has not been practised in Britain or America for a century and a half, its past popularity has left a legacy of words and expressions in the English language.

COCKPIT

Although cockfighting was an ancient sport in England, the name *cockpit* was not applied to the arena where fights took place until the sixteenth century. Early cockpits were simply depressions in the ground encircled by a mound of earth. Later pits were circular platforms with a matted surface surrounded by a low fence, and indoor pits were constructed to shelter aristocratic gamesters. Cocks brought to the pit were held beak to beak then loosed to fight. The battles were swift and bloody, the birds fighting to the death or until one of them was injured to the point where it could no longer continue. For this reason, in the early eighteenth century the term *cockpit* was applied to the area of a warship where the surgeons attended to the dying and wounded. The cockpit walls were painted red and the horrific injuries of battle were roughly tended without the benefit of either antiseptics or anaesthetics: after amputation boiling pitch was applied to the stump to prevent the spread of infection. With the advent of the aeroplane, *cockpit* was transferred from nautical to aeronautical vocabulary to describe the place occupied by the pilot in a fighter-plane. This was a small, snug space and so, in the 1930s, *cockpit* was also applied to the similarly compact area occupied by the driver in a racing car. From air travel to outer space, in the second half of the twentieth century *cockpit* describes the enclosure in a spacecraft which holds the astronaut and his navigational instruments.

PIT (PITTED) AGAINST

The source of the word *pit* is Latin *puteus*, 'well, pit'. It came into Old English as *pytt* by way of the unattested West Germanic form *putti*. The cockpit was sometimes simply known as the *pit*, and in the eighteenth century the derived verb *to pit* meant 'to put cocks in a pit to fight'. The verb was soon figuratively applied with the sense 'to match one against another, to set (one's efforts, will, etc) in opposition'.

COCK OF THE WALK

The pen where a gamecock was bred and kept was known as a *walk*. Here he reigned supreme since no other cock was ever put in the same enclosure. The term *cock of the walk* to denote the 'undisputed leader in any circle' was recorded by Francis Grose in his CLASSICAL DICTIONARY OF THE VULGAR TONGUE (1785). Grose's definition adds that the term also applied to *the best boxer in a village or district*. The fact that *cock of the walk* was included in the dictionary at all indicates that it was originally a low term which has gradually attained

respectability. The noun *cock*, however, had been used figuratively by genteel authors since at least the mid-sixteenth century to mean 'any greatly superior person', and had been used in phrases such as *cock of the club* and *cock of the school* since then.

GAME

Gamecocks were a special breed. They were large in the body but had short legs, and were especially trained to fight. They were bold, determined and mettlesome. The adjective *game* arose in the eighteenth century to describe an animal or person who showed the same plucky spirit as the noble bird.

The origin of *game*, which has cognates in other Germanic languages, probably lies in an unattested prehistoric word *gaman*, composed of the prefix *ga-*, 'together', and *mann-*, 'person', (the root of *man*), which meant 'participation, togetherness'. From this word, with its notion of people joining in and enjoying one another's company, came Old English *gamen*, 'amusement, fun, sport', a sense still preserved in the fifteenth-century phrase *to make game of someone*, meaning 'to ridicule'. The word first began to denote 'a diversion, a pastime' in the first half of the thirteenth century. All subsequent applications of the word to leisure activities derive from this basic meaning.

SHOW THE WHITE FEATHER

Every gambler likes to bet on certainties. Those attending a cockfight would be on the lookout for any white feather in a gamecock's plumage. In the words of Francis Grose, such a cock was *not of the true game breed* (CLASSICAL DICTIONARY OF THE VULGAR TONGUE, 1785) and was likely to display a cowardly temperament. Someone described as *having* or *showing the white feather* was, therefore, a coward. The eighteenth-century idiom was given a literal twist in the First World War when some women gave white feathers to men in civilian dress whom they deemed fit enough to fight in the trenches. In her novel PALE HORSE, PALE RIDER (1937) K A Porter describes the reaction of men refused for service:

All the rejected men talked like that. War was the one thing they wanted, now they couldn't have it. All of them had a side-long eye for the women they talked with, a guarded resentment which said, 'Don't pin a white feather on me, you blood-thirsty female. I've offered my meat to the crows and they won't have it.'

SPAR

The origins of this verb are a mystery, but its use dates back at least to the turn of the fifteenth century when it meant 'to move rapidly, to thrust suddenly (as with a spear)'. The word was little used and would seem, from written records, to have fallen into disuse by the mid-fifteenth century. Appearances can be deceptive, however. The term had been taken into the vocabulary of cockfighting and it reappeared in this context in the second half of the sixteenth century. Gamecocks use the spiny spurs on the backs of their legs to fight, and in the language of the sport *to spar* meant 'to strike out with the spurs or feet'. In the mid-eighteenth century the verb was borrowed as a boxing term to mean 'to practise boxing movements without landing heavy blows'. The sense 'to argue, to dispute' dates from the late seventeenth century.

WELL HEELED

It was common practice to sharpen a cock's spurs, but in the eighteenth century a cock was sometimes *heeled* as well. This meant that he had sharp spurs of steel, or sometimes silver, fitted over his natural ones. In nineteenth-century America, where cockfighting had been introduced by colonists two centuries earlier, *heeled* became a slang term meaning 'armed with a weapon', usually a revolver. In his LETTERS FROM HAWAII (1866) Mark Twain recounts how, at the start of an argument back in Virginia City, *the*

insulted party . . . would lay his hand gently on his six-shooter and say, 'Are you heeled?' Travellers in the American West were advised to make sure that they were *well heeled*, that is 'well armed' and able to protect themselves. It was around 1880 that *well heeled* was used with the sense 'well off, well-to-do', the transference to money possibly arising from the notion of possessing everything necessary to meet any situation.

BATTLE ROYAL

In the vocabulary of cockfighting a *battle royal* was a contest in which a number of gamecocks were put in the pit to fight at the same time until only one remained. The expression has been in figurative use since the seventeenth century to mean 'a general set-to, a free fight', one in which all available forces take part:

After dinner that evening there was a battle royal. Freddy was a quick-tempered man, unused to opposition, and he gave George the rough side of his tongue.
(W Somerset Maugham, 'The Alien Corn', in SIX STORIES WRITTEN IN THE FIRST PERSON SINGULAR, 1931)

• The earliest recorded use of *cock* in English (Old English had the forms *cocc*, *coc* and *kok*) dates from around the end of the ninth century. No one knows where the word came from. Although it is a common noun in both English and French, it is not found in any other Germanic or Romance languages. But, wherever it originated, the term is almost certainly an imitation of the bird's crowing, just like Chauntecleer the cockerel in Chaucer's NUN'S PRIEST'S TALE (c 1387) who *cried anon cok, cok*.

• The word *cock* is variously used in English to mean 'water-spout or tap' (15th century), 'firing mechanism in a gun' (16th century) and 'penis' (17th century). German usage correspondingly employs *hahn*, 'hen', in each of these three senses. The allusion is to the shape of a cock's head and crest. The OED suggests that the sense 'penis' may arise from a comparison with a water cock – but there again, it may not:

I have a gentle cock
Croweth me day:
He doth me risen erly
My matins for to say.

I have a gentle cock,
Comen he is of gret:
His comb is of red coral,
His tail is of jet.

His legges ben of asor,
So gentle and so smale:
His spores arn of silver whit
Into the worte wale.

His eyen arn of cristal,
Loken all in aumber:
And every night he percheth him
In myne ladye's chaumber.
(ANON, early 15th century)

• The proud strutting of the cock and his amorous advances are alluded to in the words *cocky* (18th century), 'self-important, arrogant', and *coquette*, 'flirting woman'. In the seventeenth century French *coquet*, a diminutive form of *coq*, 'cock', was applied to both men and women who were considered flirtatious and forward. By the eighteenth century *coquet* had become obsolete and the feminine form *coquette* was being used of women only.

1861-5

THE AMERICAN CIVIL WAR IS FOUGHT

••••••

A number of economic and political frictions led to the outbreak of civil war in 1861, but in the end they boiled down to two main issues: to what extent should a federal government with restricted powers be permitted to intervene in the affairs of individual states, and how far should slavery be tolerated?

The Northern states had abolished slavery and were anxious that the same policy should be adopted throughout the Union. This was vigorously opposed by the Southern states. Unlike the North, which was populated by industrialists and small farmers, the Southern states were made up of large plantations whose owners relied heavily upon slave-labour for their cotton crops. Demand for cotton especially had boomed, with new machinery making the business more and more profitable:

The production of cotton depends not on soil, or climate, but on slavery.
If slaves were freed cotton production would fall from 1,200,000 bales to
600,000 bales. Little more than two million Negro slaves set at liberty
would beggar ten million white men, instantly.
(From a speech by George McDuffie, Governor of South Carolina 1834-6)

The Southerners felt more and more under threat. When Abraham Lincoln was elected President in 1860 on the strength of his abolitionist sympathies, it was one step too far. Eleven Southern states seceded one by one from the Union, in order to preserve their slaveholdings. In 1861 they formed a Confederacy. Then, in April of that year, Southern troops opened fire on federal forces in Fort Sumter, South Carolina, opening the hostilities that were to last for the next four years (see **1865–77**, page 214).

ABOLITIONIST, EMANCIPATION

The earliest black settlers in Virginia, bought from a Dutch man-of-war in the early seventeenth century, were not slaves but indentured servants permitted to progress socially through their own hard work. But the need for labour soon hardened attitudes against the blacks and the American colonies began to restrict their rights. Already, by the 1680s, Quakers in Pennsylvania were moved to oppose slavery. Nevertheless the practice gathered momentum, particularly in the South where the need for plantation workers was pressing. It was justified on the grounds that black Africans were by nature inferior and enjoyed a better life in servitude:

The African Negro is destined by Providence to slavery. It is marked on his skin and by his lack of intelligence and ability to care for himself. They are in all respects inferior to us. They are not able to cope with freedom. People who would free the black race have only to look to those still in Africa to see how much our slaves have gained by their servitude.
(From a speech by George McDuffie, Governor of South Carolina 1834-6)

Vigorous opposition to slavery arose in Europe and America in the late eighteenth century, fuelled by evangelical revivalism and the spirit of the Enlightenment, a philosophical movement that emphasised reason, tolerance and the rights of the individual. Those who spoke out were called *abolitionists*, a name derived from the verb *to abolish,* which had been in English since the late fifteenth century. Its origins lay in Latin *abolēre. Abolēre* meant 'to grow obsolete', being a coupling of *ab,* 'off, away', and *olēre,* 'to grow'. Used transitively, the verb meant 'to do away with' and as such was borrowed into Old French as *abolir* whose stem *aboliss-* gave the English verb. The word *abolitionist* is now applied to 'a person who works to abolish a law or institution': capital punishment, for instance.

From about 1776 onwards many Northern states began the gradual *emancipation* of their black population by freeing the children of slaves at the age of twenty-one. The word *emancipation* came from *emancipātiōnem,* a Latin derivative of *ēmancipāre.* In Roman Law *ēmancipāre* meant 'to release a child from the authority of his father or guardian' so that he became legally responsible for himself. The verb was formed from *ex-,* 'out of', and *mancipium,* 'ownership' (from *manus,* 'hand', and *capere,* 'to take'). It was borrowed into English directly from Latin in the seventeenth century as *emancipate* and had the general sense 'to release from legal, social or political control'.

The noun *emancipation* had been in English since the mid-seventeenth century, where it had languished, little used. Now it had new force; it referred to the very process of liberating slaves. Indeed, its first recorded use in this context is in a letter written by future American President Thomas Jefferson on 7 August 1785: *Emancipation is put in such a train that in a few years there will be no slaves northward of Maryland.*

From here *emancipation*, *emancipate* and the participle *emancipated* were used with reference to the liberation of other groups. *Emancipation*, for instance, occurs in the title of the *Catholic Emancipation Act* of 1829, by which Irish Catholics were permitted to stand as MPs and be appointed to Irish offices of state except those of Viceroy and Chancellor. In the same period, but on the other side of the globe, *emancipated convicts* were taking their place in society in the colonies of Australia. And in the late twentieth century we dare to talk of the *emancipated woman*, supposedly free from all the prejudice traditionally shown to her sex.

HOLD THE FORT

This idiom, which means 'to stand in for someone temporarily' or 'to remain at one's post, to hold on', was inspired by an incident in the Civil War. On 5 October 1864, a Union force led by General Corse found itself hard pressed by Confederate troops in a struggle for Allatoona Pass. General William Tecumseh Sherman signalled from the heights of Kenesaw Mountain to say that assistance was on its way. The signal read *Hold out, relief is coming*, but in a subsequent report appeared as *Hold the fort for I am coming*. Undoubtedly the revised version has a more poetic ring, so perhaps the reporter may be forgiven for failing to notice that there was no fort at Allatoona. It also assured the quotation a place in the English language. Around 1870 Philip Paul Bliss incorporated the words into the chorus of one of his gospel songs:

> 'Hold the fort, for I am coming,' Jesus
> signals still;
> Wave the answer back to heaven, 'By Thy
> grace we will.'

This was often sung at mass evangelistic events led by the spirited and energetic preacher Dwight L Moody, which popularised the quotation still further. Clipped to *hold the fort*, the saying was used as an idiom in the first half of the twentieth century.

ON THE GRAPEVINE

At the beginning of the second half of the nineteenth century, due to technological advances, telegraph networks were being set up throughout Europe and America. The original *grapevine telegraph* was said to have been set up by Colonel Bee between Placerville and Virginia City in 1859. The lines were apparently attached to trees whose swaying stretched them until, hanging in loops, they had the appearance of wild vines. Whether or not this is true, the term *a despatch by grape-vine telegraph* was in use during the American Civil War to indicate 'a false report, a rumour', and a *grape-vine* simply meant 'a hoax'. According to John S Farmer (AMERICANISMS, OLD AND NEW, 1889,) *exciting news of battles not fought and victories not won were said to be received by grape-vine telegraph*. In modern English the term *on* or *through the grapevine* has come to indicate 'the means by which a piece of information, which may well be true but is usually secret or private, is made known':

> The grapevine that had brought news of
> Josie's job and the return of Matthew's
> children also reported a marked improvement
> in domestic regularity.
> (Joanna Trollope, OTHER PEOPLE'S
> CHILDREN, 1998)

SIDEBURNS

Unlike General Sherman, Union General Ambrose Everett Burnside had an unremarkable Civil War. After a crushing defeat at the Battle of Fredericksburg in 1862, his command was replaced by that of General Joseph Hooker. Dignified and charming, Burnside's chief claim to fame was his whiskers. At the start of the war he cut a dashing figure on the parade ground, sporting thick side-whiskers which merged with his bushy moustache, while his chin was clean-shaven. This style of grooming became all the rage in America and beyond. Known originally as *burnsides*, by the 1880s the alternative *sideburns* was also current, since the hair was on the sides of the face, and this is now the modern English term.

1865-77

America Undergoes a Period of Reconstruction

••••••

The American Civil War (see **1861-5**, page 211) ended in the defeat of the Confederation and, with the thirteenth Amendment to the Constitution, the abolition of slavery. It was followed by Reconstruction, a period of political and social unease during which terms for the reinstatement of the Southern states into the Union were argued over and the integration of almost four million freed slaves was begun. The Southern states constantly sought ways to circumvent hard-won black liberties. In response, the Republican Congress passed several acts and amendments, ultimately imposing military law in the South. This had some effect, but there was a drift back to former ways. A major influence was the terrorist activity of organisations like the Ku Klux Klan. White rule in the South gained special impetus from a deal struck over a disputed election. As a part of the compromise of 1877, the Republican candidate, Rutherford Hayes, acceded to home rule for the South in order to gain office as President, and black subordination was gradually re-established.

BULLDOZER

Black suffrage opened the door to black power. In some states the black population was much greater than the white and it was not long before black candidates were voted to serve in Reconstruction governments, a number of them going on to win seats in Congress. The Ku Klux Klan (whose name was derived from Greek *kuklos*, meaning 'circle') was just one of the groups which used terrorist activities against this political progress in the late 1860s. Dressed in white robes and masked by pointed hoods, Klan members would begin by burning crosses near the houses of their victims before going on to flog or mutilate those who refused to be intimidated. In the 1870s such a flogging was known as a *bull-dose* and was, quite literally, 'a dose fit for a bull'. What was fit for a bull was sometimes fatal for a human being. The SATURDAY REVIEW (9 July 1881) carried this definition: *To 'bull-dose' a Negro in the Southern States means to flog him to death, or nearly to death.* The term *bull-dose* was also spelt *bulldoze* and those who meted out such treatment were called *bulldozers*. The first recorded use is 1876. From the same date the noun was applied more widely to any thug with a mission to intimidate. This latter sense is still current, as is a parallel use of the verb *to bulldoze* used colloquially to mean 'to force (by violent means), to intimidate, to pressure':

One must ask why Labour, Liberal Democrats and a small minority of Conservative politicians, plus leaders of some of our larger companies, are so keen to bulldoze us into the euro and full integration with the European Union. Could it be that they, too, would like to get on the gravy

train and enjoy all the perks which seem to abound in Brussels?
(THE TIMES, 14 January 1999)

And so when a massive, diesel-driven, earth-moving machine thundered into existence in America around 1930, sweeping aside everything in its path, *bulldozer* seemed an appropriately brutal term.

1869

THE FIRST PEDAL BICYCLE IS PRODUCED IN ENGLAND

••••••

The earliest bicycles were rudimentary, consisting of nothing more than a beam mounted on two wheels which the rider propelled by striding along the road. In the late eighteenth century these *vélocifères* enjoyed something of a vogue amongst the affluent young men of Paris who enjoyed racing them along the flat and whizzing downhill. Steering and stopping at the bottom of the hill were significant problems which cooled their enthusiasm. The first problem was solved in 1817 by Karl von Drais, a German baron, who invented a pivoting handlebar. In April 1818 the *Draisienne* was exhibited in Paris. It immediately became all the rage and within a few months had caught on in Britain too, where the improved machine became known as a *hobby-* or *dandy horse*.

This craze, though intense, was short-lived. The next few decades saw a proliferation of cumbersome three- and four-wheeled inventions propelled by pedal systems or treadles, but it was not until 1863 that the first pedal-propelled two-wheeler eventually appeared. Its inventor was Pierre Michaux, a Parisian coach repairer. The Michaux family immediately went into production and were soon selling as many bicycles as they could turn out. In January 1869 an improved version of the Michaux machine was put on show and demonstrated in a London gymnasium by a certain Mr Turner, the Paris agent for the Coventry Sewing Machine Company. John Mayall of the magazine IXION reported the event, amazed that balance on two wheels was possible:

We were some half-dozen spectators, and I shall never forget our astonishment at the sight of Mr Turner whirling himself round the room, sitting on a bar above a pair of wheels in a line that ought, as we innocently supposed, to fall down immediately he jumped off the ground.

Judge then of our surprise when, instead of stopping by tilting over on one foot, he slowly halted, and turning the front wheel diagonally, remained quite still, balancing on the two wheels.

Mr Turner persuaded his uncle, the company manager, to produce bicycles for sale in France, but the untimely outbreak of the Franco-Prussian War forced him to sell in England. He was not disappointed. The machines were snapped up and the Coventry Machinists Company, as it then became, was soon producing for the home market.

BICYCLE

Throughout the nineteenth century any of the various machines invented that had been propelled by manpower had generally been known in French as a *vélocipède*, borrowed as *velocipede* in English. The word was coined from Latin and literally means 'swift foot'. (French still sometimes uses the shortened form, *vélo*, for 'bicycle'.) The MONTHLY MAGAZINE for March 1819 had reported on *A machine called the Velocipede, or Swift Walker. Invented by Baron Drais and patented in England by Denis Johnson, coachmaker, of Long Acre, in 1818.* And the catalogue for the Great Exhibition of 1851 listed a *Velocipede, consisting of three wheels.* In France, the Michaux invention was known as the *vélocipède à pédale*, but now the French also introduced a new word, *bicycle*, a combination of Latin *bi-*, meaning 'two', and Greek *kuklos*, meaning 'circle' and hence 'wheel'.

This new French coinage first appeared in English as *bysicle* in 1868 in an article for the DAILY NEWS which reported summer sightings of these machines in the Champs Elysées and the Bois de Boulogne. The following year Rowley Turner demonstrated the Michaux machine in London and production for the English market began. In English, as in French, the old term *velocipede* was used but *bicycle*, the new borrowing, began to vie for prominence and eventually won out. With the improvement in bicycle technology, most notably the safety bicycles of the early 1880s, cycling became an increasingly popular pastime in Victorian England. *The bicycle trade is particularly brisk,* reported the PALL MALL GAZETTE for June 1882. The term *bicycle*, now prevalent, proved too cumbersome for colloquial speech and was clipped to *bike.* In the early twentieth century this abbreviation was also used for 'motorcycle'. The first *bikers* were not youths clad in leathers and mounted on Harley-Davidsons, however, but cycling enthusiasts in the 1880s.

The early 1880s also saw the appearance of *to cycle, cyclist* and *cycling* as enthusiasm for the sport grew. A contributor to LONGMAN'S MAGAZINE for October 1883 was almost incredulous in his wonderment at the new skill of propelling oneself along on two wheels. It was as if mankind had suddenly discovered the innate ability to fly. *To the human family,* he wrote, *the art of cycling is the bestowal of a new faculty.*

• The expression *on your bike*, meaning 'go away, get lost', arose in the 1960s. It might well have faded from use were it not for a much publicised speech given by Norman Tebbit, then Employment Secretary, at the Conservative Party Conference in October 1981. In answer to criticism over government unemployment figures he said that, when his father had been out of work during the Depression in the 1930s, instead of joining in with the rioting he had 'got on his bike' and looked for work. The remark was twisted round by right-to-work campaigners who retorted with 'On yer bike, Tebbit', thus giving the expression a boost.

PEDAL
One morning in 1861 an old-fashioned hobby-horse was brought into the Michaux workshop for repair. Pierre Michaux began to consider what could be done to improve the machine and, inspired by observation of some crank handles on a vertical grindstone, hit upon the idea of attaching a pedal-driven crank axle to the hub of the front wheel. Thus the pedal bicycle was invented.

For well over a hundred and seventy years *pedal* in English had been applied uniquely to 'a lever operated by foot' on a musical instrument. It was the Italians who first used *pedale* to denote an 'organ pedal'. They had the word from Latin *pedālis*, which meant 'belonging to the foot', being a derivative of *pēs*, 'foot'. The term was borrowed into English as *pedal*, via French *pédale*, at the beginning of the seventeenth century. Later, as musical instruments developed, *pedal* was also used for the foot levers on pianos and harps. Not until the late eighteenth century did the term begin to denote 'a lever worked by foot' in a machine of any sort, but its particular application from 1869 onwards, following the French lead, was to the bicycle. In the early twentieth century the word was taken up for the foot controls of another means of transport, the motor car.

TYRE
The original Michaux bicycle had a wooden frame and wheels with iron tyres. In England, in spite of the early improvement of solid rubber tyres, the discomfort of riding the machine over cobbled streets and bad roads earned it the nickname *boneshaker*. A breakthrough came in 1888 when John Boyd Dunlop invented the pneumatic tyre, which absorbed the worst of the shock.

In the second half of the fifteenth century *tire* or *tyre* denoted 'a protective metal rim fitted around a wheel'. The word was a particular application of *tire*, a shortened form of *attire*, meaning 'accoutrement, clothing', and therefore alluded to the trappings of the wheel. Traced further back, the noun *attire* had been derived from the verb *to attire*, a Middle English borrowing of the Old French verb *atirer*, meaning 'to put into order, to array'. In the fifteenth and sixteenth centuries the spellings *tire* and *tyre* were interchangeable, but in the seventeenth century *tire* became the accepted form and is therefore established in American English. During the nineteenth century, however, British English saw fit to revive *tyre* when referring to the pneumatic rubber cushion on bicycle and motor-car wheels.

• *Pneumatic* originates in Greek *pneuma*, 'wind, breath'. From this the adjective *pneumatikos* was derived, meaning 'by or of the wind', which Latin borrowed as *pneumaticus*. In the mid-seventeenth century, the word was taken into English as *pneumatic* to describe any of the various mechanical contraptions invented whose functioning depended on the intake and expulsion of air or upon air pressure. In the 1860s the word was also used to describe inflatable things – a *pneumatic* life-boat, for instance – hence the word's application to Dunlop's air-filled tyre. French, which borrowed the adjective *pneumatique* from Latin, has *pneu* for inflatable tyre.

TANDEM
The second half of the eighteenth century saw the appearance of a light two-wheeled carriage drawn by a pair of horses. The carriage was notable because the horses were harnessed one behind the other instead of side by side. In popular parlance the vehicle became known as a *tandem*. The name was bestowed by an anonymous wag with a smattering of Latin and an enjoyment of puns, for the Latin word *tandem* is an adverb of time and means 'at length'. The term made its printed début in A DICTIONARY OF THE VULGAR TONGUE (1785), a dictionary of *Buckish Slang, University Wit, and*

Pickpocket Eloquence, where Francis Grose defined it thus:

> TANDEM. *A two wheeled chaise, buggy, or noddy, drawn by two horses, one before the other: that is, at length.*

The pun was generally pleasing and *tandem* was soon current in standard English where it was applied not just to the carriage and horses but more widely to 'any arrangement in which two or more persons or things follow one behind the other'. Not surprisingly the word was called into service in the 1880s when manufacturers of tricycles and bicycles began to produce machines designed for more than one rider. The early 1880s saw the production of 'sociable' or 'honeymoon' tricycles on which a husband and wife could pedal along seated companionably side by side. These machines were rather slow and cumbersome, however, and by the mid-1800s were giving way to *tandem* tricycles with one rider (the heavier, to avoid upsets) seated behind the other. More effective still were the *tandem* bicycles of the late 1880s. These, too, could be romantic. The young man in the music-hall song 'Daisy Bell' proposes to his sweetheart but, unable to afford a honeymoon carriage, assures her that she'll *look sweet, Upon the seat of a bicycle made for two*. This verse from PUNCH magazine, however, shows the other side of the marital coin:

> *Henpeck'd he was. He learned to bike.*
> *'Now I can go just where I like',*
> *He chuckled to himself. But she*
> *Had learnt to bike as well as he,*
> *And, what was more, had bought a new*
> *Machine to sweetly carry two.*
> *Ever together now they go,*
> *He sighing, 'This is wheel and woe'.*

BLOOMERS

Women who longed to participate in the exciting new sport of cycling found themselves frustrated. Bicycles were considered masculine and dangerous for the fair sex and, besides, the ample skirts ladies wore in the name of propriety would become entangled in the wheels. Throughout the 1880s only tricyling was considered suitable and even then a lady was advised to wear knee-length knickerbockers beneath her skirt to ensure decency. Then in the early 1890s, following the innovation of pneumatic tyres and further improvements to safety including wheel and chain guards and a dropped frame to accommodate those full-length skirts, bicycling for women was suddenly no longer taboo.

Most women continued to wear skirts but the more daring ones longed for greater freedom of movement. For them *bloomers* were the answer. The *Bloomer suit* was an outrageous and liberating style of dress for women that appeared in America in 1850. It consisted of a pair of long loose Turkish-style trousers worn beneath a shortened skirt that fell to below the knee. The outfit took its name from Amelia Jenks Bloomer who publicised its use in THE LILY, a magazine of which she was editor, arguing that it was more comfortable, practical and hygienic than the hooped and trailing skirts of the period. Amid much loud controversy the costume was adopted amongst young ladies of firm, liberated opinion, and later in the century its practicality was confirmed by those seeking comfortable cycling clothes. In time the term *bloomers* was extended to cover women's garments that were the same basic shape as the Turkish-style trousers until eventually it came to denote a pair of baggy knee-length knickers.

• There is, incidentally, no connection at all between *bloomer* meaning 'long knickers' and *bloomer* to denote 'a blunder'. The latter sense is Australian prison slang from the late nineteenth century and is a contraction of *blooming error*.

1871

The Treaty of Frankfurt Brings the Franco-Prussian War to a Close

••••••

In the second half of the nineteenth century there was increasing tension over the balance of power in Europe. In 1867 the Prussian Prime Minister, Bismarck, had succeeded in bringing the North German states into a confederation under Prussian control. He was eager to provoke the reluctant Southern states into an alliance that would complete the unification of Germany. To this end he engineered war with France, who had been growing increasingly jittery at the growth of Prussian power. The pretext was the vacancy of the Spanish throne, for which Bismarck proposed a Hohenzollern prince, knowing that this would be unacceptable to the French. Through the rewording and subsequent publication of a report which described a meeting between the Prussian king and the French ambassador, Bismarck succeeded in provoking a diplomatic incident that forced France to declare war on 19 July 1870. As Bismarck had hoped, the South German states joined the confederation in fighting the French. Crushing French defeats at Metz and Sedan were followed by the four-month-long Siege of Paris. The brief war saw the overthrowing of the Second French Empire and the proclamation of the new German Empire. The war was finally brought to a conclusion on 10 May 1871 by the Treaty of Frankfurt.

OPT

The terms of the Treaty of Frankfurt were humiliating. The Germans required a vast war indemnity of 5 billion gold francs and also demanded the northeastern provinces of Alsace and part of Lorraine. Situated on the border between France and Germany, the provinces were valuable both agriculturally and for their abundant natural resources. The inhabitants of Alsace-Lorraine were, however, permitted to *opt* between French and German citizenship. That is, they could choose whether to cross the border into France or remain at home and become German subjects. It was press reports of this decision-making that brought the verb *to opt* into English. It comes from the French *opter*, a borrowing of Latin *optāre*, 'to choose'.

By the mid-1880s the verb was no longer confined to decisions about citizenship, although this sense remained current. The Pall Mall Gazette, for instance, wrote of a political candidate being *permitted to opt for the borough of Northampton* (31 January 1885). By the mid-twentieth century *opt* was so well integrated into English vocabulary that it was given the phrasal-verb treatment that is so much a feature of the language. This resulted in *to opt into (in)*, 'to decide in favour of participating in something', and *to opt out of*, 'to decide against participating'. Just over a decade and a half later, the latter was modified still further to give the ugly, but thankfully little-used noun *opter-out* for 'someone who has decided against participation'.

• Latin *optāre* is also found in:
  adopt (16th century): from Latin *adoptāre*, 'to choose for oneself', from *ad-*, 'to', and *optāre*, 'to choose, to desire'.
  option (17th century): from French, from Latin *optiō* (stem *optiōn-*) 'choice', from *optāre*, 'to choose'.

1885

GOTTLIEB DAIMLER AND KARL BENZ USE LIGHT PETROL ENGINES TO PROPEL MOTOR VEHICLES

••••••

Built in 1770, Nicholas Joseph Cugnot's *fardier*, a three-wheeled wooden vehicle propelled by a steam engine instead of a horse, was capable of hauling its load of heavy artillery from A to B at the breakneck speed of just over two miles an hour. Even so, its progress was punctuated by stops every fifteen minutes or so to allow the engine to build up a new head of steam. This first horseless carriage was the precursor of numerous other steam-driven vehicles, for both public and private use, that were produced in France, America and Britain over the following century and a half. But the real breakthrough for motorised transport was the invention of the internal-combustion engine, initially fuelled by coal gas, in the mid-nineteenth century (see **engine**, page 199). This concept was further developed, though quite independently, by two men of vision, both German, who are credited with the invention of the first practical motor cars. In 1885 Gottlieb Daimler used a compact single-cylinder air-cooled petrol engine to propel a motorcycle, while in the same year Karl Benz launched a successful three-wheeled vehicle driven by a petrol engine of his own design. Daimler then produced the first efficient petrol-run car in 1886.

CAR
The work of Daimler and Benz excited much activity in the United States during the 1890s. By the end of the decade there were more than fifty motor-car companies turning out carefully constructed vehicles, though no one knew quite what to call them once they were finished. If one contemporary description had prevailed, the new millennium would have seen us driving *horseless carriages* up the motorway. The term sounds quaint to modern ears, but in the days of horse-drawn transport it was

no stranger than the term *automobile* which caught on in continental Europe and the United States. Coined in France in the 1870s, *automobile* was an adjective used to describe any self-propelling mechanism. The French cobbled the word together from bits of Greek and Latin: the Greek prefix *auto-* means 'by oneself' (from Greek *autos*, 'self') while French *mobile*, 'moving', came from Latin *mōbilis*, an adjective derived from *movēre*, 'to move'. In the 1890s the term was sometimes hauled into service to describe the engine-driven vehicles which were lately being produced (*automobile carriage*, for instance). And since there is always a tendency to shorten cumbersome expressions, by the mid-1890s *automobile* was allowed to stand alone as a noun. It was clipped still further to *auto* at the end of the century: the BOSTON HERALD for 9 July 1899 carried a report on an *accident to Mr W K Vanderbilt's 'auto'*.

Meanwhile, the British were getting upset. *A name has not yet been found for horseless carriages,* fretted the DAILY CHRONICLE in October 1895, and went on to discuss the latest suggestion, *motor-car*. This term became the British favourite, winning out over *autocar* which appeared in the same year. *Car* in its modern sense first appeared as a shortening of *autocar* in 1896 and was established by the early twentieth century (by this time, probably, as a shortening of *motor-car*). The word itself was not new to English, however, having been current since the fourteenth century to denote 'a wheeled vehicle'. Its origins lie in an unattested Old Celtic term *karros* which Latin borrowed as *carrus* and applied to 'a two-wheeled cart'. Late Latin had *carra*, an unattested variant of *carrus*, and this found its way into Anglo-Norman as *car(re)* and from there into Middle English. Throughout its long history *car* had been variously applied to different kinds of wheeled vehicles, more recently (1873) to a *tramcar*, before presenting itself as a solution to the vexing problem of what to call the horseless carriage (see **tram**, page 205).

• Old Northern French and Anglo-Norman had *carre* from Latin *carrus*. This noun was the basis of the verb *carier*, 'to transport on a cart', which was taken into English as *carry* in the fourteenth century.

Late Latin derived the verb *carricāre*, 'to load up', from *carrus* and this was borrowed into Old French as *charger*. Taken into English as *charge* in the thirteenth century, the verb originally meant simply 'to load' or 'to furnish with'. *Carricāre* was also responsible for Spanish *cargar*, 'to load'. From this came the noun *cargo*, 'load, cargo', which was borrowed into English in the seventeenth century.

TRAFFIC

Traffic entered the English lexicon in the sixteenth century when European trade was fast expanding. It was borrowed as a mercantile term denoting 'the transportation of goods for trade' and more generally, 'commerce'. It came into English by way of French *traffique*, itself a borrowing of Old Italian *traffico*, a derivative of the verb *trafficare*. The word evidently emerged from the trading activities of the Mediterranean in the Middle Ages since the earliest known record of the Old Italian noun and verb occur in a text on commerce originating in Pisa and dated 1325. Many etymologists consider that the term is Romanic and have identified the initial *tra* as the Italian representation of Latin *trāns-*, 'across'. Others, who have advanced the theory that the term has an Arabic origin, cite *taraffaqa*, a verb which can mean 'to seek profit'. Whatever its ultimate origin, *traffic* is still current as a commercial term and now has the added dimension of 'dealing in illegal commodities', a sense which first arose in the second half of the seventeenth century.

All this commercial activity meant merchants passing to and fro with their goods, ships and vehicles. During the 1820s the general movement of vehicles or people about their daily business began to be described as *traffic*. By 1894 *traffic* had become the accepted term for 'street movement'. Horse-drawn vehicles had caused congestion enough in the streets of cities and large towns, but the arrival of the car exacerbated the situation. And it was to worsen. In 1930 W Somerset Maugham saw fit to mention *the congested traffic of Jermyn Street* (CAKES AND ALE) while in the United States, the familiar expression *traffic jam* to denote 'total traffic congestion' had already been in use since at least 1917. The motor car has revolutionised the way we live, enabling us to go further and further afield in pursuit of work and leisure. One wonders if, when they first glimpsed the possibilities of motor transport, Daimler and Benz could ever have imagined a motorway the size of the London orbital M25, choked with early morning motorists and laughingly described as 'the world's biggest car park'.

The British may be excused for being rather slow off the mark when it comes to motor-car production. Alarmed at the speeds achieved by steam vehicles and the like, the government had sought to protect its citizens by the introduction of a Locomotive Act in 1865. This stated that machine-powered vehicles should have three drivers and should not exceed a speed of 4 mph (6.4 kph). The latter requirement was not hard to keep, since the Act also stipulated that each vehicle should have a man walking in front holding up a red warning flag. The first of the annual London to Brighton vintage car rallies was run in 1896 to celebrate the demise of the Act. The French had no such restrictions and enjoyed a head start in motor car production and design: the Peugeot company was set up in 1896 and Renault around 1899. This early French involvement in the industry ensured that a number of their motoring terms entered English. Among them are:

CHAUFFEUR

The French word *chauffeur* was derived from the verb *chauffer*, 'to heat'. A *chauffeur* was originally the 'stoker' of a furnace or the 'fireman' on board a steam train whose job it was to shovel fuel into the boiler and maintain a head of steam. Steam-powered motor vehicles worked on the same principle (it took as long as fifteen minutes to produce steam from a cold boiler and supplies of fuel and water were carried in containers to keep the engine going) but this time the *chauffeur* was often also the driver. Thankfully, the internal-combustion engine did away with the tiresome chore of heating up the engine: drivers could now simply abandon themselves to the pleasures of motoring. However, the word *chauffeur* was retained for 'driver' and is now a testimony to the evolving history of the motor car. When the word was borrowed into English at the very end of the nineteenth century it first simply denoted 'a motorist', particularly a French one. Meanwhile the affluent classes were in a quandary over what to call the servant who maintained their vehicles and drove them from place to place. According to the WESTMINSTER GAZETTE for 5 August 1902 *'chauffeur' seems at present to hold the field*. The fine-sounding foreign term stuck and the paid driver of a privately owned car has been a *chauffeur* ever since. The combination *chauffeur-driven* arose in the 1930s.

LIMOUSINE

To the modern ear, *limousine* has the ring of luxury but its origins are really very humble. *Limousin* was the name of an old French province centred upon the town of Limoges and *limousine* was the name given to a type of heavy woollen cape worn by the shepherds of that region. Around the turn of the twentieth century a car was produced whose body enclosed and protected only the passengers travelling behind, the chauffeur having to be content with the shelter afforded by a simple roof. Someone with a fine and fanciful imagination thought the shape of the car resembled that of the *limousine* cape, and the vehicle was given that name. Today that resemblance is even less evident. *Limousine* now denotes any large luxury car which is built to be chauffeur-driven; only the grandest have a rear compartment for passengers which is separate and private from that of the driver. The abbreviation *limo* arose in the United States in the 1960s, while today the ultimate status symbol, though strictly for the nouveaux riches (whoever could imagine the Queen in one?), is a *stretch limo*, a limousine with an exaggeratedly long wheel base.

COUPÉ

In the early nineteenth century the French developed a comfortable but expensive four-wheeled horse-drawn carriage which could seat just two people inside and a driver outside. Since it was shorter in design than other carriages it was known as a *carrosse coupé*, literally 'cut-off carriage', *coupé* being the past participle of the verb *couper* 'to cut'. The word *coupé* to denote such a conveyance was known in English from the 1830s. In the late nineteenth century French motor companies began to produce quality small cars designed along similar lines. The Peugeot *coupé* of 1896 had a luxurious padded interior for two passengers with a bench-like seat outside for the chauffeur. The first mention of such a car in English occurs in Arnold Bennett's BURIED ALIVE in 1908. As engines became lighter and more efficient, the shape of car bodywork changed to become increasingly streamlined so that *coupé* now denotes 'a styled and stylish two-seat, two-door car'. Advertisers are particularly good at suggesting all the nuances of the word:

> *This is a top athlete with a well-developed sense for elegance and aesthetics. A vehicle with its own distinctive image; its own style. So if you're into both sporty dynamics and uncompromising driving comfort, then you'll soon realise that the new BMW 3 Series Coupé symbolises mobility in its most beautiful form.*
> (BMW advertisement from the Taylor Auto Group, Augusta, USA, 1998)

• Although Old French *couper, colper* meant 'to cut' its primary sense was 'to strike'. The verb was derived from the

noun *colp, coup*, 'blow'. This came from medieval Latin *colpus*, which in turn was derived from Latin *colaphus*, from Greek *kolaphos*, 'a blow with the fist'. Old French *couper* was borrowed into Middle English as *to cope* around the turn of the fifteenth century. Initially this meant 'to come to blows', but by the sixteenth century *to cope with* had developed the sense 'to prove oneself against a well-matched adversary'. During the seventeenth century the verb was used figuratively with the sense 'to face difficulties with success', and hence the twentieth-century usage, 'to handle a situation effectively'.

GARAGE

Early motor cars were costly machines, and secure stabling was necessary for these expensive horseless carriages. In the early twentieth century entrepreneurs ran large establishments called *garages*, big enough for the safe-keeping of a number of vehicles. The DAILY MAIL for 11 January 1902 reported on *the new 'garage' founded by Mr Harrington Moore, hon. secretary of the Automobile Club*. The paper informed its readers that the 'garage', *which is situated at the City end of Queen Victoria-street . . . has accommodation for eighty cars*. The number of car owners increased rapidly. People wanted their cars conveniently close to home and houses were soon built which incorporated covered space for a car, also known as a *garage* even on such a small scale. Motoring services were set up, too: buying petrol in cans and relying on the local blacksmith for repairs was not practical as cars became more sophisticated and traffic increased. The word *garage* was also applied to establishments offering these services.

Although new to English in 1902 (the DAILY MAIL reporter was careful to wrap the term in inverted commas), *garage* had already existed in French before the advent of the motor car to denote 'the docking of a ship'. It was derived from the modern French verb *garer*, 'to dock'. In Old French *garer* had meant 'to keep, to protect', being a borrowing of Old

High German *warōn*, 'to protect'.

It is the notion of protection, then, that is at the very root of the word *garage*. But with the smallest runabout costing at least a third of a year's salary, who wouldn't want to protect their car and tuck it up in a garage each night to prolong its life?

1885

The First Skyscraper Is Built in the United States

••••••

In America in the mid-nineteenth century there was an unprecedented demand for commercial property in the already crowded business quarters of the larger cities. An obvious solution to the problem was to build upwards rather than outwards. At that time, however, buildings more than five storeys high were neither practical nor feasible. Two innovations in the second half of the century changed the situation: the invention of the first safety passenger lift, and the discovery and inspired use of steel as a building material.

The ten-storey Home Insurance Company Building in Chicago was constructed in 1885 by William LeBaron Jenney, an American architect and civil engineer. Instead of relying on thick load-bearing walls and iron beams to support the structure, Jenney used a framework of cast-iron uprights held together by steel beams. This was the first time that steel had been used in construction and riveted steel frames soon replaced iron altogether, being stronger and lighter. Now it was possible to build even taller buildings.

SKYSCRAPER

A hundred years before *skyscraper* was ever used to denote 'a tall building', the word was used in various contexts to describe 'something tall or high up'. *Skyscraper* was once a nautical term coined in the late eighteenth century to denote 'a light sail hoisted high during calm weather to catch any favourable breeze', a use which may have prompted a number of other subsequent applications. Around that time a horse named *Skyscraper*, which was owned by the Duke of Bedford, famously won the Epsom Derby in 1788. The name may have been inspired by the nautical coinage but was more likely suggested by the animal's great size. Whatever the initial prompting, large horses were subsequently known as *skyscrapers* well into the nineteenth century. At the turn of the nineteenth century *skyscraper* was also being applied to 'a hat with a high crown', and around the middle of the century was a slang term for 'a very tall man' (*I say, old skyscraper, is it cold up there?*). The word had travelled across the Atlantic by the 1860s when baseball fanatics used it to denote 'a ball lobbed high in the air'. But its first application to a multi-storey building occurred in 1883, two years before Jenney's building breakthrough, when an innovative correspondent in AMERICAN ARCHITECT AND BUILDING NEWS wrote that *a public building should always have something towering up above all in its neighbourhood . . . The capitol building should always have a dome. I should raise thereon a gigantic 'sky-scraper', contrary to all precedent in practice.* Such an edifice would, he said, be *refined, independent, self-contained, daring, bold, heaven-reaching, erratic, piratic,* and *Quixotic.* What enthusiasm!

Skyscraper is, of course, a compound word, being made up of *sky* and *scrape,* two Middle English borrowings which are interesting in their own right. The unattested prehistoric Germanic root *scrap-,* 'scrape', is responsible for *scrape* which came into English via either Old Norse or Middle Dutch in the early fourteenth century. It initially meant 'to erase what is written' by scraping the surface of the parchment or paper with a knife or sharp edge, a sense which persisted until rubber made the task easier.

Sky was an earlier borrowing. When it first appeared around 1220 it meant 'cloud'. It was a borrowing of Old Norse *skȳ,* 'cloud', whose origins go back to an Indo-European root meaning 'to cover'. (The Latin word *obscūrus,* source of English *obscure,* means 'covered over', the element *-scūrus* coming from the same root as *skȳ.*) Lines from Chaucer's poem THE HOUSE OF FAME (c 1385) describe how *A certeyn wynde . . . blewe so hydously and hye That hyt ne left not a skye in alle the welkene.* (*Welkin* and, more especially, *heven,* which English retained as *heaven,* were current terms for 'sky'.) *Sky* first began to be used in its modern sense at the very end of the thirteenth century. It gradually ousted *heaven* as the common word for 'sky' and had ceased to denote 'cloud' by around the mid-sixteenth century.

ELEVATOR, LIFT

Elisha Graves Otis was the ideal employee. Wherever he worked, he set about inventing mechanical devices to complete his task more efficiently. In 1852 he was sent to

Yonkers, New York, to set up a new factory. This project led to the invention of the 'safety hoist', a steam-powered freight-elevator fitted with a safety mechanism that would be triggered automatically if the load-bearing cable broke.

In 1854 Mr Otis gave a daring demonstration of his 'safety hoist' at the Crystal Palace exhibition in New York. Riding high on an elevator platform, he gave the sudden command for the rope to be cut. The safety clamps snapped into action. Mr Otis was safe and the orders came pouring in. In 1857 the first safety passenger lift was installed in a New York store, its journey between the five storeys taking just under a minute to complete.

Elevator was not coined by Mr Otis. The word had already been in agricultural use in American English since the late eighteenth century to denote 'a hoist for lifting grain in a mill' or 'a conveyor for lifting hay to the top of the stack', but was first used by seventeenth-century English anatomists to describe 'a muscle that raises a limb'. The term was borrowed from Latin *ēlevātor,* a derivative of *ēlevāre* which meant 'to raise', being a compound of *ē,* 'out', and *levāre,* 'to lighten' and hence, 'to raise'. But Mr Otis's 'safety hoist' lifted *elevator* from the specialised areas of anatomy and agriculture and made it an everyday word for millions of Americans at home and abroad:

> *These two elevators must have been among the first batch of elevators sent out to Asia by the Otis Elevator Company. The doors took forever to open and close, as if they had to wait for signals from company headquarters in New York.*
> (Thomas Hale, LIVING STONES OF THE HIMALAYAS, 1993)

Elevator proved rather too formal for the British, who immediately had recourse to the comfortably familiar *lift.* The verb *to lift* literally means 'to move up into the air'. It was ultimately derived from an unattested prehistoric Germanic word meaning 'air, sky', and came into Middle English in the late thirteenth century by way of Old Norse. *Lift* began to be used as a noun to denote 'the action of lifting' in the fifteenth century and from there developed a range of meanings. Its first application to 'an apparatus for lifting or lowering people or things from one floor of a building to another' came in the Catalogue for the Great Exhibition of 1851 at the Crystal Palace which speaks of *dinner-lifts for hotels and mansions*.

STOREY, STORY

By the late nineteenth century, elevators were required to travel between sixteen storeys, the height reached by Jenney's Manhattan Building in Chicago (1889-90). But in the twentieth century buildings really soared. Chicago's Sears Towers, for instance, built in 1974, rose to 110 storeys.

The etymology proposed for *storey* is fascinating and intertwined with that of other common English words. It goes back to an unattested Indo-European root *wid-*, 'to know' (source of English *wit*, see **remorse**, page 79). This was ultimately responsible for Greek *histōr* which meant 'wise, learned man'. A derived term *historiā* was used to denote 'learning by enquiry' and hence 'a written report of an enquiry, a narrative or history'. Latin borrowed this Greek word as *historia*, and from there it passed into English as *history* in the fourteenth century where it denoted either 'a factual account' or 'an imaginary narrative'.

Meanwhile, Latin *historia* had also been borrowed into Old French as *estoire*. This became *estorie* in Anglo-Norman, emerging as *storie* in Middle English. In the thirteenth century the term denoted 'a true narrative of significant events'. Not until the late sixteenth century did *story* begin to refer rather more specifically to 'an imaginary narrative', while *history* gradually came to mean 'a factual account'. Latin *historia* was also present in Anglo-Latin where it was applied to 'a picture or sculpture', specifically one whose subject was historical. In the Middle Ages, it was also of architectural significance, denoting 'a tier of sculpture or stained-glass windows, composed around a theme or story'. These decorated the front of imposing buildings and were as tall as one of its floors. The term for the decoration became the term for the whole floor, possibly from as early as 1400 but certainly by the latter part of the sixteenth century.

PENTHOUSE

Penthouse is a fine example of a word that has come about by the workings of folk etymology. Old French had the word *apentis* to denote 'an outhouse projecting from the side of a main building'. The word was a borrowing of medieval Latin *appendicium*, 'appendage', a derivative of the Latin verb *appendere* (from *ad-*, 'on', and *pendere*, 'to hang') which meant 'to attach, to suspend one thing from another'. When Middle English borrowed Old French *apentis* in the early fourteenth century, the initial vowel was dropped to give *pentis*. There was immediate confusion over the word's origins. Since most lean-tos are constructed with a sloping roof *pentis* was assumed to be a derivation of Middle French *pente*, meaning 'slope'. By the sixteenth century *pentis* had also fallen prey to folk etymology, when the final syllable was changed to *house*, giving the compound *penthouse*.

Penthouse continued to denote 'a smaller structure attached to a main building', with or without a sloping roof, down through the centuries. An old nineteenth-century bill of sale for the Jolly Tanner public house in Staplefield, Sussex, lists *stabling for 5 horses, a Blacksmith's shop, Penthouse and Coal House* amongst the outbuildings of that property. But this use has been eclipsed by a more recent application.

Skyscrapers were originally intended to provide commercial accommodation in overcrowded American business quarters. However, as city populations grew, land became scarce and expensive city-wide creating a need to build vertically for domestic purposes also. The term *penthouse* had already been applied to the rooftop housing of elevator shafts or stairwells – a small structure upon a large one. When it was understood that the rooftop area could provide a separate apartment affording a high degree of privacy together with spectacular views and a terrace, this extra dwelling built on the top of a high block became known as a *penthouse. Two of the elevators were designed to run to the roof, where a pent-house . . . was being built,* runs a description in COUNTRY LIFE magazine for April 1921, while on 8 December 1948 the New York SUN published a view of an *eighteen-story and penthouse apartment building* which was being erected at the south corner of Fifth Avenue and 76th Street. More recently, estate agents have begun to describe the top floor of any tall building as a *penthouse* so that the word no longer necessarily refers to an additional structure. True penthouses are highly sought after. An article in GOOD HOUSEKEEPING (March 1998) on the housing requirements of the rich and famous informs us that *penthouses are popular simply because no one can overlook them* – the actor Tom Cruise apparently *can't bear to have anyone in the room above* – but adds that *the ideal complex also includes a roof terrace for seclusion.* Nice if you can afford it.

1888

A GREAT BLIZZARD SWEEPS ACROSS THE EASTERN UNITED STATES

••••••

In March 1888 a severe snowstorm propelled by a violent wind descended from the Rocky Mountains and whipped across country as far as the Atlantic coast. The whole area was devastated and several hundred people lost their lives. New York was paralysed by snow so deep that people standing on its crust were reportedly able to touch the tops of the lamp-posts. The storm made such an impact upon those who lived through it that, for decades afterwards, reunions were organised to commemorate its anniversary.

BLIZZARD

Blizzards, characterised by bitter temperatures, fierce winds and blinding snow, are a feature of the climate in the American Midwest. Indeed, the state of Iowa claims the word for its own. *Blizzard* first appeared in the NORTHERN VINDICATOR, a newspaper of Estherville, Iowa, in 1870. Its separation from the rest of the text by inverted commas is an indication of its status as a purely local term. Over the next few years the press in neighbouring states began to pick up the word, though it was still carefully wrapped in inverted commas whenever it was used: according to the MONTHLY WEATHER REVIEW for December 1876, *very severe storms known in local parlance as 'blizzards' were reported on the 8th as prevailing in Iowa and Wisconsin.* But it was during the winter of 1880-81 that the word began to infiltrate journalistic reports further afield. The harsh weather conditions that winter were so widely felt and reported that a journalist for the NEW YORK NATIONAL (1881) wrote:

The hard weather has called into use a word which promises to become a national Americanism, namely 'blizzard'. It designates a storm (of snow and wind) which men cannot resist away from shelter.

But it was reporting of the great snow-storm of 1888 which finally confirmed *blizzard* as an accepted Americanism.

In Britain in the early twentieth century the word was famously used by the explorer Robert Falcon Scott in the journals he published of his expeditions to the Antarctic. Most poignantly memorable is an entry in March 1912, where Scott describes the departure of Captain Oates: *It was blowing a blizzard. He [Oates] said, 'I am just going outside and may be some time.' He went out into the blizzard and we have not seen him since.*

Curiously, the word *blizzard* had been used in America earlier in the nineteenth century, though in different states and with a different meaning. As early as 1829 *blizzard* was defined as 'a violent blow'. Davy Crockett later used it in a description of a hunting trip where he *took a blizzard* at a large buck. In TOUR DOWN EAST (1834) Crockett also made figurative use of the word to mean 'a piece of one's mind'. But although both senses were current in the 1870s, and the violence of the snow-squall would be a logical extension, it is generally felt that this earlier usage was too limited and too localised to have influenced the emergence of the Iowa term. It is more probable that *blizzard* is imitative in origin and the OED suggests comparison with words such as *blow, blast, blister* and *bluster*.

1901

GUGLIELMO MARCONI SUCCESSFULLY TRANSMITS RADIO SIGNALS ACROSS THE ATLANTIC

••••••

Marconi's early experiments in radio were carried out at his father's estate in Bologna, Italy where he succeeded in sending signals over short distances using a directional aerial. Convinced that this method of communication had great potential but unable to find support for his work in Italy, Marconi left for England in 1896. With the assistance of Sir William Preece, chief engineer at the Post Office, Marconi continued his research and succeeded in transmitting over ever-increasing distances: first across Salisbury Plain, then the Bristol Channel and, in 1899, from the English to the French coasts, a distance of 33 miles (50 kilometres). But Marconi still had to overcome the scientific objection that radiotelegraphy would only ever be possible over comparatively short distances because the earth's surface was curved. In December 1901 Marconi addressed the criticism and won worldwide acclaim by successfully transmitting signals from Poldhu in Cornwall to Saint John's in Newfoundland, Canada, a distance of 2,000 miles (3,200 kilometres).

RADIO

In 1792 the term *telegraph* was first applied by a Frenchman, Claude Chappe, to his invention of a hilltop signalling system. This consisted of a network of posts. Each post had a pivoting crossbar bearing indicators at each end which could be moved up and down with ropes to signal coded messages. *Telegraph*, which was coined from Greek *tele*, meaning 'at a distance', and *graphos*, meaning 'writer' (from *graphein*, 'to write'), was subsequently applied to numerous other devices for sending messages over long distances, including the electromagnetic telegraph invented by Samuel Morse in 1836. Morse's system required conducting wires to carry the electric pulses between the points of transmission and reception (see **on the grapevine**, page 213). Marconi dispensed with wires altogether and his system was therefore known as *wireless telegraphy*, which was soon shortened to *wireless*.

> The news on the wireless was a must. Each word of Alvar Liddell was savoured and recorded, not only for discussion with your peers, but to relate to your dad on his return from the pit.
> (Wartime account of a boy in Tyneside in 1940 in Westall, CHILDREN OF THE BLITZ, 1985)

Alternatively the system was known as *radio-telegraphy*, which was similarly shortened to *radio*. *Radio-* itself is the combination form of Latin *radius* which originally denoted 'a rod, a stake' but which also developed other senses, one of which was 'a ray (from any shining object)'. The notion behind *radio* (*telegraphy*) then was that of signals being transmitted by means of electromagnetic waves or 'rays'.

• A number of English words have their origins in Latin *radius*, 'rod', and its supplementary senses:

Latin used *radius* to denote 'the thicker and shorter of the two rod-like bones in the forearm'. This anatomical sense was borrowed into English in the seventeenth century.

Latin *radius* developed the sense 'ray', which became responsible not only for *radio* but also for English *ray* (14th century), *radiant* (15th century) and *radium* (19th century).

Another secondary meaning of Latin *radius* was 'spoke of a wheel'. This notion was behind the English mathematical term *radius*, used from the mid-seventeenth century to describe 'the distance from the centre of a circle to its circumference'.

MASS MEDIA

The notion of broadcasting to a mass audience had first been mooted in 1916 by David Sarnoff, an executive of the American Marconi Company. His proposal fell on sceptical ears, but within seven years radio stations proliferated in the United States and Europe. Broadcasting was immediately recognised as a powerful tool for reaching a large number of people for good or ill. No sooner had it begun, for instance, than it was exploited by the Soviet Union for disseminating propaganda (see **propaganda**, page 159). Radio, along with the written word and film, had become a new *mass medium*.

The term *mass medium* dates from the early 1920s. *Mass* goes back to the Greek *maza*, meaning 'barley cake' and by extension 'lump (of matter)'. This was borrowed into Latin as *massa* and, from there, found its way into Middle English in the fourteenth century via Old French *masse*. In English the word was first used to denote 'a lump of mouldable matter' and then more widely 'a large lump' in general. By the late sixteenth century *mass* could also denote 'a large quantity or number', hence its application from the eighteenth century to 'a multitude of people'.

Medium, on the other hand, has Latin origins, being the neuter form of the noun *medius*, which meant 'middle'. It was borrowed directly into English from Latin in the sixteenth century to denote 'a middle state or quality': *There is no concorde betweene water and fire, nor any medium betweene loue and hatred* (TELL-TROTHES NEW-YEARES GIFT, 1593). (Modern English might describe this condition as *a happy medium*, an expression which dates from the late eighteenth century). By the end of the sixteenth century *medium* also began to denote 'an intervening substance through which something is carried'. The air, for instance, was identified as the *medium* of sight and of sound. In the early seventeenth century another related sense emerged, that of 'an intermediate channel or means'. As early as the eighteenth century a magazine or journal might occasionally be referred to as a *medium* of information. Towards the end of the nineteenth century, cheaper paper and strides in printing technology brought down the price of newspapers and magazines. The resulting increase in sales attracted more advertising revenue and prices fell still further in the early twentieth century. Newspapers were now within the means of the masses. The term *mass medium* to denote 'a means of communication that reaches a large number of people' was coined in 1923, probably amongst those concerned with advertising and selling. At first the term referred to the printed word. Increasingly, however, radio was recognised as having a significant role in mass communication, and was commercially operated in the United States. Before long, radio was also identified as a *mass medium*, to be followed by television.

The Latin plural of *medium* is *media*. Strictly then, *(mass) media* should be followed by a plural verb. In practice, users of the term have been either indifferent to or ignorant of grammatical correctness. *The treatment of* media *as a singular noun . . . is spreading into the upper cultural strata*, wailed Kingsley Amis in an article for THE NEW STATESMAN in January 1966. In fact, the error dates back to the 1920s, and has become even more common since the time of Amis. It is almost inevitable that *media* will follow the path of other plurals, such as *agenda*, and be treated as singular.

BROADCAST

Broadcast was originally an agricultural term coined in the early eighteenth century, meaning 'to sow seed by scattering it widely over the land' rather than by placing it in drills. Within a century the word was being used figuratively, with the sense to 'spread abroad' information, doctrine, accusations, etc. During the First World War restrictions were placed on wireless communications, which had been largely used by shipping. When they were eased after the war, many amateurs began tinkering with radio. Soon, the possibility of every home enjoying radio was becoming a reality. As interest increased, there were different responses: the United States followed the commercial route – there were 564 licensed radio stations by November 1922 – while in Great Britain the publicly financed British Broadcasting Corporation was established in October 1922. The means were in place to scatter seeds of information, education and entertainment wider than ever before. The term *broadcast* from this date onwards became irrevocably linked to radio and later, in the 1950s, to television.

THE CAT'S WHISKERS

One explanation for this picturesque phrase is connected with the early years of radio broadcasting. When radio stations were first set up in the early 1920s their audiences listened in on crystal sets. These receivers incorporated the crystal detector patented in 1906 by American electrical engineer Greenleaf Whittier Pickard, and worked when a thin metallic wire was brought into contact with a silicon or lead sulphide crystal. The wire was so fine that it earned the name *cat's whisker*. The crystal sets were not easy to use: contact between the fine wire and the crystal was tricky and required endless adjustment. Before long crystal detectors had been replaced by the more satisfactory thermionic valves but the American slang expression *the cat's whiskers* survived. This was undoubtedly helped by a vogue in the 1920s for bizarre phrases such as *the* cat's pyjamas, *the eel's heel* and that other long-term survivor, *the bees' knees*.

The positive connotations, as in *It's the cat's whiskers*, probably came from association with the excitement and

novelty of early popular radio broadcasting. Soon, anything considered to be truly excellent was described as *the cat's whiskers*.

1914
COCO CHANEL OPENS HER COUTURE BUSINESS IN PARIS

• • • • • •

It was unimaginable that, after the devastation of the First World War and the loss of a generation of young men, society should simply pick up its former ways and beliefs and continue as before. In the 1920s the world of fashion responded to post-war sentiment with a new simplicity of style. Fashions fitted the movement towards emancipation which had been accelerated by women's contribution towards the war effort. In Britain in 1918 women had finally won the right to vote and, immediately after the war, several women were appointed to important posts in what had previously been male preserves. No career-minded woman wanted to be hampered by what she wore; no fashionable woman wanted to appear extravagantly overdressed. According to historian A J P Taylor:

Practical needs revolutionised fashion. Never again did skirts sweep the ground. The petticoat disappeared . . . Women's hats became neater. (ENGLISH HISTORY 1914-1945, 1965)

As ever, the world of fashion on both sides of the Atlantic looked to Paris for its inspiration, and thus it was that French couturière Coco Chanel came into her own. Never one for corseted formality, Chanel was already designing simple clothes which required little time and effort to put on; comfortable clothes she could *jump straight into*. In his book THE PASSION FOR FASHION (1988) Adrian Bailey describes how, as early as 1916, Chanel was presenting a soft, casual look consisting of *a jersey-fabric jumper cut across the hips, with a matching skirt and blouse tied with a sash*. Chanel's style not only inspired the world of haute couture after the war but was to continue to do so for over half a century.

SLIMMING

The Middle Dutch adjective *slim* meant 'distorted, awry', and when applied to people, 'crafty, sly'. It derived from the unattested prehistoric Germanic base *slimbaz*, which meant 'crooked, oblique'. In modern Dutch *slim* picked up the additional notion of 'meagre, inferior, small'. When the word was borrowed into English in the second half of the seventeenth century it carried all these senses with it: a *slim customer* was a 'cunning, artful fellow'; a *slim jest* was a 'malicious joke'; *slim majority* meant 'meagre, small majority', a sense which is still current. In English *slim* also meant 'slight, slender', a notion doubtless derived from this latter sense of 'meagre, insubstantial', and, with fashion swinging towards the lean look in the twentieth century, eventually became the main sense of the word. To carry off the soft, unstructured look promoted by Chanel and the severe 'boyish woman' look of the 1920s, a woman needed a straight, slender figure. Suddenly, curvy hips and bosoms were despised. Fashionable women began to diet. The verb *to slim* in its modern sense 'to use diet and exercise to achieve a slim body', and the noun *slimming* both date from around 1930:

> *Perhaps the young of today will nevah grow fat. They do slimming – ah-ha!*
> (John Galsworthy, MAID-IN-WAITING, 1931).

A slim body has been a preoccupation of the fashion-conscious ever since, with the late twentieth century seeing a booming market in slimming aids and magazines with titles such as THE BEST DIET, SLIMMING and SLIMMING WORLD.

• The word *diet* originates in Greek *diaita* which meant 'way of life'. The term was used by Greek physicians who extended it to denote 'a recommended regimen or diet'. Latin subsequently borrowed the term as *diaeta* where it came to mean 'daily ration of food', possibly through the influence of the similar-sounding *diēs*,

'day'. The word subsequently passed into the Romance languages, coming into English in the thirteenth century by way of Old French *diete*.

BRA

The figures of Victorian and Edwardian ladies had been squeezed, pinched and moulded into fashionable perfection by all-in-one corsets, confections of whalebone and lacing designed to accentuate the contours of the female body and achieve an impossibly tiny waistline. Doctors constantly warned about deformity as well as breathing and digestive difficulties, but no one took any notice. The corset had evolved over the centuries from a close-fitting bodice, laced up at the front, which had been worn as an over-garment in the Middle Ages. *Corset* is a diminutive of Old French *cors*, 'body' (from Latin *corpus*, 'body'), and was borrowed into English in the late thirteenth century.

During the late nineteenth and early twentieth centuries, however, women began to lead more active lifestyles. They longed to move freely and to feel at ease in their clothes. Gradually, a war was waged on the restrictive corset. Around 1907, for instance, couturier Paul Poiret introduced a slim, straight silhouette for women. The look was achieved by discarding whalebone and opting, instead, for a foundation garment of elastic which began below the bust and ended at the tops of the thighs. However, any reduction of the corset inevitably left the bust unsupported and the invention of the *brassière* was essential for female comfort. The word *brassière* is obviously of French origin and, indeed, some claim that the garment was the inspiration of Parisian couturière Madame Cadolle. If this is so, its uplifting presence was soon felt on the other side of the Atlantic: in July 1911 a Canadian newspaper carried an advertisement for *Brassieres of fine cambric, lace and embroidery trimmed*. (DAILY COLONIST, 5 July 1911). Curiously, though, French does not use, and never has used, the word *brassière* for the undergarment, except in Canada (instead it has the combination *soutien-gorge*, which translates as 'breast-support').

It seems that by 1912 the *brassière* was supposedly *de rigueur* for the fashionable woman, for in July of that year an advertisement in THE QUEEN was insistent that *The Stylish Figure of To-Day requires a Brassière*. In 1914 New York socialite Mary Phelps Jacob, desperate for a light undergarment to wear under her diaphanous gowns, had patented her *Backless Brassière*, a frippery which she had simply devised from a couple of handkerchiefs and some thin pink ribbon. By the time her design was in full production, Chanel's casual style was in vogue, and sales of the soft *brassière*, which supported rather than accentuated the bust, boomed.

Earlier meanings of *brassière* had referred to much more substantial garments than Mary Phelps Jacob's scanty invention. Way back in the seventeenth century the French word *brassière* had denoted 'a bodice' and, indeed, the undergarments of 1911 and 1912 were bodice-like in appearance. More recently *brassière* had also described 'a baby's sleeved vest' or 'the straps on a backpack'. Traced back still further the term appears to be from the Old French word *braciere*, 'a protective armour or guard for the arm', a derivative of *bras*, 'arm' (from Latin *bracchium*, from Greek *brakhion*, 'arm'). By the mid-1930s the *brassière* had been around for a while and was now worn by most women, and so popular usage began to shorten the now familiar, but rather cumbersome, foreign term to *bra*.

PERM
Freedom from crimping irons. This was the service offered to customers in Charles Nestlé's New York salon in 1908. The snag was that a style held in place by the Nestlé Permanent Waving technique took about twelve hours to achieve and didn't come cheap. In the first year only eighteen women were willing to sit in the salon all day and then part with the $1,000 asked. Twelve years later,

following the example of Chanel, women were shearing off their locks and trimming them into boyish bobs. Some went further and had their hair shingled. A popular song of 1924 describes the pressure to submit to the prevailing fashion:

Sweet Susie Simpson had such lovely hair,
It reached down to her waist:
Till friends sweetly told her that around Mayfair
Having hair was thought bad taste.
'Bobbed or shingled it must be dear',
Said they, 'If you wish to wed . . .'

Short hair was set into neat permanent waves with Marcel home perm kits. The word *perm*, which came into English in the 1920s, is short for *permanent wave*, too much of a mouthful for any '20s flapper (although American English does use *permanent* for this). *Permanent* comes from Latin *permanēns* (stem *permanent-*) which is the present participle of *permanēre*, 'to stay throughout' (from *per-*, 'throughout', and *manēre*, 'to remain').

Those women who opted for a *bob* chose a style named after a horse's tail which has been docked short into a knob, the word *bob*, which is of unknown origin, having denoted 'a lump, a knob' since the early seventeenth century. Both *perm* and *bob* are still current in every high street hairdresser's.

PERFUME
Along with their designs, leading fashion houses of the 1920s sought to make a statement with perfumes which bore their names. In 1922 Coco Chanel launched *Chanel No 5*, the first fragrance to have a completely chemical base (and the only thing Marilyn Monroe would admit to wearing in bed). However, the etymology of *perfume* testifies to the fact that the word has not always denoted a fragrance to be dabbed behind the ears or sprayed from an atomiser to make the wearer nice to be near. The term comes from an early Italian verb *parfumare* (from *par-*, 'through', and *fumare*, 'to smoke')

which meant 'to permeate with smoke' from incense and the like. French borrowed this as *parfumer* and from it derived the noun *parfum* which was borrowed into English in the first half of the sixteenth century.

Substances were burnt for a variety of reasons: the perfume from burning juniper berries, for instance, might be used to fumigate a room after a plague death; often the leaves of certain herbs were burned as a remedy for a cold or for breathing difficulties; and sometimes substances prepared from flowers or spices were burnt simply to sweeten the air:

Perfumes . . . fill the ayre, that we can putt our nose in no part of the roome, where a perfume is burned, but we shall smell it.
(Sir Kenelm Digby, from a treatise ON THE NATURE OF BODIES, 1644)

Thus *perfume* originally denoted 'fragrant fumes' but the term was soon applied more generally to 'a pleasant fragrance' of any sort, whether given off through burning or not: the scent of flowers, for instance. By extension, in the sixteenth century *perfume* also came to denote 'the material source of the perfume, the substance prepared for burning', a use which remained current well into the second half of the nineteenth century. Its application to a bottle of liquid scent that Chanel and Monroe would recognise dates only from the late nineteenth century.

• Like *perfume* the word *incense* has to do with burning. Incense was an important element in Old Testament ritual. The Old Testament had two Hebrew words for *incense*, one to denote the substance, a gum resin, which was burnt, and another for the sweet-smelling smoke. Both senses combine in the English word *incense*. This came, by way of Old French, from ecclesiastical Latin *incensum*, which literally means 'that which is set on fire', being a derivative of Latin *incendere*, 'to set on fire'. (Latin *incendere* was also used figuratively with the sense 'to inflame with anger', and this gave the English verb *to incense*.) The superiority of the gum resin *frankincense* is proclaimed by its name. It is a compound of *incense* and the adjective *frank* which, from the fifteenth to the seventeenth centuries, was applied to plants and medicines of exceptional quality.

Scent was not applied to a liquid fragrance until the eighteenth century. The word goes back to Latin *sentire*, 'to feel, to discern'. It was later borrowed into Old French as *sentir*, 'to feel, to smell', and from there into Middle English as *sent* around the turn of the fifteenth century. The verb was mainly used in hunting contexts, where it meant 'to track down game by following its smell'. A remnant of this usage today is in *hot on the scent*. The derivative noun *sent* also meant both 'a hound's sense of smell' and the 'odour of an animal'. Used more generally, the term also denoted 'a distinctive smell'. This could either be pleasant:

The fragrant sents of flowry banks
(Sylvester, translation of Du Bartas, THE DIVINE WEEKS AND WORKS, 1592)

or not so pleasant:

Every man rose fro the table abhorrying & eschewyng the sente and sauour of the dede man.
(Caxton, RECUYELL OF THE HISTORYES OF TROYE, 1471)

Eventually the agreeable won out, so that later the term could be unambiguously applied to liquid fragrance.

1916

IN THE FIRST WORLD WAR TANKS ARE USED FOR THE FIRST TIME AS THE BRITISH ATTACK THE GERMANS AT THE SOMME

......

In 1914 the First Lord of the Admiralty, Winston Churchill, invested £70,000 of Admiralty money in the development of motorised vehicles that could penetrate enemy lines and stand up to machine-gun fire. Wheels were useless over broken terrain and an armoured vehicle mounted on caterpillar tracks was proposed. The first tank, named 'Little Willie', was built in September 1915 and an improved model, 'Big Willie', capable of crossing wide trenches, was ready to be tested by December.

On 15 September 1916, forty-nine of these tanks were used at the Battle of the Somme. They met with little success. The 23-ton tanks were too slow, they developed mechanical faults and their protective plate was easily perforated by German artillery. They were also too few in number and thus deployed too far apart to effect a major breakthrough for supporting infantry. They did, however, have a major psychological impact, causing panic and disruption in the German ranks and surprising even the British. This is what one British soldier had to say:

> *There before our astonished eyes appeared about six of the first Mark I tanks, lurching about the country on their caterpillar tracks . . . bursting through hedges, crossing trenches, demolishing walls and even snapping off small trees.*

Undeterred, the British and the French, who had coincidentally begun to develop their own tanks at the same time, continued to work on the concept. On 20 November the following year a massive offensive was launched against the Hindenburg Line at Cambrai. Here 400 redesigned British tanks accompanied by numerous infantry plunged deep into German territory.

Both the British and the French persevered with tank design throughout the war and built several thousand vehicles. The German command were never convinced of their usefulness, however, so that only twenty German tanks were built in all.

TANK

In India many centuries ago, artificial water-storage lakes were dug out to collect the monsoon rains. Gujarati had the word *tānkh* to denote such a reservoir and Marāthi *tānken*. These words are thought to derive from the Sanskrit term *tadāga*, 'lake, pond'. When the East India Company opened trade with India at the beginning of the seventeenth century, the word *tank* came into English, initially in travel accounts describing Indian life. The extended use of *tank* for 'a large receptacle for storing liquids' began around the end of the seventeenth century but became common during the nineteenth when even fish in captivity began to live in *tanks*. And with the advent of the internal combustion engine, *tank* was, of course, applied to the 'fuel reservoir'. The production in 1915 of a heavily armoured combat vehicle, designed to crush the might of German artillery on the Western Front, was highly secretive and a code word was deemed necessary. The project was developed at Foster & Co, an engineering works at Lincoln, under the cover of an order for water tanks and, indeed, the vehicles were subsequently shipped to the Front in crates marked 'tanks'. The code name was successful because, as a reporter in THE TIMES wrote just three days after the armoured monsters' first appearance at the Battle of the Somme, *the name has the evident official advantage of being quite undescriptive.*

1920

WEEKLY PAYMENTS ARE MADE TO THE UNEMPLOYED FROM NATIONAL AND LOCAL FUNDS

••••••

A tide of optimism followed the Great War. Britain expected that the industries on which her pre-war prosperity had been based would pick up again. Sadly this was not so. New competitors who had invested in efficient modern machinery emerged during and immediately after the war years to supply Britain's former markets in cotton, shipbuilding, steel and coal. These industries began to flounder in the United Kingdom and many men lost their jobs. The high unemployment figure was increased by farm workers put out of work by cheap food imports from abroad and the gradual mechanisation of their tasks, and by domestic servants whom the middle class could no longer afford to employ. By June 1921 there were over two million unemployed.

DOLE

Old English had the word *dāl* which meant 'part, portion'. During the early thirteenth century the term was sometimes applied to 'the apportioning or distribution of gifts', in particular to food or money given in charity. By the second half of the fourteenth century *dole* had come to denote the charitable gifts themselves, and this sense is still current. After the Great War a benefit, popularly known as *the dole*, was introduced to help out demobbed soldiers. By 1920, however, the economic situation was so dire that the scheme had to be extended to alleviate the plight of the growing number of unemployed. Recipients of the dole barely reached subsistence level. In BRITAIN BETWEEN THE WORLD WARS (1975), Marion Yass quotes from the case book of a Birmingham health visitor:

Mrs J's husband's been out of work 14 weeks and there's five of them starving . . . Although Mrs J was nursing her baby, I found that all the food she had had yesterday

was a cup of tea at breakfast time, and tea and two slices of bread and butter, provided by a married sister living near, at tea-time.

By the mid-1920s the term *on the dole*, meaning 'in receipt of unemployment benefit', was current and has featured in the language ever since.

The derived verb *to dole*, meaning 'to distribute in charity' dates from the fifteenth century. It has been more commonly used with *out* since the eighteenth century and implies stinginess, having the sense 'to deal out sparingly'.

1928

ALEXANDER FLEMING DISCOVERS PENICILLIN

• • • • • •

Fleming's research into antibacterial substances was triggered by his experiences in the Royal Army Medical Corps during the First World War when he treated many soldiers dying from infected wounds. However, his discovery of the first antibiotic was in part accidental. Fleming, who had inadvertently left a petrie dish of staphylococci uncovered in his laboratory, observed that the green mould which now contaminated the dish had inhibited the growth of the surrounding bacteria. He identified the mould as *Penicillium notatum* and succeeded in isolating a chemical in it which not only prevented the bacteria from reproducing but was also nontoxic. This he called *penicillin*.

The purifying and testing of *penicillin* were developed at the outbreak of the Second World War by two British scientists, Howard Florey and Ernst Chain. The supply available for their first patient, a man dying of septicaemia, was so inadequate that the chemical had to be recycled from the man's urine.

PENICILLIN, PENCIL

Penicillin is related to the most unlikely words – and thereby hangs a tale. The Latin word *pēnis* originally meant 'tail'. For reasons that need no explanation, the term was extended to denote 'penis' and in this sense was borrowed into English in the

second half of the seventeenth century.

In Roman times, ox tails and horse tails were used by housewives and servants to flick away dust. The word for this handy 'brush' was *pēniculus*, which literally meant 'little tail', being a diminutive of *pēnis*. However, a painter would need something a little finer than an ox tail for his work and so *pēnicillum* was formed, a diminutive of *pēniculus*, to denote 'a painter's brush'. This word was altered to the unattested form *pēnicellum* in Vulgar Latin. From here it was borrowed into Old French as *pincel* (becoming *pinceau* in modern French) and then into Middle English as *pensel*, *pencel* in the fourteenth century, the spelling *pencil* emerging during the seventeenth. The use of *pencil* to denote 'an artist's fine brush' persisted until the mid-nineteenth century, but is now archaic. Its modern application to 'a graphite rod used for writing' dates from the early seventeenth century, almost fifty years after graphite began to be used as a marker (see below). The green mould in Fleming's culture dish was identified as *Penicillium notatum*. Various moulds are classed as *Penicillium*. The Latin name was applied to them in the second half of the nineteenth century because of their tufty appearance, rather like the hairs of a paint brush. The word *penicillin* was applied to the antibiotic substance by Fleming, the final suffix *-in* being common in chemical terminology:

In the rest of this article allusion will constantly be made to experiments with filtrates of a broth culture of this mould, so for convenience and to avoid the repetition of the rather cumbersome phrase 'Mould broth filtrate', the name 'penicillin' will be used. This will denote the filtrate of a broth culture of the particular penicillium with which we are concerned.
(Alexander Fleming in BRITISH JOURNAL OF EXPERIMENTAL PATHOLOGY, 1929)

• In 1565 a German-Swiss naturalist, Conrad Gesner, described a writing instrument consisting of a stick of graphite enclosed in a wooden holder – in other words, a pencil. The production of such pencils had been greatly facilitated by a discovery made in the aftermath of a great storm in 1564 when a large deposit of very pure graphite was accidentally uncovered in Borrowdale, England, beneath the roots of a felled oak. Nevertheless, the word *pencil* was not applied to the article until around 1612, the term being borrowed from the artist whose fine brush was known as a *pencil*.

The valuable Borrowdale deposit was at first thought to be a type of lead and was, therefore, known as *black lead* or *plumbago*. Not until 1779 did a Swedish chemist identify the mineral as a type of carbon, and in 1789 a German geologist, Abraham Werner, coined the name *graphite* (German *Graphit*), a word derived from the Greek verb *graphein*, 'to write'. (See **pen**, page 239)

1938

LASZLO BIRO PATENTS THE FIRST PRACTICAL BALL-POINT PEN

••••••

Ball-point pens were invented back in the late nineteenth century but they were unsatisfactory and did not catch on. The main problem was with the oil-based ink which did not always flow smoothly and took a long time to dry. Then in 1938 Laszlo Biro, a Hungarian journalist, patented a practical model whose thick oily ink kept the writing tip rolling freely.

BIRO

The early uptake in the late 1930s of Biro ball-point pens in Great Britain was assured when they were issued to the Armed Forces. They were impressed by a pen that was unaffected by either altitude or climate, could be used on many different writing surfaces and had a long-lasting supply of waterproof, fast-drying, permanent ink. The new ball-point pen was popularly named *Biro* or *Biro pen* after its inventor. At the end of the war, Biro found a British manufacturer to produce his pens and, although other models from different manufacturers soon appeared on the market, they, too, were known as *biros*, this time written with a lower-case initial letter.

PEN

By the late 1940s ball-point pens were used throughout the world, swiftly replacing the fountain pen as the most convenient writing tool. The first really practical fountain pen had not appeared until L Edson Waterman's invention in 1884. Indeed, developments in writing implements had been slow over the centuries: the quill was in use as late as the mid-nineteenth century when metal nibs at last became widespread.

A quill pen was made from the dried wing feather of a goose, crow or swan. This was trimmed at the end to a writing edge which was kept sharp by constant retrimming. Jonathan Swift, in TALE OF A TUB (1704) wrote of *A quill worn to the pith in the service of the State*. The word *pen* has its origins in Latin *penna*, which meant 'feather'. In a Late Latin manuscript of St Isodore of Seville, written in the early seventh century, *penna* was used with the sense 'quill-pen', an indication that feathers were being used to write with by that date. Old French took the word as *penne*, 'feather' and 'writing implement', and it passed into Middle English as *penne* around the turn of the fourteenth century. The modern English spelling dates from the early seventeenth century (see **pencil**, page 237).

QUILL, NIB

The origins of *quill* are more difficult than those of *pen*. The most that can be said is that the word is Germanic. It dates back to the fifteenth century when it denoted 'a hollow stalk or reed'. Its use to describe 'the hollow main shaft of a feather' goes back to the mid-sixteenth century. *Quill* (or *goose-quill*) to denote 'writing tool' is a specific application which arose at the same time.

The point of a quill sharpened for writing was slit to make the end more flexible. In the late sixteenth century this writing point was called a *neb*. This was a particular application of a word of Germanic origin which had been in English since the eighth century and which denoted 'a bird's beak' or 'an animal's snout'. *Nib* was a variant of *neb* which arose in the second half of the sixteenth century. It first denoted 'a beak' and then, in the early seventeenth century, 'the point of a pen'.

In their play THE ROARING GIRLE (1611), Thomas Middleton and Thomas Dekker permitted themselves this jibe against lawyers' venom:

> *Let not you and I be tost*
> *On Lawiers pens; they haue sharpe nibs.*

A sentiment which John Florio had previously extended to scholars:

> *A serpents tooth bites not so ill,*
> *As dooth a schollers angrie quill*
> (SECOND FRUTES, 1591).

Indeed, the damage that could be done by the written word has been variously expressed over the centuries. Shakespeare's Hamlet muses how *Many wearing Rapiers, are affraide of Goose-quills* (1602). In modern English the thought finds expression in a line from Lord Lytton's play RICHELIEU (1838) which is now proverbial: *The pen is mightier than the sword*.

INK

The Greek verb *egkaiein* literally meant 'to burn in', being a compound of *en-*, 'in', and *kaiein*, 'to burn'. In fact the term denoted a particular method of painting which was practised by the ancients. According to a first-century account in the writings of Pliny the Elder, the process involved mixing pigments with hot beeswax, brushing them on to plaster and then smoothing and fixing them to the surface with a hot iron. (English derived the word *encaustic* from Greek in the seventeenth century to describe this kind of painting.)

Whenever Greek or Roman emperors had documents of state to sign, they used an ink of imperial purple. The word for this special ink was *egkauston*, a derivative of the verb *egkaiein*. By the time the term arrived in Old French as *enque* in the eleventh century by way of Late Latin *encaustum*, it simply denoted ordinary ink. Middle English took the term from Old French as *enke* in the mid-thirteenth century. Over the centuries *ink* has been applied to various substances used for writing or painting, including the viscous paste prepared by Mr Biro.

1940

VIDKUN QUISLING ASSUMES LEADERSHIP OF NORWAY

••••••

Vidkun Quisling entered Norwegian politics in 1929. He was a fascist and admirer of the German Nazi Party, and in 1933 founded his own National Union party along similar lines. Firmly rejected by the Norwegian electorate, the party was unsuccessful. Undeterred, in 1939 Quisling made direct contact with German Nazi command and eventually, in December of that year, with Hitler himself. In April 1940 Hitler finally responded to Quisling's overtures and invaded Norway. Quisling seized the opportunity to declare himself head of government but his glory was short-lived: his regime lasted only six days through lack of support. The Norwegian leaders refused to cooperate with the occupation authorities, who were eventually forced to establish a puppet government of Nazi sympathisers with Quisling at its head. In his role as 'minister president', Quisling was strenuous in his efforts to instil Nazi ideology into Norwegian society. Rigorous in his persecution of the Jews, Quisling also terrorised supporters of the exiled king.

QUISLING

In 1939 Norway had declared her neutrality in the war and fiercely resisted the unexpected German occupation. Quisling, however, collaborated. From the moment Quisling declared himself head of the Norwegian government, his name became synonymous with 'traitor'. As early as 15 April 1940 THE TIMES called for vigilance against possible *Quislings* in Sweden and within a year was using the name as an adjective: *quisling newspapers* appeared in a report dated 11 March 1941. The term was used so frequently in war-time reports that it spawned a number of interesting derivations such as *to quisle, quisler, quislingism* and *quislingise.*

Vidkun Quisling zealously collaborated with the Nazis throughout the war. After the liberation of Norway in May 1945, the death penalty was reintroduced specifically for the punishment of traitors. Quisling was arrested by his countrymen, tried for treason and executed by firing squad at Akershus Fortress, Oslo, on 24 October 1945. His name, however, lives on and means 'traitor'.

1940
THE BLITZ BEGINS
• • • • • •

In September 1940, the German Air Force, the Luftwaffe, began a series of intensive air-raids on major British cities. London and Coventry were particular targets, but Bristol, Plymouth, Portsmouth, Southampton, Birmingham, Hull and Glasgow were also heavily bombed. The raids were intended to wipe out armament factories, to damage ports and to prepare for an eventual German invasion by weakening British resolve and resistance.

BLITZ

The years 1940 and 1941 saw the heaviest bombing of the war. Almost every night a siren gave a two-minute warning that enemy aircraft were approaching (see **siren**, page 195). Soon the sound of their engines could be heard, followed by the explosion of bombs, the crash of falling masonry and the clatter of anti-aircraft guns. Flames lit the city and searchlight beams pierced the sky. The raids could last for several hours.

Although many citizens took refuge in air-raid shelters, public facilities were crowded, smelly and noisy, and some people chose to remain at home. They preferred to face death in familiar surroundings, waiting with bated breath for the All Clear to sound. Perhaps only the very young succeeded in keeping terror at bay:

The wail of the siren brought my mother upstairs, to shepherd us down. This was great fun! We tipped our old settee on its end; this was to protect our heads, the three of us! The big old kitchen table was pushed up to it. Hey presto, a home-made air-raid shelter! We cuddled down into makeshift sleeping-bags. The living-room fire was kept on. We were cosy, warm and safe. (Account of a nine-year-old girl from Cheshire in Westall, CHILDREN OF THE BLITZ, 1985)

The air-raids were known colloquially as the *blitz*. The word was a shortening of the German *Blitzkrieg*, literally 'lightning war' (from *Blitz*, 'lightning' and *Krieg*, 'war'). Coined in 1939, the term referred to the highly successful German tactic of using aircraft and tanks to mount an intensive attack on the enemy at the rear instead of head on. The British press used the word *blitz* for the raids from the outset. From 7 September 1940, London was bombed for seventy-five nights out of seventy-six. On 9 September THE DAILY EXPRESS carried the headline *Blitz bombing of London goes on all night*, while the following day it reported that *in his three-day blitz on London Goering has now lost 140 planes*.

In present-day English, *Blitz*, written with a capital letter, refers to the historical period when the raids took place. However, there were figurative uses from the very earliest days, *blitz* now having the sense of 'intensive effort to carry out a task, such as a *blitz* on the gardening, on the paperwork or on redecorating a room.

1946

ATOMIC BOMB TESTS ARE CARRIED OUT IN THE MARSHALL ISLANDS

••••••

Situated in the central Pacific, the Marshall Islands are made up of two strings of coral atolls. They were sighted by the Spanish in the sixteenth century but are named after John Marshall, a British sea-captain who explored them in 1788. The islands were ruled by Germany from 1885 until 1914, and then by Japan. In 1944 American forces ousted the Japanese and occupied a number of the atolls, including Bikini. In July 1946 Bikini was used by the United States for two atomic bomb tests: the first to discover the effect of an atomic bomb on a naval fleet and the second to conduct a nuclear explosion underwater.

BIKINI

A bomb of a different kind rocked the world of French fashion the following year, when a scanty two-piece swimsuit was unveiled. The *bikini* had arrived. Its impact on the senses and sensibilities of the French who thronged the holiday beaches was shattering. LE MONDE ILLUSTRÉ for August 1947 revelled in its description of a garment which reduced the area of covered flesh to practically nothing, thus achieving *une minimisation extrême de la pudeur*.

The *bikini* was an immediate success, although a certain amount of courage was needed to wear it. The girl in Brian Hyland's 1950s hit song 'Itsy Bitsy Teenie Weenie Yellow Polka Dot Bikini' has trouble making it to the water's edge for fear of being noticed the first time she wears hers. Nevertheless, by 1964 the shock waves had long subsided and it was time for new eye-opener – a bikini without the top bit. But what to call it? Its designer, noting that *bikini* looks as if it begins with the Latin prefix *bi-*, 'two', cleverly substituted *mono-*, 'one'. The result was *monokini*.

1948

THE FIRST ALTERABLE STORED-PROGRAM COMPUTER IS BORN

······

In 1948, Freddie Williams and Tom Kilburn were hard at work in a small workshop in Coupland Street in Manchester. They were conscious of the race to produce a machine that had a memory, could store a program of instructions, and execute them. In the same hunt were scientists in Cambridge University and at the National Physical Laboratory at Teddington in Middlesex, and others in America. On June 21, 1948, the 'Baby', as it was known, ran its first program, ahead of all its competitors. This was a key moment in the history of the computer.

No invention springs out of nothing. The Manchester scientists had centuries of discovery and creativity behind them. One claimant to the title 'Father of Computing' is the genius Charles Babbage (1792-1871). Among a wealth of inventions and initiatives, he is perhaps best known for his calculating machine (a computing device in the limited sphere of mathematical calculation). His main claim, though, comes from his Analytical Engine. It had a mill (a unit to make the calculations), a store (the memory), input and control devices based on punched cards, and a printer. The motive power was steam. In other words, it was a general-purpose computer. It never got beyond a design, but one wonders what might have happened if Babbage had had access to electricity. Over subsequent decades, there were many incremental improvements. Burroughs patented the first commercially successful adding machine in 1892; Vannevar Bush built the differential analyser at the Massachusetts Institute of Technology in the early 1930s.

In the later 1930s and early '40s, Kruse in Germany was working on a shoestring budget to develop increasingly sophisticated devices – the Z1 machine came out in 1938, the Z3 in 1941, and the Z4 was annexed after the War by the Allies from an Alpine cellar in which he had hidden it. At the same period, all the might of Thomas J Watson's IBM was engaged in the development of a twentieth century Analytical Engine, under the direction of Howard Aiken. The Harvard Mark I, as it became known, was digital rather than analogue, and relied on electro-magnetic relays rather than valves. It was switched on briefly at IBM's headquarters at Endicott in 1943, then redesigned, modified and reassembled at Harvard. All this was a world away from the device in a Swiss cellar. The Mark I was huge. It had a million parts, was 55 feet long, 8 feet high, and was in a glossy steel and glass setting. Ex-naval officers (Aiken had been one during the War) danced it loving and very military attention. Marching, saluting and standing to attention were the norm around its cradle. The Manchester 'Baby' also weighed in at some size. A replica of it is now on view at the City's Museum of Science and Industry, and needs to be seen to be believed.

BUG

The Smithsonian Museum of American History has in its possession a logbook with the following entry for 9 September, 1947:

1545 Relay #70 Panel F (moth) in relay first actual use of bug being found.

Pasted on the page is a dead moth.

According to Admiral Grace Hopper (known for her invention of the computer language COBOL), the Harvard Mark II machine at Dahlgren, Virginia, was malfunctioning one day and a technician put it right by extracting a moth from between the contacts of one of its relays. Such is the fame of this incident that it is recorded in serious histories of computing, and in etymological works investigating the use of the word *bug* in technological contexts. Important and fêted though this moth might be, it is not the origin of the term. *Bug* in the sense of 'defect, cause of malfunction' goes back much further than a joke in a computer lab in Virginia. Indeed, the phrasing of the log entry shows that the term was already well known to Admiral Hopper and her staff.

So what is the origin? There has been considerable discussion, best summarised in Shapiro's paper in AMERICAN SPEECH in 1987 'Entomology of the Computer Bug: History and Folklore'. (It is surprising how many have seized the chance to play on the happy coincidence of entomology and etymology!) The online NEW HACKER'S DICTIONARY is also very thorough. Such sources suggest the following account.

The first recorded uses of *bug* as 'defect' are connected with Thomas Edison and his laboratories and date back to 1878. The meaning it had towards the end of the nineteenth century is evident from this entry in HAWKIN'S NEW CATECHISM OF ELECTRICITY, published by Audel in 1896:

The term `bug' is used to a limited extent to designate any fault or trouble in the connections or working of electric apparatus.

At roughly the same period, bugs were prevalent in the field of wireless telegraphy. Telephone connections were notoriously 'noisy' and interference popularly attributed to 'bugs on the line'. Moreover, an important way of sending messages then was by Morse code, which involved an operator and a device to send the signal. There were manual keyers and, for the professionals, semi-automatic ones that sent a string of dots if they were kept depressed - just as a keyboard does today. One of the most famous of these was the Vibroflex keyer, which came complete with a beetle as its logo. Of course, if you weren't a professional and got the pressure a bit wrong, you sent a string of garbled text from your 'bug'.

In the nineteenth century, radio technicians had a diagnostic device that looked for interference and harmful emissions. Early versions had a coil of wire, with two wires protruding forward and then bending back, in order to form a spark gap. Because of its appearance, the elements were called the roach body and roach antennae in American English. These and later versions were called *bugs*.

(Incidentally, it is probable that the bugs of modern espionage and surveillance take their name from this source.)

Of these various influences, Hawkin at least thought the primary source was telegraphy. He adds in his CATECHISM that bugs are *said to have originated in quadruplex telegraphy and have been transferred to all electric apparatus.*

But how did *bug* come to be used as an informal word for 'insect' in the first place? It arose in the seventeenth century with reference, for example, to tiresome bedbugs. Skeat proposes that the Middle English word *bugge*, meaning 'hobgoblin', that was current until the mid-eighteenth century, may have influenced an Old English word *budd*, meaning 'beetle', to lend it an overtone of unpleasantness that *budd* alone did not have. But this is just theorising without real proof. *Bugge* itself may well go back to Welsh *bwg*, 'ghost', which would explain its occurrence in *bugaboo*, *bogey* and *bogeyman* (see *Bug Bible* in **bible**, page 93). As for *bugbear*, it is found in Florio's Italian dictionary of 1598 and later in the works of Pope, Hazlitt and a range of other literary figures.

Bug has forced its way to public attention over recent decades in the guise of the *millennium bug*. It is an expression that has been seriously overworked. The first part of the phrase, none the less, has some linguistic interest. In Classical Latin, there existed *biennium*, 'a space of two years', which came from the root *bi-*, 'two', and *annus*, 'year'. *Triennium*, 'a space of three years', was formed on the same basis, as were *quadriennium*, *quinquennium*, etc. However, it was not until Modern Latin that *millennium* was coined by analogy, for 'a period of a thousand years'. *Mille* is Latin for a thousand. In its plural form *milia* or *millia* was borrowed into Old English and gives us our contemporary *mile* - the standard measure of a thousand steps of a Roman soldier is estimated at 1,618 yards, a little short of the modern mile's 1,760 yards. Earliest uses of *millennium* in English, mainly from the eighteenth century, focused on the Latin sense of 'a space of a thousand years'. This was undoubtedly reinforced by the debates then raging about the Millennium (note the initial capital), that is the thousand-year period when, according to the biblical book of Revelation, Christ will reign on earth. This was a hot theological issue, since there is no consensus as to whether Christ's second coming will be before the Millennium (pre-millennialism) or after it (post-millennialism). More recently, the sense of *millennium* has also come to mean 'thousandth anniversary', as in Millennium Dome and Millennium Experience. After all the hype and over-exposure of recent years, one might hope that *millennium bug* might sink back into decent linguistic obscurity, along with the Experience.

HARDWARE, SOFTWARE

Most computer vocabulary is actually an old word with a new sense. *Hardware* is a case in point. The base word *ware*, 'goods, commodities, merchandise', has been in use for over a millennium from its Old English origin *waru*. Perhaps surprisingly, it is the compound *hardwareman*, 'a dealer in ironmongery and small wares', which occurs next in texts in the sixteenth century. This is some two hundred years before *hardware* itself is regularly recorded, still in the context of pedlars of locks, scissors and other miscellaneous bits of ironmongery. From this humble beginning, it was a small leap to apply the term to weaponry in the latter part of the nineteenth century.

The computing use of the term, 'a set of physical components that make up a system', has developed over the second half of the twentieth century. The ENIAC machine was described as *hardware* in 1947, and the bits of a computer that you can touch have ever since been so called.

Some computer words are genuine originals. About 1960, *software* was coined, with the meaning 'program, instructions to make the hardware operate'. One might hope that the term's originator had a sense of humour, or possibly was prophetic, and could see all the breakdowns, losses and frustrations that *software* was going to cause, so he chose *soft* in its meaning of 'silly, stupid'. Alas, the prosaic truth is that it is a formation by analogy, soft simply being the antonym of *hard*.

One good thing leads to another. Computer programmer Andrew Fluegelman registered *freeware* as a trademark. He disappeared mysteriously in 1984, which had the effect of releasing the term for wider use. It is now common, meaning 'software produced by enthusiasts for distribution and use without charge'. A variation on this is *shareware*, 'a program for which the author requests a minimal, voluntary payment'. There are quite a few other new terms on the same model. Some are unpleasant (*wetware* means 'the human brain'); some creative (*shovelware* is dumped on to a CD, to fill up any remaining space); some show a tendency to generalise beyond the computing world (*payware*).

BIT/BYTE

To non-specialists, *bits* and *bytes* join the other mysteries of computing, and seem designed to keep the uninitiated outside the charmed circle of the true élite. In fact, this particular distinction is fairly straightforward. A *bit* is 'a binary digit, 0 or 1'. Eight of these basic units make up a *byte*, and that is all there is to it, at least by way of definition. What they can do in combination is, of course, little short of miraculous.

One day in the late 1940s, statistician and computer scientist John Tukey was out for lunch, and with friends was trying to work out what to do with the somewhat unwieldy term 'binary digit'. 'Binit' wasn't much good, but it was better than 'bigit'. Best option, they concluded, was *bit*, as it was short, neat and already in its standard English sense carried the idea of 'a small part'. This inspired bit of word coining reached print for the first time in 1949, in an article in Bell Systems technical journal by C E Shannon.

Before long, the need to name a higher unit became evident. What should a set of *bits* big enough to store or process or transfer one character be called? There is some doubt about the precise story, but it seems to be that Dr Werner Bucholz was engaged on the development of the IBM stretch computer in 1956, and introduced the term *byte* for a 6-bit unit. It was only late in 1956 that 8-bit units became standard, on the introduction of IBM's System/360. The odd thing about this is that the first mention in print in the OED is from the IBM systems journal of 1964. Blaauw and Brooks explain the new term:

An 8-bit unit of information is fundamental to most of the formats [of the System/360].

This is a surprisingly late appearance for a term coined in the mid-1950s. With regard to the form of the word, the obvious conclusion is that it is a bit of word play that attempts to retain something of *bit*, yet is different enough in pronunciation and spelling not to create confusion. One famous writer, William Safire, proposes it is short for BinarY TErm, or else BInary digiT Eight, with the I changed to Y to avoid confusion. This is, at best, speculation.

GEEK, NERD

Computer fanatics seem to attract pejorative words to describe them. (Now why should that be?). More often than not, they are words previously known in other contexts, but given new strength and life in the computer age. *Geek* and *nerd* both come into this category.

The online NEW HACKER'S DICTIONARY has this graphic description of the *computer geek*:

One who fulfils all the dreariest negative stereotypes about hackers: an asocial, malodorous, pasty-faced monomaniac with all the personality of a cheese grater.

From about 1500 up to the beginning of the twentieth century in some dialects, *geck* (originally from Low German) was used to describe a fool or simple person. It was used in several of Shakespeare's plays and by other literary masters. Its fortunes turned for the worse when it transformed into *geek* in the American slang of the early years of the twentieth century. As is so often the case with slang words, it seems to have had a variety of meanings. One of them in general slang is 'man, fellow' – Eric Partridge in his DICTIONARY OF THE UNDERWORLD guesses that it might be formed from an amalgamation of *gee*, 'guy' in slang, plus *bloke*, 'man'. This is unlikely, as the word is principally American, and bloke is essentially British. More convincing is the attribution to carnival slang. Circus performers who took to drugs or alcohol slipped down the jobs available until they reached rock bottom: the job of the *geek*. Webster's dictionary records its meaning then as being *a carnival 'wild man' whose act usually includes biting the head off a live chicken or snake*. From such a source the term reached a wider public through William Gresham's novel NIGHTMARE ALLEY. It was published in 1946 and subsequently made into a film with Tyrone Power.

Yet another sense for *geek* is recorded by Random House lexicographer Jesse Sheidlower, that of 'a socially awkward or offensive person who is overly intellectual'.

Whichever of these various meanings you take, none is particularly complimentary. Small wonder, then, that it was applied disparagingly to the *computer geek* from the start of the electronic revolution.

By an inverted twist, from about 1990 it has been used by computer people of other computer people as a term of praise. In itself it is quite a common phenomenon to take a term of abuse and use it for self-reference and protest: blacks have called themselves *niggers*, homosexuals *dykes*, *queers* and *fags*. Many highly respectable Conservatives probably do not realise that *Tory* was once a term of abuse, used alongside *robber, murderer, despicable savage, outlaw, ass* and *idiot* (to name just a few).

Nerd is similar in meaning and equally uncomplimentary. It has been around for a much shorter time, however. The first printed record is in 1950 as the name for a fanciful creature in the children's book IF I RAN THE ZOO by Dr Seuss:

And then, just to show them, I'll sail to Ka-
 Troo
And Bring Back an It-Kutch, a Preep and a Proo,
A Nerkle, a Nerd, and a Seersucker, too!

The trouble with this as the likely origin is that it is a very rapid transition from a children's rhyme to a pejorative term, for it is only one year later in 1951 that it is recorded with its slang meaning.

There are lots of other attempts to account for it. Variant spellings prevalent at Massachusetts Institute of Technology in the 1960s were *nurd* and *knurd*. The former rhymes with *turd* and the latter is *drunk* spelt backwards. Very convenient.

A slightly more convincing explanation is one concerning a ventriloquist's dummy. Edgar Bergen had a variety act featuring his brainy dummy, Mortimer Snerd. Their joint fame was such that they got a mention in 1941 in Bond and Anderson's FLYING T. DIARY:

I discussed the P-40 flying characteristics with 'Mortimer Snerd' Shilling.

The possible change of *Snerd* to *nerd* is obvious, in its form, at least. The problem with regard to the sense development is that Snerd was an intelligent dummy, yet all the quotations up to the 1970s use *nerd* pejoratively in relation to a stupid person. There are no early references to bright but antisocial students, for instance.

In this case, it seems best to admit that no one knows the origin. In any event, the current sense of 'a socially maladroit person, with above average intelligence and a tendency to obsession' lends itself well to some computer types, and explains its frequent use in this context. In fact, a *computer nerd* is not far from the striking picture of the *computer geek* in the NEW HACKER'S DICTIONARY. What a pair they make!

1950

North Korean Troops Invade South Korea

······

Following the defeat of Japan in the Second World War, Korea ceased to be a Japanese possession and was partitioned, the USSR supervising Japanese withdrawal from the North and the United States that from the South. Subsequent attempts to form a united Korean government failed, and separate governments were set up in 1948. On 25 June 1950 the Communist North Korean leader, Kim Il Sung, took advantage of unrest in the South and invaded. A conflict ensued between the North, aided by China, and the South which was supported by United Nations forces, led by US General MacArthur. The war ended in 1953 with all South Korean territory intact.

BRAINWASHING

During the Korean War the Chinese and North Koreans attempted to cleanse the minds of American and European prisoners, totally replacing their previously held political beliefs with Communist principles. This was done by isolating the men from each other, by depriving them of basic necessities such as food or sleep, and by forcing them to be self-critical and confess past misdemeanours. In BRAVE NEW WORLD REVISITED (1958), Aldous Huxley explains how *to intensify their sense of guilt, prisoners were made to write and rewrite, in ever more intimate detail, long autobiographical accounts of their shortcomings. And after having confessed their own sins, they were required to confess the sins of their companions. Thus the camp became a place of secrecy and suspicion, a nightmarish society, in which everybody was spying on, and informing against, everyone else.*

This cleansing process, *hsi nao* in Chinese, was accompanied by indoctrination with Communist ideology.

Brainwashing is a literal translation of *hsi nao* (from Mandarin *hsi*, 'to wash', and *nao*, 'brain'). The term came into American English when the Chinese succeeded in persuading a number of prisoners to denounce publicly their own governments and state their intention of embracing Communism. Although *brainwashing* was brought to Western attention in 1950, the Communist Chinese had already subjected leading Chinese dissidents to the same techniques on coming to power in 1949. *Brainwash* is a back formation of *brainwashing*. The term is used in modern English, though usually in less threatening situations:

> *In London, to admit you're a churchgoer is to invite social death. People assume you've had to invite Jesus into your life because there's no one else in your Filofax. Sophisticated style slaves despise you, and Lefty bike-riders – who see the C of E (rather flatteringly) as an agent of imperialist repression – think you're being brainwashed by neo-fascist ritual.*
> (Oenone Williams in GOOD HOUSEKEEPING, June 1999)

Of course, if you have been indoctrinated and brainwashed, especially by a cult, then help is at hand in the shape of *deprogramming.* Thanks to the images of the electronic era, the human mind is now understood to be like a computer that can be programmed, deprogrammed, and reprogrammed at will:

Some families have even arranged to have their loved one kidnapped, transported to an unfamiliar location, and forced to listen to sermons, watch videotapes and undergo other attempts at persuasion. This controversial technique is often called 'deprogramming'. (Comment on judgement in the Superior Court of the State of Idaho, 1996)

1957
THE FIRST EARTH SATELLITE IS LAUNCHED
······

The first spacecraft ever to orbit the earth was a small artificial satellite launched by the Soviet Union on 4 October 1957. The scientific theory that made the launch possible had been suggested as early as 1687 by Sir Isaac Newton. Sputnik I went round the earth every 96 minutes and emitted a radio signal that could be picked up by scientists worldwide. It had an immediate impact on science, with the extra precision it allowed in gravity studies, and in defining the shape of the earth. It was the first of many subsequent satellites that have been used to collect such scientific data.

SATELLITE

It is the way of princes or distinguished persons to surround themselves with a retinue of attendants and guards. The Latin word for such an escort was *satelles.* The term was taken into French in the fourteenth century as *satellite* (the stem of *satelles* being *satellit-*) and, from there, was borrowed into English around the middle of the sixteenth century. Thomas Blount's GLOSSOGRAPHIA (1656), a dictionary of difficult words, defined *satellite* as *one retained to guard a mans person; a Yeoman of the Guard; a Serjeant, Catch-pole, one that attacheth.* Blount's last definition, *one that attacheth,* is still current in modern English where the term often implies subservience or unscrupulousness. In his LIFE OF OLIVER GOLDSMITH (1849), Washington Irving wrote that James Boswell was *made happy by an introduction to Johnson, of whom he became the obsequious satellite.*

Early in the year 1610 Galileo, who had been exploring the heavens with his telescope, announced his discovery of the *Sidera Medicea,* secondary planets circling Jupiter. The following year the German astronomer Johannes Kepler described these planets as *satellites* and thereafter, this became the accepted term for 'any small planet orbiting a larger one'. Not surprisingly, when men began to dream of the possibility of putting a manmade craft into orbit around the earth in the last quarter of the nineteenth century, *satellite* was the word chosen for such an object.

Satellite is now found in a number of compounds where it carries the sense 'secondary' or 'dependent': *satellite state, satellite town, satellite computer.* And since there are now thousands of satellites in orbit round the earth collecting data and relaying signals, *satellite* is also used adjectivally to mean 'transmitted by satellite': *satellite television, satellite communications.*

• The Russians named their first satellite Sputnik I. The word *sputnik* means 'travelling companion' (from *s-*, 'with', *put*, 'path, journey', *-nik*, agent noun suffix). The Russian advantage over arch-rivals the Americans was a source of some satire. In 1958 Perry Como was at the top of the charts for six weeks with 'Catch a Falling Star'. One ironical version went:

*Catch a falling star
and put it in a matchbox.
Send it to the USA.*

Linguistically, there was a rash of terms ending in *-nik*. Few have lasted, except perhaps *beatnik*, and *peacenik*. Interestingly, the suffix was already known, though not particularly productive, since the Second World War from Yiddish.

1961

JOSEPH HELLER'S NOVEL CATCH-22 IS PUBLISHED

••••••

Joseph Heller, an American novelist and dramatist, is best known for his novel CATCH-22, a darkly humorous satire on the evils of war. During the Second World War Heller was a bombardier with the US Air Force in Europe and his novel is set against this background. Captain Yossarian, the anti-hero of the novel, is based on a small island in the Mediterranean during the Italian campaign. The story concerns his desperate efforts to avoid flying dangerous missions and thus survive the war.

CATCH-22

The use of *catch* to denote a 'snag' or a 'tricky situation intentionally concealed' has been current since the mid-nineteenth century. It is derived from a figurative sense of the verb *to catch* which came into Middle English as *cacchen* in the early thirteenth century. *Cacchen* originally meant 'to chase, to hunt', being a borrowing of Anglo-Norman *cachier*, 'to hunt' and Old French *chacier* (from which English gets *to chase*). These verbs in turn came from the unattested Vulgar Latin *captiāre*, an alteration of Latin *captāre*, 'to attempt to seize, to catch', which was derived from *captus*, 'captive', past participle of *capere*, 'to take, to seize'. However, *cacchen* was not long in English

before it came to mean 'to capture (by any means at all)' and this became its basic sense. As early as the fourteenth century the verb had developed the figurative application 'to ensnare, to deceive', and the noun *catch*, 'unexpected difficulty' or 'intentional trap', is a development of this. Heller's CATCH-22 describes a particular kind of snare, a knotty problem from which there is no escape because the only solution ultimately leads back to the original difficulty. The dilemma is encapsulated in an Air Force regulation, *Catch-22*, which the novel expounds like this:

There was only one catch and that was Catch-22, which specified that a concern for one's own safety in the face of dangers that were real and immediate was the process of a rational mind. Orr was crazy and could be grounded. All he had to do was ask; and as soon as he did he would no longer be crazy and would have to fly more missions. Orr would be crazy to fly more missions and sane if he didn't, but if he was sane he had to fly them. If he flew them he was crazy and didn't have to; but if he didn't want to he was sane and had to. Yossarian was moved very deeply by the absolute simplicity of this clause of Catch-22 and let out a respectful whistle.

The success of Heller's novel brought *Catch-22* into the English language where it is used as an idiom to denote any evidently nonsensical problem:

Students are caught in an impossible catch-22. High school standards are now so dreadful that a college education is required even for unskilled jobs. Graduates can expect to earn 76% more than those without degrees. So students are willing to bankrupt themselves in order to gain a college education that actually teaches them nothing except what they should have learned at school.
(James Bowman, NATIONAL REVIEW, May 1999)

Curiously, the expression might easily have been *Catch-18* as this was the original title of Heller's novel but, just before its publication, the best-selling novelist Leon Uris brought out MILA-18 and this prompted a change.

1969

THE STONEWALL RIOT TAKES PLACE IN NEW YORK

······

In the small hours of 28 June 1969, the Stonewall Inn, a gay bar in Greenwich Village, New York, was raided by police. There had been other similar raids but this time, instead of resignation, the customers resisted. The riot, which lasted just three-quarters of an hour, was the first-ever demonstration against police harassment of homosexuals and was the turning point for gay activism.

GAY

Absolon, the parish clerk, was a handsome fellow and a bit of a lad. In THE MILLER'S TALE (c 1387) Chaucer describes him as *jolif* and *gay*. In the fourteenth century people described as *gay* were 'cheery, light-hearted, full of fun' – which was all part of Absolon's charm. The word was a borrowing of Old French *gai*, 'merry', a term of uncertain origin which may be related to Old High German *gāhi*. 'Cheerful,

carefree' remains a current meaning of the word in modern English and it was still being freely used in this sense in the late 1960s:

Why should I indulge in complaints and regrets? Mark is generous, gay, good-humoured and good-looking. What more can a woman expect of a man?
(Susan Howatch, THE SHROUDED WALLS, 1968)

But, during the second half of the twentieth century, *gay* began to be used informally to denote 'homosexual'. Since this sense is now prevalent, writers have become wary of using the term in its strict sense for fear of unintentional sexual innuendo.

The unusual transformation of the adjective began during the seventeenth century when *gay* began to be applied to fellows whose happy and carefree attitude manifested itself in a self-indulgent lifestyle. It is assumed that this sense of 'recklessly carefree' was responsible for the coining of the term *gaycat*, current among the hobo fraternity in the United States from around the end of the nineteenth century. It denoted a young dropout, not yet wise to the ways of life on the road, who needed the company of an experienced tramp. Raymond Chandler defined the term thus: *A gay-cat is a young punk who runs with an older tramp and there is always a connotation of homosexuality* (LETTER, May 1950). From here the term drifted easily into underworld slang where, according to the DICTIONARY OF AMERICAN SLANG (Wentworth and Flexner, 1960), from the 1920s to the 1940s *gay-cat* was sometimes applied to *a young or inexperienced criminal or a youth who acts as a decoy, runner or lookout for criminals.* As always there was a suggestion of homosexual relationship, for in his UNDERWORLD AND PRISON SLANG, written in 1935, N Ersine defines *geycat* (an alternative spelling) as *a homosexual boy.*

By the early 1950s the reduced form *gay* had appeared and was gradually being used beyond the homosexual community in crime fiction and in dictionaries of homosexual slang. The subsequent growth in the use of the term (accelerating after the 1969 Stonewall riot) was in parallel with the prominence of homosexual issues from that period onwards. There are now many phrases resulting from this: *gay rights, liberation, pride, activism, youth, bars,* etc.

1971

GREENPEACE IS FOUNDED

• • • • • •

Greenpeace is an international charity which works to protect the environment. It was originally set up by a group of people who were opposed to nuclear armament and wanted to prevent a US nuclear testing programme in Alaska. Its activities drew international support from environmental activists, and the organisation subsequently turned its attention to another ecological concern, the protection of whales and seals which were being hunted to supply commercial markets.

Since then, Greenpeace has become involved in general conservation. Campaigners still employ the tactics of peaceful direct confrontation where necessary. On 26 July 1999, for instance, English protesters admitted to destroying government trials of genetically modified crops. But Greenpeace also invests in scientific investigation, meets with leaders of business and industry and mounts public education and information schemes. The organisation's refusal to accept money from governments or business allows it to protest freely about any environmental concern worldwide.

GREEN

The word *green*, the colour of growing vegetation, ultimately comes from *grō-*, thus springing from the same unattested prehistoric Germanic root as *grow* and *grass*. This Old English colour adjective has gathered a number of figurative applications during its long life, most of them drawn from the concept of *green* as the predominant colour of the natural world. Young grass and foliage are both tender and intense in colour. Thus, since the fifteenth century, *green* has been used to denote 'youthful':

> Green in years
> But ripe in glory
> (Joel Barlow, THE COLUMBIAD, 1807)

Green is also the colour of unripe fruit and can therefore mean 'immature': in a speech made at the Guildhall in London on the occasion of her Silver Jubilee in 1977, Queen Elizabeth II spoke of her *salad days* when she was *green in judgement*. But youthfulness and immaturity might also render a person 'gullible', another figurative application of *green*:

> Most readers . . . will think our hero very green for being puzzled at so simple a matter
> (Thomas Hughes, TOM BROWN AT OXFORD, 1861).

None of the above senses was intended, however, when THE TIMES, reporting on a drought in the Southern United States, described President Clinton as *newly green* (22 July 1998). The President, who had recently returned from a summit in China where environmental issues had been addressed, subsequently blamed global warming for the heatwave at home. The use of *green* to denote 'concerned with protecting the natural environment' arose in the early 1970s. Yet again the adjective is understood to be nature's colour. Its earliest appearance on the environmental scene in this sense comes in the name *Greenpeace* which combines the ideal of a green earth with a peaceful one. The word was concurrently taken up by European environmentalists who, first in Germany and soon after elsewhere, formed parties and lobby groups under the title *green*: *Grüne Aktion Zukunft* ('Green Campaign for the Future'), *grüne Listen* ('green lists' – of ecological election candidates). The fight for safe food, a healthy environment and a green economy continues:

> Green Party
> European Elections
>
> Proportional
> Representation
> gives you your
> first real chance
> to elect a
> Green Party MEP
>
> Vote Green Party
> on Thursday June 10 1999
> (Green Party Election Communication, South East European Electoral Region)

Over the past thirty years the lobbyists have been highly successful in educating the world about environmental abuses. But education does not always result in wholehearted application. Industry and governments alike are skilled in presenting policies with a *green* veneer so that they appear ecologically sound. Since the late 1990s this practice has rather cynically been known as *greenwashing*, a term which was modelled on the word *whitewash* in its figurative sense of 'to attempt to conceal mistakes'. Sadly, as we continue to pollute our world and squander its resources, the environmental sense of *green* shows no indication of becoming obsolete in the new millennium.

• As early as the turn of the fourteenth century the pallor of a sickly or emotionally distressed person was identified as being *green*, thus inspiring Shakespeare to describe jealousy as *green-eyed* in THE MERCHANT OF VENICE (1598) and as *the green-eyed monster* in OTHELLO (1604):

But there's a lot to be said for being out of love you know. The most undesirable side-effect of desire is jealousy. Even Green Party members can become victims of the Green-Eyed Monster.
(Sue Limb, OUT ON A LIMB, 1992)

(See also **1616**, page 153.)

1989

TIM BERNERS-LEE MAKES PROPOSALS THAT LEAD TO THE WORLD WIDE WEB

······

Following the major advances in the mid–century (see **1948**, page 243) the computer industry made huge strides forward. The vast Harvard Mark I machine reduced to desktop proportions, and computers began to be linked together in networks. Much of the development was done by rival commercial organisations or by Governments, all of which tended to secrecy and proprietary conventions, so as not to give away a commercial, military or political advantage. By the end of the 1980s, there was an obvious need to provide accessibility of one computer to another, whatever conventions they operated under, in a way that a non–specialist could handle.

Tim Berners-Lee is a graduate of Oxford University, with a background of system design in real-time communications and text processing software development. His own account of the birth of the World Wide Web is, appropriately enough, on his Home Page on the Internet:

In 1980 I played with programs to store information with random links, and in 1989, while working at the European Particle Physics Laboratory, I proposed that a global hypertext space be created in which any network-accessible information could be referred to by a single 'Universal Document Identifier'. Given the go-ahead to experiment by my boss, Mike Sendall, I wrote in 1990 a program called 'WorlDwidEweb', a point and click hypertext editor which ran on the 'NeXT' machine. This, together with the first Web server, I released to the High Energy Physics community at first, and to the hypertext and

NeXT communities in the summer of 1991. Also available was a 'line mode' browser by student Nicola Pellow, which could be run on almost any computer. The specifications of UDIs (now URLs), HyperText Markup Language (HTML) and HyperText Transfer Protocol (HTTP) were published on the first server in order to promote wide adoption and discussion.

The World Wide Web consists of millions of 'documents' stored on computers around the world, which can include text, images, sound, photos, videos and anything else capable of being defined by bits and bytes (see **1948**, page 243). Each Web page has its own address, or Uniform Resource Locator (URL), and can be accessed from other computers on the Internet. This is nothing less than a revolution, making available all the resources of the wired world to a global audience. It all goes back to the work of Tim Berners-Lee at CERN in Switzerland in 1989.

WEB

In October 1990, Berners-Lee worked on a program WorlDwidEweb, which happily soon became WorldWideWeb. The name for the project as a whole, of which the program was a product, was a matter for some debate. Two variants of a mining metaphor were possible choices: Mine of Information, and Information Mine. (Since then, *data mining* has become an industry in its own right). Another possibility was the figure of a mesh, prompted by the interlinking nature of the computers on the Internet: Information Mesh. The final choice of project name was World Wide Web. The same term is now used globally to refer to the virtual abstract information space that is figuratively criss-crossed by connections between computers on the Internet. It draws on the imagery connected with web, which is fundamentally 'a woven thing'. For an account of the linguistic background, see **spinster**, page 76.

In the years since then, there has been a burgeoning of related terms. A *webmaster*, for instance, is responsible for running the computer on which the *web pages* are found (the *web server*, or just *server*) and keeping them up to date. A reference list of sources published on the Internet is a *webliography*, a blend of *web* and *bibliography*. The number of terms, however, could not grow as fast as the number of servers. In June 1993, there were just 130; one million came by April 1997; two million by March 1998; three million by September 1998; four million by January 1999; and, it is safe to say, five million will be reached by the time of the publication of this book.

INTERNET

The Internet precedes the collection of online documents that constitutes the World Wide Web. The huge mainframe computers that were spawned by early pioneers of computing (see **1948**, page 243) became more manageable, efficient and useful. The military certainly thought so, especially when challenged by the launch of the Sputnik in the Cold War (see **1957**, page 249). Part of the electrified response to this event was the immediate creation of the Advanced Research Projects Agency in America. ARPA began a computer research programme in 1962, and published a plan for a network system called ARPAnet in 1966. In 1969, this consisted of linked computers in UCLA, Stanford, Santa Barbara and Utah. The Internet was born.

Some authorities prefer a rather later date for the birth of the Internet. Its early users were a tiny number of scientists, academics and military men, using large mainframe computers. By 1982, several things had happened. Ordinary mortals now stood some chance of access, through cheaper, smaller machines, and the commercial exploitation of the internet was beginning. The particular significance of 1982 is that TCP/IP (a common language for linking computers) was adopted as standard, thus making it possible to connect networks that were using previously competing and incompatible techniques and protocols.

Net is short for network in the context of computers. As an independent word, *net* has been in use for well over a thousand years, both literally as an open mesh used to catch fish, animals, etc, and metaphorically as a snare or trap for the unwary. *Network* is found in the GENEVA BIBLE of 1560 in the early sense of 'material shaped in the form of a mesh'. Shortly afterwards it is used to mean 'an interrelated system', which is very much its contemporary computer sense. *Inter-* is a suffix from Latin, meaning 'between, among'.

The compound *internet* in fact dates back to the nineteenth century, but the context is very different. Herschel writes in an 1883 volume of NATURE of *The marvellous maze of internetted motions*. Its prominence as one of the vogue words of the late twentieth century was jump-started by DARPA, the successor to ARPA. In 1973, it initiated the Internetting Project, which carried out research to develop the system of networks which became known as the *Internet*. More recently, this has shortened to the *Net* or *net* in more informal use. *Internet* can also be used with or without an initial capital.

There have been very many derived forms coined in recent times. *Netiquette* is how to conduct oneself properly on the Internet. People must have started behaving badly very soon in order to need

such advice, since the word is in use since early 1986. Much has been written to guide the *newbie* ('new internet user'). A well known authority is Virginia Shea, who gives these cardinal rules on line:

Rule 1: Remember the human

Rule 2: Adhere to the same standards of behavior online that you follow in real life

Rule 3: Know where you are in cyberspace

Rule 4: Respect other people's time and bandwidth

Rule 5: Make yourself look good online

Rule 6: Share expert knowledge

Rule 7: Help keep flame wars under control

Rule 8: Respect other people's privacy

Rule 9: Don't abuse your power

Rule 10: Be forgiving of other people's mistakes

One might almost believe that *computer geeks* and *computer nerds* (see **1948**, page 243) could belong to the human race if they followed these benign (and anodyne) prescriptions.

Intranet is a modern development, by analogy with internet. It is dated January 1994 on Keith Lynch's online timeline of terms. It means an internal system (within a company, for example) that uses the same protocols and applications as the *Internet*, but is separated from it. This is usually for security purposes. The Latin suffix *intra-* means 'within'.

CYBERSPACE

If pressed to name a word typical of the internet age, most people would probably come up with *cyberspace*, or one from its family, such as *cybercafé* or *cybernetics*. In fact, the word has an old international history and is not as modern as people think. The Greek word *kuberman*, 'to steer', resulted in the English verb to govern. The same Greek word, along with the attendant noun *kubernetes*, 'steersman', led to the coining in 1834 of the French term *cybernétique*, 'the art of

governing', by A-M Ampère in ESSAI
SUR LA PHILOSOPHIE DES SCIENCES. It is
probable that this use influenced Norbert
Wiener, a mathematician at the
Massachusetts Institute of Technology, in
1948 when he introduced *cybernetics* to
English in his book of that name:

> *We have decided to call the entire field of*
> *control and communication theory, whether*
> *in the machine or in the animal, by the*
> *name Cybernetics.*

The thread of meaning concerning
control and human capabilities surfaces in
1960 in *cyborg*, 'an advanced fusion of man
and machine' as Alvin Toffler defines it in
FUTURE SHOCK ten years later. The
word itself is a fusion of *cybernetics* and
organism. The 1970s vogue word *Psycho-*
Cybernetics is in the same tradition.

As for *cyberspace*, it was coined by
William Gibson in his 1984 science
fiction novel, NEUROMANCER. Its early
sense was closer to what has become
called 'virtual reality', a world separate
from our own, experienced through 3-D
headsets and other interfaces. More
recently, it is used as a synonym for
internet. The NEW HACKER'S
DICTIONARY points out Gibson's relation
to other writers, particularly Vernor
Vinge's TRUE NAMES. . .AND OTHER
DANGERS, and John Brunner's 1975
novel THE SHOCKWAVE RIDER.

Cyber- has become a very productive
suffix. Words like *cybernaut, cybermall* and
even the clever *cybotage*, 'undermining the
infrastructure of the state through
computers', jostle with such modern gems
as *cybercrud* and *cybersex*.

BIBLIOGRAPHY

......

This Bibliography does not include standard works of reference such as the *Oxford English Dictionary* or *Encyclopedia Britannica*. Nor does it attempt to be completely comprehensive, as many additional sources were referred to – both in print and on line – but attempts to give an indication of the types of sources we used. These are also the sources of much of the primary material quoted in the text.

(1987). *Reader's Digest Universal Dictionary*, Reader's Digest.

(1991). *The Merriam-Webster New Book of Word Histories*, Merriam-Webster.

Allen Brown, R 'First Castles' in Winston Churchill, *History of the English Speaking Peoples*, Cassell.

Anon.'Murder at Canterbury' in Winston Churchill, *History of the English Speaking Peoples*, Cassell

Ayto, J (1990). *Bloomsbury Dictionary of Word Origins*, Bloomsbury.

Bagley, J J (1960). *Life in Medieval England*, Batsford.

Bailey, A (1988). *The Passion for Fashion*, Dragon's World.

Baugh, A C and Cable, T (1935). *A History of the English Language*, Routledge.

Bennet, W R (1965). *The Reader's Encyclopedia*, A & C Black.

Blacker, I R (1966) *Cortés and the Aztec Conquest,* Cassell

Bray, W, ed. (1907). *Diary of John Evelyn*, J M Dent and Sons.

Brooman, J (1985). *The Great War*, Longman.

Cadbury World Souvenir Brochure, 1991.

Chronology of British History, Brockhampton Press, 1995.

Cooper, G (1998). *The New Forest*, on Hantsweb.

Davis, H W C, ed. (1928). *Medieval England*, Oxford University Press.

Deeson, E, ed. (1991). *Dictionary of Information Technology*, HarperCollins.

Dowley, T, ed. (1977). *The History of Christianity,* Lion.

Drabble, M, ed. (1985). *The Oxford Companion to English Literature*, Oxford University Press.

Evans, C, ed. (1981). *The Making of the Micro*, Victor Gollancz.

Flexner, D (1995). *The Optimist's Guide to History*, Avon.

Friar, S (1991). *The Batsford Companion to Local History,* Batsford.

Galbraith, V H 'Domesday's Meaning' in Winston Churchill, *History of the English Speaking Peoples*, Cassell.

Gossling, W (1970). *A Time Chart of Social History*, Lutterworth.

Green, V H H (2nd edition, 1964). *Renaissance and Reformation*, Arnold.

Greimas, A J (1968). *Dictionnaire de l'Ancien Français*, Larousse.

Grose, F *Dictionary of the Vulgar Tongue* (reprint of 1811 edition), Digest Books.

Grun, B (1991). *The Timetables of History*, Simon & Schuster.

Harpur, P, ed. (1982). *The Timetable of Technology*, Michael Joseph.

Heer, F (1961). *The Medieval World*, Weidenfeld.

Hey, D (1996). *The Oxford Companion to Local and Family History*, Oxford
    University Press.

Hibbert, C (1987). *The English, A Social History, 1066–1945*, Grafton.

Hibbert, W A, ed. (1983). *The London Encyclopaedia*, Macmillan.

Hinde, T, ed. (1985). *The Domesday Book*, Phoebe Phillips Editions.

Hughes, G (1988). *Words In Time*, Blackwell.

Ichikawa, S, ed. (1964). *The Kenkyusha Dictionary of Current English Idioms*. Kenkyusha.

Jancey, M (1994). *Mappa Mundi – a brief guide*, The Dean & Chapter of Hereford.

Jones, J A P (1979). *The Early Modern World, 1450-1700*, Macmillan.

Kelly, R S (1998). *Black Peoples of the Americas*, Heinemann.

Kendall, A (1970). *Medieval Pilgrims*, Wayland.

Kightly, C (1987). *The Perpetual Almanack of Folklore*, Thames & Hudson.

Lagard, A and Michard, L (1970). *Moyen Age*, Bordas.

Lawson-Dick, O (1949). *Aubrey's Brief Lives*, Mandarin.

Lenman, B P, ed. (1993). *Chambers Dictionary of World History*, Chambers Harrap.

Lewis, G 'The Early Printers' in Winston Churchill, *History of the English Speaking
    Peoples*, Cassell.

Little, C E (1900). *Cyclopedia of Classified Dates*, Funk & Wagnalls.

Lockett, A (1974). *The Wool-Trade*, Methuen Educational.

Lockyer, R (1964). *Tudor and Stuart Britain, 1471–1714*, Longmans.

Messadié, G (1991). *Great Inventions through History*, Chambers.

Middleton, H (1988). *The Age of Chivalry*, Oxford University Press.

Muir, F (1976). *The Frank Muir Book: An irreverent companion to social history*,
    Heinemann.

Müller, K & García-Oropesa, G (1991). *Mexico* Insight Guides, APA Publications.

Petroski, H (1993).*The Evolution of Useful Things*, Pavilion.

Reynoldson, F (1980). *War at Home*, Heinemann.

Ridley, A (1971). *Living in Cities*, Heinemann.

Rienits, A T (1968). *The Voyages of Captain Cook*, Hamlyn.

Rowe, L A, ed. (1993). *The Hutchinson Dictionary of Science*, Helicon.

Sale, K (1992). *The Conquest of Paradise,* Macmillan.

Skeat, W W (1879-1882). *Etymological Dictionary of the English Language*,
    Oxford University Press.

Stevenson, B. (1947). *Stevenson's Book of Proverbs, Maxims and Familiar Phrases*,
    Routledge.

Stimpson, G (1948). *Information Roundup*, Harper.

Tannahill, R (1973). *Food in History*, Penguin.

Uden, G (1968). *The Dictionary of Chivalry*, Longman.

Vess, D (1995). *Virtual Tour and Brief History of Fountains Abbey*. The World
    Civilization Virtual Library, Georgia College and State University.

Vincent, B (1906). *Haydn's Dictionary of Dates and Universal Information*, Ward Lock.

Warren, W L 'Knights and Barons' in Winston Churchill, *History of the
    English Speaking Peoples*, Cassell.

Warrington, J, ed. (1924). *The Paston Letters*, Dent.

Warrington, J, ed. (1953). *The Diary of Samuel Pepys*, Dent.

Wentworth, H and Flexner, S B (1967). *Dictionary of American Slang*, Harrap

Wilkins, F (1975). *The Shopkeepers*, Allman.

Wilkinson, F (1977). *The World's Great Guns*, Hamlyn.

Wilson, J D, ed. (1911). *Life in Shakespeare's England*, Penguin.
Woodforde, J (1970). *The Story of the Bicycle*, Routledge.
Wright, L (1960). *Clean and Decent*, Routledge
Yass, M (1975). *Britain between the World Wars*, Wayland.
Zarnecki, G '12th Century Craftsmanship' in Winston Churchill, *History of the English Speaking Peoples*, Cassell.

WEBLIOGRAPHY

Websites are by no means as stable as the printed word. The following addresses are current at the time of publication, but may well alter in the future. The intention is to show some of the Internet resources available to those interested in etymology.

Brewers Phrase and Fable, 1894 Edition
http://www.bibliomania.com/Reference/PhraseAndFable

Dave Wilton's Etymology Page
http://www.wilton.net/etyma1.htm

Jesse Sheidlower's Random House Site
www.randomhouse.com/jesse/

Evan Morris's Etymology Site
http://www.users.interport.net/~words1/index.html

A Word With You
http://www.accessone.com/%7Elparos/archives/archive.htm

Melanie's Etymology Magazine
http://bay1.bjt.net/%7Emelanie//take.html

Morgan's Etymology
http://www.westegg.com/etymology/

Fun with Etymology
http://www.compassnet.com/mrex/etymol-2.htm

Multilingual Language Resources
http://www.utas.edu.au/docs/flonta/

AmeriSpeak – expressions of our American ancestors
http://www.rootsweb.com/~genepool/amerispeak.htm

Outrageous Aussie Sayings
http://www.peg.apc.org/~malcolms/sayings.html

The Etymology of First Names – the origin and meaning of first names
http://www.pacificcoast.net/~muck/etym.html

INDEX

......

Entries in roman type refer to main headings in the text; those in *italics* to subentries.

269